Hollywood
Independents

Commerce and Mass Culture Series
Justin Wyatt, Series Editor

Hollywood Independents: The Postwar Talent Takeover
DENISE MANN

Making Easy Listening: Material Culture and Postwar American Recording
TIM J. ANDERSON

Citizen Spy: Television, Espionage, and Cold War Culture
MICHAEL KACKMAN

Hollywood Outsiders: The Adaptation of the Film Industry, 1913–1934
ANNE MOREY

Robert Altman's Subliminal Reality
ROBERT T. SELF

Sex and Money: Feminism and Political Economy in the Media
EILEEN R. MEEHAN AND ELLEN RIORDAN, EDITORS

Directed by Allen Smithee
JEREMY BRADDOCK AND STEPHEN HOCK, EDITORS

Sure Seaters: The Emergence of Art House Cinema
BARBARA WILINSKY

Walter Wanger, Hollywood Independent
MATTHEW BERNSTEIN

Hollywood Goes Shopping
DAVID DESSER AND GARTH S. JOWETT, EDITORS

Screen Style: Fashion and Femininity in 1930s Hollywood
SARAH BERRY

Active Radio: Pacifica's Brash Experiment
JEFF LAND

Hollywood
Independents

The Postwar Talent Takeover

Denise Mann

Commerce and Mass Culture Series

University of Minnesota Press
Minneapolis ◆ London

Published by the University of Minnesota Press
111 Third Avenue South, Suite 290
Minneapolis, MN 55401-2520
http://www.upress.umn.edu

Library of Congress Cataloging-in-Publication Data

Mann, Denise.
    Hollywood independents : the postwar talent takeover / Denise Mann.
      p. cm. — (Commerce and mass culture series)
    Includes bibliographical references and index.
    ISBN-13: 978-0-8166-4540-4 (hc : alk. paper)
    ISBN-10: 0-8166-4540-X (hc : alk. paper)
    ISBN-13: 978-0-8166-4541-1 (pb : alk. paper)
    ISBN-10: 0-8166-4541-8 (pb : alk. paper)
      1. Motion picture industry—California—Los Angeles—History. 2. Motion pictures—United States—History. I. Title.
    PN1993.5.U65M29 2008
    384'.80979494—dc22
                                                                        2007036955

Printed in the United States of America on acid-free paper

The University of Minnesota is an equal-opportunity educator and employer.

15 14 13 12 11 10 09 08   10 9 8 7 6 5 4 3 2 1

Contents

Acknowledgments

Bringing to life the axiom "let no good deed go unpunished," after Vincent Brook thanked me in his acknowledgments for teaching a graduate seminar on television history that inspired his book *Something Ain't Kosher Here,* I turned to him for editorial help with this book. Therefore, first and foremost, I thank Vincent for his "inspiration, guidance, and good karma," and for serving as a voice of reason and rigor during the final months of writing. I also thank Jason Weidemann and the other members of the first-class editorial board and staff of the University of Minnesota Press, as well as my series editor, Justin Wyatt, for his precise notes and for always encouraging me to express my ideas with ever-greater clarity and precision.

Many colleagues at UCLA offered support, but none more than Janet Bergstrom, Nick Browne, and John Caldwell, who each provided provocative suggestions and invaluable inspiration on early drafts of the manuscript. For their support of my fledgling scholarly career, I'd like to thank Janet Bergstrom (again), Elizabeth Lyon, and Connie Penley for inviting Lea Jacobs, Candace Reckinger, Lynn Spigel, Janet Walker, and me to join *Camera Obscura* in the late 1980s while we were mere graduate students. In addition, I'd like to thank Dean Robert Rosen, Associate Dean Vivian Sobchack, and Chair Barbara Boyle for supporting my "cross-programmatic" interest in theory and practice. Other colleagues and allies who provided assistance and encouragement along the way include Daniel Bernardi, Raquel Cecilia, Tito Deveyra, Maria San Filipo, Jess Flores, Anne Friedberg, Jackie Frost, Laura Gabbert, Ben Harris, Caroline Libresco, Lael Loewenstein, Ron Mangravite, Mary Martin, Chen Mei, Cheryl Rave, Kevin Sandler, Ellen Seiter, Lorraine Houssain Sullivan, Shaoyi Sun, Cyril Tysz, Tsuei Wei, Sabine Werk, Eden Wurmfeld, Kris Young, and the more than ten generations of MFA, MA/PhD, critical studies, and undergraduate students who have endured my ongoing passion for talking and writing about the vicissitudes of popular culture in relationship to American culture and social history.

I owe a special debt of gratitude to my mentor and guide, Howard Suber, who allowed me a means to indulge my fascination with the inner workings of the contemporary Hollywood entertainment industry by asking me to assume his role as head of the UCLA Producers Program after his early retirement in 1994. Since that time, I have had the privilege of working closely with many of Hollywood's best and brightest. I am grateful to the various studio heads, network heads, heads of talent agencies, major producers, executives, and attorneys who have helped educate the next generation of UCLA filmmakers, including Peter Bart, Eric Baum, Emmanuelle Borde, Steve Fayne, Alan Friel, Tom Garvin, Jim Gianopulos, Geoffrey Gilmore, Peter Guber, David Hoberman, Jerry Katzman, Paul Nagle, Charles Newirth, Tom Nunan, Terry Press, Arnold Rifkin, Joe Roth, Cathy Schulman, and Ken Suddleson. For their mentoring, I'd like to thank the UCLA Producers Program Advisory Board members Donald De Line, Denise Di Novi, Lindsay Doran, Tom Jacobson, Anne Kopelson, Kevin Messick, and Jennifer Perini. For their extraordinary "roll up the sleeves" commitment to the UCLA Producers Program, to their students, and to me, I especially thank my constant allies, Sheila Hanahan Taylor and Meg LeFauve.

If it is not amply clear from my extensive list of colleagues and supporters, I have been blessed with the generosity of many friends, scholars, mentors, and most of all my sister Linda during the lengthy process of bringing this book to press.

1.

Charting a Path of Independence
in a Corporate Wilderness

By setting up stars as their own producers . . . MCA has
revolutionized the whole economy of the film capital and turned
it into a wilderness of expensive enterprise. . . . They have sold
Marilyn Monroe to Billy Wilder and Billy Wilder to United
Artists. They have sold automobiles, batons, bandstands, and
annuities to band leaders and their inventory of supplies has also
included, at various instances, Gregory Peck, swizzle sticks, Audrey
Hepburn, short-term loans, Dean Martin, and Torchnose Lee
and the Joy Kings. . . . But their chief business is show business.
"They own it," Jerry Lewis joked.

—DAVID GELMAN AND ALFRED G. ARONOWITZ,
"MCA: Show Business Empire"

The decline of the old studio system and the resulting transformation of the
American film industry that took place from 1947 to 1960 are frequently
characterized as the end of the golden era of Hollywood. In 1951 famed
independent producer David O. Selznick *(Gone with the Wind, Rebecca,
Spellbound)* went so far as to compare the by-then-already-antiquated studio system to the crumbling ruins of Egypt.[1] In contrast to Selznick's
rather morbid, if colorful, assessment, the decade is just as frequently championed as the inauguration of a New Hollywood—an era when independent production increased, factory-like production techniques receded (in
the movies, if not in television), and greater autonomy for actors, writers,
directors, and other members of the creative community was attained.[2] In
using "New Hollywood" in this context, I am well aware of the term's several permutations. From an initial designation for the New Wave–inspired
counterculture films of the late 1960s and early 1970s (e.g., *Bonnie and Clyde*
[1967], *The Graduate* [1968], *Easy Rider* [1969], and *The Last Picture Show*
[1971])—now more commonly termed the Hollywood Renaissance—the
label has subsequently been attached to the post-1975 blockbuster era
characterized by innovative marketing techniques, burgeoning box-office

1

success, and what Gerald Mast calls "the return of the myth" film (e.g., *Jaws* [1975], *Star Wars* [1977], and *E. T.: The Extraterrestrial* [1982]). But even with the latter usage, some see the difference it identifies more as one of degree than of kind. Most historians agree, however, that a definite paradigm shift in Hollywood's business practices occurred in the late 1940s and 1950s. Thus, the terms "Old Hollywood" and "New Hollywood" will be used here to indicate this historic break.[3]

So defined, this book explores the unique ideological and industrial circumstances attending the rise of independent production in the New Hollywood era, and the conflicting oppositional and recuperative forces this radically changed filmmaking climate brought to bear on a group of prominent talent-turned-producers. By examining a range of industry insider accounts, and paradigmatic film texts, I consider how these drastically altered conditions and the contradictory impulses they generated in both independent-minded filmmakers and studio management contributed to two divergent but ultimately related trends: an art cinema and a blockbuster cinema.[4] This bifurcated structure did not emerge full-blown from the crumbling classical studio system, nor was the development of such a striation anything but nonlinear and uneven. The Hollywood studios would not begin to formalize distinct production, distribution, and exhibition strategies for these two types of films until the late 1960s and early to mid-1970s, with several detours and roadblocks before and after.[5] But the origins of the seismic shift in creative and business practices that would lead, in fits and starts, to the contemporary two-tiered system are readily apparent in the late 1950s and can be traced back even further, to the late 1940s and early 1950s. In their often-fierce and ultimately inconclusive debate over the comparative autonomy of contemporary independent cinema and the extent of this cinema's interdependence on the more commercial blockbuster film, media scholars as well as industry insiders have generally located the former's genesis in the unprecedented rise of auteur directors during the Hollywood Renaissance and the latter in the wide-release, mass-marketing, high-concept period that followed. Precious few, however, have closely examined the seeds of these two integrally related developments in the extraordinary confluence of reactionary politics and industrial crisis of the early post–World War II era.[6] Indeed, far from giving the New Hollywood period its creative due, the prevailing tendency has been to demonize it as a low point, from an artistic standpoint, in American film history, with the blacklist figuring prominently in the equation. While not denying the devastating impact of direct and indirect political repression in the McCarthy era on the American film industry and U.S. society as a whole, this study adds its voice to those seeking to broaden our understanding of this highly complex period.

An examination of the specific historical and "behind-the-scenes" context of the emergent American art cinema movement reveals a contentious mix of competing interests—some economic, some ideological, some institutional, some aesthetic—all of which severely qualify a narrowly auteurist conception of the New Hollywood independent. Any textual engagement with these filmmakers' work must therefore also seriously consider the specific industrial and ideological conditions from which they sprang. As David James reminds us, media scholars considering independent filmmaking, like any other form, must recognize that "aesthetics and politics, industries and ideologies, are [always] linked."[7] While previous histories of this contentious period have identified striking examples of artistic innovation in the midst of industrial crisis, few have found a satisfactory means of shedding light on the concrete ways in which independent-minded filmmakers, who were actively charting a path of artistic autonomy in the midst of an increasingly corporate Hollywood, were constantly adjusting their aesthetic goals in response to rapidly evolving industrial-ideological circumstances. Using self-referential and reflexive films as the focus of this study provides a tangible means of exhuming evidence of the types of internal debates and subtle negotiations about the state of the industry that later generations of independent filmmakers (from the Hollywood Renaissance on) had largely internalized.

One of the defining features of the Old Hollywood studio system was a division of production into two basic categories, A and B films, typically separated according to budget, production values, types of stars, potential running time, and distribution strategy.[8] A films, among the major studios, were further divided into so-called Specials and Super-Specials, the latter including Oscar-oriented "prestige" films on the one hand and big-budget musicals and epic spectaculars on the other. Another, in-between category consisted of "programmers": low-end A films or high-end B films that could play either side of a double bill.[9] In the New Hollywood era, with the drop in movie demand, the increase in independent production, and the emergence of exploitation film and TV markets for lower-budget fare, the A/B film system gave way to a more fluid, less rigorously defined structure derived, in large part, from the old Super-Special category. Out of this emerged the bifurcation delineated above, between artistically ambitious films that experimented with classical norms and ever bigger-budget films comprised of highly marketable elements to attract a mass(ive) audience. The "programmer" survived in the form of medium-budget "genre" pictures (westerns, melodramas, crime thrillers), but increasing emphasis was placed on the art film and blockbuster strands, both of which fit into an overall campaign to re-engage the "lost" movie audience. Both sides of the equation were celebrated in the popular and industry press in the mid-1950s: the blockbuster in a *Fortune* magazine article titled "The Comeback of the Movies" (1955), which proclaimed that "big movies are back," and the art film in the critical and box-office success of the eventual Oscar-winning *Marty* (1955), for which the trades praised distributor United Artists (UA) for discovering the value of the "small picture."[10]

The Rise of the Independent Producer

The term "independent," when applied to cinema, is a notoriously slippery designation.[11] While it applies, perhaps most rigorously, to the exploitation, documentary, and avant-garde cinemas functioning outside the studio system, the expression has been used variously to describe a period, a movement, a persistent style, or a production, distribution, and exhibition pattern in American movies. It has also been assigned retroactively to describe certain New Hollywood producers such as Stanley Kramer, Billy Wilder, Burt Lancaster, and Kirk Douglas, who began making films influenced by Neorealist and other European art films, which veered from the classical norm in style and/or subject matter but, unlike the European films, still relied on studio financing and distribution and which played in mainstream theaters.[12]

While truly alternative or independent film practices (sexploitation, documentary, avant-garde) began in the 1910s and have persisted to the present, the focus here is on the more *qualified* independence that grew out of the transitional phase in Hollywood following the 1948 Paramount decree and the rise of independent package productions. As film historian Paul Monaco notes, "The major studios might have invested in nearly all of these productions and might have reached a distribution agreement with the producers of practically all of them before filming began. Still, the overwhelming majority of the productions were correctly called independent because they were produced outside the direct creative control of the studio."[13] One of our main tasks here, beyond examining the nature of this New Hollywood independence, is to determine how this altered industrial structure factors into the types of films and filmmakers that emerged in the early post–World War II period.

In the Old Hollywood era, the "Little Three" studios—Universal, Columbia, and UA—as opposed to the "Big Five"—Paramount, MGM, Twentieth Century–Fox, Warner Brothers, and RKO—lacked theater chains and therefore struggled to compete with the Big Five; after divestiture, however, these lesser majors benefited from their more streamlined, flexible operations and less burdensome overhead costs. UA, under its new co-heads Arthur Krim and Robert Benjamin, was particularly well positioned to take advantage of the new industrial conditions. Innovative but economically precarious when it was instituted in 1919 by the company's filmmaker-founders—Mary Pickford, Douglas Fairbanks, Charlie Chaplin, and D. W. Griffith—UA's method of offering creative autonomy and generous terms to independent-minded stars- and directors-turned-producers (e.g., Billy Wilder, Joseph Mankiewicz, Kirk Douglas, Burt Lancaster) flourished in the more conducive postwar era. In addition to requiring less restructuring to adjust to the changed circumstances, the UA approach allowed the studio to provide more of the type of A pictures preferred by many theater owners, now that the end of block booking no longer obliged exhibitors to show whatever dross the studios heaped upon them.[14] Universal and Columbia, meanwhile, used their familiarity with lower-budget, factory-like B pictures to segue into telefilm production starting in the mid-1950s. The B-film market, given the majors' focus on bigger-budget films and TV, became increasingly relegated to upstart companies like Samuel Arkoff's American International Pictures (AIP) and Allied Artists, and Roger Corman's New World, independent production/distribution houses that found a niche in the 1950s and 1960s by targeting an increasingly potent youth demographic for their exploitation and/or teen movies.[15] These independently produced, though still occasionally major-studio distributed, films (e.g., *I Was a Teenage Werewolf* [AIP, 1957], the *Gidget* [Columbia] and *Beach Party* series [AIP, 1959–65], *Invasion of the Body Snatchers* [Allied Artists Pictures Corporation, 1956, produced by Walter Wanger], *Teenage Doll* [Allied Artists Pictures Corporation, 1957, produced and directed by Roger Corman], *Night of the Living Dead* [Walter Reade Organization, 1968])[16] had trouble accessing the A theaters and would therefore appear in less-appealing theaters and drive-ins, but this type of fare was emerging as a lower-cost, commercially viable alternative to bigger-budget films by cultivating the growing (both in raw numbers and discretionary income) youth population spawned by postwar prosperity and the baby boom.[17]

A second alternative postwar creative and business practice, which established its own distribution and exhibition network, was the emergence of an American art-house cinema derived from the postwar audience's new interest in foreign art films and classic revivals of Old Hollywood genre films. An early instance of an alternative release strategy was employed outside the studio system by independent distributor Cinema V, founded in 1957 by Don Rugoff, whose interest in the early art-house business began in the early fifties after he started showing international art films and American classics in his two New York–based, small theaters, Cinema I and Cinema II.[18] Justin Wyatt explains how Cinema V is "often cited as a model for such later 1990s independents at Miramax and New Line, operated in part by establishing an identity based on its otherness from the major studios. This otherness—through products and business practices—greatly aided the continued presence of the art cinema."[19]

These alternative trends in marketing and distribution were accompanied by a more diversified, segmented movie-going audience, which was also related to the surge in the youth market as the baby boom generation came of age and large numbers of college-bound youth and scholars were increasingly focused on the art-house cinema that came to fruition in the late 1950s and 1960s. As art-house audiences became attuned to the "alternative" strategy, the outlines of a sophisticated "soft-sell" approach directed toward the highly committed, "advertising-averse," specialized film audience—as opposed to classic "hard-sell" techniques adopted for the mass-audience film—began to emerge.

Although the art-house phenomenon wouldn't fully blossom until the late 1950s, the European art cinema began to feed into an emerging American art cinema as early as the mid-1940s, when Italian Neorealist films began winning awards and critical acclaim at major international film festivals. In their effort to reassert America's cultural supremacy in the face of the growing global influence of the European art cinema, several journalists from key industry trade magazines and popular arts magazines began celebrating the artistic ambitions of its own notable, award-winning directors. The cross-pollination and competition between the two continents and their respective national cinemas became more pronounced in the late 1950s and early 1960s as American audiences' interest in the sexual imagery, dark themes, and the countercultural aesthetic of the French New Wave prompted yet another volley of articles expressing concern that Europe's sexually frank cinema and modernist style was going to compromise the commercial viability of the American "family" (i.e., mass appeal) film model; however, what followed was yet another round of Hollywood-based experiments (e.g., *The Apartment* [1960], *The Manchurian Candidate* [1962], *Irma*

La Douce [1963], *Dr. Strangelove* [1964], and *The Pawnbroker* [1965]), suggesting that the alternative aesthetic strategies of the emerging American independent cinema had already taken hold.

The alternative production, marketing, and distribution practices taking place both inside and outside the studio system would eventually coalesce in the post–Production Code era around a larger mainstream movement that would retroactively be assigned the title of an American New Wave or Hollywood Renaissance: a group of major-studio but more personal films featuring innovative technique, provocative themes, sexually or socially progressive views, and which frequently challenged Hollywood's entertainment-centric cinema. The most astounding thing was that many of these films made money, often more than the big-budget Hollywood fare, until another business downturn and the rise of the blockbuster in the 1970s spelled the demise, for the foreseeable future (with notable exceptions), of the large-scale, studio-backed auteurist experiment.[20]

Package Productions and *Über*-Agents

The precipitous decline in movie attendance beginning in 1947, and the theater divestiture mandated by the Paramount decrees of 1948, forced the Hollywood majors to sell their theater chains and release most of their contract players, creating significant new opportunities for independent producers, distributors, and exhibitors. As the studios dismantled most of their in-house-controlled producer-units and shifted, by 1955, to a predominantly "package-unit" system, an era of qualified independent production emerged. Newly released from their onerous studio contracts, many stars and directors—ranging from newcomers like Burt Lancaster, Kirk Douglas, and Elia Kazan, to established talent like Jimmy Stewart, Bette Davis, Alfred Hitchcock, John Huston, and Billy Wilder—consolidated their increased power by forming their own production companies, asserting creative control, and, most disturbing for the studios, demanding lucrative profit participation deals. In these and other, less-overt ways, the power dynamics binding the studios and talent were reversed: the studios, rather than dictating all the terms, were forced to cater to the whims of a numerically limited yet culturally potent talent pool in order to obtain a product that both sides hoped would lure enough viewers away from their suburban homes, baby-boom families, and television screens to turn a profit.

The tables were not completely turned, however; for the newly entrepreneurial filmmakers, still dependent on the studios for financing and distribution, knew that their creative and monetary survival depended on their ability to navigate an increasingly complex and precarious entertainment universe. Confronted with this climate of heightened bureaucracy and aggressive deal-making that began its exponential climb in the 1950s, Billy Wilder, in the mid-1970s, expressed nostalgic yearning for the comparative simplicity of the contract era: "We made pictures then, we didn't make deals. . . . Today we spend eighty percent of our time making deals and twenty percent making pictures."[21]

During this era of vast industrial transformation, when independent filmmakers became the primary producers of content for studios that had lost their monopolistic control over the film industry, talent agencies stepped into the power vacuum. A significant portion of this book charts the paradoxical collusion between many of the new breed of talent-turned-independent-producer and the newly empowered talent agencies, epitomized by MCA (Music Corporation of America), the agency most responsible for negotiating—quite literally—the postwar Hollywood paradigm shift to an increasingly commodified and synergistic corporate enterprise. Chapter 2, which is devoted entirely to the MCA juggernaut and the agency's imposing CEO, Lew Wasserman, focuses on how, in the first half of the 1950s, industry trade papers and magazines attacked MCA for its cutthroat, draconian style of doing business; however, by the second half of the decade, the same trades congratulated the mega-agency for having revamped and revitalized an outmoded entertainment industry model. Indicating the extent to which these changes had been internalized by the early 1960s, industry insider accounts show filmmakers blaming themselves if they were not skilled enough to avoid being double-crossed by MCA's *über*-agents.

From the outset, the conditions and the stakes of the Faustian bargain were clear to both sides. The filmmakers recognized that the agencies they had employed to further their creative and monetary interests were also using their famous clients as leverage to help fulfill the agencies' larger mission of maximizing corporate efficiency and profitability through business mergers and cross-platform convergences. Starting with MCA's 1959 purchase of Universal Studios to supplement its television production arm, Revue Studios, and the 1962 (government-mandated) divestiture of its talent agency, the move to cross-media synergy was underway. Since then, with an interim period of "loose diversification" in which movie studios were purchased largely by nonmedia companies, most major film and television production entities have been absorbed by "tightly diversified" transnational conglomerates, with films and television programs being valued primarily as branding opportunities for ever-expanding ancillary markets (video/DVD, books, magazines, CDs, video games, toys, clothing, theme-park rides, and so on). Under Wasserman's rein, Universal also contributed heavily to the evolution of the blockbuster trend with *Jaws* (1975), the first major studio film to employ high-concept marketing and a wide-release, saturation-booking strategy.

After establishing the structural basis for the institutional sea change from the side of the agency-turned-powerbroker, subsequent chapters focus on the more ambivalent role and reaction of postwar talent-turned-producers such as Billy Wilder, Joseph Mankiewicz, Elia Kazan, and Burt Lancaster. For these and other newly independent filmmakers, the silver lining of creativity and financial reward came with a dark cloud of renewed subservience to the agency-turned-powerbroker, MCA/Universal in particular, which rapidly gained a stranglehold on the operations of the postwar entertainment industry.[22] In a 1962 article about MCA in *Show* magazine, journalist Bill Davidson comments on the strained relationship:

> Kirk Douglas, an iconoclastic rebel, did not have a permanent agent until a few years ago, when he formed his own filmmaking company, Bryna Productions. Then he signed with MCA. When I asked him why, he said, "Because they have most of the top stars and now I won't have to go through a big hassle every time I want one of them for a picture. I was an MCA client myself for several years, and I must admit they did very well by me with screenwriting contracts, until my soul rebelled against the cynical, syndicate atmosphere and I moved elsewhere."[23]

The problems newly independent talent confronted in dealing with the New Hollywood's corporatized mode of doing business is further elucidated by film scholar Robert Phillip Kolker:

> The promise of "artistic freedom" offered when the old Hollywood structure collapsed has turned into something of an economic nightmare where costs, salaries, profits, and reputations are ruthlessly juggled and manipulated, with the film itself all but disappearing in a mass of contracts and bookkeeping.[24]

Then there was television. Given the big agencies' focus on the quantity of package deals closed over the quality of the productions they led to, TV became an increasing priority given the volume of business it generated. As a result, the independent film production companies and movie studios often found themselves in rivalry with television not just for audiences but for stars and writers.[25] Ultimately, then, although a layer of dependence on the studios was removed for artistically inclined filmmakers, several more had been added due to the agents, publicists, attorneys, and a host of professional middle-managers needed to negotiate (and in the case of the studios, to pay for) production deals in an increasingly competitive marketplace.

More complex power relations also were forged between talent and studio in the New Hollywood era. The studios granted greater creative autonomy and profit participation to filmmakers, but in exchange for certain guarantees—namely, that the risks associated with alternative, art-film production would be offset by the occasional star vehicle or big-budget genre film. Hecht-Lancaster's production deal with UA personifies this strategy. Burt Lancaster forged an extremely successful production company partnership with his former agent Harold Hecht, forming Hecht-Lancaster in 1948, and eventually Hecht-Hill-Lancaster (H-H-L) once the team was joined by producer James Hill in 1956.[26] The deal UA struck with their first big star-turned-producer, Lancaster, did not come cheaply. As Tino Balio notes in *United Artists: The Company That Changed the Film Industry*, UA "nearly had to give away the store," granting Lancaster terms that no other star since Chaplin had received.[27]

Lancaster balanced the agendas in a time-honored way, however, alternating between films that satisfied his liberal political and artistic leanings and films that benefited his entrepreneurial interests. Some of the films he produced were clearly aimed at an adult, more sophisticated audience through their complex explorations of institutionalized power and their unconventional casting that undermined traditional star turns: for example, *Marty* (1955, with Ernest Borgnine and Betsy Blair), and *Sweet Smell of Success* (1957, with Burt Lancaster and Tony Curtis in unflattering roles).[28] Other of his company's films pursued a broader audience through familiar genres, best-selling books, Broadway plays, and casting according to commercial type: for example, *Vera Cruz* (1954), *The Kentuckian* (1955), and *Trapeze* (1956).[29] In following this somewhat schizoid strategy, Lancaster and H-H-L were, to a certain extent, emulating the Old Hollywood ploy of leveraging a few commercially risky "prestige pictures" with a preponderance of B films and programmers. Columbia head Harry Cohn was perhaps most notorious in this regard, reminding his top director, Frank Capra, in the 1930s that it was the studio's fifty "programmers" a year that financed Capra's one Oscar nominee.[30] Or as Lancaster said about his two types of films: "I make one for the pope and one for me."[31] The difference was that UA's "pope" in the postwar era wielded a lot less power than Columbia's had in the classical period, and that the strategy of alternating art films and blockbusters was now being replicated on a far narrower ratio.

Liberal/artistic producers with an entrepreneurial bent like Lancaster flourished in the changed conditions of postwar Hollywood by creating a highly profitable and efficiently run independent production company that diversified its portfolio and adapted its budgets and marketing strategies to maximize the potential audience for each film. The H-H-L business model reveals an emerging corporate ethos of the 1950s that would culminate in the late 1960s/early 1970s with a system that required independent producers to balance the major studios' agenda of making fewer, larger-budget, broadly appealing feature films with auteur filmmakers' goals of engaging in alternative film practices.

In contrast to H-H-L's cooperative but compromised relationship with UA, the writer-director team of Elia Kazan and Budd Schulberg saw their independent production company, Newtown Productions, as a mechanism to protect the creative autonomy of artists (which for them meant writers and directors only) from studio interference. Ironically, however, the studio marketing teams responsible for selling Kazan's films learned to emphasize his status as an autonomous artist whose credibility depended on the impression that he was bucking the studio and its industrial organization. Eventually, the studios went further, discovering an indirect, institutional means of controlling content by developing an alternative promotional strategy that also allotted smaller production and marketing budgets for films whose oppositional elements undermined their commercial appeal. Thus, at the same time that high-brow magazines like *Theatre Arts* were celebrating Mankiewicz's *A Letter to Three Wives* (1949) by comparing him favorably to European art-filmmakers, the Fox studio marketing team was starting to target an older, sophisticated adult audience for this film by emphasizing its high-art pedigree—that is, its serious themes, positive reviews, Academy Awards, and noteworthy acting and directing.

Art Cinema versus Blockbuster

Postwar films associated with the emerging American art cinema ranged widely in budget, from $300,000 (slightly higher than the average B film) to A-film prices of $2–$4 million.[32] In contrast, the early 1950s historical-epic blockbusters ranged from $5 million to $15 million and frequently earned two to four times their budget (e.g., *Quo Vadis* [1952], $7-million budget, $10.5-million domestic box office; *The Robe* [1953], $5-million budget, $20–$30-million domestic box office; *Ben-Hur* [1959], $15-million budget, $39.1-million domestic box office).[33] The huge expense and risk involved in these films prompted studios to focus increasingly on a global audience through spectacular subject matter and international stars, and to defray costs through international coproduction/cofinancing arrangements, foreign location shooting, and the use of foreign, nonunion crews.[34] The definition of the emerging blockbuster style can also be applied to bigger-budget, A-film productions that also incorporated highly marketable elements such as the latest technologies (CinemaScope, VistaVision, Todd-AO, 3-D, and so on), top stars, broadly appealing storylines (often based on presold literary properties), and, increasingly, contemporary settings, fashions, furnishings, and décor, or the opposite, nostalgic representations of the past.[35]

In his seminal historical analysis of the blockbuster phenomenon, Schatz argues that two 1946 independent productions, Sam Goldwyn's *The Best Years of Our Lives* and David O. Selznick's *Duel in the Sun,* presaged the blockbuster trend, with Selznick himself calling *Duel* "an exercise in making a big grossing film."[36] To this list one could add subsequent studio productions as *The Greatest Show on Earth* (Cecil B. DeMille/Paramount, 1952) and *From Here to Eternity* (Buddy Adler/Columbia, 1953); independent productions such as *Trapeze* (Hecht-Hill-Lancaster/UA, 1956), *Around the World in Eighty Days* (Michael Todd/UA, 1956), and *The Bridge on the River Kwai* (Sam Spiegel/Columbia, 1956); and several of Darryl Zanuck's "prestige productions" for Fox, including *How to Marry a Millionaire* and *Gentlemen Prefer Blondes* (both 1953), and *Woman's World* (1954), among others. Notably, these early blockbusters were just as often made by the new postwar generation of independent producers (Hecht-Hill-Lancaster, Sam Spiegel, Michael Todd), as the older generation of established "showman" from the classical era (Goldwyn, Selznick, Zanuck, DeMille, Adler)—suggesting the willingness of at least some of the New Hollywood independents to conform to the entertainment-centric policies of the dominant cinema.

As for the art film, film historian James Harvey points to the increase in the number of dark, provocative, and original films during the 1950s. This shift signaled, for Harvey, the end of the studio era and the beginning of what he terms a postclassical era, in which largely independent art-filmmakers "emphasized and aestheticized" genre and when "individual films became more self-conscious and more complex."[37] These early art films can be broken into several overlapping categories. One is the low-budget, black-and-white production dubbed the "new American realist" film (e.g.,

On the Waterfront [Horizon/WB, 1954] and *Marty* [Hecht-Lancaster/ UA, 1955]), which was influenced by the Italian Neorealist movement and made predominantly by left-wing New York–school filmmakers. Several films in this category were adapted from live teleplays (e.g., *Marty, Patterns* [Jed Harris/Michael Myerberg/UA, 1956], *Twelve Angry Men* [Orion-Nova (Henry Fonda, Reginald Rose)/UA, 1957] and *The Miracle Worker* [Playfilms (Fred Coe)/UA, 1962]).[38]

A second category is the star-studded adaptations of significant literary or theatrical properties that explored the politics of class and gender and often contained sexually provocative themes (e.g., *Streetcar Named Desire* [Charles K. Feldman Group/Kazan/WB, 1951], *The Rose Tattoo* [Hal B. Wallis/Paramount, 1955], *Baby Doll* [Kazan/WB, 1956], *Suddenly, Last Summer* [Horizon/Columbia, 1959]).[39]

A third category is the stylistically ambitious, proto-postmodernist reversals of accepted A- and B-film genre formulas (e.g., *Kiss Me Deadly* [Parklane/UA, 1955], *Sweet Smell of Success* [H-H-L/UA, 1957], *A Face in the Crowd* [Newtown/WB, 1957], *Touch of Evil* [Albert Zugsmith/Universal-I, 1958], *The Manchurian Candidate* [Howard W. Koch/UA, 1962]).[40]

A fourth category is the films made by director-auteurs (e.g., Wilder, Huston, Hitchcock, Nicholas Ray, John Ford, Frank Tashlin), who were being singled out by the international press, in particular, for works that demonstrated a unique visual style, compelling themes, and distinctive sensibilities (e.g., *Vertigo* [Hitchcock/Paramount, 1958], *Some Like It Hot* [Mirisch/UA, 1959], *The Apartment* [Mirisch/UA, 1960], *Will Success Spoil Rock Hunter?* [Frank Tashlin/TCF, 1957]).[41]

Finally, one could include the politically and/or socially provocative films by talent-turned-producers like Elia Kazan, Kirk Douglas, Hecht-Lancaster, Otto Preminger, and Stanley Kramer, which challenged the implied or direct content restrictions imposed by the House Un-American Activities Committee (HUAC), the Production Code Administration (PCA), and the Catholic Legion of Decency (e.g., *High Noon* [Stanley Kramer/UA, 1952], *Viva Zapata!* [Darryl F. Zanuck/Fox, 1952], *Baby Doll* [Elia Kazan/WB, 1956], *The Moon Is Blue* [Otto Preminger, 1953], and *The Man With the Golden Arm* [Preminger, 1956]). Indicating the extent to which the independently produced package production approached true creative autonomy, George Axelrod, who in partnership with Frank Sinatra produced *The Manchurian Candidate* (1962) for United Artists, said, "Once they'd ok'd [a project], they'd say, 'Goodbye, bring us a print.' It was a lovely way to work. . . . We were allowed to do 'wild things.'"[42]

Further elaboration of Harvey's distinction between classical and post-classical is required, however, if we are to properly gauge the comparative "wildness" of the New Hollywood. Theoretical debate over the definition of the classical Hollywood cinema began with André Bazin's scholarly writing on the subject in the 1950s. Bazin broke down the classical period, which he saw as beginning in the sound era and ongoing, into two categories: the "classicism" of the 1930s, and a "baroque" cinema of the late 1940s and 1950s, characterized by greater self-consciousness and stylization, such as in "superwesterns" like *Duel in the Sun* (1946), *High Noon* (1952), and *Shane* (1953).[43] Most contemporary scholars follow, with some qualification, David Bordwell, Janet Staiger, and Kristin Thompson's influential but not uncontroversial *The Classical Hollywood Cinema* (1985), which describes the "mature" period of classical Hollywood production as taking place during the 1930–60 period and rejects Bazin's "baroque" distinction, claiming instead that "Hollywood films of the 1940s and 1950s intensified or 'maximized' the themes and formal possibilities established in the 1930s" and that the style has embraced any and all variations that emerged within certain "bounds of difference."[44] Most all scholars agree, however, that there was a decisive shift away from the classical Hollywood style after 1960, a period variously called "the New Hollywood, the New New Hollywood, post-classicism, and more indirectly, post-Fordism and postmodernism."[45]

Since this book focuses on films made in the late 1940s and 1950s (Bazin's "baroque" phase), but also indicates how many of these films forecast the more pronounced shifts of the Hollywood Renaissance of the late 1960s, these theoretical distinctions are pertinent. For instance, Bazin's notion of a "baroque" phase may usefully apply to the New Hollywood's attempt to construct more expensive and elaborate versions of the "classical" A films in the face of changing industrial conditions. By the same token, the studio-based A "art film" favored by Mankiewicz, Wilder, and Huston, for example, and nonstudio-based B "art film" favored by Welles, Kubrick, Ray, and Aldrich, reflect the way artistically minded filmmakers sought (and were enabled) to reinterpret classical conventions or, in some cases, to radically deconstruct them. The Bazinian model, while certainly not a template for the Old Hollywood/New Hollywood binary, can serve to facilitate understanding of how 1950s filmmakers, working at each end of the filmmaking spectrum, art cinema and blockbuster, were starting to reenvision the classical style in divergent but also overlapping ways.

The Studio-Distributed Art Film

The New Hollywood's double-pronged business model is exemplified in the approach of Fox's Darryl Zanuck, a hands-on studio chief who had, already in the classical period, managed to balance broadly appealing extravaganzas (e.g., the Shirley Temple musicals and Errol Flynn swashbucklers) with provocative social dramas (e.g., *The Grapes of Wrath* [1940] and *Tobacco Road* [1941]).[46] Zanuck's interest in the social-problem film persisted into the late 1940s and 1950s, albeit with a decisive shift in focus away from the plight of the working class and onto the concerns of the middle classes in a series of commercially liberal films (e.g., *Gentleman's Agreement* [1947], *Pinky* [1951], *Woman's World* [1954], and *The Man in the Gray Flannel Suit* [1956]). Zanuck is also credited with helping launch the careers of at least two major directors, Elia Kazan and Joseph Mankiewicz, whose ambitious and original works contributed to the studio-based art-film phenomenon. By the mid-1950s, however, Zanuck was becoming increasingly intolerant of what *Hollywood Reporter* owner/columnist W. R. Wilkerson described as the occasional "little picture [that] has what it takes to attract audiences," gravitating instead to "big pictures" that possessed the wherewithal to attract a mass audience.[47] In this way, as later chapters dealing with Mankiewicz and Kazan describe in greater detail, Zanuck would play a decisive role not only in the emergence of the art film but, by shifting the studio's thrust toward such broadly appealing, entertainment-centric films as *Gentlemen Prefer Blondes* (1953), *How to Marry a Millionaire* (1953), and *Woman's World* (1954), also facilitate the evolution of the blockbuster.

Fox's and other studios' mid-1950s' tilt toward the "big picture" constrained but did not extinguish the more cinematically innovative and politically progressive art-film trend that was concurrently emerging in the New Hollywood. Instead, directors like Mankiewicz, Kazan, and Wilder increasingly sought creative asylum by forming or aligning with independent production entities—Figaro, Inc., Newtown Productions, and Mirisch Productions, respectively—or in the case of Lancaster's H-H-L, by accelerating a strategy of producing both "big" and "little" pictures. As these newly empowered filmmakers demanded and ultimately were granted greater independence from studio intervention, not only were a number of aesthetically daring and thematically complex films produced, but the seeds of the Hollywood Renaissance were sown.

The origins of a clearly identifiable strategy for the studio distribution of an independently produced art film can be traced to 1955 when UA released the H-L production of *Marty,* a film based on an Emmy-winning television drama that the foreign press would celebrate as the first in the "new American realist" film cycle and that would become, according to Lancaster biographer Kate Buford, "a model of modern movie marketing."[48] While studio marketing teams understood, from long practice, how to sell A films and "prestige" films to a mass audience, they had less expertise in selling what was essentially a new category of small-scale, unassuming art films without stars. The nut was cracked when, through a series of press screenings in New York where the film was showing in a single East Manhattan theater, noted columnist Walter Winchell wrote that *Marty* would become one of the great sleeper hits of all time. Multiple rave reviews in major newspapers followed, creating word of mouth that propelled the film's initial success. Mass appeal beyond urban centers still lagged, however, until the film was submitted to the Cannes Film Festival in "a deliberate effort . . . to win the cheap publicity of 'international acclaim.'" After winning the prestigious Palme d'Or, unprecedented for an American film, *Marty*'s "prestige" status was affirmed—both for U.S. and, just as important, international audiences. It was the first time, Buford notes, that "America had joined the *realismo* company of real people, real 'art' movies."[49] Building on the Cannes imprimatur, the film's ad budget was tripled to $150,000 and the independent art-film success story was assured, capped by the film's garnering four Academy Awards, including Best Picture, the following year.

Their experience with *Marty* gave H-L and studio partner UA unique insight into how to tap a highly invested adult audience that shares its discoveries with like-minded viewers, thereby generating positive word-of-mouth that amounted to free publicity—a marketing tool that would become the mainstay of independent distribution in the decades to come. Notably, however, despite the film's phenomenal critical and financial success, H-L's Lancaster was the first to point out that the "little picture," made for a mere $360,000, had grossed half as much ($6 million) as *Vera Cruz* (1954), one of H-L's blockbuster-style films.[50] Whether hubris (Lancaster was the star of *Vera Cruz*) or obtuseness prevented Lancaster from acknowledging *Marty*'s epochal significance from a marketing standpoint, the handwriting was on the wall: trade industry analysts, filmmakers, and studio executives all began pointing to the need for alternative forms of production and targeted marketing like those that *Marty* had back-handedly pioneered.[51]

Other small- and medium-budget art films followed, with studio marketers focusing on the film's dark, provocative themes, the presence of a movie star in a nonstar turn, or, increasingly, the visual style of the director. Whether the art films that emerged were Old Hollywood–style in-house productions or New Hollywood package-style works, studio heads and filmmakers alike were starting to conceptualize a form of quasi auteurism as "a commercial strategy for organizing audience reception."[52] In its 1950s variation, however, before *la politique des auteurs* had crossed the Atlantic via *Village Voice* critic Andrew Sarris, Hollywood's proto-auteurist marketing component, particularly in its youth orientation, was carried just as often by actors as directors. Popular and news magazines like *Look, Saturday Evening Post, Life,* and *Time,* as well as industry trades like *Daily Variety* and *Hollywood Reporter,* tried, often unsuccessfully, to mediate the revised, cult-like attachment that youthful audiences felt for "edgy" new stars like Lancaster, Douglas, Marlon Brando, James Dean, Marilyn Monroe, and others, whose public persona emphasized rebelliousness and independence.[53] Partly by choice, partly by default, then, the independent-minded, newly empowered filmmakers were constructing, or having constructed for them, the parameters of a nascent alternative cinema. For their part, studio heads were learning to adjust their production budgets and distribution strategies to distinguish between films that deviated, in divergent ways, from classical Hollywood's established norms: comparatively low-budget films aimed at select audiences (art films), and bigger-budget films that had the potential to hit the box-office mother lode (blockbusters).

Postwar Ideological Battles—A "Hot" War Turns Cold

In 1947 Charlie Chaplin, who had pioneered a more independent, if anomalous, Hollywood production practice as cofounder of United Artists in 1919, told the London press that he welcomed an end to the old studio system's standardized product and single-minded pursuit of profits:

> I, Charlie Chaplin, declare that Hollywood is dying. . . . Hollywood is now fighting its last battle, and it will lose that battle unless it decides once and for all to give up standardizing its films—unless it realizes that masterpieces cannot be mass-produced in the cinema, like tractors in a factory. I think, objectively, that it is time to take a new road—so that money shall no longer be the all-powerful god of a decaying community.[54]

While the New Hollywood would heed Chaplin's call for independence in significant ways, truly autonomous expression would be impeded as well, not least of which by the anti-Communist campaign that blacklisted many, led to the self-censorship of many more, and banished Chaplin altogether after the British-born filmmaker, who had never obtained American citizenship, refused to testify before HUAC in 1952.[55]

The ideological struggles that marked the post–World War II period in the nation as a whole were magnified in Hollywood, given the staunch conservatism of most of the studio moguls and the disproportionately liberal (-to-radical) composition of the filmmaking community. Postwar movie-industry leaders like Eric Johnston, head of the Motion Picture Association of America (MPAA), and Ronald Reagan, head of the Screen Actors Guild (SAG), used their leadership positions to promote anti-Communism as a way of delegitimizing the postwar Hollywood labor movement. This was in stark contrast to the strong support given to labor unions in the Hollywood of the 1930s, when a commitment to both above-the-line (creative) and below-the-line (crafts) workers' unions mirrored a thriving, if also fiercely resisted, labor movement in the United States as a whole. But the populist spirit of the early FDR years was curbed during World War II, when a moratorium on social activism was established in the name of presenting a unified patriotic front in the war against fascism. As the war wound down, both union and antiunion activity picked up, with some studios resorting to red-baiting tactics against the reformist Conference of Studio Unions (CSU), which had begun to strike on behalf of crafts workers in 1945. The studios retaliated by locking out CSU the following year, not only crushing the union and seizing control of production but essentially blacklisting thousands of union members.[56]

More widespread blacklisting affecting Hollywood's creative personnel would result from the HUAC hearings of the late 1940s and early 1950s into alleged Communist infiltration of the film industry. Due to the hearings, many filmmakers who had briefly experimented with Communism or other radical causes (or merely sympathized with them) were denied work, forced underground, and/or moved abroad during this period. A few suffered heart attacks or committed suicide. As one of the exiled directors, Joseph Losey, who went from ostracized B-film director in Hollywood to esteemed auteur in England, summarized (as recounted by Thom Anderson): "[T]he Left in Hollywood was utterly demoralized by Truman, the atomic bomb, and the HUAC investigations, and it was beginning to recognize 'the complete unreality of the American dream.'"[57]

Some filmmakers who were opposed to the McCarthyist witch hunt compromised their principles for the sake of their careers.[58] In *The Hollywood*

Writer's Wars (1982), Nancy Lynn Schwartz observes how the Hollywood Left was effectively "purged" through a two-pronged censorship campaign. The first entailed "objective" pressure via organizations such as the Production Code Administration (PCA), the MPAA, HUAC, the Tenney Committee in the California Senate (a state version of HUAC), the Hearst press, and the Motion Picture Alliance for the Preservation of American Values (MPAPAV, a right-wing anti-Communist group formed by Hollywood personnel in 1944). The second came from the creation of an insidious atmosphere of self-censorship or "before-the-fact editing of writers and other creators in the industry who found themselves avoiding the controversial."[59]

Reactions among the Hollywood Left to the anti-Communist hysteria were as varied as the political makeup of its members. Some of the more radical leftists like director Robert Rossen and screenwriter Clifford Odets vowed that they would never capitulate to the reactionary pressure and became shadows of their former selves when they finally did.[60] Others, like German playwright/screenwriter Bertolt Brecht, were ashamed that they fell short of open defiance and serving time in jail; instead, Brecht fled to Communist East Germany, where he was welcomed with open arms.[61] More moderate liberals like writer/director Wilder escaped the ordeal unscathed but continued to feel pressure to conform to an unspoken rule of behavior if they wanted to work in Hollywood.[62] Former Communist Kazan, who spared his directing career by disavowing his past association with the party, channeled his residual ambivalences into his films. While never a member of the Communist party, the left-leaning Lancaster was singled out by several right-wing organizations.[63] All liberal filmmakers who wanted to continue to work during this period of Cold War tension had to learn to balance their social concerns with the demands of mainstream Hollywood and of the capitalist ideology that undergirded it.[64] Compromised liberal filmmakers like Odets, Wilder, Kazan, Schulberg, Mankiewicz, and Lancaster—the men whose work is the focus of this book—were forced either to self-censor, to express their critical views indirectly through allegory, or to engage in stylistic and structural innovation that acted as an aesthetic "frame" for an emerging auteurist cinema.

Some Hollywood liberals went beyond the muffling of their views and opted actually to reinforce the status quo. Indeed, one of the more striking changes of the postwar era was the altered ideological function of the Hollywood star. The popularity of patriotic crossover movie/TV stars like Bob Hope and Bing Crosby, as well as the new conservatism of once-liberal movie stars like William Holden and Ronald Reagan, was emblematic of the shift from the pro-union radicalism of the 1930s to the capitalist cheerleading of the wartime and postwar eras. This moderate to right-wing group of actors perceived themselves as spokespersons for Hollywood and the nation and sought to present a positive and uplifting portrait of American life both in the United States and abroad.[65] In addition, MPAA chief Johnston, SAG president Reagan, and other key industry leaders helped extend the international reach of American capitalism by justifying the continuation of a wartime emergency agenda after the war through the European Marshall Plan (initially a liberal agenda that took on conservative political overtones as the Cold War escalated). These leaders also openly challenged the pro-union positions of remaining outspoken liberal stars like Katharine Hepburn, John Garfield, and James Cagney. Hope famously reinforced Cold War politics while performing with other entertainers for the troops abroad, claiming that the United States was fighting for a moral victory by spreading democracy and upholding Americanism, what Hope called the American "Shangri La."[66] In all, conservative Hollywood leaders and their star supporters used their power within the industry to ward off dissenting voices and to create the image of a unified American front. Yet, paradoxically, despite the McCarthyist national and Hollywood-specific pressures to conform to a consensus view of America, the late 1940s and 1950s managed to generate a remarkable collection of creative and progressive Hollywood films, often with the full cooperation of the studios.[67] A prime aim of this book is to examine and attempt to explain this and related paradoxes.

Self-Referentiality and Ideological Reflexivity

Despite the formidable challenges associated with working in the reactionary McCarthy era, one might have expected the recently empowered movie directors, writers, and stars to take advantage of their comparative freedom to focus on an oppositional or alternative cinema, one that expressed the progressive, quasi-socialist ideals that prevailed in the 1930s and, despite considerable resistance, persisted through the 1940s and beyond.[68] Further encouraging political and aesthetic boldness was the postwar Italian Neorealist movement, which insisted on confronting difficult social issues head on and shunned stars and spectacle in favor of nonprofessional actors and documentary grit. In fact, most histories of the early postwar era emphasize the politically charged social-problem films in the social-realist tradition made by soon-to-be or already-blacklisted filmmakers, or else they track "film noir and youth culture movies [that] reflected the tension and anxiety [of this period] and created the outlines of a distinct postwar culture."[69] While acknowledging these influences, I take a different tack by looking at a group of "insider texts": literary ones drawn from industry trades, and cinematic ones drawn from self-referential and ideologically reflexive entertainment-business films of the period. These cinematic critiques of the culture industry are especially pertinent to our analysis because they expose both the personal and the societal stakes involved in the rise of the New Hollywood independents.

"Self-referential" films, in this schema, are those whose narratives and themes are related in a self-conscious way to the business aspect of the entertainment industry; "ideologically reflexive" films are those that go beyond mere referentiality in subject matter, incorporating formal deviations from the classical Hollywood norm not for their own sake but to foreground, deconstruct, and challenge the media's hegemonic methods of meaning construction.[70] Self-referential films were occasionally low-budget (e.g., *The Star* [1952] and *The Big Knife* [1955]), but most were expensive A productions (e.g., *The Hucksters* [1947] and *It Should Happen to You* [1954]) that featured big stars, were heavily marketed, widely distributed, and generally favorably reviewed by the trades and popular press, and that typically scored at the box office. A select group of big-budget A films (e.g., *Woman's World* [1954] and *The Man in the Gray Flannel Suit* [1956]) were expressly designed as potential blockbusters by the studios. Ideologically reflexive films, including *Sunset Boulevard* (1950), *Ace in the Hole* (1951), *A Face in the Crowd* (1957), and *Sweet Smell of Success* (1957), were generally fairly big-budget, featured big stars (although typically not in heroic roles), yet veered from standard Hollywood fare by engaging a range of genres and aesthetic approaches that dissolved boundaries between high art and low art and acerbically critiqued an increasingly corporatized mass media. While many of these films also received critical accolades, they were not yet singled out by the trade, popular, or even scholarly press as independent or art-house films.[71] Nonetheless, retroactively, much like certain postwar film noirs, they can be seen as "liminal products . . . that . . . eventually came to occupy a borderland somewhere between generic . . . and art movies."[72]

The self-referential and ideologically reflexive film cycle is subsumed under two, sometimes overlapping genres: the social-problem film and its occasional adjunct, the big-business film, both of which have long histories in American cinema. While the social-problem film has a consistently progressive political pedigree, the business film has played it both ways, sometimes challenging, sometimes recuperating the status quo. Chapter 3 considers how several postwar big-business films sought to resolve workplace anxieties and rebelliousness linked to the emergent "organization man" mythos by reasserting old-fashioned domestic ideologies.[73] Chapter 4 focuses on a group of prominent entertainment-business films made between 1947 and 1960, which typically deflect their anticapitalist critique onto the "antitelevision" discourse of the period. Given the shadow cast by the anti-Communist crusade over films that appeared too openly critical of U.S. society, the assault on TV provided a means for politically liberal filmmakers to attack one aspect of the larger society while at the same time affirming, via modernist aspirations, the film industry's "high culture" pedigree. An examination of self-referential and ideologically reflexive entertainment-business films thus allows for a focused analysis not merely of postwar sociocultural conditions but also of the New Hollywood independents' engagement with a culture industry and corporatized capitalist system in which the filmmakers themselves were embedded.

While many of the politically and cinematically challenging films that emerged in the postwar era were the result of politically liberal, artistically inclined filmmakers becoming or teaming up with independent-minded producers and/or studios, not all the self-referential and ideologically reflexive films discussed in this study follow such a straightforward pattern. The lines of demarcation between studio and independent productions are not now nor were they ever so clear-cut.[74] For instance, *A Face in the Crowd* (1957) may have been the work of two controversial leftist filmmakers—Group Theater expatriate Elia Kazan and cynical, disaffected "industry brat" Budd Schulberg—but it was grand old Warner Bros. that released their highly unconventional and polemical film. Other films critical of big business—for example, *A Letter to Three Wives* (1949), *Executive Suite* (1954), *The Man in the Gray Flannel Suit* (1956), and *Will Success Spoil Rock Hunter?* (1957)—were also studio-based productions, several from Twentieth Century–Fox under studio chief Darryl F. Zanuck.[75] Thus, it is an overstatement to presume that the studios had a consistently conservative agenda and the independent production companies a progressive one. Indeed, one could easily argue the opposite: since liberal filmmakers working for their own independent companies were themselves responsible for earning a profit in order to maintain their independent power base and access to studio marketing and distribution, they may have been even more inclined to compromise principle for profit or, as we have seen with Lancaster, to alternate between more controversial films and more mainstream fare.

My study culminates with a close look at two of the period's most aesthetically challenging, thematically provocative ideologically reflexive films, *A Face in the Crowd* and *Sweet Smell of Success*, both of which represent calculated attempts to articulate a form of American art cinema in an era of heightened competition and industrial crisis. Situating the origins of an American art cinema in the early New Hollywood era, while not unique, does go against the prevailing wisdom, which, as previously mentioned, points to the Hollywood Renaissance period as the source of the art-film movement. One historian, Timothy Corrigan, actually trumps both the mainstream and the alternative ontology, tracing the genealogy of the American art film back to certain B films of the 1940s and 1950s, "the public precursor of [modern-day] cult movies."[76] While I am not in agreement with Corrigan's thesis *in toto*, one of his observations intersects significantly with my analysis: the contemporary art-film audience's cult-like fascination with classic B movies extends to their stars and directors, preeminently Orson Welles, whose American work in particular (e.g., *Citizen Kane* [1941], *The Magnificent Ambersons* [1942], *The Lady from Shanghai* [1948], and *Touch of Evil* [1958]) exhibits a (post)modernist mix of traditional "genre" and "art" tendencies in single works. Following Welles's lead, several of the postwar talent-turned-producers focused on here similarly sought to break the classical Hollywood mode by choosing challenging story material, attaching innovative writers and/or directors, casting character actors instead of movie stars and/or casting stars against type, yet also seeking studio marketing and distribution for work that melded the unconventional with the generic.[77]

For New Hollywood art-filmmakers, even those who ran their own companies, charting a path of independence was paradoxically linked to the rise of the blockbuster mentality, converging film and television industries, and the rise of a new breed of high-powered talent agencies.[78] Independence was, in this equation, never more than comparative and highly circumscribed.[79] Filmmakers who had gained qualified independence in the postwar era and maintained decent box-office track records did experience unprecedented creative autonomy, but this increased freedom was tethered to increased fiscal responsibility for films in which they now had a direct financial stake. The pressure to succeed financially was heightened by the fact that continued independence hinged on continued financial success. For liberal filmmakers ideologically at odds with conservative studio heads and the inequities of the capitalist system, the tensions produced by their own privileged working conditions were particularly acute. These tensions, in turn, were exacerbated by a reactionary political climate that had caused their more radical colleagues to be blacklisted, forced underground, or exiled. And yet the remarkably subversive films the liberal independents managed to make emerged not in spite but because of these ambivalent social and industrial circumstances.

Text Meets Context: A Note on Methodology

In combining political economy with textual analysis—that is, by examining a group of paradigmatic film texts in relation to their industrial settings— this history of New Hollywood independent filmmaking foregrounds the intrinsic symmetries between the cultures of production and the production of culture. While this basic approach may not be new, the added dimension here is the selection of films *about* the production circumstances of the entertainment media in the New Hollywood period, films whose inner tension and creative force derive as much from a manifestation of as from a resistance to these circumstances. The ambivalence among film practitioners toward the changed entertainment industry landscape during the tumultuous postwar period can be traced both in the self-referential films and in the inherently self-explanatory, self-critical industrial texts (e.g., *Daily Variety, Weekly Variety, Hollywood Reporter, Fortune, New York Post, Television Magazine, Show*). In cross-referencing the filmic, television, trade, and popular press discourses, the book also, more specifically, applies John Caldwell's notion of the industry "inter-text": "practitioner discourses [which function] as a means of charting the critical-theoretical competencies and marketing imperatives behind the textual practices."[80] Employed by Caldwell to address the hyperconsciousness of the postmodern mass-media complex, the methodology can be usefully adapted to the increasingly "knowing" participation of independent filmmakers in the proto-postmodern New Hollywood.

Hollywood Reporter owner/columnist W. R. Wilkerson's daily column proved an especially valuable "industry-intertextual" source, given his staunchly politically reactionary and, for the most part, pro–Old Hollywood stance. By the mid-1950s, however, Wilkerson's initial ideological and industrial intractability gave way to reluctant acceptance of the corporation-dominated, talent agency–dependent, television-infused New Hollwood.[81] Equally valuable are the reviews, articles, interviews, photo-essays, and other more mainstream analyses of industrial practices that prevailed in a number of popular magazines (e.g., *Saturday Evening Post, Look,* and *Life* magazines). As my analysis in chapter 2 of the evolving industry and popular discourse on talent agencies suggests, popular magazines, although betraying shifting alliances, consistently revealed their interconnectedness with the New Hollywood infrastructure.

Explaining the significance of these insider textual accounts of practitioners' activities or what he calls evidence of "low theory" being articulated by industry insiders in the contemporary period, Caldwell argues, "A close examination of industrial textual practice . . . shows how the industry theorizes its presence in moving image form, even as it teaches the film audience . . . by publicly circulating [sanctioned] insider knowledge about the [televisual and film production] apparatus."[82] Similarly in the New Hollywood, the growing interest among postwar viewers in "behind-the-scenes" depictions of industrial trends is evident not only in the self-referential and reflexive films to be examined in later chapters, but also in the mid-1950s' proliferation of behind-the-scenes TV programs about Hollywood (e.g., *Toast of the Town, MGM Parade, Warner Brothers Presents,* and *Twentieth Century–Fox's Front Row Center* [for General Electric], as well as Disney's *Disneyland* and *The Mickey Mouse Show*).[83] Further cultivating audience competency in industrial matters were the growing number of publications providing insider accounts of not just the stars' film roles, fashions, romances, and domestic lives—as had long been the case—but now of their business practices as well. For instance, despite the article's focus on Rita Hayworth's troubled romantic life, *Look* magazine also integrated news about her new production company, H-H-L, which Hayworth joined after marrying James Hill, one of the principles. Epitomizing the increasing overlap between gossip and "behind-the-scenes" industry reporting, as well as the growing interdependence between industry trades and popular magazines covering Hollywood, is a 1959 *Hollywood Reporter* full-page ad celebrating *Saturday Evening Post's* "in-depth" analysis of Marilyn Monroe's new production company in a feature article titled "Blonde, Incorporated."[84]

The growing popularity of "behind-the-scenes" exposés of Hollywood practices and practitioners emerged simultaneously with two major changes in studio publicity department operations. The first change, prompted by the declining number of star contracts with the studios, was the studios' relinquished control over the New York–based fan magazine publications, which for several decades had been contractually obligated to adhere to predictable (and often fanciful) formulas when describing movie stars' lives in order to protect these valuable, studio-owned properties. The second major development was the waning popularity of the powerful newspaper entertainment columnists (e.g., Hedda Hopper, Louella Parsons, and Walter

Winchell), who had dominated the Hollywood- and New York–based gossip circuit throughout the 1930s and 1940s. In their place, a new generation of vaudeville and nightclub-entertainers-turned-film-and-radio-stars-turned-TV-hosts (e.g., Milton Berle, Jack Benny, Bob Hope, Dean Martin and Jerry Lewis) dispensed often highly cynical "insider information" from the bully pulpits of their popular 1950s' TV shows (e.g., *Texaco Star Theater, The Jack Benny Show,* the Bob Hope specials, and the *Colgate Comedy Hour*).[85] Insider references were most frequent on such variety shows, but they also became a regular feature of several successful situation comedies set in the world of show business (e.g., *I Love Lucy, The Burns and Allen Show, Make Room for Daddy*).[86]

The "instructional value" of television's insider perspectives for both film and television industry practitioners and average viewers during the postwar period of crisis and transformation cannot be overestimated. These gossipy shows mediated unresolved tensions associated with television's corporate address and enhanced the public's knowledge of how *both* the film and television industries functioned. The stand-up monologues and narrative skits articulated the changing and increasingly convoluted power dynamics among the various "players": TV hosts, costars, and guest stars; talent agents and managers; studio and network heads; show sponsors and magazine-spot advertisers. Equally important, the interwoven monologues and skits instructed average viewers on how to receive and integrate the new medium of television in their home décor and family rituals.[87] In sum, these shows used the contained irreverence of comedy to expose and then defuse sociocultural disquiet associated with television's erosion of the public/private divide and its insertion of consumer capitalism into the domestic sphere. Self-referential and reflexive television thus functioned quite differently from the self-referential and reflexive film. As we have previously discussed and will explore further in our case studies, the films served a disciplining function in regard to the perceived threat posed to the movies by TV— they sought to put television in its place. The films' mediating function had more to do with the quasi-independent filmmakers themselves (as well as the movie studio heads), and their ambivalent relationship to the New Hollywood (including, of course, TV) they had helped to fashion.

The paradox of rivalry and synergy between the two mediums, as well as the New Hollywood's ability to theorize its own relations, was revealed quite clearly, and colorfully, in an incident surrounding a 1952 episode of *The Colgate Comedy Hour.* The show's cohosts, Dean Martin and Jerry Lewis, created a major industry scandal that threatened their budding TV and movie careers when they made fun, in their opening monologue, of the movies' box-office crisis. Interspersed with the monologue were film clips of ushers running from a theater screaming they were lonely inside, and a cashier doing a striptease to lure customers into the empty movie house. In response, Arthur Mayer of the Council of Motion Picture Organizations fired off a wire to RCA president Frank Folsom:

> In depicting motion picture theaters as places shunned by the public, both the producers of the show and NBC have done serious damage to this industry. . . . We ask you to take steps to see that this scene is not repeated on other stations.

The council even proposed a boycott of Martin and Lewis's films by exhibitors. The comedy team quickly recanted:

> We're relatively new to motion pictures, and equally new to television and radio. Our principal experience has been in the intimate atmosphere of night clubs and personal appearances, where satire is accepted always in good fun. . . . We now realize . . . that such is not always the case with respect to radio, TV or the movies which reach vast audiences.

The debate, which played out for several days in the trades, shows how precarious the balancing act between waxing and waning, yet mightily interdependent industries, was, and how necessary the "intertextual discourse" had become to maintaining at least a semblance of equilibrium.[88]

Given the starkly contrasting economic trajectories of TV and the movies in the postwar period, it is not surprising that the intertextual discourse would diverge as well. Indeed, a distinct double standard prevailed, by which TV's criticism of the movies became taboo, while the movies' demonizing of TV was pursued with impunity if not active encouragement. Thus, trade reviews for *A Face in the Crowd* and *Sweet Smell of Success*—both released in 1957 and both scathingly critical of television—instruct studio marketing teams to capitalize on the growing interest in this type of film by targeting the narrow demographic of highly engaged, well-educated, more-sophisticated, urban viewers (i.e., the emerging art-house audience). The trade journals' comments are suggestive of the significant and paradoxical role which insider texts (whether from the political economic perspective of trades and the studios, or the mostly politically liberal perspective of most filmmakers) played during this transformative moment in postwar industry practices. The paradox is heightened on the macro level by the fact that these films with a decidedly anti–big business message were being produced, promoted, and praised by an industry in crisis during a period of severe political reaction.

A Face in the Crowd and *Sweet Smell of Success* are emphasized in this study because they highlight a number of the most important themes that run through the book: the antitelevision debate, the anti-"organization man" ethos, and the New Hollywood opportunity/dilemma for the politically liberal, artistic-minded filmmaker. These films, coming at the far end of the self-referential business-film cycle of the late 1940s and 1950s, are also striking in their proto-postmodernist coupling of a "high art" modernist aesthetic with "low art" mass-entertainment elements. Other postmodern attributes include the films' ironic tone, self-reflexivity, simultaneous critique and indulgence in that which is being critiqued, and blatant pastiche—both in form and content—of various mass media: vaudeville, nightclub, newspaper, magazine, pop music, radio, television. Both films can be said to function as liminal, or border, texts, and as such serve as prototypes for the brazenly postmodern product of more recent vintage: from David Lynch's *Blue Velvet* (1986) to Quentin Tarantino's *Pulp Fiction* (1994) to Robert Rodriguez's *Sin City* (2005).[89]

The analyses of *A Face in the Crowd* and *Sweet Smell of Success*, and other self-referential and reflexive films in the chapters to follow, are not meant to be exhaustive; rather, they are intended to highlight paradigmatic sociocultural and industrial concerns that emerged in the New Hollywood era. The goal of this book is not to replicate previous studies of the postwar era that emphasize the evolution of a modernist, self-reflexive trend by analyzing large numbers of films from the postwar era.[90] The aim is rather to isolate how media insiders (filmmakers, studio executives and marketers, industry trade analysts, agents, and film critics) were engaged in a complex and ongoing dialogue about the relationship between industry and culture a decade before Andrew Sarris and others had popularized their French-based, "high theoretical" auteurist theories prioritizing artistic autonomy without factoring in the historically specific impact of institutional-industrial forces on the filmmaking process. Indeed, at about the same time that critics at *Cahiers du cinéma* and *Positif* were beginning to assign authorship, most controversially, to both American A *and* B film directors of the classical period, newly independent U.S. filmmakers-turned-producers such as Wilder, Mankiewicz, Kazan/Schulberg, and Lancaster were themselves articulating and putting into practice an American art cinema that combined the best of European art cinema and postclassical Hollywood models by creating ideologically reflexive films that underscored the impact of a market-driven film and television industry on artistic decision making.

As for the remainder of the book's overall structure: following an examination in chapter 2 of mega-agency MCA—the business entity that, more than any other, laid the foundation for the New Hollywood—subsequent chapters interweave the textual and the extratextual. Industrial and societal forces, insider, popular and scholarly discourses, and a select group of self-referential and ideologically reflexive entertainment-business films are examined as both reflections and reproducers of the "industry intertext." Additionally, those readers with some understanding of contemporary industry practices—for example, the primacy of talent packaging, the mega-concentration and convergence of media enterprises, the twin economies of art-house/exploitation film and blockbuster—may discern in this postwar American film history the first manifestations of these postmodern markers. While the ancestral line is not straight, or the connective tissue unfrayed, salient characteristics of the contemporary mass-entertainment scene are traceable, to a significant degree, to the seismic 1940s/1950s shift from the Old to the New Hollywood.

2.
Backstage Dramas:
MCA and the Talent Takeover

A Hollywood saying has it that "if MCA isn't God, nobody in
the company knows it." It would be hard to blame MCA executives
for playing God occasionally, for that's how many important
entertainment-industry executives treat them.

—EDWARD T. THOMPSON, "There's No Show Business
like MCA's Business"

The years 1942 to 1962, and especially the postwar years when the Old
Hollywood studio system began to crumble, marked a major transition in
the way the film industry did business. When the movies began experiencing serious economic difficulties in 1947, the three top talent agencies—
MCA (Music Corporation of America), the William Morris Agency
(WMA), and Famous Artists—became an increasingly powerful presence
in the industry because of their formidable relationships with newly independent above-the-line talent: writers, directors, and, especially, the stars.[1]
Studio executives found themselves ever more at the mercy of the elite
agencies if they wanted to access big-name talent, which the moguls believed
they needed to sell their movies to the public.[2] MCA and its head, Lew
Wasserman, in particular, pioneered this new relationship between studio
and agency and exploited it to the fullest, thereby altering forever the power
dynamics in Hollywood. Furthermore, according to Gomery, "Through
the 1950s and 1960s Lew Wasserman re-crafted the independent mode of
filmmaking and brought broadcast television production and exploitation
into the Hollywood 'film' industry."[3]

The groundwork for the agency "takeover" in Hollywood was laid by a
series of postwar institutional changes. The most significant of these was
the government-mandated divestiture of studio-owned theaters brought
about by the Paramount decrees in 1948. This, in combination with reduced domestic attendance and protectionist measures abroad, forced the
studios to cut back on production, which in turn created excess studio space

and overhead, and altered distribution patterns. Given these no-longer-functioning economies of scale, the studios were forced to lay off personnel, sell off props and studio property, and rent out office space, soundstages, and back lots to independent producers. In the thirties and forties, the seven major studios with talent under contract (only UA did not) each kept a stable of 300 or 400 high-salaried stars, featured players, directors, writers, producers, and cameramen. As a result of drastically reduced production, the 742 actors under contract in 1947 were reduced to 229 by 1956.[4] The forty producers with studio deals in 1947 became 165 by 1957. A 1953 *Hollywood Reporter* article titled "Long-Term Deals on Way Out" reported on the drop-off in contract-talent:

> Paramount is down to three in the star division—Crosby, Hope, and Holden—but has another 12 others with young players. . . . Twentieth-Century Fox has only [director] Henry King and [actor] Clifton Webb holding what might be termed "long deals" with the company. . . . RKO has only 5 term-contracts operating.[5]

MGM held out longer than most, but soon even it was forced to give up most of its star contracts. While studio heads Jack Warner, Darryl Zanuck (Fox), Harry Cohn (Columbia), and Louis B. Mayer (MGM) struggled to maintain their hold on power in the post-1948 era, Hollywood's leverage was increasingly shifting to the new generation of agents and attorneys who had access to stars suddenly cut loose from the long-term studio contracts of old.

As early as 1945, a federal judge who was presiding over a $3.3-million antitrust case against MCA nicknamed the organization "the Octopus" to describe its monopoly stranglehold over the big-band industry.[6] The name stuck, although this early antitrust charge did not. By 1957 MCA had extended its tentacles to the movies and television, further justifying the derogatory nickname to describe the extent of its dominance over every aspect of the entertainment industry. That same year the owner and lead columnist for the *Hollywood Reporter*, W. R. "Billy" Wilkerson, expressed his pessimism about the studios' ability to develop new stars in the face of the competition represented by the newly omnipowerful agencies. Even if the studios found new talent, he lamented, "when that time arrives there is still a chance that player and agent maneuverings might jerk some of these aces away for a dive into their own production companies, or outside pictures, shoving the studios back to where they are now."[7] This possibility made it seem fruitless for a studio to spend time and resources to develop a big star because even if the studio succeeded, the agents would swoop down and entice the talent to forge their independence.

The second most significant institutional crisis confronting postwar Hollywood was the emergence of television. Here also the new emerging powerhouses, the agencies, were able to adapt to and capitalize much more quickly on this changed circumstance than the moribund studios whose moguls had been accustomed to conducting business in a set pattern for a decade. As Anderson points out in *Hollywood TV,* the studios responded to the potential threat of television by seeking to replicate their current strengths as distributors in the new medium. When federal regulators blocked the studios from entering the television industry via distribution outlets already dominated by radio, most major studios didn't gravitate immediately to the next big opportunity open to them, television production. Had they done so, they would have been able to capitalize on their production facilities, their factory-like production capabilities, and their backlog of films to help fill the new medium's voracious need for content. Instead, some studios created further roadblocks to entry into the booming TV industry because they were reluctant to allow their remaining studio contract players to appear on regular television series. This resistance to the new medium was not monolithic, however. Columbia, Universal, and Disney became involved in TV production early on; Paramount actually co-owned (with DuMont) several early TV stations before the FCC and the consent decrees nixed the deals; and the film industry encouraged, as it had previously with radio, numerous synergies including promotional appearances by film stars.[8] Nevertheless, Hollywood's overall attitude toward television, initially at least, was ambivalent at best, hostile at worst.

In contrast, the agencies, and Lew Wasserman in particular, aggressively pursued television, seeing it as a means of getting work for their clients in an era when Hollywood film production was in decline. Wasserman offered lucrative television production and profit-participation deals to both established talents like Jack Benny and to new, prospective clients like George Gobel, and offered MCA's aging movie-star clients roles as guest stars on ongoing series. Furthermore, the agency began purchasing already aired television shows (those that had been filmed instead of kinescoped) for reruns and purchased pre-1949 movies (from those studios which would permit it) to release through syndication to sponsors and local networks.[9] Unique among the Big Three agencies, MCA also became a primary producer of television programming through its production subsidiary Revue Studios.

Finally, and the overriding factor in its near-monopolistic hold over the television business, MCA gained a ten-year "head start" over other TV production companies by wangling a Screen Actors Guild waiver that allowed the company to both represent talent and produce the shows in which those writers, actors, and directors appeared. Hollywood's once-dominant studio system reeled from the effects of these changes, as the stars, major directors, and their handlers almost overnight usurped the power long held by the studios.

The Transformation of the Hollywood Star System

Starting as early as 1942 with the formation of Bette Davis's independent production company, B.D., Inc., MCA began forging lucrative talent deals on behalf of its clients, using them as leverage and causing agents to emerge as key decision-makers in Hollywood. MCA helped other middle-aged movie stars such as Joan Crawford, dubbed "box-office poison" in the trades by exhibitors, to revitalize their careers.[10] MCA helped Crawford rebound from her career slump in 1945 by negotiating with Warner Bros. to secure her role in the Academy Award–winning *Mildred Pierce*. The agency accomplished similar successful career makeovers for John Garfield, Jimmy Stewart, and countless others. In fact, Wasserman couldn't have been happier when older stars started walking away from their contracts with the studios and forming their own companies.[11]

Wasserman also understood, better than the studio bosses, that accepting and adapting to the neuroses and "childish whims" of his high-priced clientele was part of the mainstream filmmaking process. For instance, Bette Davis flagrantly rebelled against Warner Bros. by refusing to grant interviews to the press or, if she did, she complained about the rotten dialogue she was forced to deliver. Jack Warner insisted that Wasserman "control his client." Instead, Wasserman backed Davis, citing her right to freedom of speech. Jack Warner tried to punish MCA for turning the studio's best contract players like Bette Davis into "freelancers" by threatening to ban MCA agents from his lot. However, like other studio heads who were initially baffled and angered by MCA's newly acquired ability to assert control where previously the studios held sway, Warner eventually had to give in if he wanted access to MCA's burgeoning talent roster.[12]

While some of the old studio actors who formed production companies with the help of the agencies used the companies primarily as corporate shells and tax shelters, a new breed of actor emerged—those who were anxious to take a more entrepreneurial role in their companies and their careers. In 1945 Joan Bennett formed Diana Productions with husband/ producer Walter Wanger and director Fritz Lang.[13] In 1948 Burt Lancaster formed Hecht-Lancaster with his former agent, Harold Hecht. Their independence from the studios granted Lancaster and Bennett, and the large numbers of actors who followed suit from the late forties on, a greater choice of projects and greater responsibility for managing their images and maintaining their status as desirable commodities in a highly competitive marketplace. On the other hand, other factors compromised that independence, the primary one being the need to take advantage of the studios' still comparative largess and resources during this period of severe box-office decline.[14] Nonetheless, the assets of a major studio, including a physical plant and technical departments, an apparatus for distributing films to theaters, and the ability to borrow money for financing, were now rented out on a film-by-film basis to enterprising independent companies as the stars increasingly arranged deals themselves.[15]

In 1950 MCA changed the Old Hollywood rules once again by creating a lucrative percentage deal on *Winchester '73* (1950) for its star Stewart, whose acting career, after he returned from active duty in World War II, was nowhere near its prewar stature. While star percentage deals had been in place as early as 1919, they had grown out of favor during the thirties and forties when seven-year studio star contracts became the norm. Even the most successful stars under contract during the "old studio" era, stars whose salaries rose as high as $5,000–$6,000 a week by the early forties, lost up to 90 percent of their earnings to taxes. The combined impact of the independent production companies and star profit participation deals irrevocably altered the way business was conducted in postwar Hollywood by granting stars greater creative autonomy and deal-making leverage with the studios, as well as considerable tax benefits. These agency-engineered production companies, lucrative percentage deals, and tax shelters restored the careers of an older generation of movie stars and launched the careers of a new generation of movie and television talent. The stars' greater independence, once they had broken free from their rigidly paternalistic studio contracts, was not without negative consequences. The trade and popular-press discourse of the time opined that the glamour associated with the Old Hollywood star system was being tarnished by a heightened emphasis on the stars' finances and their increasing control over their careers.[16]

The new professional class of bureaucrats, brokers, and handlers—exemplified by super-agents like Stein and Wasserman—was a crucial component of the evolution from the Old to the New Hollywood, and of the emerging self-referential, anti–big business film. Given its proximity to talent and its often unscrupulous tactics, this new breed of power player radically altered the way stars and other members of the creative team—writers, directors, and producers—were perceived during the postwar era. The MCA team, as we have seen, worked hard to preserve the impression that the stars, in particular, still maintained their aristocratic otherness, but it became an increasingly difficult subterfuge to maintain.

The changing political landscape also contributed to altered perceptions of the role and function of the stars, and the movie industry in general, in the postwar era. Former *Time* magazine entertainment reporter Ezra Goodman, for example, pointed to the contrasting political persona of fifties star William Holden to thirties/forties star John Garfield: "Holden, in his businesslike, clean-cut way, was representative of the Eisenhower era (Holden was a Republican) in the same sense that John Garfield, for instance, typified the turbulent, proletarian Thirties."[17] Stars like Garfield, Chaplin, Eddie Cantor, and others, spurred by the anticorporate and populist sentiments of the thirties, helped unionize Hollywood's actors. Given the high-profile status of its members, the organizing activities of the Screen Actors Guild (SAG) helped capture public attention and, most significantly, represented a significant shift in attitudes toward the members of the crafts unions.[18]

Whereas previous union activities in Hollywood had been associated with the crafts (grips, prop masters, electricians, editors, and the like), whose members largely stemmed from the underpaid, blue-collar classes, SAG members (at least the famous minority of established movie stars) were comprised of well-paid, white-collar "talent." Spotlighting the abundantly wealthy and successful movie stars in the guild could have been seen as detrimental to the cause of the working class. However, the actors' highly publicized pro-union activities, along with those of writers and directors, helped forge significant alliances across class lines and furthered the cause of the crafts, which could use the boost.[19] Prior to 1937, the mob had come to control the major crafts union, the International Association of Theater and Stage Employees (IATSE), and coordinated its activities with studio heads and producers who agreed to pay off union leaders in order to keep wages and labor unrest in check. Starting in 1937, in an effort to wrest craft-union control from the mobs, left-leaning talent-guild members supported the efforts of leftist organizer Herbert Sorrell to form the Conference of Studio Unions (CSU) as a progressive alternative to the corrupt IATSE. The guilds' and the CSU's combined efforts helped to put both the mobsters involved with IATSE and some of their corrupt producer allies in jail.[20]

Lary May further demonstrates how these early union developments unified talent and crafts workers against those moguls and producers who tried to use "red-baiting" as a way to undermine union efforts during this politically turbulent period. However, the tide shifted during the forties when producers, stars, union leaders, and others in Hollywood felt a responsibility to join forces during the war effort to boost domestic morale and to enhance the image of America abroad. William Holden typified this patriotic attitude. According to Goodman, "He traveled extensively abroad on behalf, he said, of his studio, Paramount, and of the movie industry in general, as 'an ambassador of good will.'" Holden viewed liberal stars like Humphrey Bogart and his "Holmby Hills rat pack," which Goodman describes as "an aggregation of fun-loving profiles with Dead End kid inclinations," as making his job doubly hard.[21] When he went abroad to Japan or India or France and was asked about the rat pack, Holden replied,

> Not all actors are bad. It might sound stuffy and dull, but it is quite possible for people to have social intercourse without resorting to a rat pack. . . . People have worked for years to lend some dignity to our profession and it [the rat pack] reflects on the community and on my children and on their children and everybody's children.[22]

The unbridled patriotism which Holden, Bob Hope, Bing Crosby, and other prominent stars attributed to their role as Hollywood spokespersons and representatives of the acting profession took on a reactionary cast as the Cold War gathered steam. Eric Johnston, the new head of the Motion Picture Association of America (MPAA), published an article in 1946 titled "Utopia Is Production," which called upon the SAG leadership to continue to further the cause of American capitalism here and abroad after the war was over. Johnston's position argued for a reversal of SAG's newly forged political alliance with the crafts unions and urged all Hollywood players to align themselves instead with big business and corporate leaders in an attack on labor militants. The reactionary demand for once-liberal filmmakers to drop their affiliations with unions to support big business reflected the shifting Cold War climate and mirrored developments taking shape at the national level in Washington, events that would propel the HUAC hearings of 1947 that specifically targeted left-wing elements in Hollywood. Whereas in the late thirties SAG and other key unions had denounced red-baiting during HUAC's initial foray into Hollywood, now the ideological shift enunciated by Johnston and carried out by HUAC paved the way for a reinvigorated brand of anti-Communism made suddenly more palatable by Cold War concerns about national security and the survival of American capitalism.

The paradigm shifts in the postwar political landscape, coupled with the institutional sea changes already delineated, contributed in the late forties and fifties to a revolution in the Hollywood star system. The remainder of this chapter examines the most dynamic mover and shaker of this New Hollywood system, MCA, and the man who made it move and shake, Lew Wasserman.

MCA, Phase One: Contending with an Image Problem

Whereas most movie stars recognized that their financial circumstances improved once they were represented by MCA, many talented and successful directors under contract to MCA, including Alfred Hitchcock and Billy Wilder, wrestled with the problem of how to manage the agency's power over them. Their contempt for the agencies was evident not only in their films but also in veiled insults such as a painting Hitchcock gave to Wasserman in the sixties. As Wasserman biographer Dennis McDougal describes the incident:

> Hanging in the Wasserman house, along with the other expensive art, was a gift from Hitchcock—an exaggerated oil portrait of somber Lew Wasserman. "Lew looked like some stern-faced personification of evil in the painting," said a senior MCA executive during the sixties. I once asked Hitch, "Doesn't he get it?" And he just blinked at me, as if he didn't quite understand what I meant. But I'm sure he did.[23]

Who had the last laugh? The agent who earned steady profits from a favored client or the director who felt both gratitude and disdain for the strong-arm tactics of the middleman who was able to garner both greater financial rewards and increased creative autonomy for the director?

Further facilitating filmmakers' willingness to accept the business arrangements of the new breed of "moguls" was Wasserman's ability to transform the image not just of the agencies but of Hollywood itself by refashioning the status of the agent from unmitigated scoundrel to sophisticated businessman. This was no easy task, given the stereotypical view of agents as hustlers, flesh-peddlers, and glorified car salesmen that had persisted since the earliest days of Hollywood (and continues to this day). Adding to the shady reputation of these backroom go-betweens was the perception that they tended to operate "in the dark" and through invisible means. Given the agency's penchant for keeping its business practices a secret, the trade press would often draw unsavory conclusions. For instance, when Frank Sinatra opted to leave his agency voluntarily and join MCA at the height of his career, the trade press assumed it was another instance of client theft.[24] Agents were not creative talent themselves, nor did they get credit on the screen for their accomplishments. But given their access to and contractual relationship with talent, they were key to every transaction. As MCA historian Connie Bruck notes, when MCA went into business in the early forties, "it was surprising, in a way, that there were so many sellers; some may have felt it was an offer they couldn't refuse, [the alternative being MCA's stealing of all their clients and leaving them with nothing]."[25] Thus, as the ambivalence toward agents may have risen as their power within the industry increased, so did respect for their ability to maintain a low profile while both managing their top-dollar talent and maximizing everyone's bottom line.

By 1949, after Wasserman negotiated Jimmy Stewart's landmark gross percentage deal on *Winchester '73*, every star in Hollywood wanted him to do the same for them, and Wasserman's dominion within the industry was secure. But in 1942 MCA was still a sleeping giant and agents were viewed in Hollywood with undiluted derision, variously known in the industry as "tapeworms, leeches, bloodsuckers, parasites, flesh peddlers and various technical terms borrowed from the underworld."[26] The first in a series of popular-press articles on talent agents emerged the same year, indicating that the public perception of agents was similarly negative. The articles by Alva Johnston in the *Saturday Evening Post* depicted agents as the bottom of the Hollywood food chain. Oddly, the series made little mention of MCA specifically, even though it had been a prominent agency since the thirties, a striking omission that is probably due to the fact that the *Saturday Evening Post* was reluctant to criticize this powerhouse given the magazine's dependence on MCA as an inside source for its frequent articles about Hollywood talent.[27] Johnston's 1942 articles were lighthearted, but the negative perception of agents was clear enough in the portrait of them as low-level salesmen who handle, along with unknown actors, also mules, rats, and other lesser beasts. Zeppo Marx, Johnston pointed out, moved back and forth between being an agent and joining the madcap antics of his brothers on screen as the fourth Marx Brother, implying that he engaged in clownish behavior on and off the screen. The articles also underscored agents' relative lack of power by focusing on the small-time agent who had to spend years "scouting amateur theatricals" in search of the newest personality and fostering that talent only to have a bigger agent come along and steal the client away. Johnston reported that movie stars were advised by studio publicity departments regulating the public perception of their clients "to cut low-level agents from their circle and mix only with the aristocracy."[28]

The popular discourses on agents in the early 1940s were closely linked to the studio-controlled publicity campaigns used to promote stars under contract. These campaigns sometimes featured "behind the scenes" looks at movie stars' lives on the job or at home but the goal was to encourage fan identification rather than envy. The publicity circulating around Joan Bennett, for instance, typified the "bourgeoisification" that film theorists Edgar Morin and Richard Dyer suggest took place in the late thirties and forties so that stars would seem more ordinary, their lives closer to that of the fans.[29] The campaigns also emphasized the hard work associated with becoming a star. Prewar studio-era publicity departments helped foster the myth that most stars' success was the result of a "rags-to-riches" story.[30] However, once they had ascended the ranks of stardom, publicity releases often reinforced the actors' aristocratic separation from the sordid world of business. In the case of Joan Bennett, her domestic image as wife, mother, and hostess was balanced with her glamorized star image perpetuated through her wearing expensive clothes and holding well-publicized parties at her large Holmby Hills home. Once she formed her own production company, the publicity avoided compromising prescribed gender roles for postwar women by emphasizing that her professional responsibilities never took precedence over her domestic duties. Few references were made to salaries, profit participation, or other "behind-the-scenes" activities.[31] Studio publicity departments made every effort to separate out and hide what many perceived as the stars' excessive salaries or aristocratic lifestyles so as not to encourage envy among fans.[32] All this subterfuge and contradiction did not prevent the studio owners from reaping additional revenues by capitalizing on their stars' allure through commercial tie-ins and merchandising schemes once a star's publicity campaign was established and the star had taken off.[33]

One aspect of stars' financial lives that began to be scrutinized more closely, and more critically, in the forties was agents' unseemly association with their clients' income. Johnston made clear in the 1942 *Post* articles that she disapproved of agents because they earned their living by squeezing money from the pockets of the "hard-working" stars. One photo shows Bob Hope standing with his pockets inside out, along with a quip he delivered to his agent, Louis Shurr: "Look at all the money you're going to make, Louis." In yet another photo, noted William Morris agent Johnny Hyde, described as being "short and plain," "highspots" himself (i.e., enhances the value of a client through some manufactured public relations scenario) by appearing in public with a star who is tall and beautiful—Linda Darnell, with whom Hyde is shown dancing while staring at her décolletage (Hyde later became famous for orchestrating Marilyn Monroe's early career). The common point of these images is that agents are "cads" or "hangers-on" who stand to benefit in financial and perhaps other fleshly ways through their association with glamorous stars. The agent's actual work is devalued as well, described as playing "nursemaid to Hollywood stars for ten per cent of their salaries."[34]

The *Post* articles damn agents with faint praise by describing the slight recent improvements in the profession, such as agents trading in their once-outlandish garb for more respectable-looking offices and clothes (described as "more Wall Street" now than before). Johnston reminds us that all these improvements are paid for courtesy of their star clients, once again circulating the notion that agents do not do "real" work to earn their living.[35] To counter what the star clients and Johnston clearly saw as highway robbery, Johnson added that the star "still puts in much of his [or her] spare time inventing jests to make the agents look ridiculous." For instance, Carole Lombard created an elaborate practical joke in which she took the small-print contract her long-time agent Myron Selznick had given her and returned a different contract that stated the agent was required to pay *her* 10 percent of what *he* made. Another popular anti-agent joke of the day prevented agents from drinking tomato juice in public to avoid jabs about them squeezing blood from their clients.[36]

An even more elaborate prank involved the successful writing team of Billy Wilder and Charles Brackett. Small to medium-size agents had to pay a hefty fee (in the *Post* article, it ranged from $17,500 to $25,000) for a piece of big-name talent. This left the agent vulnerable if the talent "died." Therefore, when Leland Hayward bought an agent's contract for the prize writing team of Brackett and Wilder, he sent a physician to give them a medical examination first. To mock this blatant (and morbid) act of objectifying their "value," Wilder and Brackett sent a psychiatrist to examine the agent.[37] While this joke is an early example of Wilder's famous acerbic wit regarding the industry he knew so well, it is also a telling portrait of a time (early forties) when talent could still make a mockery of its agency representatives without fear of repercussion.

In contrast to the crassly negative photos and anecdotes about agents in the 1942 *Post* article, another photo in the same article shows Jimmy Stewart dining at Ciro's with Ginger Rogers. Her agent, Leland Hayward, looking elegant and dignified, is seated at a respectful distance, thus conveying a more complex ambivalence about the difference in status between stars and their handlers. Stewart and Rogers share what seems to be an intimate moment, exchanging looks and conversation; Hayward is not included in the exchange but merely looks on. Another photo whose tagline emphasizes Hayward's economic ties to another client, his future wife, Margaret Sullavan, also underscores the combined proximity and implied separation of the star and her opportunistic business manager.[38] The article goes on to point out that when Hayward married Sullavan, he received a wire, "Congratulations on getting the other ninety per cent." This nasty joke at the agent's expense contains an added slight of his masculinity in referring to the inversion of the normal gender role of the breadwinner husband.

Whitney Stine's 1985 historical account of talent agents helps clarify the contradictory meanings associated with Hayward's image in 1942 and helps explain Hayward's contribution to the transformed perception of agents. Hayward was perceived as well bred, intelligent, well read, a supposed "rarity among agents," according to various popular magazine accounts. A wide range of clients from stars Sullavan, Hepburn, and Merle Oberon to author Ernest Hemingway admired Hayward, calling him the "best agent in the world."[39] Furthermore, Hayward was credited with having initiated the postwar acting and writing talent raids among the major studios, something Wasserman also would later be credited/accused of pioneering. Louis B. Mayer of MGM, for instance, was annoyed when Hayward convinced Jimmy Stewart to leave MGM after he returned from World War II, a decision that later prompted Wasserman to step in and resuscitate Stewart's career through the orchestration of the epochal *Winchester '73* deal. In other words, Hayward served as a precedent and role model, both in terms of his business savvy and his fashion sense, for all agents in the forties and fifties, but none more than Jules Stein and Wasserman at MCA. However, as aggressive businessmen, none surpassed Stein and his protégé Wasserman.

Bruck notes that after talented agents Leland Hayward and Nat Deverich decided to merge with MCA in 1945, turning MCA overnight into the most powerful agency in the world, the hard part, according to Hayward's assistant, Larry White, was getting Hayward-Deverich's clients (e.g.,

Jimmy Stewart, Greta Garbo, Myrna Loy, Ginger Rogers, Margaret Sullavan, Fred Astaire, Joseph Cotten, Oscar Levant, and Fredric March, as well
as producers and directors like Billy Wilder and Joshua Logan) to move to
the more cutthroat operation. Hayward told White, "Getting some of the
artists to go there was hell—send them flowers, candy, do whatever you have
to do." White added, "Generally speaking you had an agent like Leland,
he took 10 percent. But with MCA, you didn't know what they would take.
And the artists were afraid of them. They [MCA] let you know they could
destroy your career."[40]

A final example from Johnston's 1942 *Post* article reveals a latent climate
of political conservatism in Hollywood that accompanied the heightened
focus on big business. When Orson Welles refused to "play ball" with the
bigger agents, preferring to remain loyal to a young New York agent, Albert
Schneider, the Hollywood agents "soon lost interest in the boy genius" who
wasn't interested in money. According to Johnston, Welles became known
as a "dangerous Red" after *It's All True,* his second film project after *Citizen*

MCA buys out the Hayward–Deverich Agency in 1945: *(left to right)* Leland Hayward,
Lew Wasserman, Jules Stein *(center)*, Nat Deverich, and Taft Schreiber. Courtesy of Screen
Actors Guild Foundation / Gene Lester Collection.

Kane, was shelved (after the studio "wasted" a good deal of money on it), and Welles offered to make another picture for nothing.[41] But Welles's forgoing an income was considered anti-American and caused him to be dubbed a Communist years before Cold War politics and blacklisting would be formally implemented.[42] On the one hand, Johnston's relating this incident reinforces her theme that agents were only interested in making money off their celebrated clients. On the other hand, it speaks to the complex, increasingly reactionary wartime political climate in Hollywood that threatened liberal filmmakers like Welles who preferred to see filmmaking more as a selfless act of artistry and possibly even of political engagement rather than as a purely profit-making enterprise.

Lew Wasserman understood the business/politics distinction early on when he warned the then-liberal actor Ronald Reagan not to engage in an antinuclear rally in 1945. "Like other left-leaning clients, Reagan had to be convinced that political convictions were irrelevant when it came to staying employed."[43] The agent implicitly understood that his leverage with talent depended primarily on his ability to capitalize on stars' financial and career ambitions. Because Welles operated outside the economic parameters of the business, it followed that he could not be controlled by the system and was thus expendable. Welles would spend much of the remainder of his career in Europe. But the problem of reconciling artistic integrity and political belief with financial success would not go away; indeed, it would increase in intensity in the "independent" atmosphere of the New Hollywood, as we will see in subsequent chapters' discussion of particular films and filmmakers.

MCA, Phase II: Dealing with Pre-eminence

The second phase in the popular media's efforts to explain agents to the public began in 1946 in a second *Saturday Evening Post* series.[44] Whereas the 1942 series carefully omitted any references to the sleeping giant, MCA, the agency was forewarned that it would be foregrounded in the 1946 article. The agency was terrified about what might be revealed in this second article. As it turned out, when *Post* reporter David Wittel published "The Star-Spangled Octopus" in 1946, Wasserman and his boss, Jules Stein, were relieved with the result. While the articles reasserted the pejorative name "octopus," which would stick to MCA for the next twenty years, the article was largely adulatory in its treatment of the powerful agency.[45] Wasserman, Stein, and Sonny Werblin, the key members of the MCA power elite, were given sympathetic public personalities for the first time. Wasserman, in particular, using the same "rags-to-riches" story studio publicists had used with their star clients, was described as having moved from the Jewish ghetto to the top. Stein, accorded a bit more mystique, was called "Mr. Big of show business . . . who remains a mystery."[46] A comparison of the 1942 and 1946 *Post* articles suggests the vast change in perception that agents had undergone in only four years; largely through its increased power and prestige in the industry, MCA had managed to banish its lowly "flesh-peddler" image.

Part of the business strategy adopted by MCA to engineer this image makeover was to downplay its own business strategies and avoid publicity, preferring to operate, even more stealthily than usual in the business, behind the scenes. Instead, MCA emphasized results, showcasing the great deals engineered on behalf of their most famous clients, the stars. Movie stars have always personified, if ambivalently, the American Dream to many people. Richard Dreyer, among other media scholars dealing with the concept of stardom, has demonstrated the extent to which stars are products of media industries: "Hollywood controlled not only the stars' films but their promotion, the pin-ups and glamour portraits, press releases and to a large extent the fan clubs."[47] However, equally important was the creation of a notion of individuality. Therefore, in the thirties and forties, studio publicity departments sought various means to bridge the gap between the star's persona (the cumulative impression created by a string of movie roles) and their individual or private lives to emphasize this impression of a larger-than-life "individualism." Wasserman used his initial famous client conquests like Bette Davis, Jimmy Stewart, and Lana Turner to draw other big-name stars to the agency, making every effort to capitalize on the aura (the heightened impression of glamour and uniqueness) associated with stars during the golden era of Hollywood, while downplaying the role of the agent. MCA was able to court stars like Davis and Stewart by offering them an enhanced if largely illusory sense of power and autonomy through the formation of corporations in their names (although the ploy did help them tax-wise). In this way, the entertainment business shifted from the paternalistic system of the old studio days to one in which the stars now appeared to hold the power, a power linked to their status as glorified "individuals." However, because most of the agency's actor-clients were not accustomed to handling their own negotiations, Wasserman, Stein, and other super-agents ended up becoming the new patriarchs—potent, behind-the-scenes strategists, managing not only the stars' transactions with the studios but also their overall investment activities, whether in terms of optioning a screenplay or book, negotiating profit-participation deals, or advising on lucrative real-estate transactions.

One of the ways Wasserman ensured that public attention went to the stars rather than to MCA or its agents was to turn his agents into "team players" who were expected to work on behalf of the agency rather than for individual gain. Wasserman insisted on regimenting the agency to enhance his control over the information flow. According to Bruck, "Wasserman had also instituted a system, unique to MCA, in which agents covered not only their clients but a particular studio"—an industry standard at most large agencies today.[48] All agents were expected to write daily reports on their activities to the MCA executives, reports that were discussed at weekly meetings. The company's uniformity of dress—the requisite dark suit, white shirt, and dark tie—long hours, and a detached, unemotional demeanor were all part of the "gray flannel" trend that at this stage of the agency's evolution (late 1940s/early 1950s), and it turned out to be a winning strategy. Indeed, the trend persisted into the 1980s and 1990s, when super-agent Michael Ovitz formed Creative Artists Agency (CAA) and steered it to preeminence in the industry. Emulating Wasserman, Ovitz required CAA agents to dress uniformly, avoid publicity, and emphasize teamwork in their work ethic—what Ovitz, in a New Age twist, identified as an "Oriental style" of doing business, in contrast to the Western focus on individual ambition. Of course, Ovitz and CAA, like Wasserman and company before him, rode this "modest, unassuming" style all the way to the bank, swank resorts, and mansions in Beverly Hills. As McDougal notes, "[CAA heads] Michael Ovitz, Ron Meyer, Rowland Perkins, Bill Haber, and Michael Rosenfield employed exactly the same star power, packaging pressure, and publicity techniques that MCA had pioneered close to half a century earlier."[49]

Not everyone was willing to go along with Wasserman's tyrannical rules in the early postwar era, however, which included catering to the client's every whim, whether "it meant giving them pedicures, personally picking up their dry cleaning or giving their dressing room a new coat of paint." Irving "Swifty" Lazar (who later became an independent super-agent himself) was one MCA acolyte who refused to sublimate his ego and conform to Wasserman's mandates. Whereas Wasserman's new-style of agenting required total selfless devotion to the job, old-school agent Lazar felt that agents should only be expected to negotiate contracts, settle disputes with directors, and handle similar types of business. So Lazar quit.[50]

Wasserman also wanted his agents to keep out of the limelight for another reason: MCA was operating on the fringes of unethical if not illegal business practices. Given the studios' and production companies' desperate need to access the agency's ever-growing roster of bankable clients, MCA could strong-arm the former into doing business with the agency on the agency's terms. Thus the agency gained nothing by grandstanding about its deals in public. Furthermore, MCA's ability to exert control over the entertainment industry was enhanced if MCA's competitors were in the dark about how MCA did its deals. Such furtiveness also guarded against other agencies' poaching of MCA's clients and prevented these agencies from countering MCA's draconian demands on behalf of its clients.

While Wasserman remained tight-lipped about MCA's insider operations when dealing with the popular press, he was less successful in preventing the industry trades from documenting his business activities. After all, Wasserman had almost single-handedly transformed the nature of deal making in postwar Hollywood by taking into account complex tax laws and arcane legal principles previously unexplored by nonstudio personnel. Wasserman received accolades from a variety of industry professionals from tax accountants to entertainment attorneys who "marveled over his mastery of the hidden rules of show business." A business columnist for *Hollywood Close-Up* magazine wrote, "An acute student of facts, figures and trends and percentages, Wasserman reduces moviemaking to the science of the slide rule." Another wrote in *Show Business Illustrated*, "Wasserman . . . the most potent single figure in show business today is mightily admired for his imaginative approach to taxes." A top theatrical lawyer stated, "Without formal legal training he knows more about taxes than any of us. Show business contracts have jumped from two to a hundred pages since the war, partly to accommodate the deals devised by Mr. Wasserman."[51] These industry-trade quotes indicate the extent to which a cadre of high-priced lawyers, accountants, and especially agents had taken over an industry previously orchestrated by a handful of studio moguls.

The infiltration of layers of bureaucrats into people's daily lives in an increasingly corporate America did not begin in, nor was its entrenchment limited to, the New Hollywood. And the pejorative "organization man" description that came to characterize big-business board rooms across the country would ultimately tarnish—from a position of dominance, this time, rather than of subservience—the more positive agent's image Wasserman had worked so hard and so successfully to fashion. In addition, despite Wasserman's best efforts to avoid publicity, the negative ramifications of his company's complex, back-door deals engineered by a new breed of "gray-flannel" professionals were starting to become visible to the public at large given the agency's high-profile role in administrating the careers of the public's favorite stars.

The MCA Star Treatment

Among the first movie stars to get the "MCA treatment" were Bette Davis and Jimmy Stewart. As one of the big earners from the studio contract days, Davis was among the elite players who had been losing 90 percent of her salary to taxes until Jules Stein helped the Oscar-winning actress form her own corporation. As a corporation, she paid a much smaller fraction of her earnings in capital gains taxes than she would if taxed directly on her personal income (in 1945, for example, Davis earned $328,000 from Warner Bros. but kept only $90,000 after taxes).[52] Davis, meanwhile, was the high-profile "magnet" MCA needed to pursue other stars, who soon came clamoring for Wasserman or Stein to turn them into corporations. The strategy was not based purely on a humanistic desire to help movie stars, of course, but was another way for MCA to extract more money from its clients by gleaning 10 percent of the star's corporate profits as opposed to the typical 10 percent fee based on the star's salary on individual movies.

For the studios, having their studio contract players under the sway of a powerful agency like MCA created a problem by introducing a burdensome middleman. Now they had to negotiate with shark-like manipulators like Wasserman and Stein rather than the individual actor who was often inept when it came to negotiating on his or her own behalf. Even before 1942, agents understood the unwritten principle that actors and other talent should not negotiate for themselves. Indeed, once they had achieved their palace coup with the studios, the agencies adopted the same policy: "Unless the client is gagged, he is likely to spoil everything by jumping at a moderate figure instead of holding out for a handsome one."[53]

While the decline of studio dominance freed writers, producers, directors, and actors from studio contracts, it was a circumscribed independence. Much of the control over their careers simply shifted from the studios to representatives of the above-the-line talent. As the agencies gathered more power in the wake of the movie-theater divestiture and movie attendance, they increasingly insinuated themselves into studio business transactions by acting as the gateway to talent. So how independent, in the end, were the New Hollywood stars, directors, and other above-the-line talent? Had they simply traded one oppressor for another? Some stars like Clark Gable or Kirk Douglas, who were known as industry renegades, were hesitant to align themselves with the aggressive agencies but ultimately acceded because it granted them greater leverage as producers—who themselves became engaged in high-stakes negotiations with talent.

The changing climate of Hollywood impacted the lives of the new, more-powerful breed of freelance talent in various, not always positive, ways. Agencies were more interested in a volume business—in creating large numbers of deals on behalf of many clients—than in keeping individual clients happy. MCA agents, for instance, were notorious for coddling talent in the beginning but once the actor was represented by the agency, the agent would move on to the next conquest. As *Fortune* reported in 1960, "According to Hollywood producer George Stevens, '. . . They are very adept with the velvet-glove technique.' Obviously, the velvet-glove technique is enough when you represent so much of the cream of show-business talent that everybody in the industry fears your slightest frown of displeasure."[54] Whitney Stine, in *Stars and Star Handlers: The Business of Show*, provides an anecdote that was in circulation in the late forties. MCA agent Phil Berg was at the Trocadero nightclub when he was introduced to screenwriter Thomas Monroe. The music was so loud that he did not catch the writer's name. Later, when Monroe complained about not being able to reach his agent, Berg asked him the agent's name. The writer replied, "Phil Berg."[55]

An old-style agent, Henry Wilson, described his role in grooming a star like Rock Hudson, only to have a more unscrupulous MCA agent step in to reap the economic benefits. "An agent often becomes a sort of father after discovering and grooming a personality," Wilson said during a 1985 interview, recalling the circuitous way in which he lost Hudson to MCA:

> I've paid to get teeth fixed, ears pinned back, and contact lenses fitted. I've shown which fork to use and which wines to order and taught all the amenities. After educating them in every way possible, and eventually wrangling a long-term deal at one of the major studios, then when it appears that the box office years are in the making, another agent comes along and takes over.[56]

The actors may have lost the personal touch of their old agents, but what they gained was the sophisticated savvy of trained businessmen in their new MCA agents. Their attitude may have been, "Let someone else develop them. We'll grab them once they start earning money."[57] But stars knew this was an attitude that also promised them a windfall down the road.

Winchester '73: The Gross-Profit Deal

Jimmy Stewart's profit-participation deal on *Winchester '73* (1950) is perhaps the best known of the lucrative agency-concocted star deals. *Winchester '73* is part of the Lew Wasserman legend, marking a significant and irreversible shift in the dynamics between the studios, stars, and agents. Yet earlier star profit-participation deals for actors can be traced back as far as 1919, when Douglas Fairbanks and Mary Pickford, Charlie Chaplin, and D. W. Griffith together formed their own studio, United Artists, in order to gain greater artistic autonomy and reap fuller profits for their work. More typical talent-participation deals on behalf of Howard Hawks and Gary Cooper were negotiated as early as 1943 by Charles Feldman of Famous Artists. He forced RKO to guarantee both the director and the actor a minimum fee of $350,000 per picture plus 50 percent of profits. Gross deals assume the talent receives first dollar out even before the studio. The more-typical deal on behalf of talent is known as a "net" deal, which has long been deemed virtually meaningless in view of convoluted studio accounting procedures that allow the studios to postpone evidence of paper profits indefinitely.[58] What distinguished Wasserman's gross-participation deal for Stewart from previous profit deals was the fact that Wasserman revitalized the fading star's stature virtually overnight, therefore making it a deal all actors subsequently wanted.

Wasserman pulled a rabbit out of a hat (pun intended) when he tied the high-profile Broadway play *Harvey* to a seemingly lackluster Western in his deal with Universal. He speculated, correctly, that the latter would pay off royally by gathering huge audiences and the former would be a box-office flop. Prior to this fortuitous turn of events, Jimmy Stewart had lost his leverage in the early postwar period following his brief absence from the screen due to his service in World War II. His youthful successes in movies like *Mr. Smith Goes to Washington* (1939) and *The Philadelphia Story* (1940) had made Stewart a huge star.[59] The films that followed in the late forties, however, were uneven in their critical and box-office success. In 1947 Stewart left Hollywood for Broadway stage work, including a role as an alcoholic with an imaginary rabbit named Harvey. When Wasserman negotiated the deal with Universal, he gave the studio the film rights to *Harvey* for next to nothing while guaranteeing Stewart half of the profits of *Winchester '73*, for which the studio had no high hopes. The studio expected *Harvey*, the successful stage play, to do good business and the Western to do none. In exchange for gross points, Stewart agreed to take no salary. When *Winchester '73* became a surprise smash hit, no one was more surprised than Universal. The film made Stewart a wealthy man.[60]

The *Winchester '73* deal may have been a boon for Stewart and MCA but it was anathema to the studios. It established a precedent of granting stars far greater power and creative control over projects in which they appeared. Besides profit participation, Stewart was granted the unheard of privilege of determining "everything from director to cast."[61] What the arrangement meant to MCA was that the agency could henceforth require the studios to accept "package" deals, which meant forcing them to take in several MCA clients (more than one actor, perhaps even a director and a writer) on the same film. The package deal became a standard agency strategy for reaping multiple percentages from clients' salaries, rather than only a single actor's, director's, or writer's salary. These extortionist tactics meant that studios were often forced to hire lesser or unsuitable actors, directors, and/or writers on packaged films. Despite the added financial and structural costs of doing business with agencies like MCA, the studios relented— by default, given the sagging state of the industry and the agencies increased power—letting go of all but their most lucrative stars and paying the top prices demanded by the agents. The only alternative to succumbing to the extortionist tactics of the agencies was for studio heads to rely on their remaining contract players whether they were appropriate for the film or not.[62] On the other hand, Stine states that Universal studio head Bill Goetz was so desperate to cast Jimmy Stewart, he was willing to pay the price: "Goetz knew that he could cast the picture with low-salaried Universal stock players like Rock Hudson and Shelly Winters, give the picture a class 'A' production, and still come out on top, but he wanted Stewart, so he accepted the deal."[63]

These talent package deals were not the exclusive domain of MCA. For instance, in 1961 when director Frank Capra wanted to make *Pocketful of Miracles,* he had to resort to a similar New Hollywood–style deal. Abe Lastfogel, a WMA agent, represented four clients in the package for the film: "producer-director Frank Capra (a hired man), Frank Capra Productions (a hiring corporation), actor-star Glenn Ford (a hired man), and Ford's Newton Productions (a hiring corporation)."[64]

WMA, like all talent agencies that made package deals, collected 10 percent of the respective salaries for both the employers (the corporations) and the employees (work-for-hire contracts). Capra was unnerved to discover that even though he was producer-director, he had no more power over decision-making than any of the other partners in the co-venture. In contrast, Capra discovered that star Glenn Ford had the power to demand his own makeup man, wardrobe man, secretary, chauffeur, publicity man, and still photographer. He also had the power to have his clothes tailormade, to choose special props and furniture, and, most important, to choose his leading lady. For a prestigious director like Capra, whose career had reached its height during the prewar era, these concessions to the new way of doing business seemed not only insulting but highly detrimental to the creative process. Whether this was true or not, the ramifications of these studio concessions to the agency's hardball negotiations in the fifties remain clearly evident in Hollywood today, given the even greater leverage high-voltage stars like Tom Cruise, Tom Hanks, Jim Carrey, and Julia Roberts have with the studios.[65] The balance of power that shifted in the fifties from the studios to the stars and other high-profile talent (and, by extension, to the agents who represented them) is a fait accompli today. The only difference is that studio heads have started complaining that movies are no longer a profitable business given the exorbitant salaries and gross-point profits today's talent commands—a complaint that might be taken seriously were it not that movies are now only one slice of a much larger entertainment pie, and studios themselves but one facet of giant multinational conglomerates running the bakery franchise.

The SAG Waiver, 1952–1962

In 1946 Jules Stein resigned as president of MCA and handed control of his kingdom to Lew Wasserman. A year later, as television was poised to make its grand entrance on the media scene, MCA began asserting control over this new industry as it had previously with the music and film industries, using the same aggressive, legally obfuscating business tactics. It was MCA's ability to couple its near-monopoly hold on talent with its leadership in television production through its Revue Studios that would expand MCA's dominance of both the film and TV industries. It was not until 1952, however, when Wasserman negotiated a so-called blanket waiver from the Screen Actors Guild, signed by SAG president (and MCA client) Ronald Reagan, that MCA's absolute hegemony over television commenced. Bruck wrote about this infamous deal that "in early 1952, Wasserman navigated this process in ways so characteristically deft and traceless that even FBI and grand jury investigations undertaken later would be unable to fully reconstruct it."[66] By virtue of this unprecedented and legally questionable agreement, MCA agents were granted an exclusive exemption from the rule precluding them from both representing talent and hiring the same talent to work on Revue Productions films and TV programs—a practice that seemed, given that MCA owned Revue, an obvious conflict of interest.[67] With this exemption, MCA was able to "clean up" in terms of its combined agency and television production activities in the fifties.[68] As

New York Post reporters David Gelman and Alfred G. Aronowitz recalled in 1962:

> The waiver shocked, amazed, distressed, bowled over and annoyed large and various segments of the entertainment industry, including MCA's competitors, who attacked the agreement as "mysterious" "secret" "monopolistic" and patently favortistic to MCA. SAG has defended the agreement with just as much heat and an equal number of adjectives, saying it was necessary at the time to stimulate employment in Hollywood.[69]

Given its control not only of talent, a major TV production company, and a synergistic link between the two, MCA's power over the TV networks became even greater than over the movie studios. Moreover, this talent/production "double bind" made it difficult for even successful independent television production companies like Desilu Productions and Screen Gems, Revue's primary competitors, to compete.[70] In the early sixties, the press finally began to reveal both the details of MCA's style of doing business and the professional community's combined awe and ire. While Wasserman would publicly disavow any preferential treatment given to Revue Productions by the MCA Artists agency, everyone knew that MCA talent would be offered to Revue before other independent production companies. In the 1962 antitrust trial forcing MCA to divest either its agency or production capabilities, when most industry witnesses feared saying anything negative about MCA, archrival Desilu disclosed the difficulties it had encountered in negotiating with MCA when vying with the agency for favorable prime-time slots. Even this attack was rather soft, however, given that Desilu was no doubt up against MCA in nearly every one of their business transactions.[71]

In 1986, Dan E. Moldea wrote a dark portrait of Wasserman and MCA, alleging the company's collusion with organized crime and linking this to Ronald Reagan's term as head of SAG in the fifties. Some of the facts in Moldea's book were hastily compiled to meet a publisher's deadline and, for better or worse, the truth does not appear to justify the conspiratorial thrust of Moldea's text. However, more recent books on the subject like Bruck's *When Hollywood Had a King: The Reign of Lew Wasserman, Who Leveraged Talent into Power and Influence* (2003), Dennis McDougal's *The Last Mogul* (1998), and David F. Prindle's *The Politics of Glamour* (1988) provide painstaking accounts of these events that do confirm a link at least between Reagan's tenure as head of SAG, his subsequent television deals, and MCA's all-important SAG waiver.

Whatever the darker ramifications may have been, television industry players in the fifties understood that the game was rigged against them. Not only were the networks at MCA's mercy and rival agencies and production companies shortchanged; MCA's deal with SAG was frequently disadvantageous for its own clients. MCA agents would not necessarily negotiate as good a rate for talent at Revue as they would if they were negotiating with Screen Gems or Desilu. While these patently unfair practices were well known among industry insiders, most went along either for fear of reprisals, or because they were impressed with Wasserman and company's business savvy and unparalleled success. Or perhaps it was a bit of both.

The statistics regarding MCA's dominance of television in the fifties are staggering:

> MCA's take from TV has been leaping forward at an annual increase of from $7 to $10 million over the last seven years. Its income from television in 1954 amounted to $8.7 million. This shot to $17 million in 1955, $23.7 million in 1956. And the spiral has continued: $30.4 million in 1957, $38.6 million in 1958, $48.1 million in 1959 and $57.6 million last year [1960]— steadily about 80% of total income for the entertainment colossus.[72]

These figures are essential to understanding the magnitude of MCA's penetration of the television industry. At the end of the war, MCA's primary source of income was the movies, big band music, and radio. After the war, MCA's impact on television was immediate and overwhelming because it was able to move with ease from radio to the new medium. "'Rape,' some MCA critics have since cried, although MCA's dominance over television production was an inevitable union."[73] Granted, this comment came from a television industry trade magazine whose agenda was to further the interests of television. However, the fact remains: MCA was "good" for television, at least in the capitalist sense of helping propel a fledgling industry toward enormous profitability and phenomenal growth.[74]

Symptomatic of the ambivalent attitudes about MCA's role in the rise of TV were those directed at super-agents like Sonny Werblin, who elicited combined wonder at his business acumen and ingenuity and shock at his hard-driving ambition. In his 1961 *Television Magazine* profile on Werblin, journalist Arthur R. Kroeger explained why Werblin and others had come to admire MCA:

> Historically—during the boom days of network radio and the early days of television—advertising agencies put shows together. They were peeved

at MCA and other entrepreneurs for moving into the area, mad at their dealing directly with sponsors and short-circuiting agencies. The peeve today has largely vanished.[75]

Most of Werblin's professional associates interviewed for the *Television Magazine* article were reticent to say anything bad about him except for one disgruntled ex-employee who ventured, "Sonny has a morbid lack of trust in everyone around him and a flair for eviscerating the hired hands." The employee added that Werblin was "infuriated by non-acceptance" and was therefore "basically insecure and unhappy . . . a nervous wreck."[76] As testament to the growing stress on Werblin and other MCA agents, Werblin suffered a serious heart attack at the age of twenty-eight and from that point on looked a decade older than his years.

Much like the 1960 *Fortune* and 1961 *New York Post* articles about Wasserman, the 1961 *Television Magazine* article on Werblin focuses on his skills and work ethic and ignores his unscrupulous practices. The writer marvels at Werblin's grueling twenty-four-hour schedule which left him only a few hours a night to sleep. His compensation for this rugged work schedule, the writer notes, was a huge salary that rivaled that of a network president at $100,000 a year. Wasserman and Stein made nearly twice that amount. To put these salaries in perspective, a more typical midlevel executive salary in 1956 was $7,000–$9,000; for instance, Tom Rath was pulling in $7,000 for his public relations job at the fictional network in the popular mid-1950 novel and film *The Man in the Gray Flannel Suit* (to be discussed at length in chapter 4). Nonetheless, even Kroeger recognized the cost in health and well-being of such obsessive behavior. Whereas the film industry had previously been seen as a dream factory populated by glamorous stars and run by a handful of colorful moguls who loved the movies and the masses and made seat-of-the-pants decisions, the New Hollywood entertainment industry was increasingly viewed as a cold, calculating, speculative business in which only the most hard-bitten, hard-driving executives succeeded.

Jack Benny: MCA's "Mr. Nice"

As it had with Bette Davis, Jimmy Stewart, and other movie stars, MCA was instrumental in boosting Jack Benny's broadcasting career by signing him in 1946, the height of his radio career, and advising him to form a corporation, Amusement Enterprises, when he entered television. To further enhance this moneymaking scheme, and to avoid the appearance of having created a shell company simply to save on taxes (paying capital gains rather than personal income taxes), MCA also advised Benny to produce other television shows—on which he would benefit whether the shows made profits or he wrote them off as losses. Through such Byzantine deals with talent—setting them up as corporations, selling their shows, and eventually buying back their corporations from them—MCA was able to far exceed the normal 10 percent agent's commission from their television clients. As if this weren't lucrative—and devious—enough, MCA devised any number of additional revenue streams, often making themselves equal partners in the corporations they had set up with the actors.[77]

As for ruthlessness, McDougal describes in some detail MCA's manipulation of talent for its own ends in the case of George Gobel. The agency had gotten Gobel a job as a summer replacement for a television variety-show host. Reviews called Gobel mildly promising. Werblin negotiated a contract for Gobel with NBC that in five years would be worth $6–$7 million, turning an obscure nightclub comedian into an overnight celebrity phenomenon. Next, MCA made Gobel even more money by creating a corporation for tax purposes. On the way to an NBC meeting concerning Gobel, Werblin and his MCA associates, knowing they would be asked about Gobel's company, came up with the name Gomalco on the spot. NBC told MCA that Gomalco needed to get involved with more TV projects, so MCA watched for other properties they could develop into TV shows for Gomalco. One of the most popular of these turned out to be *Leave It to Beaver*, whose writers were also MCA clients. Thus, while Gobel himself had little or nothing to do with the creative aspects of this highly successful show, "his" company became a vehicle for creating additional revenue streams, from which his agency, of course, earned a percentage. After five years of hefty returns on *Leave It to Beaver* in a fifty-fifty arrangement with the writers, MCA sold it back to MCA's Revue Productions for a million dollars, making Gobel a millionaire several times over.[78]

Given his greater success and longevity in the entertainment industry, Jack Benny's dealings with MCA were even more lucrative than Gobel's. But in 1959 he was faced with a crisis because the second corporation he had formed under MCA's stewardship, J&M Productions (for Jack and Mary, his wife), was being scrutinized by the IRS. The government claimed that J&M was an empty corporation because it sold only Benny's services and had no other properties. So once again, as it had with Gobel, MCA helped Benny acquire more properties for his corporation when he was negotiating his contract renewal at CBS. In order to keep their biggest moneymaker happy and out of trouble with the government watchdogs, two new properties were added: *Checkmate,* a drama series, and *Ichabod and Me,* a situation comedy. McDougal notes,

> When Benny's CBS contract expired in 1959 and both the network and his sponsor, Lever Brothers, wanted the comedian back for another season, Sonny Werblin told them Benny would quit unless CBS and Lever Brothers launched a new detective series called *Checkmate.* With Benny as a wedge, Werblin forced the network to take show after show from J&M Productions . . . the new company MCA had created for the comedian.[79]

Both new shows disappeared the following season, but they had put Benny in a position where he had an "estate," which is the term and ploy MCA used to lure clients into the fold. Afterward, MCA bought out Benny's corporation in an exchange of stock. As McDonald notes of the agency's often shady tactics: "MCA blithely wielded a star against the networks like a blunt instrument, with or without the star's permission. If the star's interests coincided with MCA's, as they did in the case of Jack Benny, so much the better."[80] This was the MCA pattern. Performers became corporations, their shows produced other shows, and finally MCA reabsorbed the whole conglomerate. As Gelman and Abramowitz put it, "The economic tracery is so intricate that only a tax lawyer could figure out who's on first, and MCA, by acknowledgement of everyone in the trade, is 'the world's greatest tax lawyer.'"[81]

The Government Comes Knocking on MCA's Door

In preparing for the prosecution of its antitrust suit against MCA in 1962, the Justice Department had to work through all the agency's labyrinthine business transactions and determine which ones were legal and which were not. The trial focused on Jack Benny and J&M's *Checkmate* deal along with almost every other MCA-Revue operation, but it was a long and cumbersome process. As we have seen, even though many in Hollywood were negatively impacted by MCA's invasive practices, many had also been helped by the company and few were willing to speak out against it. As Gelman and Aronowitz describe it, the FCC had to fight not only MCA but also the entertainment industry's combination of fear and blithe complacency:

> "I've never seen anything like this in my life," Federal Communications Commissioner Frederick W. Ford once complained to Bill Davidson. "It

seems as if you can't even go to the bathroom in Hollywood without asking MCA's permission." What upsets me most is the way people tell me that MCA says, "Nobody in Washington can touch us."[82]

The period leading up to the trial played out in the trade press in such a way that MCA, rather than being castigated for its unfair business practices, was largely rewarded for its industriousness and ingenuity in revitalizing one industry, the Hollywood movie (now also TV) studios, and building another from scratch, the television industry. The trade papers gave the agency a near blanket endorsement during the trial, turning MCA into hapless victims and the government antitrust team into heartless predators. Television executives and studio heads alike were quoted as praising the admirable work ethic and business savvy of Wasserman and his team.

But the Justice Department itself was partly responsible for the surprisingly forgiving and even adulatory treatment MCA received, given the government's own decade-long delayed reaction to the talent agency's antitrust violations. While an earlier antitrust case against MCA had been undertaken unsuccessfully in 1945, the agency, rather than being chastened, actually increased its untoward practices, most notably with the SAG waiver of the early fifties. Why the government chose to look the other way then and throughout the fifties and then suddenly trained the spotlight back on the company in the early sixties has much to do with changes in the political economy over this period. Permissible antitrust violations are often the result of government leaders looking the other way in order to bolster a flagging economy or reinforce a pro-business agenda, as was the case with the Republican administration of Dwight Eisenhower. With the election of Democrat John F. Kennedy in 1960, and especially with the appointment of his firebrand brother Bobby Kennedy as attorney general, the pendulum shifted decidedly back toward more aggressive enforcement of antitrust law. At first, Attorney General Kennedy thought that MCA would be an easy target as one of the most flagrant of the big-business antitrust violators. But he was soon to discover that industry players, journalists, and even the public were reluctant to find fault with MCA, given its ties to the celebrated luminaries of the entertainment industry. Bobby Kennedy discovered that in taking on MCA, he had inspired the public's ire by attacking, if only indirectly, their beloved stars.

Widespread admiration for Wasserman's style of doing business was another reason MCA was granted partial immunity in Hollywood circles despite its questionable business practices. As one agency chief put it, "I think the whole thing about MCA can be summed up in this way: Can the business that really is everybody's secret dream—is it ruined when somebody comes in and makes it really a business?"[83] Another industry insider praised MCA for revolutionizing the business through teamwork, in contrast to the autocratic control the studio moguls asserted over decision making:

> The thing is ego. The whole business is ego. In show business, everything is ego. At every other studio, they're playing a role. Ego. They're playing the role of being in this business. At Revue, they're not playing! No games. Just business. There's a maturity there you don't find in any other studio.[84]

Another factor in the support MCA received during and in the period leading up to the antitrust trial was the fact that many in the industry—especially the talent represented by the industry—had themselves become embroiled in the agency's shady dealings. By creating corporations for television stars as fronts for a complex array of businesses above and beyond television production (real estate ventures and other outside business interests), MCA's clientele felt not only beholden but also complicit in these often-unethical practices. The net result was a series of compensatory gestures that deflected potential public hostility from their ill-gotten gain.

Emblematic of this deflection were the backstage comedy-variety shows like *The Jack Benny Show*, which adopted a posture of comic self-deprecation toward the business side of television. Benny's monologues and skits pulled back the curtain on the show, but only so far, revealing a carefully circumscribed portrait of the industry's seamier side. One typical ploy was to encourage home audiences to welcome television's "homey" stars into people's living rooms by emphasizing rather than camouflaging the medium's lackluster technology and shabby reliance on corporate sponsors.[85] After all, as long as TV hosts were willing to admit that their paychecks were paid by such common, unglamorous (yet all-American) products as Jell-O pudding, Grape Nuts, and Firestone tires, attention was drawn away from the hosts' more troubling affiliations with the agencies and their network counterparts.

As a companion strategy, however, countless insider jokes on *The Jack Benny Show* made indirect and innocuous references to MCA's get-rich-quick schemes. To cite one example, in one of the Lucky Strike–sponsored shows, Jack Benny is writing his life story at his Beverly Hills home with his all-purpose servant Rochester doing the typing. Don Wilson, Benny's sponsor announcer, enters with the Lucky Strike singers humming the commercial theme song for the product. Benny tells Wilson that he's writing his life story, ignoring the fact that at the top of the show Wilson had announced this to the audience from the stage—indicating the split realities operating in the backstage show format. In the scene playing out in the living room, Wilson remains the show's announcer but now is simultaneously also a "character" in Benny's backstage family of employees. Benny makes a joke about Wilson's weight that is a running gag on the show but that also indirectly references Benny's independent corporation's complex behind-the-scenes business practices: "Don, with you a dinner could be capital gain." This simple joke condenses the various layers of textual and extratextual reality that convey both a seemingly refreshing honesty about Benny's financial status while neutralizing its potentially damning underside. The subterfuge works to distill any residual hostility the audience may feel toward the television star's participation in the corporate culture of 1950s America. In other words, by humanizing and trivializing the complex corporate finances underlying his celebrity and by making his moral lapses appear comparable to those of the average viewer, the show helped dispel social tensions associated with the burgeoning commercialism of postwar America and to deflect any adverse associative connections to MCA.

MCA did not receive a blank check from the industry or the press during the pre-antitrust trial period, however. In the more negative press that started to appear from 1959 to 1962 (mostly supplied by ex-agents), what emerges is a portrait of a cutthroat competitive environment in which agents were encouraged by the agency heads to fight one another. One former MCA agent-turned-movie-producer stated:

> When I went to work as an agent for MCA a few years ago, it was like stepping into another world. It was pure, naked, ruthless power every day. The MCA executives I dealt with were efficient, hard, and completely lacking in compassion. Their stock-in-trade was creative, gifted human beings, but they handled their clients' lives as if they were so many inanimate objects, like bales of cotton or crates of furniture. . . . At least the "pieces of talent" were respected as valuable merchandise, however. We MCA agents commanded no respect at all—unless we were dedicated to the MCA principle of sell, sell, sell, make that buck for the agency no matter how tasteless the product you are selling or how pitiless the methods you use.[86]

Another former agent, who had since become a journalist, had this to say of his former employers:

I found that my most ruthless enemy was the man in the next office at MCA. . . . We were pitted against each other by the nature of the agency, and it was like living in a snarling, cannibalistic, primitive society where your survival depended on your brutality and your guile. . . . We got comparatively small salaries plus a big Christmas bonus. . . . The bonus was based on what you had sold during the year to contribute to the profits of the company. . . . Spying, memo-stealing, eavesdropping were all common practice.[87]

And yet, in the next breath, the above agent-turned-journalist praised MCA for injecting new life into a fading film industry and fledgling television industry. These conflicting views convey the ambivalence felt by many in the industry as a result of residual McCarthyist anxieties, MCA's immense power, and the postwar discourse of big business boosterism.

Fortune, Show, and *The New York Post* all published hard-hitting articles in the years leading up to the trial that contrast sharply with the fawning, superficial coverage of the MCA by *Saturday Evening Post* in 1946. Even here, however, given the seriousness of the charges leveled against the agency, it is surprising how forgiving these later articles are as well, justifying much of the company's unethical practices in the name of competition.[88]

Another significant factor in the widespread, if ambivalent, support MCA received from within the industry in the years leading up to the trial was the fear of ostracism and reprisal. That such fears were warranted is demonstrated by the incident in 1959 when Wasserman refused to talk to *Time* magazine. The publication sought out one of Wasserman's clients instead, actor Tony Curtis, who offered up a few bits of information, mostly of minor consequence, but told the reporters that Wasserman and his wife did not sleep in the same bed. Wasserman's response was not to speak to Curtis for the next four decades, despite the fact that their relationship formerly had been like father and son.[89] When the government stepped in to challenge MCA's antitrust activities and a parade of talent was brought in to testify against them, the fear of reprisals caused one witness after another to say only favorable things about the organization and their business techniques (a climate remindful, in reverse, of the HUAC and McCarthy hearings).[90]

When the dust finally settled on the antitrust trial in 1962, the federal case pitting the U.S. Justice Department against MCA was resolved in favor of the government. But as Bob Hope quipped right after the news broke, "The government better be careful. MCA might declare war, and then they won't get any more movies or television in Washington."[91] Indeed, the government may have won the case, but the ten-year reprieve the FCC had granted Hollywood's most powerful agency by turning a blind eye to its monopolistic practices had allowed MCA to transform show business beyond recognition. There was no turning back to the pre-1948 studio contract days when the movie studios had singular control over the entertainment industry. As thirty-eight-year-old Wasserman boasted as early as 1951, upon turning down an offer to run MGM, "I run all the studios."[92]

But the MCA case would leave its mark on the Octopus, chopping off some of its tentacles and loosening its industry stranglehold. MCA had had no real competitors in TV until 1962, when new government regulations brought to a close the agency's near-complete control over television production. While WMA's overall profits were comparable to MCA's in 1957, in the television area they were a distant second. WMA had also tried to repeat the MCA formula, forming the TV production company Four Star and using a majority of WMA clients in its shows. But because MCA had had the playing field to itself for most of the first decade of television, pickings were slim and all latecomers only achieved modest successes.[93] Contemporary authors like McDougal, Lary May, and Stephen Prince have noted that Ronald Reagan, in the eighties, applied the SAG waiver lessons of 1952 well—if with decidedly mixed results—when, as newly elected president of the United States, he turned a blind eye to antitrust violations and fostered deregulation nationwide in hopes of stimulating a drooping economy.[94] However, while his actions as U.S. president may have been motivated by national interest or overweening ideology, his complicity with MCA on the SAG waiver appeared to be based, at least in part, on his own personal ambitions as an out-of-work actor. Immediately following his signing the waiver, MCA got him a spot hosting the General Electric Theater television show and later negotiated extremely lucrative real estate deals on his behalf. Not surprisingly, when asked to testify against MCA at the 1962 trial, Reagan (pre-Alzheimer's) pleaded to memory lapses about these events.[95]

Wasserman also learned his political economic lesson well, about the implicit connections between business and government policy, tax laws, and antitrust allowances designed to foster corporate capitalism. Wasserman (himself a registered Democrat) remained linked to various Washington administrations (Republican and Democratic) throughout the subsequent decades, including even the Kennedy administration whose Bobby Kennedy–led Justice Department had engineered the antitrust case against MCA. Wasserman became especially close to Lyndon and Lady Bird Johnson, visiting them in the White House and Camp David. He helped place Jack

Valenti into the Johnson administration and, soon thereafter, facilitated Valenti's appointment as head of the Motion Picture Association of America (MPAA), a post he maintained from 1966 though 2004 (the longest term by close to twenty years, of any MPAA chief).[96]

The MCA Legacy

In contrast to backstage television shows like *The Jack Benny Show*, which backpedaled their complicity with MCA, big business, and the consumerist ethos, self-referential films like *The Hucksters* (1947), *The Man in the Gray Flannel Suit* (1956), *A Face in the Crowd* (1957), *Sweet Smell of Success* (1957), and *The Apartment* (1960) foregrounded and harshly critiqued the corporatization and commodification of the advertising and broadcasting industries—and by extension, the New Hollywood film industry, given the extent to which the aggressive breed of middlemen, epitomized by the talent agents, had penetrated the entire entertainment business. The divergent attitudes of filmmakers and television's creative teams toward these unseemly industry practices of the New Hollywood can be traced back to television's deep roots, via radio, in the network corporate structure and on government incentives favoring the television over the film industry in the post-1948 era. Added to this was a new factor, MCA, which had come to serve as a broker and bridge within and across both the TV and film industries.

The liberal political tradition in Hollywood of the thirties and forties may have prompted certain postwar filmmakers like Billy Wilder, Joseph Mankiewicz, Frank Tashlin, and Elia Kazan to use their films to demonize television as a merchant of false consciousness; however, they also found television a useful subterfuge to engage in a more comprehensive critique of a corporate structure and consumer culture from which they benefited but which they also dreaded and despised. The conundrum facing liberal members of the filmmaking community in postwar Hollywood—especially those with strong memories of and affinities with the New Deal populism of the thirties—was the extent to which writers, directors, and actors should preserve the progressive potential inherent in an art form which was also transparently a business. But then, as the old studio system began to crumble, MCA stepped into the power vacuum and offered a compromise solution to the filmmakers' dilemma—one that allowed them greater freedom to express their liberal views in exchange for an even greater embroilment in the capitalist system. This, of course, created a new dilemma, as the newly "independent" filmmakers ironically found themselves interchangeable cogs in the MCA mass-media machine. MCA understood the intricate interconnection between the culture industry and consumerist capitalism. Whereas many in Hollywood were appalled at the agency for treating its stars like poker chips, Wasserman and company saw their approach not as a gambling enterprise but rather as a way of turning the infamously undisciplined entertainment industry (a charge that had always been based more on myth than fact) into a more stable and rational business operation.[97]

3.
The Gray Flannel Independent:
New Hollywood's New Organization Man

The era of hard-fisted, colorful pioneers is past. . . . Everywhere the
producers . . . are beginning to have a gray-flannel look. Even the
actors are sweating over taxes and account books.

—RICHARD DYER MACCANN, *Hollywood in Transition*

An Empire has fallen, but something better than an Empire is
rising up. . . .

—ERIC HODGINS, "Amid Ruins of an Empire a
New Hollywood Arises"

The previous chapter, through a case study of the rise of MCA, examined
the radical restructuring of the Hollywood film industry in the early post–
World War II period. This development led to the infiltration of the "organization man" and "gray flannel" ethos into the business operations of the
industry and also, paradoxically, facilitated the rise of independent filmmaking. This chapter looks at the more constructive side, from a progressive, ideological, and creative cinematic standpoint, of the New Hollywood
ledger. As the two epigraphs to this chapter suggest, the rise of the "independents" and the rise of the "organization man" are integrally related, given
that independent filmmakers ended up having to take on the mantle of
the businessman once they had set up their own companies.[1] Following a
detailed discussion of the postwar independent "movement" and of the
"organization man"/"gray flannel" phenomenon in its broader, sociological
context, the chapter tracks the evolution of big-business films from the late
1940s through the end of the 1950s—films that emphasized not so much
the corporatization of Hollywood as that of the United States as a whole.
The "something better," cited in the *Life* magazine quote above, from this
book's perspective, was the rise of independent production that encouraged—at least for a select few—more, not less, creative filmmaking. However, even for those filmmakers still working within the studio system, a

number of the big-business and self-referential films that emerged during this transitional era function as key barometers of the contradictions and ambivalences of this turbulent period.

When Worlds Collide: The Rise of the Postwar Talent-Turned-Producer

A world war may have ended for the United States in 1945, but for Hollywood the postwar period was anything but peaceful. Labor unrest, the HUAC hearings, sagging box-office returns, television looming as a major competitor, and then, in 1948, another crushing blow: the Paramount decrees. The decrees mandating the break-up of the Big Five studios (Paramount, MGM, Warner Bros., Twentieth Century Fox, and RKO) ended these companies' vertically integrated, oligopolistic control over production, distribution, and exhibition. The resulting power vacuum created an opportunity for television to emerge as the vanquishing hero, given its network corporate takeover facilitated by Federal Communication Commission (FCC) incentives and other preferential treatment. The economic and structural crisis within the film industry extended over two decades, as audiences declined, theaters closed, and the studios underwent massive restructurings, asset sales, ownership changes, and mergers. The advantages enjoyed by the Old Hollywood studios included their rationalized coordination of operations within a single physical plant, their control of an apparatus for distributing and promoting films to domestic and international markets; their ownership of contracts binding writers, directors, and stars; and their ability to procure financing. These advantages were undermined, at least for the Big Five, when these studios lost control of exhibition. In addition, the termination of block booking (another monopolistic practice ended by the Paramount decrees) meant that the studios could no longer force independent theater owners to accept the studios' cheaper B pictures, sight unseen, in order to acquire their more-coveted A pictures, thereby ending the studios' assurance that all of their films (400–500 a year during the "golden age") would receive a return on investment.[2]

One of the most significant consequences of the difficulties befalling the movie studios during this period was a major overhaul in production practices, which, in conjunction with new business practices, transformed the entire industry. Before 1948, the studios mass-produced films using in-house personnel via a system of organization called the "producer-unit," in which the studio's top production executive oversaw several "A" producers, several "B" producers, and so on, who together were responsible for producing the studio's total output of films.[3] After 1948, the reduction in output made such a factory system unviable and it was replaced by a "one-off basis" (also known as "package productions"), in which studios forged deals with independent producers who put each individual film together by assembling financing, key above-the-line talent, and other members of the freelance production team.[4] During the first half of the 1950s, most studios started aggressively signing talent-driven production deals. For instance, Warner Bros. signed studio deals with directors-turned-independent-producers Mervyn LeRoy, John Ford, Alfred Hitchcock, Howard Hawks, Raoul Walsh, William Wellman, John Huston, Elia Kazan, and Billy Wilder, and with stars-turned-producers Burt Lancaster, Doris Day, and John Wayne. By 1957 71 percent of all of the studio releases were independently produced.[5] David Bordwell, Kristin Thompson, and Janet Staiger argue that the postwar transformation from the "producer-unit system" to the "package-unit system" constitutes the single most significant change in the structure of the industry over this period. The adoption of the "package-unit system" meant that:

> Rather than an individual company containing the source of the labor and materials, the entire industry became the pool for these. A producer organized a film project: he or she secured financing and combined the necessary laborers (whose roles had previously been defined by the standardized production structure and subdivision of work categories) and the means of production (the narrative "property," the equipment, and the physical sites of production).[6]

This is not to say that independent producers didn't exist prior to the 1950s or that it was without challenges—the primary being locating the creative elements needed to secure financing. Throughout the 1930s and 1940s several nondirecting independent producers served as presidents of their own production companies and were behind some of the golden age's most highly regarded and successful films: *Gone with the Wind, Wuthering Heights, Stagecoach, Rebecca, Duel in the Sun, The Best Years of Our Lives,* to name only a few. These independent producers—for example, Samuel Goldwyn, David O. Selznick, Walter Wanger, Alexander Korda, Walt Disney, and Hal Roach—were responsible for securing financing and typically released their product through a major studio, making only a few pictures a year (typically one to five).[7] Most of the major independent producers from the old studio era continued their successful careers after 1948, but not without also having to adapt their business practices to the changed circumstances of the New Hollywood. Like the studio bosses, they now had to negotiate with the newly independent talent and their agency representatives, and, most significantly, on the latter's terms.

As for the other "fly in the ointment," television, while many among the old guard initially expressed hostility toward their upstart rival (Warner Bros. went so far as to bar television sets from appearing in any Warner movies!),[8] this did not prevent established independent producers or two of the non–Big Five majors (Columbia and Universal) from enthusiastically embracing the lucrative new field of TV production and the New Hollywood system in general. Among the producers, Selznick and Disney were the most aggressive, and successful, at making the transition from the Old to the New Hollywood.[9] In fact, they helped usher in the new system not only by playing ball with television but by wresting power from the studios by replicating the studios' centralized base of operations and becoming distributors themselves. Disney, in particular, only a minor player in the golden age, became a model for the new corporate-run industry by controlling all aspects of production and cross-promoting media product through interlocking businesses (such as its theme park, Disneyland) and across multiple platforms, capitalizing in particular on the synergistic benefits of television programming (*The Wonderful World of Disney* and *The Mickey Mouse Club*).

Whether one fiercely resisted, actively promoted, or remained torn about the new system, it was clear by the early 1950s that the glorious studios of old had become shadows of their former selves. As the decade wore on, the erstwhile dream factories would become part of a shell game, alternately bought and sold as "subsidiaries of transnational media and leisure conglomerates."[10] The purchases began officially in 1959 when MCA bought Universal Studios. A series of corporate takeovers ensued, with the financially strapped studios providing ripe pickings for the burgeoning multinationals: Gulf and Western purchased Paramount in 1967, Transamerica bought United Artists in 1967, Kinney National became Warner Communications in 1969, and Coca Cola swallowed Columbia in 1982 (RKO had been sold to Desilu already in the mid-1950s). Of the eight Old Hollywood majors, only MGM and Twentieth Century Fox remained in the hands of individual owners, although these changed frequently.

Established independent producers like Disney, Selznick, Goldwyn, and Wanger were joined in the early postwar period by a new group of independent producers (Sam Spiegel, the Mirisch brothers, among others), each of whom needed more than ever to secure talent in order to gain access to financing and distribution for their films.[11] The bottom line was clear for

New Hollywood producers and studio heads alike: above-the-line talent with a successful track record at the box office held the trump card in contract negotiations. These new power relations couldn't help but create a situation in which the new breed of entrepreneurial actors, directors, and writers began behaving like—and in many cases became—producers themselves, with a greater sense of fiscal responsibility and a focus on the bottom line of profits. Director Alfred Hitchcock, for instance, despite engaging in what his former producer Selznick considered occasional lapses in judgment upon becoming his own producer (such as "the shocking [and expensive] Dali figures [in *Spellbound*]"), was acutely aware of the importance of budgets, shooting schedules, and how to maximize the results on the screen.[12]

While Schatz, Staiger, and other media historians have charted the profound changes taking place in the postwar Hollywood film industry, few histories look specifically at the talent-turned-independent-film-producers working in the postwar era.[13] A noteworthy contribution is J. A. Aberdeen's *Hollywood Renegades: The Society of Independent Motion Picture Producers* (1994). Aberdeen focuses on a little-known organization called the Society of Independent Motion Picture Producers (SIMPP), which played a crucial, if behind-the-scenes role in ushering in the New Hollywood. Formed in 1941 by Disney, Chaplin, Goldwyn, Wanger, Selznick, Mary Pickford, and Orson Welles, SIMPP provided information and impetus to the government in its prosecution of the Big Five studios in the case that eventuated in the Paramount decrees.[14] Aberdeen's survey of the attempts by talent to forge an independent path during the studio-contract era of the thirties and forties also helps contextualize developments that took place after the war. Examples include James Cagney, Constance Bennett, her younger sister Joan, and Orson Welles. Cagney created Cagney Productions in 1942 with his brother and business partner, William Cagney, after years of fighting the studios for creative autonomy.[15] Constance Bennett's turn as an actress-turned-independent-producer demonstrates an ability, in her negotiation with tough-minded studio heads and agents alike, that defied stereotypical gender roles of the era. Welles's landmark film *Citizen Kane* (1941) was independently made under his Mercury Productions (together with RKO). Yet Old Hollywood independents faced certain obstacles their New Hollywood counterparts didn't. Proprietors of the studio-owned theater chains were notorious for mishandling independently made films in favor of studio productions. Welles suffered most famously from this bias, starting with many theater owners' refusal to exhibit *Citizen Kane* (granted that the animus in this case was heavily overdetermined given the anti-*Kane* campaign mounted by newspaper magnate William Randolph Hearst, on whom the unflattering portrait of Kane was based).[16]

One of the more significant points of continuity between Old and New Hollywood is the "producer-director": a director with a track record of successful films who is granted full authority over the production of his/her films. Examples of producer-directors who flourished during the studio era include Capra, Howard Hawks, Ernst Lubitsch, and Gregory La Cava. Capra established Liberty Pictures in the late thirties, formed in partnership with William Wyler (though Wyler eventually returned to the studios). Also during this period, Howard Hughes and Preston Sturges briefly formed California Pictures, and Hawks later formed his own company, as did Hitchcock and John Ford. Despite Ford's early success as an independent director-producer (both in terms of profitability and critical notices in the case of *Stagecoach* [1939]), his independent stint didn't last long.[17] Deciding that he wasn't willing to gamble his entire future on independence, at the same time he was operating his own production company, he simultaneously signed a multipicture deal with Twentieth Century Fox. Ford's pattern of alternating between working as an independent and under studio contract persisted in the late 1940s and early 1950s with filmmakers like Kazan, whose complex and highly controversial case forms the basis of chapters 6 and 7. As we will see there, the postwar independent producer-director was a risky enterprise, since financing the next picture depended on the commercial viability of the previous one. Whereas the studios could balance their losses against their occasional hits through a process called "cross-collateralization," for independents lacking the studio's financial resources, a single high-priced A picture that failed at the box office could jeopardize the future of the entire independent production company—a fact of filmmaking life that continues to the present, as the "indie prod" burial grounds amply attest.

A compromise solution for the independent-minded but financially fearful director was to work with another independent producer who would handle the financial end yet give the director free creative rein. Certain established producers like Goldwyn or Selznick, for example, were known for their tendency to micromanage all aspects of the production process to the dismay of strong-minded and talented directors like Ford, Wyler, and Hitchcock. Postwar independents like Sam Spiegel, meanwhile, who formed successful collaborations with Welles, Huston, and later Kazan, were valued as producers because of their hands-on financial/hands-off creative approach. Well versed in the ways of the New Hollywood, Spiegel considered his primary function the ability to assemble financing based on the credentials of the talented actors and directors he packaged for his movies, talent he was additionally able to attract, in turn, by offering them a percentage of the profits.[18]

Stanley Kramer and United Artists are two anomalies in the Hollywood independent matrix. Kramer is the only major pre- or postwar producer-director who started as a producer and became a director rather than the other way around. His first film as a producer, *The Champion* (1949), helped reverse the trend among newly independent producers toward exorbitant "prestige pictures" with often disastrous results at the box office.[19] Using this successful low-budget film as a springboard, Kramer launched Stanley Kramer Productions in the fifties under the new UA management team of Arthur B. Krim and Robert S. Benjamin. In the mid-1950s, entertainment attorneys Krim and Benjamin had bought a majority stake in UA from the studios' only two living original owners, Charles Chaplin and Mary Pickford. Krim and Benjamin retained UA's decades-long reputation as the studio of choice for Hollywood independents throughout the 1950s, financing and distributing the work of producers as varied as Chaplin, Selznick, Goldwyn, Wanger, Korda, Roach, James Roosevelt, and Edward Small, among others.[20] As for the UA/Kramer partnership, the most successful film Kramer made under the arrangement was *High Noon* (1952), which won an Academy Award nomination for Best Picture. Despite the critical and financial success of *High Noon*, after several years of struggling to raise money for films which he produced independently under his own label, in 1952 Kramer decided to give up some of his creative autonomy in exchange for guaranteed financing by moving his production company to Columbia. The studio deal was neither creatively nor financially successful, given that all of the films he produced at Columbia, except for *The Caine Mutiny* (1954), failed at the box office. He terminated the arrangement at Columbia in 1954 and henceforth shifted his focus to directing films, often with a socially conscious bent, such as *The Defiant Ones* (1958), *Judgment at Nuremberg* (1961), *Ship of Fools* (1965), and *Guess Who's Coming to Dinner* (1967).

Enterprise Studios, which specialized in socially conscious films, was perhaps the greatest of all Hollywood anomalies, Old or New. Formed in 1946 by three executives (one formerly at Warner) who secured revolving credit, Enterprise leased studio space and forged a distribution agreement first through UA, then MGM. Leftist-inclined talent was attracted to the studio for the chance to make more challenging fare but also, as with Sam

Spiegel, "by the chance to participate in the profits." John Garfield, who had come to Hollywood via the left-wing Group Theater, formed his own company, Roberts Productions, in the early postwar period. He began providing Enterprise with product, including *Body and Soul* (1947), a hard-hitting exposé of corruption in the fight game and one of the seminal film noir/social-problem films of the postwar period (and a model for Kramer's *The Champion*). The film's impact was diluted somewhat by a heroic ending (added by director Robert Rossen over the objections of writer Abraham Polonsky). This ending, however, no doubt contributed to the film being Enterprise's only "major commercial success from its nine productions, released between 1947 and 1949." As Robert Aldrich, one of the radical/liberal directors who worked with the maverick studio, commented, filmmakers were attracted to Enterprise as a "communal way to make films" but "there was no one at the head of the studio to bring us all up short."[21] Although the studio's days would have been numbered in any case, given HUAC and the impending blacklist, this grand experiment in creating a platform for leftist filmmakers committed the cardinal Hollywood sin: failure to satisfy the bottom line of profits.

With agents emerging as major power players in the 1940s, it isn't surprising that they, too, would begin forging independent production partnerships with their former clients, as Charles K. Feldman did with Howard Hawks in 1944 and Harold Hecht did with Burt Lancaster in 1948. During World War II Feldman and Hawks created H-F Productions as a way for Hawks to command greater leverage in his negotiations with Warner Bros. and other studios. According to Aberdeen, H-F sought out story rights, developed material, attached talent, and created package productions that they then sold to one of the studios with Hawks as producer-director. Two well-known films that were made in this fashion at Warner Bros. were *To Have and Have Not* (1944) and *The Big Sleep* (1946).[22] However, the full impact of the newly empowered talent on independent production would not be felt until after the post-1948 Paramount decree when potent agencies like MCA swooped down on actors and directors, recently freed from their contracts, to help each of their new clients negotiate lucrative production deals with the studios. Former agent-turned-producer Harold Hecht went one step further by leaving the agency to partner with his former client, rising movie star Burt Lancaster, using the studio's dependency on talent to extract highly favorable terms for his company.

The fact that talented and thoughtful filmmakers like Lancaster, Wilder, and Hitchcock were able to gain unprecedented leverage over the studios (and, in Hitchcock's case, over the networks as well) is symptomatic of the changed power dynamics between studios and talent in this era.[23] Another contributing factor, however, is the professional association between each of these three individuals and their powerful agent, MCA's Lew Wasserman, whose grasp of the altered circumstances attending independent production in postwar entertainment industry, including the advent of television production in Hollywood (circumstances he had helped forge), allowed MCA, as we have seen, to insert itself (and its clients) into virtually every entertainment transaction. In many respects, Wasserman's leveraging of talent to monopolize the newly integrated film and television industries and create a more pragmatic and interconnected set of businesses epitomizes the business shift in Hollywood, and in the nation as a whole, during the Eisenhower era of deregulation. Similarly, given their indirect contribution to and benefit from the newly corporatized Hollywood, it is not surprising that newly independent liberal filmmakers would find the business and self-referential entertainment film a fitting means of mediating tensions arising from these conflicted professional arrangements that mirrored, to a striking degree, those confronting the society at large. Before turning to a close examination of the 1950s business films, it is necessary to consider the body of literature, fictional and nonfictional, dealing with the mounting social anxieties linked to the growing numbers of professional-managerial workers in postwar America. The emergent social critique present in the 1950s' "anti-organization man" literature resonates in both the business films addressed later in this chapter and in the self-referential films (about Hollywood's collusion with big business) that will be the subject of all subsequent chapters.

"The Organization Man"

In 1956 William H. Whyte Jr., an editor at *Fortune* magazine, wrote *The Organization Man*, a hugely popular and influential book-length treatise whose title has become a part of the American lexicon. The title referred to an emergent species of middle-class white-collar worker that Whyte saw as being turned into a faceless, robotic cog in the relentless corporate machine. A damning sociological critique of the ideology, training, and "neuroses" of both the anonymous, male-dominated workplace and the white, suburban lifestyle, the book ended with a rousing call to action:

> He must fight the organization. Not stupidly, or selfishly, for the defects
> of individual self-regard are no more to be venerated than the defects of

co-operation. But fight he must, for the demands for his surrender are constant and powerful, and the more he has come to like the life of organization the more difficult does he find it to resist these demands, or even recognize them. It is wretched, dispiriting advice to hold before him the dream that ideally there need be no conflict between him and society. There always is; there always must be.[24]

The book was especially critical of the way corporations prioritize the status quo and demand employee dedication to the organization over and above their individuality. According to Whyte, organizations "fight against genius" and in so doing create the "bureaucratization of the scientist" and, by extension, of the artist and the entrepreneur, encouraging a sameness among men that defeats individualism and uniqueness. As trenchant as Whyte's critique is of the emergent corporate culture, it also is a nostalgic effort to reassert the residual values held by the 1930s populist hero, whose self-interest was outweighed by his selfless concern for his fellow worker. Whyte naively celebrates a traditional view of the self-made man who, like the fabled Horatio Alger, no longer existed in the (post)modern world of corporate America. According to Jackson Lears,

> Whyte's attack on corporate-induced conformity was pointed and well placed; the problem was that he presented few clear alternatives. Although he preferred cranky entrepreneurs to well-adjusted corporate executives, his ultimate ideal seemed to be a conception of individual autonomy that was as reified as the ideal of organization he aimed to resist. Here as elsewhere in postwar social thought, the lack of larger frameworks of meaning left the reader wondering, "Nonconformity for what?"[25]

Whyte's premise speaks to the implicit contradiction of life for many working men in 1950s America. On the one hand, the decade's popular discourse on success still valorized the American myth of Horatio Alger, the prototypical American ideal of the self-made man, as an independent thinker, the type of daring, forward-thinking entrepreneur who had built America into a bastion of free-market capitalism. At the same time, however, the rugged individualist ethos was giving way to a generation of dehumanized bureaucrats and to a debilitating uniformity that invaded not only the business environment but the worlds of science, education, art, and religion as well, nullifying the "self-made man" myth by emphasizing the need for teamwork. Whyte's fusillade against the fifties' subservience to the organization was not limited to the workplace but extended to the ramifications of "selling out" in one's home life as well. The organization trend, he argued, had spread to people's private lives via the postwar phenomenon of suburban living. The suburbs engendered "sameness" and uniformity in ones' homes, clothing, vehicles, and values. The very consumer paradise and world of abundance celebrated in the postwar media created, in actuality, a less-than-fulfilling community life, one motivated by the "empty prospect of taking part in the marketplace of personal exchange."[26] Whyte's account also critiques 1950s' popular media representations of the "organization man" via Hollywood films, Broadway plays, and best-selling books.[27] Whyte takes these representations to task for attempting to "resolve" larger social tensions through the narrative trope of the couple: "He [the fictional hero] may tell the boss to go to hell, but he is going to have another boss, and, unlike the heroes of popular fiction, he cannot find surcease by leaving the arena to be a husbandman."[28] Whyte offers no alternative to the social ideals on display in these films and other popular works, however, namely that of the self-made man and the homemaker wife whose charge was maintaining the home as safe haven.

Whyte's indictment of the "organization man" was not the only attempt to puncture the popular myth of contentedly conformist men and women showcased in advertisements and popular 1950s television sitcoms like *Father Knows Best, The Adventures of Ozzie and Harriet, Leave It to Beaver,* and *The Donna Reed Show.*[29] Other counternarratives to middle-class optimism and affluence include *The 1950s: America's "Placid" Decade,* "The Morale of the Cheerful Robots," and "Arise, Ye Silent Class of '57."[30] John Cawelti's "Dream or Rat Race," a chapter of his mid-1960s book *The Apostles of the Self-Made Man,* analyzes the plethora of 1950s and early 1960s popular literature, both fiction and nonfiction, dealing with "changing attitudes toward individualism and success in the twentieth century."[31] Cawelti organizes this voluminous body of writing into two broad categories: the *celebratory* and the *critical.* Within the first category Cawelti identifies three broad areas: the "positive thinking" approach, practical moneymaking schemes, and satire. All three areas are seen as reflecting a wavering yet resilient conservative faith in American capitalism, mainly proffering practical "self-help" strategies for getting ahead. Even the satirical strand, while introducing a subversive subtext, ultimately offers only light-hearted parodies of the American ideal of success.[32] The quasi-mystical "positive thinking" approach is exemplified in the unabashed boosterism of Dale Carnegie, Norman Vincent Peale, and Napoleon Hill. The "money-making approach" delineates particular strategies and devices for getting rich, such as William Nickerson's *How I Turned $100 into a Million in Real Estate in My Spare Time* (1959) and E. Joseph Cossman's *How I Made $1,000,000 in Mail Order* (1963). The quasi-satirical literature includes Shepherd Mead's *How to Succeed in Business without Really Trying* (1952), Mark Caine's *The S-Man* (1961), and William J. Reilly's *How to Make Your Living in Four Hours a Day without Feeling Guilty about It* (1955).

The critical category in Cawelti's schema, which marks for him the beginning of a liberal critique of postwar American capitalism, includes nonfiction works such as C. Wright Mills's *White Collar: The American Middle Classes* (1951) and *The Power Elite* (1956), David Riesman's *Individualism Reconsidered* (1955) and *The Lonely Crowd: A Study of Changing American Character* (1955), Michael Harrington's *The Other America: Poverty in the United States* (1962), and Whyte's *The Organization Man*.[33] These other critiques went further than Whyte's, however, in not only attacking a conformist and alienating success model linked to corporatization and suburbanization, but in linking this model to its advanced American capitalist base.

The fictional writers Cawelti lists in the critical category include the cream of pre- and postwar American literature: William Faulkner, F. Scott Fitzgerald, Thomas Wolfe, John Dos Passos, John P. Marquand, Arthur Miller, James T. Farrell, Ralph Ellison, Budd Schulberg, Norman Mailer, and Saul Bellow.[34] These authors, many of them leftists, were reacting to the failed promise of the American dream and, in particular, to privatized capitalism and its emphasis on economic individualism. Many of them, like many of the leftist filmmakers who worked in the social-realist tradition, invoked the quasi-socialist vision of New Deal populism as a possible solution. Cawelti, however, like Kazan, Mankiewicz, and other filmmakers explored in this and later chapters, saw the inclusive social ideals of the 1930s as incompatible with the postwar economy. Cawelti, specifically, questions whether organized labor, social security, and other social services associated with the 1930s were sufficient to meet the structural changes of the 1950s. Cawelti describes what he perceives to be the shortcomings of the New Deal:

New Deal benefits like social security, the political recognition of organized labor, farm price supports, wage and hour legislation, and other New Deal measures raised the living standards of many lower and lower-middle-class groups ... [but] accomplished little for Negroes, unskilled laborers, migrant workers, and other groups who were barred from the same opportunity by prejudice, cultural deprivation, regional backwardness, or mental and physical handicaps.[35]

In a larger sense, Cawelti doubts whether extending the middle-class standard of living to a broader portion of the population would necessarily serve the greater good of the community, since to do so merely perpetuates an ideology of success measured exclusively in terms of income level and consumption.[36] Cawelti's break from Whyte's uncritical nostalgia for the fading republican ideal associated with the New Deal calls attention to the schism between cultural representation of postwar life and real social events in which the business and self-referential film also partake.

Capitalism's Boom and Bust Cycles

Post–World War II America's dominant ideology of affluence, predicated on the myth of the self-made man, obscured the fact that the U.S. economy was by then, and had been since the start of the New Deal, largely maintained, if not always successfully, on a Keynesian economic model of government intervention to artificially stimulate business activity and foster economic growth. Whereas mass-media representations tended to reinforce the romantic ideal of the man who pulls himself up by the bootstraps toward self-sufficiency and success, in reality the individual entrepreneur was not the prime pump of American capitalism; rather, alternating periods of federal regulation and deregulation as well as governmental infusions of capital provided the main stimulus for production and consumption. To cushion capitalism's inevitable boom and bust cycles—despite comparative postwar affluence, America experienced multiple recessions in the 1950s— the federal government (both Democratic and Republican administrations) attempted to control fluctuations in the economy by alternately boosting and cutting military spending, encouraging production through corporate incentives, and encouraging consumer spending via lowering interest rates. While a decade-long depression, wartime sacrifices, and government-encouraged advertising campaigns led to a feverish desire to purchase consumer goods immediately after World War II, by 1948 consumer spending was faltering. The government attempted to correct the situation by artificially stimulating consumer purchasing, and corporations introduced a small item with major consequences: the credit card.

Consequently, consumer spending surged and, after a temporary hiatus during the Korean War, resurged, with housing construction and car sales reaching record highs. The same frenetic pace was evident in the huge numbers of television sets and other home appliances purchased during this period. This heated consumerist trend topped out in 1958, however, resulting in one of the more damaging recessions of the 1950s. The automobile and home appliance industries, as well as the related steel and aluminum industries, had expanded faster than the market could bear. Unemployment rose in 1958 to almost 7 percent, in contrast to its all-time low of 1.8 percent in 1953. These statistics reveal the volatile nature of the upward and downward economic spirals in the U.S. economy, even during a period of comparative overall growth and consumer confidence. Despite these sporadic fluctuations, the general affluence of the postwar era lasted two decades. For many Americans who had lived through the deprivations of the Depression and World War II, the postwar boom was viewed as an extraordinarily optimistic moment in American history. *Life* magazine's early postwar observation, part assessment and part prophesy, would be realized many times over: "The year 1946 finds the U.S. on the threshold of marvels, ranging from runless stockings and shineless serge suits to jet-propelled airplanes that will flash across the country in just a little less than the speed of sound."[37]

One of the negative by-products of all this private spending, however, was a neglect of public services. For instance, every American's coming to own a car and driving it twice a day between the suburbs and the city, in the 1950s, created serious congestion on city streets and on the newly constructed highways and freeways, as well as air pollution in the surrounding areas. The highway patrol, hospitals to care for the injured, and other public services necessary in an automobile-centered society lacked the resources to address the situation.[38] Thus, paradoxically, as the buying power of most Americans was rising, the quality of life was deteriorating both externally, in terms of public services, and internally, in terms of the psychological and emotional stress that accompanied the heightened struggle to compete. This competition, meanwhile, also had a public and a private component: the former relating to workplace production, the latter to domestic consumption.

In general, and certainly compared to the Democratic administrations that preceded it, the Eisenhower administration favored unimpeded corporate growth unhampered by government regulations. This trend is particularly evident in the FCC deregulation of the networks during the early days of television, and the government's blind eye in response to MCA's antitrust violations that allowed the agency to monopolize the television industry from 1952 to 1962. Military spending and overseas investments were additional means of beefing up the production of goods and services and thereby boosting the economy. To further guard against overproduction and underconsumption at home, the credit industry was revitalized, as were incentives for advertisers to keep consumers spending at all-time highs. To guarantee the effectiveness of these incentives, it was necessary to re-educate the public about the virtues of spending, counteracting previous decades (indeed, centuries) grounded in the Protestant ethic of moderation and thrift.[39] Credit cards, which encouraged consumers to spend above their means, exacerbated economic pressures on the breadwinner husband and on the homemaker wife who, as the family's primary consumer, was expected to keep up with the neighbors. Psychoanalytic techniques were incorporated into advertising by motivational sociologists such as Dr. Ernest Dichter, who felt it was advertising's mandate to "give people the sanction and justification to enjoy it [the postwar boom], and to demonstrate that the hedonistic approach to life is a moral one, not an immoral one."[40]

Government intervention to foster growth on the domestic front extended to the international front through the Marshall Plan for Europe and a cultural and economic Americanization process of unprecedented proportions for much of the rest of the world. At the end of the war, capitalizing on its economic strength and wartime advantages in Germany and Japan, the "United States quickly solidified its hegemony over both the world market and global politics . . . presid[ing] over the integration of Europe into a North Atlantic community, the integration of Japan into a North Pacific community, and the Cold War isolation of the Soviet bloc."[41] On the homefront, the impact of the Cold War and U.S. economic and military expansion contributed to and in some ways made intractable a blind faith in the American way of life, even though the hegemonic rhetoric was not always matched by circumstance, especially for ethnic and racial minorities, or by the academic, artistic, and popular discourses, as we have indicated.

Mollifying Critique with Melodrama

As this brief socioeconomic survey suggests, the ideology of free enterprise and the self-made man was contradictory in two fundamental ways: first, American capitalism remained viable only through substantial government intervention; second, the rhetoric of rugged individualism was at odds with structural imperatives that demanded the sublimation of personal needs to those of the corporation. The mass media helped to negotiate these contradictions by circulating master narratives that attempted to uphold the dominant ideology not just through content but also through classical Hollywood conventions of narrative coherence and character consistency. Yet the disparities between the idealized image of the economic system and practical reality could not be completely papered over, and in some cases—as in the 1950s' self-referential and reflexive business films—these disparities were quite patently, if ambivalently, revealed.

With the precipitous decline of box-office returns beginning in the early postwar period, studio production heads began tolerating significant breaks from classical Hollywood conventions as a means of winning back audiences they were losing to the baby boom, to suburbanization, to increased leisure alternatives, and, eventually, most of all, to television. Liberal independent filmmakers were the main beneficiaries of the studios' greater openness to unconventionality. Thus while several of the business films examined in this chapter gave expression to what Lary May terms a shift from political to "cultural radicalism," the controversial thematic concerns and modernist aesthetics of these films were largely consistent with, or at least not overly threatening to, the vested interests of the studios that agreed to market and distribute them.[42] As May explains: "[T]he trade reporters recognized that the remaining audiences [not yet lost to television] wanted a product that did not so much reinforce as undermine official values."[43]

One of the givens of mass media, the "genius of the system," in Thomas Schatz's phrase, is its pliancy in the face of change. One way of theorizing this cultural dynamic is through Antonio Gramsci's concept of hegemony, which argues that in order to perpetuate itself, the mass media must adapt to an ever-changing audience. As Lynn Spigel and Michael Curtin explain, "Gramsci's concept of hegemony . . . shows us how powerful institutions like media are involved in a perpetual struggle (never fully won, always ongoing) to incorporate social conflict and reach popular consensus."[44] When all was said and done, it seems, the needs of the liberal independents and those of the New Hollywood were compatible. This glaring paradox fuels this revisionist history of the New Hollywood independents working during the postwar era.

Another way to locate the political dimension of classical narratives, Staiger suggests, is by viewing cultural signs as discursive sites that function as a locus for "a resurgence of power and pleasure and potential transformation from one meaning to another."[45] In other words, one should look at the implicit meanings inherent in conventional texts that appear to superficially resolve complex social issues. For instance, it is difficult to reconcile the upbeat and romantic resolution of the couple in the business film *The Apartment* with the fact that just moments before, protagonist Bud Baxter appeared to have committed suicide in a scene that echoes his beloved Fran

Kubelik's earlier actual suicide attempt. Staiger argues that such "transfer points" tend to represent two opposing semiotic strands: normative, ideologically fixed meanings; and sites of social change, given that transfer points are not fixed and static but evolve over time. Similar transfer points are evident in non-entertainment-industry business films such as *Executive Suite* (Robert Wise, 1954), *Woman's World* (Jean Negulesco, 1954), *The Solid Gold Cadillac* (Richard Quine, 1956), and *Patterns* (Fielder Cook, 1956), where a social critique of overvalued cultural markers linked to the ideal of success in both the workplace and at home (e.g., the "self-made man," the "true-woman" ideal, the home as safe haven) are combined with melodramatic storylines.

Executive Suite, for example, depicts a power struggle among a group of executives that arises when the corporate boss dies and one of the remaining executives (played by stars William Holden, Fredric March, and Walter Pidgeon) must take over the company. However, the battle in the boardroom is often overshadowed by domestic digressions that overlap with the business issues: these involve Holden's character's wife (played by June Allyson), and the boss's long-time, self-sacrificing girlfriend (played by Barbara Stanwyck), who is, however, a controlling stockholder in the company. Thus, as in other business films, the cultural supremacy of the suburban-headquartered, professional-managerial classes falls back on as it reinforces traditional gender, race, and sexual orientation ideals centered on the white male breadwinner husband who seeks success in a profession and a companion-wife who supports his efforts from the home base. In an era when the looming threat of HUAC curtailed the production of social-problem films that appeared even remotely critical of capitalism, the subset of films critical of big business survived by conforming to the basic outlines of the commercial melodrama; the looming and often unsolvable problems associated with the corporate workplace were subsumed within the more manageable problems of the couple. In other words, postwar business filmmakers were able to balance their artistic ambitions and commercial instincts by introducing the mollifying tendencies of classical Hollywood formulas.

The Big-Business Film Cycle:
From Self-Made Man to Organization Man

While the business films focused on here may have been more acerbic in content and more unconventional in style, American films centered in big business have a long and distinguished history. Yet particular representations of business in its relation to working people have shifted significantly over time. Prior to World War I, business films tended to idealize the young man who starts with nothing and fulfills the American Dream by climbing his way to the top. This idealization of the nineteenth-century Horatio Alger myth persisted, with rare exceptions, until the Depression burst the capitalist bubble and films began portraying businessmen as unethical and exploitative of those who worked under them. Frank Capra's films exemplify this trend, depicting heroes who staunchly defend the populist principles of Jacksonian democracy against the venal depravations of monopoly capitalism, for example, *You Can't Take It with You* (1938), *Mr. Smith Goes to Washington* (1939), and *Meet John Doe* (1941). A corollary view is expressed in the tragic portraits of businessmen who sacrifice their friends and family while seeking success, as in *The Power and the Glory* (William K. Howard, 1933), *The World Changes* (Mervyn LeRoy, 1933), and *A Modern Hero* (G. W. Pabst, 1934). Screwball comedies of the thirties and early forties also featured class conflict, although generally for the purpose of showing how rich and poor could get along, such as in *It Happened One Night* (Capra, 1934) and *My Man Godfrey* (Gregory La Cava, 1936). An occasional screwball comedy like *Holiday* (George Cukor, 1938) or *Sullivan's Travels* (Preston Sturges, 1941) had a harder edge, the first presenting the hero as a self-made man and aspiring millionaire who rejects the business world for a permanent holiday, the second depicting a successful comedy director who learns firsthand about the harsh realities of the Depression.[46] The proworker film matured to peak, not surprisingly, in the wake of the Depression in two films by John Ford, *The Grapes of Wrath* (1940) and *How Green Was My Valley* (1941), both of which explicitly indict exploitation of the working class and champion worker solidarity; and in Sam Wood's *The Devil and Miss Jones* (1941), about a rich department-store owner who becomes a lowly shoe salesman in his own store to discover who among his employees are organizing against him, only to join them in the end.[47]

Films about business made during World War II tended to reflect Office of War Information (OWI) and other governmental campaigns for national unity and therefore generally reverted to the pre–Depression-era American success story of starting from scratch and achieving success.[48] According to May, "Disagreements would surface between the OWI and producers concerning how best to dramatize a society free of 'want' and 'race war,' but it was clear that moviemakers proved willing allies."[49] As the war drew to a close, and despite the even more reactionary climate, the pendulum swung back to the darker view of business life, with society in general portrayed as corrupt and the businessmen as dishonorable. Indeed, film noir and/or social-problem films like Rossen's *Body and Soul* (1947), Chaplin's *Monsieur Verdoux* (1947), Polonsky's *Force of Evil* (1948), and Ray's *They Live by Night* (1949) emphatically challenged the American Dream.

Capra's career, once again, provides a clear example of the shift in political orientation. Capra's postwar career, working under the independent banner of his Liberty Films production company, did not restore his prewar popularity—in part because the New Deal populism and overly optimistic themes that prevailed during the Depression failed, as Cawelti suggests, to capture the ambiguities of postwar life. Fueled by anti-Communist hysteria, the very real threat of nuclear apocalypse, and by the "organization man" phenomenon, the mood of the country—*Father Knows Best* to the contrary—darkened, as did representations of the corrupt and treacherous businessman. The Dale Carnegie–type captain of industry, popularized in the popular press since the turn of the century clashed with the 1950s' image of the stress-filled, angst-ridden "organization man."[50] In a postwar world of comparative abundance, dubbed a "consumer paradise" by historian Warren Susman, the downside was the undue pressure placed not just on the wealthy but also on lower- and middle-class Americans to maintain a level of affluence at or above that of "the Joneses."[51] Workers up and down the corporate ladder thus found themselves devoting countless hours at dehumanizing jobs that encouraged ruthlessness if not outright backstabbing to get ahead. Blue-collar workers, meanwhile, suffered the demeaning psychological effects of popular press reports and sociological studies that championed social ideals associated with the white-collar worker and the rising middle class. As for gender relations, the impact of the new consumer culture and its heightened regimentation of male and female roles in the workplace and the home gave rise to a competitive spirit across classes that frequently poisoned family relationships and created friction when women and men married for money rather than love (or the reverse, when they married for love and insufficient money became an issue). Postwar films situated in corporate settings, however—including those to be focused on here—presented complex amalgams of these opposing tendencies. Critiquing the excesses and corrupt practices of big business on the one hand, they reserved a space on the other hand for the heroic businessman who ultimately rises above the fray.

Decoupling Gendered Ideologies

A primary thematic concern shared by postwar films set in the business world is the increasing bureaucratization of the workplace, which caused white-collar males to lose not only autonomy and control over their work lives but also a sense of dignity and self-worth as human beings due to the impersonal corporate culture. A revitalization of the romantic ideal of marriage and a more rigid definition of women's role in the home tempered this loss. Roland Marchand, in "Visions of Classlessness, Questions for Dominion," argues that the emphasis on the domestic and romantic ideologies became prevalent in the 1950s because they represented the last arenas in which most Americans could assert some dominion over their lives. This dominion was realized in large part by the mass exodus of the middle class to the suburbs where ranch-style homes, notwithstanding their homogeneity and inexpensive design, emulated the parceled "estates" of gentry from another era.[52] The work of Serafina Bathrick, Lynn Spigel, and others analyzes the ways in which the popular media reaffirmed these rigidly defined male and female identities as they were expressed in the public and private spheres. According to Spigel, "In particular, popular discourses on television were organized around the social hierarchies of family life and the division of spheres that had been the backbone of domestic ideology since the Victorian age."[53]

A similar organizing principle underlay much of postwar Hollywood cinema, although, as we have seen in the business film at least, gender ideals associated with the male breadwinner and his dutiful homemaker wife are expressed far more ambivalently. For both sexes, in these films a new postwar enemy emerges: corporate culture and an overly competitive capitalist marketplace that are blamed for turning ambitious individuals with a strong sense of self into interchangeable "organization men" and subservient "companion wives." And while melodramatic conventions were offered as partial antidotes for the workingman's increasing powerlessness in the face of a corrupt and dehumanizing business world, the ideals of romance and domesticity no longer provided easy narrative solutions. Not that the earlier model didn't hang on tenaciously—especially in the studio-produced film.

Even with some of these, however, the strain of the effort is revealed in the inversion of the public and private spheres that is resorted to in an effort to maintain the woman's role as humanizing influence. In *The Solid Gold Cadillac*, for example, Judy Holliday plays a small stockholder in a large corporation who falls for a business executive, played by Paul Douglas, and works from the inside both to reform the once-corrupt businessman and to subvert the efforts of a crooked board of directors. Rather than guide Douglas's character and the other executives from her home base, Holliday's character does end up working for the company, but she never wavers from her childlike faith in a moral universe, and the idealistic ending (the black-and-white film shifts to color as the couple step into their gold Cadillac) represents a wish-fulfillment fantasy about her working alongside her husband and sharing in his success. In two other business films, *Executive Suite* and *Woman's World,* June Allyson plays virtually the identical role as Holliday of the long-suffering, noble wife who protects her husband from the moral depredations of the corporate jungle.[54] Allyson's roles as the wife of William Holden in *Executive Suite* and of Van Heflin in *Woman's World* emphasize the housewife's humanizing impact on her businessman husband as the latter competes for a coveted promotion at his corporation. The businessmen husbands in each film must engage in treacherous battles to climb the corporate ladder, while observing the unspoken moral rules conveyed by their wives at home. Both June Allyson "wives" are rewarded for standing by their men whether or not they receive their coveted corporate promotions. Thus, we find that while in the first half of the 1950s, female film characters still largely adhered to their Victorian-era stereotype as selfless caretakers, by the second half of the decade the "new" woman could no longer be trusted because her newly individualized ambition caused her to act in her own self-interest.

Patterns, written by Rod Serling, adapted from his 1956 *Kraft Television Theater* production of the same name, and notably not a major studio production, also includes a number of significant, if secondary, women characters, both at the office and at home. Here, however, they are presented not as docile, moralizing handmaidens but as "new" women whose self-interested ambition, not unproblematically, mirrors that of the men. *Patterns* also remains the most overtly anti–big business of the nonentertainment business films for examining in-depth the greed and abuse of corporate America and the political compromises associated with career advancement. When *Pattern's* autocratic boss (played by Everett Sloane) torments the aging liberal-humanist, pro-union executive (played by Ed Begley) into quitting, he creates a moral crisis for the newly transferred executive (played by Van Heflin), who is offered a promotion in Begley's character's stead. The crisis is heightened when Begley's character suffers a heart attack after a vicious verbal attack from his heartless boss. Heflin's character desperately wants the promotion but is torn, given the inhumane treatment of his fellow worker. In contrast to the silent, if supportive wives in the other big-business films, Heflin's wife in *Patterns* (played by Beatrice Straight) is blamed for misrepresenting his accomplishments to the boss in order to secure his promotion, thus providing a far more complex and contentious portrait of the relation between gender roles and corporate capitalism. His wife defends herself against this accusation by pointing out that her husband made no effort to correct the boss's misunderstanding. In other words, the "companion wife" in *Patterns* is no longer working behind the scenes to keep her husband on a righteous path or taking responsibility when he strays. Instead, she reminds him of their shared complicity in wanting to get ahead at any cost. The film therefore represents a radical departure from the conventions of the business film on two fronts: it strays from the mollifying conventions of the commercial melodrama by daring to portray the erosion of the "true woman" stereotype and in so doing exposes without qualification many of the corrupt practices employed by the professional-managerial classes to quash workers' rights.

In the preface to the published version of his teleplay, Serling discusses the paradox of his blatantly anticonsumerist/anti–big business drama's success. After the show aired to rave reviews, Serling received twenty-three firm offers for television writing assignments, three offers to write film screenplays, fourteen requests for interviews with leading magazines and newspapers, lunch with several Broadway producers, and as many meetings with publishers to discuss novels.[55] Given his liberal, anticapitalist political agenda in this and other teleplays like *Requiem for a Heavyweight*, Serling apologizes in the preface for giving in to the financial rewards and "perks" of commercial success. As advocates for the disempowered working and middle classes, Serling and his wife were embarrassed and defensive when they bought their first new car: "I drive a 1957 white Lincoln convertible, so long, so garish, so obvious, that my wife blushes when she looks at it in the driveway. It's the first big luxury car I've ever owned, and it's one of the few overt gestures of ostentatiousness on my part."[56] Serling's acknowledgment of the disparity between his teleplay's anticapitalist critique and the financial rewards for replicating these views for a mass audience within the Hollywood film and television industries are the first overt sign we have seen, but far from the last, of the ideological crisis confronting liberal filmmakers in the postwar era.

4.
Self-Referentiality:Mediating TV's Incursion
into Hollywood and the Home

> In this self-referential world, such films [as *Ace in the Hole, Sunset
> Boulevard,* and *Double Indemnity*] appear to serve as a form of
> self-criticism. Both Wilder and Huston helped create the
> American myths of class consensus and the consumer democracy
> that Cold Warriors manipulated to repress dissent. In response,
> several of their films feature characters whose rational plans end
> in entrapment.
>
> —LARY MAY, *The Big Tomorrow*

This chapter examines a subset of postwar business films that employ strategies of self-referentiality, satirical irony, and other distancing devices, including often highly self-critical references to the filmmakers' own ambivalent
experience as industry players. These films are *The Hucksters* (Jack Con-
way, 1947), *The Man in the Gray Flannel Suit* (Nunnally Johnson, 1956),
and *The Apartment* (Billy Wilder, 1960).[1] A separate section examines the
idiosyncratic self-referential anarchic comedies of Frank Tashlin, to which
much of Wilder's work bears significant comparison. Each of these self-
referential entertainment films represents a distinct type of postwar studio
release registering an industry in transition, and a distinct cinematic style
illustrating an aesthetic shift from classical to postclassical. *The Hucksters* is
a standard, black-and-white A drama, adapted from a presold literary property, cast with a major star, and produced by in-house MGM producer
Arthur Hornblow Jr. *The Man in the Gray Flannel Suit* represents a calculated attempt by Fox chief Darryl Zanuck to create a larger-budget,
blockbuster-style "prestige" film, also engaging an all-star cast and a presold literary property but projected now on an epic scale (the setting ranges
from wartorn Europe to downtown Manhattan to a Connecticut suburb)
and with the new "not-TV" technologies of color and CinemaScope. *The
Apartment* is an artistically ambitious, genre-bending mix of satiric comedy and realist drama, shot in black and white in the "new realist" style by

writer-director Wilder, produced by him in association with the independent Mirisch Company and distributed by UA.[2] Unlike the other two films,
which take place inside the advertising-sponsored broadcasting industries,
the self-referential aspect of the insurance company milieu of *The Apartment* is self-consciously metaphorical: one of Wilder's inspirations for writing the screenplay was a behind-the-scenes scandal involving MCA.[3]

As Lary May proposes in this chapter's epigraph, the postwar self-
referential films superficially replicate a consensus view of America by
focusing on the concerns of the white-collar worker while giving indirect
expression to the filmmakers' malaise at their working conditions within
the New Hollywood, a split agenda that marks the beginnings of a decisive
break from the more fully consensual narratives of the past.[4] The earliest
of these films, *The Hucksters*, while representing in many ways a typical, in-
house star vehicle from the classical era, injects two potentially controversial themes: a topical returning-veteran subject matter, made popular by
the Academy Award–winning *The Best Years of Our Lives* (1946), *and* an
unseemly portrait of advertising.[5] However, these thorny social issues were
managed, in the film's narrative, by resorting to old-fashioned genre formulas and nostalgic images of womanhood and family life. With *The Man
in the Gray Flannel Suit*, the managing strategies moved in the blockbuster
direction, as Zanuck and his studio-based creative team neutralized this
film's potentially controversial social themes by employing familiar, yet highly
exaggerated, genre formulations. In *The Apartment*, one of the last films
in the postwar self-referential film cycle, New Hollywood–independent
Wilder, while superficially adhering to mainstream consensual narrative
conventions, mixed a range of genres (satiric comedy, realist drama, and
melodrama) that accentuated rather than glossed over these social anxieties.
By forging a unique style of storytelling and modernist inclination that
depart significantly from classical Hollywood norms, Wilder's film, along
with others to be discussed later, provides evidence of an emerging American art-film impulse.

Despite their various industrial circumstances and representational
strategies, however, all three self-referential films clearly invoke a rite of
passage from an uncritical acceptance of corporate capitalist and Old Hollywood values to the more liberating but also alienating "independence" of
the New Hollywood. This shift is evident extratextually as well, such as in
the ironic treatment of Old Hollywood's desire to maintain a strict separation between the big-name star and the New Hollywood's new "organization man" as underscored in an insider joke about David Lash, a character

in the novel version of *The Hucksters,* who was based on the then-head of MCA, Jules Stein:

> The guy says, "Monday I went swimming with Gable." So the friend asks, "Clark Gable?" "No, no, no," the guy answers, "Max Gable. Then Tuesday I went swimming up to the Goldwyns." So the friend says, "the Sam Goldwyns" and the guy says, "no, no, no, the Irving Goldwyns." "But last night," the guy says, "I had the best time of all, I went to the Lashes for cocktails." So the friend says, "the Dave Lashes?" And the guy says, "yes."[6]

The joke depends on the perception that in the New Hollywood, high-powered agents, though no longer represented as bottom-feeding flesh-peddlers, were still "organization men" lacking the glamour of Old Hollywood's power elite. Given their anxiety about challenging the powerhouse agency MCA and its head Jules Stein (upon whom David Lash is based), MGM excluded all overt references to MCA.[7] Notably, this included Norman's joke about agents (the joke also would have disrupted the cinema's fourth wall by self-reflexively calling attention to Gable's status as a movie star). However, as my subsequent analysis reveals, the filmmakers and marketing teams had to grapple with the unsavory connotations not only of the talent agent's job but also of Gable's ad-agent position, since both occupations are tied to selling. In other words, in the purportedly less flashy world of the New Hollywood, agents, by forming production companies and brokering tax incentives and gross-participation profits for their star clients, were now seen as crass middlemen—not unlike those in the advertising-sponsored broadcasting industry—evincing the "gray flannel" world of commerce. By 1960, *Hollywood Reporter* journalist Don Carle Gillette claimed that even the movie stars, writers, and directors had lost their allure:

> The glamour is being taken out of the movies in more ways than one. . . . [T]he tinted aura has been swept away from a lot of star personalities as a result of their widely publicized wrangling over money and involvement in other mundane matters. . . . There is a point in the upper strata of the salary spiral where squeezing more money out of a producer cannot materially benefit the star, writer or anyone else. . . . The narrowing margin of profit and expanding element of risk . . . present the biggest threat ever faced by Hollywood and its battle for survival.[8]

The banality, along with the venality, of big business, this view would have it, had invaded the royal court of the Old Hollywood studio system, turning it into a commercially oriented organization like any other. This structural shift is reflected (and deflected) textually primarily in the postwar filmic critique of the early television industry, and other less high-profile enterprises like advertising, public relations, and insurance; extratextually, however, as the insider discourse clearly shows, the film industry did not regard itself as free from the "organization man" stigma.

The New Hollywood's critique of television served an aesthetic and an economic purpose, both of which attempted to differentiate the film industry's product and persona from those of television. In this transitional period, the West Coast studio production executives struggled to adapt to their newest competitor and chafed when forced to deal with the new breed of middle managers, the newly empowered talent agents and admen who were getting it "both ways" by encroaching on the film industry and also actively engaging with TV. One of the initial strategies the trades and popular press adopted in reaction to this "conflict of interests" was to seek to aggrandize the still-dominant (but threatened) film industry at the expense of the fledgling TV industry by arguing that the former was inherently superior because it did not rest on an advertising base. This view relied on a popular assumption—not far from the "culture industry" theories of Adorno and Horkheimer—"that advertisements are the voice of big industry, a voice that instills consumer fantasies into the minds of the masses."[9]

Christopher Anderson argues that one of the reasons previous film historians have portrayed the relationship between the film and TV industries as predominantly antagonistic is due in part to the lingering impact of a group of satirical antitelevision films, including *Callaway Went Thataway* (1951), *It's Always Fair Weather* (1955), *A Face in the Crowd* (1957), and *Will Success Spoil Rock Hunter?* (1957). For Anderson, these films' narrow critique of television, while representing one aspect of a longstanding liberal, "high art" tradition in Hollywood, were also crucially informed by a more general 1950s' "anti-mass culture" debate that portrayed television and its advertising agenda as having corrupted traditional morals and aesthetic values, which Hollywood filmmakers saw themselves preserving. As a result, these self-referential films tended to demonize television as the "merchant of false consciousness, a medium irredeemably compromised by its devotion to advertising."[10] In many respects, this book was prompted by Anderson's provocative comments about this group of films being "more a product of the Frankfurt School than Tinsel Town"—in other words, anomalous instances of oppositional texts that reinforced the anti-mass-media debate.[11]

I argue something slightly different: many of these self-referential and reflexive films (especially the late 1950s and early 1960s experiments with classical Hollywood's genre and narrative conventions) were actually the product of an ironic juxtaposition of Frankfurt School and Tinsel Town; in other words, these films contributed to the "antitelevision" debate while also avoiding "the condescension toward mass culture characteristic of 1950s educated opinion";[12] they engaged instead in a quite sophisticated discourse about the complex interplay of politics, entertainment, and consumer culture in general in the context of an increasingly corporate-run society. This more nuanced critique derives not from an elitist attitude toward television, but rather from the filmmakers' intimate knowledge of the narrowing gap between the consumerist impulse behind television and that which was engulfing Hollywood as the two industries—film and television—were becoming one. Postwar filmmakers could no longer afford to construct a position of moral superiority over broadcasting as the cross-promotional synergies between the two industries intensified.[13]

The following examination of a number of industry "insider texts" drawn from the trade magazines reveals that postwar media practitioners were less certain than their "high theory" counterparts about the negative impact of television. This is not to say that the pressure to reassert the modernist, "high art" principles advanced by the Frankfurt School had not penetrated the rank-and-file of Hollywood through a range of popular and scholarly discourse, but, rather, that many filmmakers were ultimately pragmatic about the need to adapt to rapidly shifting industrial circumstances in order to remain competitive. Ultimately, film industry leaders, studio heads, industry trade journalists, and postwar filmmakers all needed to arbitrate, from varying if overlapping perspectives, their ambivalent attitudes to an ever-expanding entertainment complex that both encouraged autonomous narratives and subsumed them within a system of total merchandising.

Hollywood's Industrial Shift to a Commodified Aesthetic

From 1947 to 1953 industry trade analysts gave early, pragmatic expression to the antitelevision discourse in the pages of *Hollywood Reporter* and *Variety*. As Anderson encapsulates, "Throughout the early 1950s, the industry trade press debated whether television ultimately would reveal itself to be friend or foe of the movie studios."[14] Notably, however, in the second half of the decade, from about 1953 to 1957, the trades began taking the opposite tact, emphasizing the direct, economic benefits for the studios and independent producers that cooperated with television. Two *Hollywood Reporter* columnists, owner-editor W. R. Wilkerson (in his "Trade Views" column) and TV commentator Dan Jenkins ("On the Air" column), personified the shift. Previously having chided the studios to restore the fading tradition of hosting glamorous Old Hollywood–style premieres when opening their films, Wilkerson altered his strategy in 1953, using his column to try to find an acceptable means of bringing together Old and New Hollywood techniques. By then a seemingly outmoded event, once staged by studio publicity departments, the lavish movie premiere had been attended primarily by Hollywood insiders to celebrate the opening of a film and showcase its stars. These extravaganzas were featured in newsreels shown before the main theatrical feature, but after the decline in movie attendance, the value of these expensive spectacles was called into question, given that their boost to distressingly low box-office returns proved negligible—that is, until the studios allowed television to air them. Recognizing the benefits of this new trend, Wilkerson reminded studio heads that these televised events combined a nostalgic regard for the outmoded, albeit still glamorous, big studio premiere with the improved selling opportunities offered by television: "The Ken Murray TV show . . . recorded . . . the premiere [of the Twentieth Century–Fox big musical *Call Me Madam*] and sent out the message to better than THIRTY MILLION people throughout the U.S. and will reach the principal cities of Europe, South America, Australia and parts of Asia." In a subsequent column, he summarized: "Hollywood premieres sell the pictures, sell Hollywood, sell the industry to millions and millions of people. Our studios have plenty of good pictures to premiere, so let's have them and plenty of them—they pay off."[15]

Jenkins, writing from the television industry perspective, not surprisingly echoed Wilkerson's sentiments:

THE MOVIE PEOPLE are really beginning to wake up to TV's strength as a drawing card, albeit it's been a long and slow awakening. At first it was a sort of tentative thing, with one or two studios trying out a TV campaign for a specific picture—and discovering that it paid off. Then the trickle of stars appearing in guest spots to plug their current releases suddenly began to take on the proportions of a young flood, with even the majors allowing their bigger names not only to take a bow on TV but to perform as well. And now we have the final and most important stage of the awakening— the use of TV personalities as box office bait for motion pictures.[16]

While many of Hollywood's less-powerful producers and smaller studios immediately recognized the benefits of television production as a way to compete with the studios in a new arena, the studios at first narrowly focused on television as yet another distribution arm. After being barred from entry into distribution by early postwar FCC rulings that favored the networks, the studios did not move as efficiently as they might have into television production. In contrast to the reluctant studio heads, three long-time independent producers, Walt Disney, Samuel Goldwyn, and David O. Selznick, seized early opportunities to participate in the television industry, prompting Goldwyn, in particular, to explain to his peers that Hollywood was entering the third phase in its history: the first being the silent era, the second being the sound era, and the third being the television age.[17]

By 1953 a prescient Walt Disney had not only entered into television production but began adopting a range of corporate practices that would eventually become part of the studio arsenal during the blockbuster era of the mid-1970s. The cultivation by the industry as a whole of these corporate strategies, which Eileen Meehan summarizes as the "commercial intertext," would eventually allow Hollywood to restabilize "after some thirty years of uncertainty and disarray."[18] Among the strategies Disney initiated were the creation of branded entertainment, cross-promotion across different media platforms, elaborate merchandising and licensing agreements, and an in-house strategy devised to quantify audience demographics for Disney films. While the studios were already employing scientific means of quantifying audiences in the 1930s primarily through the Gallup poll, in 1953 Disney began "testing" films in-house using company employees.[19] Acknowledging the need to assess the popular taste of a broad-based audience as distinct from the "professionals" who were responsible for making and selling these media products, Disney used his secretaries and other members of his nonexecutive, noncreative team to stand in for the typical audience member. (Notably, for the corporate-minded Disney, the professional-managerial classes included *both* the executives and filmmakers.) Furthermore, by 1954, Disney had perfected the cross-promotional strategy of selling his film properties on his television shows (*Disneyland* being the most prominent example), using each of these distinctive mass-media formats to motivate attendance in his theme park—another major innovation—and to enhance his merchandising/licensing businesses.[20]

By the mid-1950s, cooperative ventures between the movie and television industries gave way to a more profound and lasting institutional alliance when TV production abruptly shifted from largely "live" New York–based production to Hollywood-based telefilm production and, not coincidentally, television syndication rights for series re-reruns became a huge new source of revenue for the studios. In turn, the relationship between studio film-making and consumer capitalism, symbolized by television's advertising base, became more and more pronounced.[21] Many aging or lesser film stars, recently divorced from their studio contracts, contributed to the "culture of commodification" by readily opting for liaisons with radio and television.[22] Proven media crossover talent like Bob Hope and Bing Crosby went one step further by readily adapting their talents to a range of synergistic mass-media formats and moving freely from one industry to the next, not all of them directly related to entertainment. Crosby became one of the first and most successful of the entrepreneurial actor-turned-producers, parlaying his success in the movies and recording studios to produce programs for radio and television. He and his brother Bob formed Bing Crosby Enterprises, which, according to Christopher Anderson, "diversified successfully into a number of unrelated businesses, producing orange juice, ice cream, sport shirts, and a wide variety of endorsed merchandise." In addition, another politically conservative celebrity, William Holden, decided to cash in on his movie-star cache by adding two additional companies to his original independent film production company, Toluca Films: Toluca Enterprises, Inc., to handle his television productions; and Toluca Publishing Company, to handle the publication and distribution of original music from his feature and television films, and also to oversee any licensing tie-ins for merchandising.[23]

By 1956 a number of politically liberal independents such as Stanley Kramer were aggressively using television to sell their films.[24] H-L's Lancaster and Hecht had also become conversant with the more aggressive marketing and distribution strategies being developed for highly commercial "blockbuster" entertainment. A 1956 *Hollywood Reporter* headline states: "*Trapeze* Set in 375 Dates: $2 Million Ad Campaign Sets Up Expected Greatest First Week of Any Pictures: New York." The article goes on to report: "With a blockbuster master plan of distribution, advertising and promotion now blueprinted on an unprecedented scale, United Artists anticipates the biggest first week's business in the history of motion pictures of Harold Hecht and Burt Lancaster's *Trapeze*."[25] Lancaster and costar Tony Curtis actively campaigned for the film by appearing on such high-profile television shows as the *Ed Sullivan Show* to publicize their latest release. In addition to live appearances by the stars, the show included film clips from a star-studded, behind-the-scenes event about the making of *Trapeze* called "The Wonder Show of the World."[26]

The synergistic turn in movie-television relations was not entirely smooth, however. In the first half of the 1950s, TV exploited the allure of Hollywood to widen its audience base by encouraging film stars to appear on variety shows and situation comedies and by launching a number of behind-the-scenes series celebrating Hollywood.[27] However, by the mid-1950s, and in the face of Disney's and other studios' increasingly aggressive marketing, advertisers began questioning whether it still made sense to grant the film industry a free ride. Charles Sinclair, writing for *Sponsor* magazine, an industry trade targeting advertisers, asked: "Should Hollywood Get it For Free? . . . Every kind of plug imaginable has been used to boost the new Disneyland amusement park"—a state of affairs that prompted one ABC network official to paraphrase Churchill: "Never have so many people made so little objection to so much selling."[28]

On the Hollywood front, MPAA head Eric Johnston began making the rounds in 1957 in an effort to bring together studio heads, their studio publicity directors, and East Coast advertising heads to smooth over differences and foster a stronger and more effective alliance between the film and television industries. Johnston's speeches encouraged studio heads "to consider better liaisons between Hollywood and New York [the two industries' respective capitals] on the business-building program." The best way to expand their domestic and global reach (while also promoting the larger cause of consumer democracy), Johnston suggested, was to integrate their selling strategies with those of the television industry.[29] Moreover, Johnston insisted linkage with television ultimately would enhance, not take away from, the film industry's overall prestige.[30]

Given the incontrovertible evidence of the growing interdependence of the film and TV industries and the proliferation of talent-turned-corporate-entrepreneurs in nonentertainment-industry settings, how are we to interpret the residual antitelevision (and antiadvertising) bias that prevailed in much of the popular literature and permeated the self-referential business films? The following discussion of three of the most prominent and paradigmatic of these films explores varying responses to the increasingly divisive social tensions linked to the emergence of the New Hollywood and to postwar consumer culture in general.

The Hucksters, The Man in the Gray Flannel Suit, and *The Apartment*

These three films, spanning the period from the late 1940s to the late 1950s when antitelevision, antiadvertising, anticorporate sentiments were at their height, are each set in an entertainment industry setting, as in *The Man in the Gray Flannel Suit* and *The Hucksters,* or in a metaphorically related setting, as in *The Apartment*. Each of the film's protagonists is a mid-level executive of some sort: Vic Norman (played by Clark Gable) is a radio ad man; Tom Rath (Gregory Peck) works in public relations for the head of a television network; and Bud Baxter (Jack Lemmon) is a junior executive in an insurance firm. Each film's (in some ways quite potent) critique of the male hero's single-minded pursuit of entrepreneurial success in a corporate capitalist America is ultimately diffused by a relatively "invisible" style and contained by a classical consensual narrative structure that affirms the patriarchal, middle-class, heteronormative family. Of the three, *The Apartment* offers the strongest, if still commercially compliant, challenge to the status quo through a departure from classical genre formulas that combines and contrasts ("mixes and explodes," in New Wave parlance) several normatively incompatible genres.

Both *The Hucksters* and *The Man in the Gray Flannel Suit* focus on the problem of the returning World War II veteran and the anxiety of the male with getting a job and coping with marriage in this period of social upheaval and transformation. Both films were based on popular novels published in 1946 and 1955, respectively—the former written by Frederic Wakeman, the latter by Sloan Wilson—and therefore provide a comparison of views a decade apart on the same subject. *The Hucksters* represents a set of traditional values associated with hearth and home colliding with postwar values associated with the pursuit of success in business at any cost. In this regard, *The Hucksters* represents a crossroads in Hollywood's representations of success in the context of the corporate culture of the postwar era. Set contemporaneously in 1947, the film posits an old-fashioned value system still held firmly in place by the "good wife" whose potential disapproval forces her businessman-fiancé to question his blackmailing of a colleague to further his own career.

Vic Norman (played by Clark Gable), the fiancé, is a returning veteran determined to preserve his integrity among the "yes-men" working at a leading radio-advertising firm in New York City. The crisis point in the narrative occurs at the precise moment when Norman, suddenly vulnerable because he needs the job to support his fiancée, Kay Dorrance (Deborah Kerr), and her kids, caves in and becomes a "yes man" himself. Ultimately, the narrative resolution is left to Kay, who gives Norman permission to balance his will to succeed with his desire to be a good provider for her and her children without selling out to the boss. It is an overly optimistic portrait, for those or any times, one that neatly ties up Norman's moral conundrum by ignoring any of the harsh economic or social realities. In the end, he is able to walk away from his advertising job and keep his soul intact while Kay smiles her approval of his moral choice.

This Pollyannaish worldview had become less plausible by 1956, the year *The Man in the Gray Flannel Suit* was released. The postwar protagonist of this film, Tom Rath (Gregory Peck), is ten years into his suburban marriage and his boring and frustrating work-life. In order to comprehend the extent of the social changes in America between 1947 and 1956, it is important to look at the "Man in the Gray Flannel Suit" phenomena that reflected and helped reproduce, through both the film and the novel, the era's "gray flannel angst" over the fate of the working man. As Rath states in the novel:

> I was my own disappointment. I really don't know what I was looking for when I got back from the war, but it seemed as though all I could see was a lot of bright young men in gray flannel suits rushing around New York in a frantic parade to nowhere. They seemed to me to be pursuing neither ideals nor happiness—they were pursuing a routine. For a long while I thought I was on the side lines watching that parade, and it was quite a shock to glance down and see that I too was wearing a gray flannel suit.[31]

While in the novel Rath expresses his self-loathing and relates it directly to his unease at being an "organization man," the film only has Rath's wife Betsy (Jennifer Jones) verbalize this negative view, critiquing her husband not for the challenges facing all middle-class working men in his situation, but rather for his specific lack of ambition and enthusiasm since his return from the war. In both the novel and film, she states, "I don't know. It's just that you've lost your guts and all of a sudden I'm ashamed of you." Her harsh words end up compounding rather than relieving Rath's predicament, when she chastises her husband for no longer being the daring, free-spirited man she married. Since his return from the war to an administrative job in public relations, he has lost his edge, his nerve. This was a criticism that clearly resonated with other men returning from the trauma, but also the drama and intensity, of wartime experiences to safe but uninspiring administrative jobs. The implication was that men who worked for corporations lost their individuality and their identity not only inside but also outside the workplace. As *Look* journalist George B. Leonard Jr. wrote in 1958:

> The American Male: Why is he afraid to be different? Group pressures are making U.S. men give up individuality for conformity. The company where Gary worked as a junior executive certainly was no place for individuality.

There, teamwork and personnel relations reigned over all. This meant you had to like everyone, give careful consideration to every proposal, no matter how trivial, handle every employee with the velvet gloves of insincerity.[32]

By the end of the fifties in *The Apartment*, "gray flannelism" had become ripe for satire. On the one hand, Bud Baxter's (Jack Lemmon) anomie is portrayed by introducing him as one of a hundred faceless executives sitting at a sea of identical desks; on the other hand, Wilder has given this critique of corporate culture a comic patina by depicting Baxter with a bad case of the sniffles. At the conclusion of the film, Baxter's being granted the key to the washroom outside his own office, an ionic trope for the "brass ring," epitomizes how trivial the pursuit of corporate achievement has become, especially in view of the fact that Baxter distinguished himself from his peers solely by having given the key to his apartment to his superiors for their extramarital affairs.[33]

Contrasting shifts in the twin ideologies of success and romance tied to preferred gender roles are also evident in comparing *The Hucksters* and *The Man in the Gray Flannel Suit*. The 1956 film is a glossy, high-production-value movie based on Wilson's critically acclaimed novel about a Madison Avenue executive struggling both to get ahead economically and to find meaning in his home life. Contract director Nunnally Johnson adapted the novel and directed, receiving steady input from Fox production head and producer Darryl Zanuck, whose wife, Jennifer Jones, was cast as Rath's wife Betsy. In a lengthy, fourteen-page memo to Johnson, Zanuck listed each of the changes that Jones had requested: "Jennifer feels that from the very beginning Betsy is too pat and sure of herself, and that she seems to place all the blame on Tom instead of feeling that she, too, is somewhat at fault. She feels there is a real danger of audiences disliking Betsy if she is so damned positive and so damned sure of herself." Later, Zanuck summed up Jones's overall concern: "As written in the script she thought she became too much the 'nagging' wife."[34]

Despite Zanuck/Jones's requested changes, however, many of Betsy's unsympathetic qualities remain intact in the finished film. Affirming the legitimacy of the production head and star's concern, one reviewer at the time asked why Tom doesn't leave the nagging Betsy in favor of Maria (played by Marisa Pavan), who personifies the less-threatening, tradition-bound image of nurturing femininity in her role as the long-suffering and highly sympathetic Italian prostitute with whom he had an affair during the war.[35] The affair is visualized through a flashback of Rath's to his tortured past as a soldier in World War II when, following the killing of his best friend, Rath embarks on the "foreign affair." Both the battle and romantic incidents impinge on the happiness of his life in the suburbs. In early post-war business films like *The Hucksters*, the typical narrative antidote to the male protagonist's enslavement to his stultifying corporate job was his retreat to the suburban home and the waiting arms of an attractive, understanding wife. In this way the mythos of the white-collar breadwinner is tied neatly to the mythos of the companion wife. As the postwar period progresses, however, the breakdown of this narrative convention, as exhibited in *The Man in the Gray Flannel Suit*, reveals how business films were beginning to challenge the status quo for men and for women trapped by social ideologies that once promised fulfillment. In all three films, the corporate culture of alienating and dehumanizing materialism, exemplified in the advertising and related industries increasingly dominating U.S. society in the postwar era, is the prime villain.

Precedents for Television's Commodified Address in the Home

In his comprehensive study of the advertising industry in America from 1920 to 1940, Roland Marchand details the myriad ways in which advertisers carried their consumer messages to a public comprised mainly of women, at first primarily via magazine advertisements that relied on the visual cliché of the family circle to pictorially situate consumer products in the sanctity of the home. These images often included emotionally charged, soft-focus scenes of mother and father watching their child play as all gather around the fireplace as a way of engaging nineteenth-century values associated with the home as a safe haven "in which men could experience sympathy and tenderness and refresh themselves to sally forth into the harsh 'real' world outside." The image of the family circle relied on feelings of nostalgia about the past to reconcile the harshness and uncertainties of modernity and, in particular, to pave the way for the new consumerist technologies of radio (and later television). Therefore, the pictorial convention of depicting parents, child, and product—"a radio, phonograph, room heater, or clock"—was part of a marketing strategy designed to make technologies with a utilitarian purpose appear interchangeable with those serving a commercial purpose. Another method of using a time-honored technique to sell the new and potentially threatening was the venerable testimonial or endorsement, which, according to Marchand, "had gained new popularity during the 1920s as advertisers searched for a personal approach. . . . Moreover, the eternal 'search for authority' led people to revere whomever in a

democracy could best fill the traditional role of aristocracy . . . from business tycoons and society women to athletes and movie stars."[36]

What was at stake at this early crossroads of determining what consti-
tuted acceptable marketing practices was how to protect against the untoward encroachment of commercialization into the moral sanctity of the
home. Two decades later, as rampant commercialization, following a Depres-
sion- and World War II–induced hiatus, took a quantum leap, Hollywood
began grappling with the commercialization issue head-on. *The Hucksters*
exemplifies the confrontation in the descending character arc of Vic Norman, who transmogrifies from a decorated vet to a crass ad man pandering
to the whims of his fatuous and autocratic bosses, thereby doing further
damage to the already compromised division between public and private
spheres. *The Hucksters,* both novel and film, portrays a hero who also has
mixed feelings from the start about the advertising business in which he is
employed. He describes himself repeatedly as a "huckster"—the pejorative
term for an aggressive salesman engaged in petty bargaining who lies to
convince others to do his bidding. Norman's ad man attaches gendered
connotations to the term in both economic and sexual ways when he describes how he sells women on the idea of buying the goods he's peddling
on behalf of the corporation, and how he, as a gigolo, gets women to fall
for him.[37] He tells Kay, "I won't huckster you"—implying that he has huck-
stered numerous other women in the past both in his public and private lives.
He is angry that he has been forced to take the job of a radio advertising
man because it requires him to sell out to the system and jeopardizes his
sense of individual self-worth. However, he is also aware that advertising
is a fast track to success. In the 1946 novel, Norman says,

> I hate this job. . . . I guess I took it because I'd rather be a winner than a
> loser. . . . A man cooks up some fat and presses it into a bar of soap. He
> perfumes it. Wraps it up fancy. Then he needs a barker to sell this mirac-
> ulous combination of herbs, roots and berries. So he calls me in to bark for
> him. But not at him. I don't like peddling and I don't like cringing. And I
> don't like men who have to think, dream, and yes, by God, eat soap. I just
> don't like myself.[38]

Whereas both novels, *The Hucksters* and *The Man in the Gray Flannel Suit,*
have their heroes express their negative feelings about their professions
inside the advertising-sponsored broadcasting industries, the filmmakers,
in both cases, appear reluctant to tarnish the images of their leading men

by having them indulge in such pessimistic speeches about their occupations. The open hostility that both novels express toward the advertising profession is redirected in the films, therefore, to very specific antagonists: the sponsor and the head of the network, respectively. Adding intertextual resonance to the compromised businessman character, Norman portrayer Clark Gable's mystique as a romantic lead was linked to his Hollywood star image as a "self-made man" who takes orders from no one, traits inherited from his films of the thirties (and forties) like *It Happened One Night* and *Gone with the Wind.* The MGM publicity production stills for *The Hucksters* reinforce Gable's reputation as a ladies' man by portraying him in a series of romantic clichés with each of his two leading ladies: Kerr and Ava Gardner. The ad copy states: "A Man's Man . . . and a Woman's too . . . The 'King of the Screen' [plays] . . . Vic Norman, fast-talking advertising salesman deluxe, a go-getter who has his way with women but who finds his destiny in the love of Kay Dorrance."[39]

Norman's qualities as a "man's man" are underscored early on when he accidentally meets a glamorous woman from his past—a singer, Jean Ogilvie, played by the sultry Gardner—in front of his boss-to-be, adding to his desirability as a prospective hire. Ogilvie is Norman's counterpart: ambitious, driven, and showing all the optimistic can-do traits of the self-made man. In 1947 she also was coded as a "loose woman," someone Norman apparently had slept with in the past and who expects him to resume the relationship. Her makeup, costume, and demeanor all speak to her sexual allure. Norman's boss is clearly impressed with Norman's status as a "ladies' man." For the boss, Norman's being single and sexually experienced is evidence that he has not yet sold out to the organization or to marriage. While Norman and Ogilvie share equal status in terms of amorous skill and ambition, they are worlds apart in terms of how these attributes are coded. Whereas Norman will eventually be rewarded for staying true to himself, unfettered by the institutional controls imposed by his corporate bosses, Ogilvie is evaluated by a different set of moral standards and found wanting. By the mid-point in the film, it is evident that she is deemed less socially acceptable than Kay; one woman is marriage material and the other is not.[40]

While Kay may be the winner in this articulation of early postwar romantic ideology, something happens in subsequent business films to suggest that married women, too, have been devalued. This degeneration of the domestic ideal can be traced to the conflation of commercialism and romanticism taking place in popular culture's representation of women in the 1950s. The emerging split between the commercial priorities of the studios and the counterhegemonic tendencies of certain filmmakers are evident when examining MGM's marketing strategy for *The Hucksters*.[41] In contrast to the book and the film's incipient critique of an intensified corporate culture devoted to consumerism, MGM's marketing team were able to downplay this negative view by emphasizing traditional gender roles using conventional publicity approaches derived from the Old Hollywood star system. However, in spite of MGM's conservative ad campaign, this image of rugged independence that made Gable sexually attractive to female audiences is compromised in *The Hucksters* by his character's job as an ad man under the thumb of multiple corporate bosses and by his disingenuousness in his relationships with women, demonstrated most clearly through his hypocritical disdain for obnoxious, manipulative commercial jingles that target women.

The climate of cynicism associated with "selling" in the New Hollywood is typically coupled with anxiety about "selling out" to management. *The Hucksters* reenacts the rite of passage from Carnegie-style individualism to that of the new businessman willing to sell out to get ahead. Gable's self-assured "man's man," Vic Norman, is contrasted sharply with the meek whimpering of the other executives in the film when in the presence of their tyrannical boss, Evan Llewellyn Evans (played to the odious hilt by Sydney Greenstreet), CEO of the Beautee Soap company—the primary client of the advertising agency where Norman works. The efforts to maintain the audience's empathy with Norman as the old-style employee is complicated when he is asked to go out on his first assignment: the dubious task of exploiting a war widow to help the company sell its soap to the masses. Norman gladly agrees to dupe the woman into this unseemly activity in order to secure the job he so desperately needs, until he realizes he is not dealing with a member of the easily duped public, that is, the typical American housewife who falls for radio ads. He is taken aback by (his future fiancée) Kay's aristocratic bearing, air of sincerity, and moral strength. Thus the ad man is caught at his own game, unmasked by the very image of "true woman" femininity he uses to sell products to that other 1950s stereotype, the easily duped consumer housewife. Everything Norman has previously achieved as a duplicitous ad man suddenly changes, based on his newfound admiration and eventual love for this saintly woman. In the scene following his comeuppance, he shifts the ad from the tasteless pandering to "cheesecake" images of women in lingerie to a "tasteful" ad that features Kay in an elegant gown, seated with her two children. Norman justifies his actions by stating that women would rather see themselves idealized, identifying with the image of motherhood.

The morality lesson Norman learns (and subsequently teaches), in consultation with this "true woman," requires a delicate balancing act between his continued rise up the corporate ladder and maintaining his integrity in the clearly amoral environment of the radio advertising business. What is most effective in the corporate jungle is not necessarily appropriate to the moral universe of Christian marriage. It is this moral dilemma and the hero's resolution of it that form both his character's narrative trajectory and the thematic center of this and the other self-referential films discussed here.

Mediating the Shift from Self-Made Man to Organization Man

The anticorporate cultural climate registered in films like *The Hucksters* is narrowly focused on a pronounced antibroadcasting sentiment that obscures its critique, more broadly speaking, of big business and capitalist culture. *The Hucksters* is also the first postwar self-referential film to reveal the emergent discordance between the "self-made man" and the "organization man," with Gable's ad man Norman representing the first phase of the transformation of the Horatio Alger type into the gray flannel fraud. Clearly an "operator" skilled in the ways of the corporate battlefield, Norman engages in a complicated set of power games with his prospective employer, pretending not to need the job that he is in fact desperate to obtain. The job begins on an insincere, duplicitous pretense. But his ploy works and he is hired—in fact, due to his talent as a con man. However, the old-fashioned view that Carnegie types like Norman will engage in acts of individual self-interest but never cross the line into selfish disregard for others is rarely an option for the cinematic white-collar workers that follow *The Hucksters*.

Several of the postwar self-referential films dealing with the new theme of male anxiety rely on audience familiarity with traditional gender ideologies to indirectly facilitate the passage from the self-made man to the organization man ethos that was deemed necessary for any smoothly running corporate enterprise.[42] This ideological sleight-of-hand is evident in sequences that link Norman as the enterprising young Carnegie-style entrepreneur to Ogilvie's sexually dynamic singer, in contrast to sequences that link Norman as the more sober and cautious organization and family man to the supportive, maternal Kay. Ogilvie is repeatedly aligned with Norman when he is engaged in unscrupulous activities as an advertising executive (e.g., she is admired by Norman's advertising agency boss as she performs a sexy number on stage; she helps Norman score points with the despicable sponsor who admires her singing on his radio ad; she serves as Norman's accomplice so he can outmaneuver a savvy talent agent during a crucial negotiation). His alignment with Kay, on the other hand, is chaste and up-lifting. In a later scene, he invites Kay to join him at his favorite location (a once-quaint resort hotel by the water), and carefully orders two, nonad-joining rooms so that he may propose marriage in a romantic setting; instead, through a series of miscommunications, Kay arrives to find a tawdry hotel whose indecorous clerks put her in the room next to Norman's. When she leaves before he's had a chance to explain, Norman finally understands the extraordinary precautions he must take to protect the "true woman" virtu-ousness of his future wife in contrast to the more casual, fun-loving behav-ior he exudes with his other female acquaintances.[43] By encouraging the viewer to side with the earnest, wifely Kay, at the expense of the quasi-femme fatale Ogilvie, the film reinforces Norman's segue from man's man and business climber to domestic partner and team player.

The familiar outlines of the traditional melodrama formula end up play-ing a major role in mediating any residual anti–mass media instabilities as well. A subplot of the film focuses on Norman's artistic ambitions being temporarily derailed by the corrupting influence of an untalented but well-connected radio star whom Norman is saddled with if he wants to make the radio show that will earn him a promotion and win the hand of his fiancée. This mediating function is accomplished in a lengthy sequence depicting Norman and the rest of his creative team rolling up their sleeves in a dark, smoky motel room while everyone else at the sunny resort frolics around the pool—but the motivation behind his self-sacrifice and hard work derives not from himself (the self-made man) but from his job concerns that are tied to Kay (the organization). Tellingly, however, the scapegoat in the ideological exchange is the obnoxious and untalented radio personality Norman is forced to hire. During these motel scenes, the fading radio star played self-reflexively by Keenan Wynn (the real-life son of Ed Wynn, a well-known vaudevillian-turned-radio and later TV celebrity who was known for his career ups and downs) arrives and pitches several bad jokes that he wants Norman to include in the show. Norman pretends to listen and then escorts the washed-up comedian out of the room in order to keep work-ing on the show as originally planned. In this way, Norman demonstrates but also manages his frustration with the commercial constraints of produc-ing for radio. He will heroically sweat blood and tears to ensure the quality of a radio program made by his company even when burdened by the spon-sor's questionable choice of talent. The implicit message is that the laudable work done by film professionals in commercial broadcasting is often accom-plished in spite of the "brand" of inferior talent the advertising-based medium provides. *The Hucksters* thus incorporates a Frankfurt School–style critique by indicating the split between the high-minded artist and the commercial hack, a split that necessarily compromises the mass-media product.

Television as Scapegoat for Society's Ills

A comparative analysis of the function of space in self-referential and reflexive business films provides another means of illustrating the changes occurring in postwar U.S. society. In regard to the public and private spheres, specifically, typically represented in these films through sites related to business and home/romance, we find the distance between the two spheres increasingly narrowing and the distinction between them blurring as the postwar period progresses.[44] As previously conveyed, *The Hucksters, The Man in the Gray Flannel Suit,* and *The Apartment* each avoid the overt appearance of a controversial, anticapitalist critique of corporate culture by relying heavily on certain mollifying aspects of the traditional melodrama formula and its idealization of the home. However, a closer examination of the articulation of the two spheres, public and private, in each of these three films reveals that the political economic concerns of the workplace have increasingly permeated the home base by the end of the decade with Wilder's *The Apartment,* in particular introducing a postclassical, modernist, and anti-Fordist critique into the self-referential business film tradition.

Whereas the actions and problematic character traits of the corporate boss in *The Hucksters* are confined to the workplace, by the time of *The Man in the Gray Flannel Suit* they have extended to the home—and beyond. For in his capacity as the head of a television network whose messages and values are transmitted to millions of people in the "comfort of their homes," Ralph Hopkins' (played by Fredric March) spatial penetration collapses not only the private and the public spheres but the personal and political ones as well. And yet, this omnipresence, if not omniscience, of the network boss was fraught with ambivalence. The combined mystique and hostility associated with this "all-powerful" figure is underscored in the film's negative assessment of Hopkins, who has sacrificed everything to run a network, including the well-being of his wife and adult daughter; on the other hand, the film humanizes Hopkins when Rath reminds him of his son who was killed in the war. This more "balanced" perspective (in contrast to *The Apartment*'s blatantly nihilistic stance toward corporate bosses) is indicative of a blockbuster strategy whose impulse to smooth out the social critique is driven by the need to make these expensive productions be all things to all people.

The goal of the white-collar working man in this, as in other self-referential entertainment business films, remains wanting to become the boss, but the goal is undermined to an increasing degree as the 1950s progress, with wife and family no longer the cure-all for the job's impossible demands and the boss's questionable ethical standards. What prevents the classical antidote from achieving its traditional healing powers is television. A *Hollywood Reporter* reviewer of *The Man in the Gray Flannel Suit* intimated as much by deflecting the film's critique of corporate capitalism in general onto that of television specifically. The reviewer cautiously praised the film for its "disturbing and thought provoking social comment (though with no political propaganda)." Political controversy was eschewed, at least for this reviewer, by attributing Hopkins's failure in the film, both in the workplace and his marriage, not to his position as corporate boss per se, but rather more narrowly to that of TV network head. This scapegoating of television turns to outright demonization in the reviewer's claim that Hopkins "makes a tragically grotesque marriage, to accomplish the grand scale triviality of filling the minds of the children of the nation with moronic westerns. [As a result, he is a]t the height of his financial success and personal failure."[45] Lost in the shuffle is the fact that the film's protagonist, Tom Rath, grapples with far more complex issues, such as a war veteran's struggles to save his marriage and advance in his work, than those purportedly connected to the commercial and aesthetic problems of television.

This review is not anomalous, however, but representative of the way most industry insiders were narrowly interpreting Frankfurt School critical theory when responding to the decade's popular self-referential and reflexive films. Despite these films' overt critique of a vast array of social ills linked to corporate dehumanization and consumerist excess, trade reviews tended to focus on how they reinforced a pejorative view of television. The *Hollywood Reporter*'s Wilkerson took the antitelevision bias in another direction in regard to *The Man in the Gray Flannel Suit,* celebrating studio boss Zanuck for making this type of big-budget, star-driven, Cinemascope film as a means of re-engaging audiences lost to television.[46]

The antitelevision discourse and its spatial component, far from disappearing in the later reflexive entertainment business films such as *A Face in the Crowd* and especially *Sweet Smell of Success,* actually expands to the point of near-parody. For instance, the television celebrity–cum–fascist demagogue Lonesome Rhodes in *A Face in the Crowd* is portrayed as a lonely, desperate philanderer operating from his penthouse apartment above his television studio. Sidney Falco, a press agent who services newspaper/radio/TV celebrity J. J. Hunsecker (modeled on Walter Winchell) in *Sweet Smell of Success*, keeps his one-room bedroom apartment next to his one-room office and changes clothes while conducting business with his secretary; later Falco uses the same bedroom/office to get his girlfriend to sexually extract a professional favor from a competing columnist. Hunsecker's gossip columnist, meanwhile, is frequently portrayed wielding his dubious influence via various forms of electronic communication: from the phones at every desk at home, in the nightclubs where he conducts business, and at the television station where he enacts his personal vendettas under the pretense of "educating" the public about the proper role of mass media. This perverse collapse of private and public realms and concomitant abuse of power is portrayed most graphically in a scene in which Hunsecker uses the phone in his home-office to instruct press agent Falco on how to sabotage his sister's fiancé, while Hunsecker secretly (and incestuously) observes his sister asleep in the next room. After Falco plants contraband (first drugs, then Communist literature), Hunsecker announces the fiancé's "crimes" in his column and on his television show. These technologically reflexive scenes not only display the extent to which electronic culture—from the telephone to the television broadcast—has erased traditional spatial divisions; they argue compellingly that this erasure—accomplished, paradoxically, in the name of communication—has led to the breakdown of meaningful and supportive social and interpersonal relations.

The reflexive film's role in challenging melodramatic formulas and classical narrative resolution, not to mention its scathing indictment of postwar U.S. society, will be explored in depth in later chapters. What is already evident with the self-referential films focused on here is that for all the hand-wringing over the incursion of television into the postwar Hollywood business world and American life, this new medium also paved the way for filmmakers to experiment with, question, and partially discard some of Old Hollywood's aesthetic and industrial imperatives. Just as the introduction of sound in the late 1920s produced a series of sweeping changes in studio practices, prompting studio personnel to accommodate alternative narrative practices and acting styles,[47] so too, the introduction of television in the late 1940s (as with subsequent new technologies: video and cable in the 1980s; DVD and the Internet in the 1990s) helped create a climate conducive to cinematic innovation—at least until the studios adjusted their production, marketing, and distribution strategies to the changed circumstances.

Theorizing Industrial Change: Truth Is Stranger Than Fiction

The self-referential entertainment business film marks a decisive break from the past by no longer suppressing the commercial underpinnings of mass-media products but rather by calling attention to the means of production.[48] For example, in Charles Eckert's often-cited article "The Carole Lombard in Macy's Window," Eckert describes how Old Hollywood publicity departments seamlessly bridged the gap between celebrity and selling by enjoining Bette Davis to ride in a gold Pullman train as a way of adding mystique and allure to a display of General Electric appliances. Fifteen years later, *The Huckster*'s Vic Norman/Clark Gable was riding on another Super Chief express train from New York to Hollywood where, we are told, most Hollywood agents and Madison Avenue types conduct their deals. Indeed, this is where the sponsor of the radio show Norman is producing for an ad agency has instructed him to secure a low price for a second-rate comedian to serve as host of the show. In contrast to the coordinated 1930s publicity-advertising stunt designed to efface its origins as a means for the studio to sell its star (while earning additional income from corporate tie-ins), this postwar film opted instead to foreground the "behind-the-scenes" negotiations between the stars, their agents, the advertisers, and other corporate middlemen.[49] Eckert's nonfictional description of Davis's 1931 cross-country train conveys Hollywood's facility with the "smooth operation of the production-consumption cycle by fetishising products and putting the libido in libidinally invested advertising."[50] In contrast, the fictional scene in *The Hucksters* emphasizes the flip-side of the Faustian bargain: namely, the commercial compromises and cutthroat behind-the-scenes negotiations necessary to secure even substandard talent for a sponsor-controlled/ad agency-produced radio show.

The Hucksters' author Frederic Wakeman based his descriptions of these transactions—such as the train scenes of Norman and Ogilvie hobnobbing with other media middlemen in the dining car and over drinks—on his own experiences working for Madison Avenue in the 1940s. Norman entertains Ogilvie by explaining how he plans to outmaneuver the master negotiator, top agent Dave Lash, and his protégé, whom Wakeman modeled on MCA kingpin Jules Stein and his then-right-hand man, Lew Wasserman.[51] The public at the time remained largely ignorant of "the Octopus" and its far-reaching tentacles (which as of the late 1940s had not yet extended quite so far), but the workings of the powerful agency were well known in the entertainment community and had become a frequent target of satire.[52]

The satire had turned nasty by the end of the 1950s, as the match in *The Apartment* between the MCA regime and Sheldrake's cold, calculating executive reveals. As McDougal notes, "*The Apartment* became a somber tribute to the Jennings Lang testicle affair," a heavily publicized incident that involved actress Joan Bennett's affair with her MCA agent, Jennings Lang, a notorious womanizer. When Bennett's husband, producer Walter Wanger, discovered his wife and Lang *in flagrante* in his car, he shot the agent in the groin. The notoriously press-shy MCA tried to bury the scandal; however, the private investigator, whom Wanger had hired to follow his wife during her affair, leaked the information to the press, including the fact that Bennett and Lang were meeting at an apartment belonging to young agent-in-training Jay Kanter. Kanter later admitted to investigators that he had originally been asked to lease the apartment for MCA client Marlon Brando; however, whenever the actor was out of town, other agents *might* have used the apartment for their romantic liaisons. Wilder took this juicy morsel of an idea and simply moved the setting of his film, *The Apartment*, from a talent agency to a less reflexively conspicuous insurance firm.[53] Just as with *The Hucksters'* train-trip allusion, Hollywood insiders got the connection.

Vic Norman (Clark Gable), Jean Ogilvie (Ava Gardner), David Lash (Edward Arnold as a Jules Stein look-alike), and Freddie Callahan (George O'Hanlon as a Lew Wasserman look-alike) play cards on the Super Chief from New York to Hollywood while they negotiate a talent deal in *The Hucksters* (1947).

Another "gray flannel" connection between Lew Wasserman and the postwar self-referential film can be deduced from a 1960 *Fortune* magazine article by Edward T. Thompson. In describing the strategies adopted by MCA to turn its Hollywood operation into a well-oiled machine, Thompson reveals the extent to which Wasserman controlled everything his employees did on and off the job: "Wasserman has no outside interests. He has little home life, rarely goes to parties . . . he works seven days a week often sixteen hours a day, and so do most of his top executives." Wasserman apparently even slept on a couch so he could start his early morning calls without disturbing his wife. The similarities between Thompson's description of the work-obsessed Wasserman and the network boss Hopkins in *The Man in the Gray Flannel Suit* are striking. Both MCA's chief and his fictional counterpart are consumed by business and expect their young executives to serve as protégés. Both emphasize long hours, the bottom line, and crushing the competition, thereby emulating and helping foster a new American business model. Finally, Wasserman's protégés were given the same offer that Tom Rath receives at the end of *The Man in the Gray Flannel Suit:* to learn the trade by "acting as private secretaries to Wasserman . . . read[ing] Wasserman's mail, listen[ing] to his phone conversations, and generally watch[ing] him operate."[54]

In another case of life imitating art, Clark Gable, in his casting for *The Hucksters,* was asked to play a role that replicated his own experience of negotiating a contract with a Wasserman protégé. Gable was one of the primary benefactors of MCA's New Hollywood business practices. "I never really made any big money until [MCA agent] George [Chasin, a Wasserman favorite] took over the handling of my career," Gable admitted. Similar to Bette Davis's experience once she went independent at MCA's behest, Gable had never earned more than $300,000 a year with MGM. "With MCA representing him as an independent, he earned twice as much on a single picture." In *The Hucksters* Gable's Vic Norman is made to look heroic for pulling the wool over his opponent's eyes to get a deal favorable for his boss. He negotiates a cut-rate price for his boss's favorite comedian, Buddy Hare, by feigning disinterest (just as he feigned disinterest to win his job in the first place). What is amusing, given the film's reticence to reveal the actual state of the culture industry in 1947, is that Norman goes on to reveal his strategy to his counterpart on the other side of the table right after they close the deal. Yet Norman's deal-making is nothing like the notoriously backhanded games of manipulation engineered by MCA. Already in 1947, fears about reprisals from MCA led to *The Hucksters'* "cleaning up" the portrait of Jules Stein's fictional counterpart, Dave Lash.[55] In a later scene, Lash becomes an added source of Norman's moral crisis when Norman threatens to reveal damaging information he has on Lash to engineer a sweeter deal; Norman eventually apologizes to Lash to redeem himself.

What prompts Norman to go for the jugular with the high-powered agent Dave Lash in this watered-down version of real MCA-style deals? Norman's threat to expose the agent's troubled past would have compromised Lash's reputation among the young boys for whom he created a community center. This boy's club is designed to portray the agent's humanitarian effort to give back to the community that helped him through his own underprivileged childhood and that contributed to his achievement of success. The altruistic act also provides a means of softening both the portrait of the ruthless agent, modeled on the real-life Stein, and Gable's "self-made man." Notably, in the novel, Lash (who in real life was Jewish) donates money "to help the Jews in Europe—and to fight the forces of intolerance against them in this country."[56] Norman, in the novel, blackmails Lash, who tried to back out of the Buddy Hare deal, by telling him that if it gets out about his double-dealing, the industry won't blame the agent or the agency, but its figurehead, Lash, and will say it is because he is a Jew. The novel complicates Norman's morality by demonstrating his willingness to use anti-Semitism against Lash to secure his deal. In the film, the anti-Semitic allusions are excised; Norman kicks himself for stepping on a fellow businessman by leveraging information about his personal life (no mention of his Jewishness) to get ahead. The novel, of course, was closer to the truth, as indicated in the real-life incident in which Frank Sinatra expressed his hatred of Stein, Werblin, and Wasserman over a failed deal by letting "every bartender from L.A. to Manhattan know exactly what he thought about the 'Jew bastards' at MCA."[57] In both the novel and the film, Norman rationalizes his actions by telling Lash that his act was that of a desperate man who has something to lose, namely, the virtuous widow Kay and her two children. But the distinction made in the film is simply between two aggressive businessmen fighting over turf in the workplace and about whether blackmail that involves encroaching on an opponent's "safe haven"— his private life—is justified.

Much of the characters' ambivalence in the self-referential films seems an uncanny match with artistically minded postwar American filmmakers' internal and external conflicts in regard to their own "organization man" status in the New Hollywood. Largely of a liberal political persuasion, the most prominent of these filmmakers—director- or star-turned-producers like Wilder, Mankiewicz, Kazan, and Lancaster—were now also members of the professional and managerial classes they were attacking. Along with their agents, attorneys, and other middle-managers, they were part of the new generation of entertainment industry power players. In *The Apartment* (1960), for example, the most deeply cynical of the self-referential films surveyed here, Wilder valorizes the cause of the powerless middle-class workers, Bud Baxter and Fran Kubelik, against their oppressor, senior executive (and MCA-stand-in) Jeff Sheldrake. Unlike Capra's 1930s populist everymen, and even Norman and Peck's put-upon but resilient heroes, Baxter and Fran are portrayed as ill-equipped social misfits (despite Baxter's cunning and Fran's sexual adultery). In real life Wilder played gin rummy once a week with Lew Wasserman and knowingly allowed MCA to use its extortionary tactics to secure MCA talent for his films. For instance, MCA created an extraordinary package deal when it put together four clients—Wilder, Lemmon, Tony Curtis, and Marilyn Monroe—for *Some Like It Hot* (1957). In large part because he was a WMA client, Danny Kaye was ruthlessly excluded from the deal at a moment when he desperately needed the film to re-ignite his career.[58] Each of these extratextual factors complicates Wilder's position as a liberal filmmaker critiquing the culture industry, while conversely contributing to his films' status as liminal texts somewhere between traditional genre and art-house films.

Notably, Wilder very deliberately characterized himself as "anti-art" in a 1959 *Sight and Sound* interview with him and Ingmar Bergman. In a *Variety* summary of a press conference in 1960 about his acquisition of the rights to *Irma la Douce*, Wilder complained about the artistic pretensions of "the New Wave" and in the next breath described how invaluable the effect of television comedy has been on film comedy. This extratextual discourse on Wilder, in which the director denies artistic affiliation with the countercultural tendencies of the European New Waves while affirming kinship with and respect for American commercial television, is either a calculated put-on by a notoriously cheeky filmmaker or evidence of an explicit strategy of balancing the tenets of the Frankfurt School and Tinsel Town. From what we know (and don't know) of Wilder's complex persona, one would have to presume a combination of both.[59]

The Self-Referential Anarchistic Comedy

Another New Hollywood filmmaker who seems to have shared Wilder's penchant for "getting it both ways" was Frank Tashlin, whose self-referential anarchistic comedies were particularly suited for such a duplicitous strategy.[60]

No matter what this specific genres' oppositional intent or ultimate impact might have been, it was easy for studio publicity departments and affiliated product advertisers to pursue a conservative agenda by trading on Old Hollywood's generic and/or high-art pedigrees. Early television creative teams had employed the reverse tactic, reinforcing TV's populist entertainment while emphasizing the film industry's risky, high-art attributes by keeping, according to Caldwell, "the art-and-(im)morality specter of both high culture and Hollywood at arm's length."[61] Frank Tashlin's anarchistic comedies—for example, *Artists and Models* (1955), *Hollywood or Bust* (1956), and *Will Success Spoil Rock Hunter?* (1957)—provide access to both dominant and progressive readings, by creating an unstable (post)modern recycling of familiar tropes from a vast array of popular media formats using formal reflexivity and stylistic excess (accepted practices within the anarchistic comedy genre). These devices would offer French New Wavers like Godard and film historians a means of celebrating the films' breaks from the realist text, yet also provide both studio publicity departments and advertising firms a means of foregrounding Hollywood's familiar stars, stories, and genres.[62] For instance, Eastman Kodak Company aligned their product, without irony, with Tashlin's blatant send-up of the Hollywood/advertising axis, *Will Success Spoil Rock Hunter?* Appearing in *Hollywood Reporter,* the Kodak ad featured several poverty-stricken women selling baskets of food on the streets of Guatemala; displayed between them is a huge poster for Twentieth Century–Fox's latest blockbuster film and their new, buxom star, Jayne Mansfield, dressed in a low-cut evening gown, fur, and jewels. The extreme culture clash and capriciousness toward class inherent in the incongruous juxtaposition of rich and poor are superceded, at least in the advertisers' minds, by the image's underscoring of Hollywood's ability to sell not just a single film but the American way of life abroad. In this way, Kodak was able to use the glamour and glitz of Hollywood to sell both their film stock and MPAA head Johnston's project of extending the international reach of Hollywood and corporate capitalism.[63]

The potential effectiveness of Tashlin's type of film was such that one trade reviewer chides Hollywood for not producing more of this kind of upbeat entertainment:

A recent week's schedule for a reviewer consisted of five motion pictures and two stage presentations, every one of which was concerned with drug addiction, juvenile delinquency or race relations. There is nothing wrong with dramatic consideration of any one of these themes, but on the other hand, why can't there be more pictures like Frank Tashlin's *Will Success Spoil Rock Hunter?*[64]

This review is most significant, for our purposes, for signaling the beginnings of a studio backlash against independent-minded films that pursued topical subject matter or explored darker social themes as part of the "new American realist" cycle, such as *On the Waterfront* (1954), *Marty* (1955), *Blackboard Jungle* (1955), and *The Man with the Golden Arm* (1955)—films that appeared openly critical of the status quo. In contrast to the superficially mollifying effect of the anarchistic comedies, there was far less tolerance for the more overt subversion in the "realist" social-problem, film noir, or melodrama genres, not least of which because these films provided little opportunity for studio publicity teams to carve out the more conservative of the two available "readings" and thus to broaden audience appeal. As a result, postwar "realist" filmmakers had to fear not only HUAC, but also negative reviews that could undermine the studios' already weak commitment to their admittedly more demanding but not necessarily commercially unviable films.[65]

In the end, like other anti-big-business and antibroadcasting films, Tashlin's and Wilder's films are symptomatic of the divided political loyalties of their filmmakers. Tashlin was a union activist who used self-reflexivity and modernism in his films as a subterfuge to engage in often scathing indictments of American consumer culture.[66] His early career indicates the perils for postwar filmmakers working in the social realist as opposed to the anarchistic or musical comedy traditions. Whereas he was celebrated in the trade press for his later, hugely popular farces that dealt self-reflexively with the culture industry, his earlier, more "realist" domestic comedies, in particular *The First Time* (1952/Norma-Hecht), prompted greater controversy. *The First Time* provides early evidence of Tashlin's trademark reflexivity, his critique of socially defined gender roles, and his subversive tone (for instance, just as a dead man narrates *Sunset Boulevard* in the 1950 Wilder film, an unborn baby narrates the young couple's story in Tashlin's *The First Time*); however, the film used a social realist rather than comic approach in its critique of married life.[67] Notably, Jean Rouverol and Hugo Butler, the authors of "And Baby Makes Three," the original story upon which the screenplay was based, were blacklisted that same year for their past political activities. Gun-shy from this close brush with HUAC, Tashlin, while not a Communist Party member but definitely left-leaning shifted increasingly to the "safer" anarchistic comedy mode after 1954.[68]

A brief comparison of the two types of Tashlin comedy, realist-domestic and anarchistic, sheds light on why, despite similar themes, one was perceived as controversial while the other wasn't. *The First Time* tells a story of a young couple who are having their first child and combines social realism and moments of cartoon illogic (e.g., an out-of-control washing machine) that are familiar to most Tashlin fans. A telling moment of social critique occurs when the young wife (played by Barbara Hale) lashes out at her placidly smiling, if unnerved husband, explaining how impossible it is for women to fulfill the conflicting demands of having to serve simultaneously as wife, mother, housekeeper, and sexual goddess.[69] Tashlin conveys a similar, if even more troubled portrait of marriage and middle-class life under capitalism in the later anarchistic comedy, *Hollywood or Bust* (1956), starring Dean Martin and Jerry Lewis in their last film together as a team. For example, Martin's character's response, when his love interest (played by Pat Crowley) asks why he is still single, is hopelessly nihilistic:

> Better odds at the race track. . . . The minute you leave the starting gate the odds are six to four because you're furnishing a rundown apartment. Then the odds drop to seven to three because you need a larger place, an extra room for the little monster that your ever lovin' comes up with. Then the little monster grows, becomes a big monster. School expenses. Now you got to start taking everything that the crummy boss hands out cuz you can't afford to lose your crummy job. Li'l junior's got to go to college. "Dear Pop, need money, met a girl." The odds are now nine to one you haven't even hit the far turn yet. By the time you get to the finish line you gotta hurry up and die so you have time to pay for your own funeral expenses. That's a bad deal.

How are we to explain HUAC's interest in the screenwriters of the former film and their decision to overlook the even more seditious content of Martin's character's speech? As for the realist text, it allows no aesthetic "escape hatch" for its provocative themes. The anarchistic comedy, however, tends to turn its controversial ideas into fodder for a series of comic reversals as, for example, in the closing portions of *Hollywood or Bust*. In the final scene at Grauman's Chinese Theater, Tashlin brings together the disparate characters from each of the previous scenes, including the unlikely romantic coupling of Jerry Lewis's rabid and awkward movie fan and the elegant movie star played by Anita Ekberg. Ignoring Martin's character's previous reservations about the viability of marriage as an institution, he and his girlfriend are portrayed as happy and in love in the final scene. Both "couples" are swept off stage with the boys "winking" at the camera after appearing in this, the final, show-stopping, self-reflexive musical number. Such "direct address" to the camera was a typical feature of 1950s television's variety shows (including Martin and Lewis's own *Colgate Comedy Hour*), whose host(s) and other performers were licensed to form a conspiratorial alliance with a knowing home audience by calling attention to, and breaking, the "fourth wall."[70] Similarly, this film's eye-popping, convention-shattering finale deflects attention away from any of the film's previous social critique both by providing and calling attention to the "constructedness" of the Hollywood happy ending.

Frankfurt School Meets Tinsel Town

Given the reactionary postwar climate, most liberal filmmakers would have been leery of incorporating intact the Marxist thrust of Frankfurt School critical theory, its critique of state and monopoly capitalism in which, according to Douglas Kellner, "the state and giant corporations managed the economy and in which individuals are being submitted indirectly to state and corporate control."[71] However, certain aspects of Frankfurt School theory can be traced in the cultural backlash taking place in postwar society against enhanced corporate, consumer society via the "antiorganization man" and "antitelevision" literature that was filtering into popular mass market magazines and mainstream Hollywood filmmaking alike. Postwar filmmakers like Wilder and Tashlin can therefore be seen indirectly advancing the Frankfurt School's high theoretical critique of "the homogenizing regime of capital [that] produces mass desires, tastes, and behavior" while simultaneously negotiating the "critical-theoretical competencies and marketing imperatives behind the[ir] textual practices."[72] In other words, by simultaneously embracing aspects of an anti-Fordist, modernist critique *and* embracing the mass appeal of popular culture, certain postwar filmmakers, such as Wilder and Tashlin in particular, were setting the stage for future developments in the theory-praxis hybrid associated with the films of the Hollywood Renaissance.

Textual analysis can help shed light on how media practitioners enacted the passage from a classical to a postclassical period (and intimated the post-Fordist, postmodernist period still to come); for instance, one need only consider *The Hucksters'* normative version of the private sphere, in which Norman relishes the time he spends with Kay and her children and away from the "rat race" of the advertising business, which contrasts with the 1956 representation of the working man in *The Man in the Gray Flannel Suit;* Rath appears equally oppressed at home and at the office, given the unremitting pressure placed on him to earn more money by his discontented, nagging wife. Finally, in *The Apartment,* Wilder invokes the total collapse of the division between the two spheres by portraying Baxter working twenty-four hours a day to extract a promotion from his supervisors. Whereas the safe haven once provided the working man with sustenance so that he could engage in the type of "individual thought and action [that act as] the motor of social and cultural progress," by the end of the decade we see the same deadening routine or sameness at home or at the office.[73] At first glance, Wilder appears to be narrowly reinforcing the Frankfurt School's anti–mass culture industry theory in scenes portraying Baxter's nightly routine: sitting alone, eating uniformly wrapped frozen TV dinners in front of his television set; however, television here functions more like a red herring than as a viable explanation for Baxter's oppression given the number of other institutional forces that also serve as powerful instruments of social control and domination in *The Apartment.* While the critical community and industry trades narrowly blamed television for a host of social ills, filmmakers like Wilder and Tashlin, among others, were embracing aspects of television's populist, mass appeal as a means of balancing their modernist agenda.

The self-referential themes and self-reflexive strategies that Tashlin, Wilder, and other of MCA liberal clients favored were motivated and complicated by the need to survive New Hollywood's cutthroat world. For instance, whereas some of these filmmakers make disguised reference to MCA, Stein, and/or Wasserman to signify Hollywood's changed working environment, even the most powerful of the newly independent filmmakers had to finesse their critique so as not to jeopardize their own standing in the industry. One fairly safe line of attack was to engage the antitelevision discourse,

Bud Baxter (Jack Lemmon) is frustrated by the TV commercials in *The Apartment* (1960).

using it as a stand-in and narrative subterfuge for a broader critique of corporate capitalism and thereby shielding themselves from the fallout from government agencies and entertainment industry forces.

The paradox of this strategy, not lost on Wilder in particular, as we have seen, was that the anti-TV critique was accomplished employing aesthetic elements—stylistic excess, self-conscious irony, and hyper-reflexivity—derived from TV, and thus distanced from "high art" pretensions. *A Face in the Crowd* and *Sweet Smell of Success*, by contrast, represent a type of (post)-modern art film that revels in its bold mixture of generic conventions and artistic effects, "blurring the lines between exploitation and sophistication,"[74] but ultimately landing on the side of aesthetic pretense. Tashlin's films and Wilder's *The Apartment*, especially, boldly juggle familiar genres and joggle ideologically fixed views while adhering, superficially at least, to comedic amelioration and classical narrative resolution.

Wilder Than Most

Billy Wilder's unique insights into the contradictions inherent in modern American life were attributable in part to his outsider's perspective. Born in Austria, Wilder began his film career at the cusp of the German golden age of the 1920s. Fleeing the Nazis in the 1930s, the Jewish Wilder worked briefly in France before coming to Hollywood, where he rapidly established himself as one of Paramount's premier writer-directors. By the end of the 1950s, European and American film scholars began to herald Wilder for his contributions to an American art cinema, although, as we have seen, he was consistently dismissive (at least publicly) of such assumptions, emphasizing instead his films' status as commercial entertainment.[75]

According to James Naremore, Wilder's work shows a great debt to Weimar cinema, but less in regards to its photographic style (which is typically not expressionistic), but rather in its portrait of a "Fordist Amerika." Naremore describes how in films ranging from the film-noir classic *Double Indemnity* (1944) to *The Apartment*, Wilder makes similarly scathing references to modern industry, such as when, in describing his crime, *Double Indemnity's* Walter Neff (another insurance salesman!) likens it to a car or a moving train (e.g., "the machinery had started to move and nothing could stop it"; he'd "thrown the switch"; the "gears had meshed"; "the last stop is the cemetery"). Wilder's visuals that do resonate with expressionism frequently reinforce a negative portrait of American society that can be traced to several silent Weimar or Weimar-inspired classics such as F. W. Murnau's *The Last Laugh* (1924) and *Sunrise* (1927), Fritz Lang's *Metropolis* (1927), and King Vidor's *The Crowd* (1927). In each case, the anti-Fordist message is clear: capitalist society "has turned workers into zombies or robots"—a message that is mirrored in the opening shot of *The Apartment* showing Baxter sitting at one of a sea of identical desks.[76]

Wilder's reluctance, in the face of such evidence, to identify with any aspect of the European art cinema can be traced in part to his fears about compromising his status as a commercial filmmaker. He had weathered the flak over his attack of his own industry and the lowly status of writers in *Sunset Boulevard* (1950), but after the box-office and critical failure of his next film, *Ace in the Hole* (1951, aka *The Big Carnival*), a scathing indictment of the news media, he knew that he needed to find another, safer hit or risk losing his newly acquired creative autonomy.[77] *Ace in the Hole* co-writer Charles Brackett tried to come to the rescue, claiming in a 1952 interview that reviewers were missing Wilder's "peculiarly American sense of humor" and his inheritance of the "long standing tradition of American self-criticism." But as Wilder biographer Ed Sikov states: "Like Chuck Tatum [in *Ace in the Hole*], Wilder was prone to bragging. He'd always enjoyed rubbing the noses of others in his own success, but now the tables had turned.... [T]hanks to *Ace in the Hole*, Billy's boat had just sprung a severe leak." Film scholar Colin Young surmises that "Wilder stopped making personal films because of the failure of *Ace in the Hole*." What is clear is that the newly empowered yet also beleaguered filmmaker would henceforth seek to balance "art and industry" in his American films; more specifically, he began to cloak his anti-Fordist critique in self-consciously ironic, self-reflexive strategies influenced heavily by 1950s television comedy.[78]

Notably, each of the variations on the self-referential films that followed *Ace in the Hole*, including *Sabrina* (1954), *Seven Year Itch* (1955), *Some Like It Hot* (1959), and *The Apartment*, incorporated elements of satirical and/or highly reflexive comedy, which granted Wilder greater license to critique social norms given the allegedly less-threatening subversion inherent to the comedy genre. While his films do not fully embrace what J. Hoberman calls the "vulgar modernism" inherent in Tashlin's films, Wilder's films share certain traits with the former's work, such as the employment of comic reversals and ironic juxtapositions of stars, stories, and themes from various popular media forms including vaudeville, radio, television, and film.[79]

Wilder's film's are bubbling over with ironic and joking references to other Hollywood (and foreign) films, star personas, and technologies. *One, Two, Three* (1961) references *Grand Hotel* and *Potemkin* (1925); *Some Like It Hot* sends up Cary Grant and George Raft; Gary Cooper and James

Cagney spoof themselves in *Love in the Afternoon* (1957) and *One, Two, Three*, respectively; *The Seven Year Itch* lampoons CinemaScope and stereophonic sound and mocks the melodramatic pretensions of the Burt Lancaster/Deborah Kerr beach kissing scene in *From Here to Eternity* (1953). In a moment of near-postmodern hyperconsciousness in *The Seven Year Itch*, the hero-narrator Sherman (Tom Ewell) responds to his own rhetorical question about the woman in his kitchen by saying, "Wouldn't you like to know? Maybe it's Marilyn Monroe." As Wilder biographer Steven Seidman astutely observes, however: "[These techniques do] not function to radically deconstruct the narrative (à la Godard)." Instead, much like his contemporary Tashlin, Wilder employed such devices primarily for their broad comedic effect and a means of investing audiences in the formal exercise or joke and diverting attention away from any social critique. The added bonus of this strategy, as with more recent postmodern pastiche, is the feeling of superiority granted viewers for their knowing "insider" awareness of the pop cultural references.[80] A contemporary trade review explains in layman's terms how Wilder was able to achieve this careful balance of Karl and Groucho Marx:

> Wilder combines "the façade of a romantic comedy-melodrama . . . and delivers a blistering commentary on contemporary anti-hill society and its amoral inhabitants. . . . Whatever the implications, there is humor and romance to please the least perceptive, and aside from its commercial aspects, *The Apartment* is an important provocative film."[81]

Commercial compromises and personal disclaimers notwithstanding, self-referential filmmakers such as Wilder and Tashlin were beginning to experiment with the radical deconstruction and sexually provocative themes of European art cinema on the one hand, and with the proto-postmodernist reflexivity of television and the anarchic comedy tradition on the other. Ultimately, and with the help of the more radically reflexive 1950s films to be discussed in subsequent chapters, these two strands would coalesce and effloresce in the hip, personal, countercultural cinema of the Hollywood Renaissance.

5.
Two Emergent Cinemas:
Art and Blockbuster

Twentieth Century–Fox [was] an example of a studio [that was]
learning that bigger was better. . . . While the big-budget profit
mongering led to record gates, it also led to increased conservatism:
reliance on bankable stars, "safe" subjects, and "presold" stories was
diluting films designed for mass-audience appeal. Independent
filmmakers, on the other hand, could keep their budgets down
and appeal to smaller and perhaps more sophisticated elements
of the public, minimizing financial risk and experimenting with
techniques, subjects and even performers.

—THOMAS SCHATZ, *Old Hollywood/New Hollywood*

The early work of writer–director Joseph L. Mankiewicz offers another variation on the theme of an emerging art cinema in the "new Hollywood," an
emergence, as we saw with Billy Wilder, which would hardly follow a smooth
linear course. The focus here is primarily on Mankiewicz's *A Letter to Three
Wives* (1949), made for Fox under the stewardship of studio chief Darryl
Zanuck and yet one of the more artistically ambitious of the anti–big busi-
ness/anti–mass media films. This film is compared with another Fox offering, the star-studded, fashion-laden, CinemaScope blockbuster *Woman's
World* (Jean Negulesco, 1954). Initially conceived as an attempt to replicate the provocative woman-oriented, financially and critically successful
Mankiewicz film, Negulesco's effort, with Zanuck's hands all over it, ended
up reverting to simplistic melodramatic conventions and affirming traditional gender roles, consumer culture, and big business.

In the restructured studio system of the post–Paramount decree period,
the majors began to abandon B films and to rely almost exclusively on A
films, concentrating in particular on two distinct types of A film: the
medium-budget art film that targeted a more sophisticated, adult audience
and was prone to challenging genre conventions and accepted social norms;
and the big-budget blockbuster that aimed for a broader spectrum of the

public and carried on classical narrative and aesthetic traditions that rein-forced dominant myths.[1] *A Letter to Three Wives* and *Woman's World*, both Twentieth Century–Fox studio productions made under Zanuck's steward-ship, exemplify these two approaches. A comparative analysis of them sheds considerable light on how post–World War II American filmmakers, given the changing circumstances of the New Hollywood, either were enabled to break with classical norms or compelled to reinforce them.

The impulse, and capacity, for making art films in Hollywood was stim-ulated by market considerations, by directors' and stars' enhanced power and independence during the early postwar period, and by the influence of the European art cinema. Analogously, the evolution of the blockbuster trend, besides responding to reduced box-office returns and competition from television, can be traced to a backlash among studio executives to the growing independence and iconoclasm of the filmmakers, and to efforts to extend Hollywood's global reach by adding to elements that had long been that cinema's calling card—lavish spectacle and production values—with new ones oriented to the global marketplace—international cofinancing arrangements, international stars, and foreign locations (the latter, not coin-cidentally, often allowing for nonunion crews).[2]

Zanuck's long career as a studio head at Fox (with a brief foray into independent producing from 1957 to 1962) traverses this shifting industrial terrain, and his own personal strategic adjustments to it provide an insight-ful micro-organizing framework for viewing the macro-institutional devel-opments. For instance, Zanuck was instrumental in launching the careers of several award-winning, artistic directors, including Mankiewicz and Kazan.[3] Once a film writer and ever one of the more hands-on of the stu-dio producers, Zanuck was predisposed to accommodate a fair amount of aesthetic, and even political, rebellion among the new generation of auteur-directors; yet as one of the venerable moguls who had risen to prominence during the "golden age" of the studio era, he also nursed a desire to re-establish the type of in-house production that had prevailed during that period. This schizoid inclination is evident in his cutting loose Kazan and writer Budd Schulberg in 1954, the year of *Woman's World*'s release and a year after that of *Gentlemen Prefer Blondes*, when the directing-writing team presented him with the screenplay for the topical but complex social-realist drama *On the Waterfront*. Zanuck explained that no one was interested in a film about dockworkers and went on to describe the type of broadly appeal-ing films the studio was now looking to make.[4] (The "dockworker film," of course, besides turning a handsome profit at the box office, went on to win the Best Picture, Best Director, Best Writer, Best Actor [Marlon Brando], Best Supporting Actress [Eva Marie Saint], and three other Academy Awards.)[5]

Zanuck's (in this case short-sighted) swing toward the blockbuster versus the art film in the mid-1950s was indicative of the increasing marginalization of the newly empowered auteurs and part of a last-ditch attempt on the part of the major studios to reassert control over the production process.[6] One year prior to the Kazan-Schulberg sacking, Mankiewicz, seeing the writing on the wall and tired of Zanuck's micromanagement of his projects, left Fox to form his own production company, Figaro Inc., distributing through the most pro-independent of the old studios, United Artists.[7] As if to show Mankiewicz that he could thrive without him, Zanuck attempted, with *Woman's World,* to make a new, improved version of Mankiewicz's *A Letter to Three Wives.* His misguidedness (at least artistically) in this endeavor nearly matched his shortsightedness (artistically and financially) with *On the Waterfront.* But our goal here is not to question Zanuck's instincts as a studio head; rather, it is to more fully understand the dynamics of the Zanuck-Mankiewicz relationship and how these dynamics reflect larger industrial and cinematic developments. For this we must first examine the historical context surrounding the two emerging (and diverging) cinemas of the New Hollywood era: the art film and the blockbuster.

The Studio-Distributed Art Film

While the term "auteur" wouldn't enter the general lexicon until the early 1960s, already in the earlier postwar period, as we have begun to show, certain independent-minded directors (e.g., Mankiewicz, Wilder, Kazan, Huston), many still working under studio contract in the late 1940s and early 1950s, began capitalizing on the studios' ebbing control of the production process and the PCA's weakening grip on censorship to engage in more personal creative expression. The studios themselves, as we have seen as well, saw some strategically economic benefit to the more artistic film. Additionally important to the cultivation of a proto-American independent cinema was the growing awareness among industry insiders of a European art-cinema movement. At the end of the war, as Europe began to restabilize and a number of provocative European films began appearing on American screens (particularly those of the Italian neorealists), the influence of their pointedly anticlassical approach began to seep into the more creatively ambitious studio releases. Huston's *The Treasure of Sierra Madre*

(1946), *The Asphalt Jungle* (1950), and *The Red Badge of Courage* and *The African Queen* (both 1951), all exhibit the director's keen interest in photographic naturalism, location shooting, and social themes—albeit the latter still cloaked in genre trapping. A similar neorealist sensibility can be found in Kazan's *Panic in the Streets* (1950) and *Viva Zapata!* (1952), as well as in Mankiewicz's *Letter to Three Wives* and *House of Strangers* (both 1949). In response to changing public tastes, the studios grudgingly absorbed the added expense of location shooting in order to achieve the era's greater emphasis on realism through which films "gained the look of authenticity by being shot in an actual locale, or in one closely resembling it, rather than on a studio set or a back lot."[8]

Countering the notion of such an early infusion of European aesthetics into American cinema, film historian Paul Monaco has observed: "The aesthetics of the art film (e.g., neorealism, auteurism, New Wave, engaged cinema) were rooted in Western European philosophy and collective experience in Western European nations after World War II in ways that Hollywood could neither duplicate nor imitate."[9] While it is certainly true that Hollywood was not instantly or completely "made over" by the European art cinemas, it is also the case that U.S. filmmakers (themselves often immigrants) have, since the beginning of the movies, routinely absorbed aspects of other national cinemas and, in classically hegemonic fashion, adapted them to their own, admittedly more commercial ends—and the same goes, even in negation, for these cinemas in regard to Hollywood. The American horror film's indebtedness to German Expressionism and film noir's to Expressionism, French Poetic Realism, and Italian neorealism is well documented. To cite another postwar example, *Ace in the Hole* showed Wilder's embrace not only of the "new realism" but of other foreign art cinema influences such as the decidedly antiheroic leading role, fatalistic ending, and controversial social themes. To be sure, the film's box-office failure moved Wilder to a more careful balance of art and genre, but despite this and other financial missteps, several New Hollywood films that experimented with European art styles and themes turned a profit, such as *Joan of Arc* (1949), *High Noon* (1952), *Come Back, Little Sheba* (1953), *Rear Window, On the Waterfront* (both 1954), *The Blackboard Jungle* (1955), *The Man With the Golden Arm, The Rose Tattoo,* and *The Bad Seed* (all 1956).[10]

Another deterrent, besides the profit motive, to European-influenced U.S. filmmaking was the political pressure placed on the industry by the HUAC hearings, which singled out politically liberal filmmakers who had been making social-problem films in the realist tradition. As a result, the emerging generation of auteur-directors who survived HUAC and success-fully managed the transition from the classical to postclassical era tended to be those who balanced genre and art film, experimenting with but never straying too far from classical convention, yet also managing to comment self-consciously on these conventions.

U.S. filmmakers deliberately setting out to release commercially risky art films through major studios (as opposed to films balancing art and genre and/or cast with marketable stars) have proved a challenge in any Holly-wood era. How great the obstacles could be even in the ostensibly more art-friendly climate of the New Hollywood is indicated in the case of *Marty* (1955).[11] Determined to adapt the award-winning Paddy Chayevsky–written, Delbert Mann–directed teleplay to the screen, coproducer Harold Hecht had to convince not only UA, a studio known for its comparative indulgence of independent-minded talent, but also Hecht's skeptical pro-ducing partner, Burt Lancaster. It wasn't until the "small film" began win-ning major awards here and abroad (including the Best Picture Oscar), that Hecht achieved sufficient credibility to be able to start building a case for his vision of an alternative set of film practices in the new climate of stu-dio distributed package productions. "[S]omewhere in between Hollywood's so-called 'blockbuster' entertainment and the quickie-type melodramas and westerns," Hecht stated in the *Hollywood Reporter* in 1955, "there lies what should be a fertile field." Quoting Hecht, Lancaster biographer Kate Buford adds, "The great middle area was thought to be where 'the classes and the masses are in step,' where intelligent movies with an emotional heat cross over into art. These movies, [Hecht] thought, should cost no more that $300,000, ensuring that they have a shot at earning back twice the movie's cost."[12] Savvy to the bottom line, Hecht was promoting the idea of having independent production entities create art films in association with the stu-dios made at B or "intermediate" (i.e., B+) film prices. These budgetary distinctions are significant in order to isolate Hecht's calculated attempt to define a new, industrial category of art film (as distinct from the designation of art film retroactively assigned by contemporary film scholars, myself in-cluded). Nevertheless, art films in both categories helped set the stage for an emerging American independent cinema.

Highbrow versus Lowbrow in the Emerging Art-House Movement

Simultaneous with the studio-released art film, a more truly independent American art-house distribution system featuring the works of American and European auteurs also was emerging. While an extensive system of theaters wouldn't be in place until the late 1950s and early 1960s, the American art-house movement was unofficially launched in the mid-1940s when a number of small theaters in New York began screening two significant Italian neorealist films: *Open City* (1945), *Paisan* (1946), both by Robert Rossellini. One of the factors contributing to the growing interest in films made outside the United States was the growing circuit of major international film festivals. The Venice International Film Festival (formed in 1931) inaugurated the trend by screening the first batch of neorealist films, noted for their low-budget, working-class narratives using distinctively non-studio locations and non-professional actors in major roles. In particular, the publicity and critical acclaim showered on the two Rossellini films after their success at the Venice International Film Festival led to their release in the United States, with each earning over $1 million in box-office dollars (a tidy sum in those days, especially for a foreign-language film). When the Cannes and Berlin festivals were added to the list of showcase festivals in 1947 and 1950, the impact of European and other non-U.S. art films grew exponentially. Another significant development that opened doors for American filmmakers to explore controversial themes was the 1952 "Miracle decision," in which the U.S. Supreme Court ruled against censoring Rossellini's *The Miracle*, which several New York officials had deemed sacrilegious. This decision, which countered the 1915 Mutual decision, established, for the first time, that filmmakers were protected under the First Amendment's freedom of speech clause.[13]

During the first half of the decade, a wave of foreign films including the Japanese and Indian classics *Rashomon* (Akira Kurosawa, 1950) and *Pather Panchali* (Satyajit, 1955), as well as key art films from Italy, France, Britain, Scandinavia, and elsewhere, began appearing in small theaters in America's urban centers. At the same time, local film societies and universities started to show foreign films. Once a system of distribution was in place and a committed audience began flocking to these screenings in record numbers, the foundation was established for the next wave of international films to arrive. In addition to screening mostly subtitled foreign films, art-house theaters began adding American-made "classics" from the studio era to the mix, as well as B film noirs and recent films made for lower budgets at the margins of the industry by filmmakers being touted as auteurs by maverick young French critics who themselves would later found the French New Wave.[14]

Although it had risen in prominence by the mid-1950s, the American-produced strand of the art-house movement still faced significant resistance from the mainstream industry. James Naremore shows how two 1955 low-budget thrillers—the Allied Artists release *The Big Combo,* by Joseph H. Lewis, and especially the UA release *Killer's Kiss,* by Stanley Kubrick, who raised the modest $75,000 budget himself—stood at a historical crossroads between the decline of B-film production and the emergence of the art-house movement. Kubrick, for example, was forced to employ cost-cutting techniques that resulted in an "abstract or symbolic effect, reminiscent of the avant-garde" as well as "the style of art-ful, New York-school street photography."[15] Yet while Kubrick's, Lewis's, and other American "art-movie noirs began to appear with some regularity on the international scene" around this time, the films being released through second-tier distributors like Republic and Allied Artists were not receiving adequate promotion, access to A theaters, or the critical recognition they would have received in the late 1950s once scholarly writing on auteurism had crossed the Atlantic from France.[16] Instead, because the B-picture industry was essentially dead by 1955, these artistically ambitious and often subversive genre films were caught in a peculiar limbo—neither part of the studio system proper, nor able to benefit from an art-house distribution system that was not yet fully in place in the United States.[17]

Another aspect of the American-European art-house relation may have worked to the American's advantage. Jean-Luc Godard's seminal New Wave film *Breathless* (1959) pays homage to the pulp-genre "B pictures" favored by Old Hollywood independent production companies like Monogram Pictures at the same time that sophisticated American audiences were beginning to embrace in art houses both the New Wave and these same American-made B pictures. Both Godard and the art house theaters, Naremore suggests, "were symptoms of an emerging postmodernism . . . an intellectual hedonism that dissolved distinctions between highbrow and lowbrow. . . . [American auteur critic] Andrew Sarris contributed to this phenomenon . . . [by wryly observing that] the [French] auteurists were vulnerable to the charge of preferring trash to art," because they took iconoclastic pleasure out of announcing that a film like *Kiss Me Deadly* was superior to *Marty;* in effect, they were employing the classic highbrow gambit of elevating low-brow art at the expense of middle-brow art.[18] Although Godard and Sarris take us into a somewhat later period than our focus here, similar highbrow/lowbrow distinctions clearly already apply, as we will see in later chapters, to *A Face in the Crowd* and *Sweet Smell of Success,* two 1957, independently produced "art films" that play off against genre conventions. Moreover, the beginnings of an ironic posture toward the "high art"/"low art" binary can be seen, even at the studio level, as early as the late 1940s, as we will see shortly with Mankiewicz's *A Letter to Three Wives*.

Further encouragement for the U.S. art film had a negative source: the politically and economically motivated attacks of American trade analysts, film critics, and even certain filmmakers against their European competitors. This xenophobic reaction, beginning in the late 1940s and lasting through the early 1960s, generated a climate of greater tolerance for U.S. filmmakers to experiment with A-film genres in an effort to create a uniquely American art-cinema style that combined the commercial attributes of classical Hollywood with the high-art aesthetics of European and other foreign filmmakers. One of the filmmakers who benefited earliest and most from this qualifiedly tolerant climate, through his anointment, by the trades and literary magazines alike, as the avatar of an as-yet-undefined American commercial art cinema, was Joseph Mankiewicz.

The Roots of the Highbrow/Lowbrow Distinction

A 1949 *Theatre Arts* review of Mankiewicz's *A Letter to Three Wives* (appropriately titled, given the magazine's high-culture pedigree) is indicative of an early effort by film critics to articulate the postwar clash in values between an Old Hollywood devoted to entertainment-centric formulas and a New Hollywood open to a more artistic cinema. The anonymous reviewer deemed *A Letter to Three Wives* one of those rare films whose artistic merits made it comparable to (or even superior to) the latest crop of highly foreign art films being celebrated at the big film festivals and screened at U.S. art theaters.[19] Especially pertinent to our discussion, the reviewer identified two categories of alternative product: art and exploitation, both of which s/he saw emerging from within the Hollywood studios and as distinct from the studios' more commercial fare. "Art," in this instance, however, referred exclusively to A films with artistic aspirations, while "exploitation" encompassed lower-budget independent genre films. As a telling case in point, the reviewer lauded the satiric tone and social themes explored in the studio-produced and polished *A Letter to Three Wives,* while glossing over those in the Humphrey Bogart–starring *Knock on Any Door* (1949), an independently made (by Bogart's 1947-formed Santana Pictures) film noir directed by Nicholas Ray. Despite Bogart's status as an A-list star, the reviewer was eager to establish a pecking order separating films with "serious" literary credentials from those with pulp-fiction roots and based in the B films of a bygone era.[20] This New Hollywood hierarchizing of "high" and "low" art categories reinforces the notion that directors like Mankiewicz,

Wilder, Kazan, and others, making what could be termed "A art films," were initially privileged by critics and industry analysts over filmmakers like Ray, Kubrick, and Aldrich (at least in their early careers), working in what were regarded as B-film genres. High-art/low-art distinctions were here being awarded largely on the basis of genre: films belonging to what Schatz calls "the more visible and ideologically self-conscious realm of the 'social-problem film'" carried more critical cachet than the often more stylistically and thematically subversive offerings of film noir or the rebel youth film.[21] As the reviewer stated, "Mr. Bogart's new producing firm would have done better to leave 'Knock On Any Door' to someone who really appreciated its possibilities, while they went ahead on a routine film on delinquency."[22]

Aesthetic considerations also were key to the high-art/low-art dichotomy. Displaying an awareness of the emerging neorealist approach, the *Theatre Arts* reviewer instructed cultured filmgoers to learn to appreciate films that featured character actors over movie stars. Bogart, specifically, was castigated for capitalizing on his star power in *Knock on Any Door* to distort "the story to make Bogart's part the important one"; newcomer Paul Douglas, meanwhile, a character actor from the New York stage featured in *A Letter to Three Wives*, was praised for lending dignity and integrity to the Mankiewicz film.[23] Such overstated sensitivity to neorealist principles did not carry over into a preference for European art cinema, however. To the contrary, the xenophobic tendencies discussed earlier are in full evidence in the *Theatre Arts* review, which went so far as to scold the U.S. government for allowing so many foreign films to enter the country in the first place:

> What goes on behind the scenes in international trade and film quotas is far beyond the mental scope of a film reviewer. But something unusual must be happening in these shadowed fields, for more new foreign films than ever before seem to be appearing on the scene—so many, indeed, that we can give space only to two.[24]

The two films singled out for the reviewer's abuse were two French art films, *The Chips Are Down* (*Les jeux sont faits,* Jean Delannoy, 1947), an adaptation of Jean-Paul Sartre's treatise on existentialism, and *Devil in the Flesh* (*Le diable au corps,* Claude Autant-Lara, 1946), a sexually provocative melodrama. Since one could hardly slight the first film's literary credentials, the reviewer instead criticized *The Chips Are Down* for, on top of its deadening two hours of philosophical dialogue, failing to provide "one sentence at the end [that] might bring it all together." Maintaining his antigovernment line but also showing that he was no prude, the reviewer capped his pan of *Devil in the Flesh* by mocking the U.S. Customs' office for holding up the film's release because of its risqué title.[25]

The *Theatre Arts* reviewer's solution to the foreign competition points to that expressed by Harold Hecht a few years later: namely, that American art cinema should follow Mankiewicz's lead by combining the sophisticated aesthetic of the European art cinema with the entertainment attributes of the Hollywood A film. This hybrid approach is implicit in the reviewer's expressed preference for *A Letter to Three Wives* over *The Chips Are Down* because the U.S. film understood how to provide a more satisfying ending (even if Mankiewicz admitted later that his ending was unintentionally ambiguous).[26] Taken together, the views of the *Theatre Arts'* reviewer (which predate *Cahiers du cinéma's la politique des auteurs* by a few years and Sarris's auteur theory by over a decade) are indicative of early attempts by American intellectuals to theorize an American auteurist cinema. The crucial difference, for better or worse, is that such a cinema was predicated precisely on those high-art principles—the "well-made film," the "tradition of quality"—that Bazin, Truffaut, Godard, and company would reject in favor of the lowbrow crudeness but also greater freedom and boldness of the so-called exploitative noir thriller, rebel youth film, and other largely B genres.

During the first half of the 1950s, the *Hollywood Reporter's* Wilkerson attempted to further articulate the parameters of the emergent American art cinema. While he initially voiced dissatisfaction with the proliferating talent deals forcing studios to share gross profits and pay out huge salaries, as the decade progressed, as he had in relation to television, Wilkerson adjusted his views. By 1954 he was arguing that the added talent costs were well worth it because "the studio is presented with an opportunity of getting creators of importance in something they believe in and want to do." He chided major studios further for still perceiving themselves as factories: "Any studio that turns its back on [talent] is a plant not reaching for the progress these deals create."[27] Finally, Wilkerson lauded independent companies, at the expense of the studios, for their risk-taking and production of "quality" films:

> Which of the majors, for example, would have gone for "African Queen" [1951; John Huston directed; Sam Spiegel produced]? . . . Who of our major outfits would have bucked labor relations with Budd Schulberg's "On the Waterfront"? . . . And who . . . would have gone for "The Moon Is

Blue" [1953] other than an independent?... And how far would you think
the idea of doing a picture with a 100 percent Negro cast would have gotten in a major plant [referring to Otto Preminger's *Carmen Jones*, made in
1954]?[28]

As the decade progressed, the film critical and trade discourse on behalf
of an emerging U.S. art cinema was joined by artistically inclined filmmakers themselves, some of whom were responding both to the art-house
movement and to the high-theoretical observations of the Frankfurt School
(in its American-émigré incarnation), the latter of which argued for a modernist alternative to the cultural degradation and political subjugation puta-
tively purveyed by most mass media. This convergence of low and high
theory is evident in the discussions among figures like Mankiewicz, Kazan,
Arthur Miller, Bertolt Brecht, Harold Clurman, Odets, and others, most
of whom came from the New York theater, who saw an analogy between
the commercial Hollywood/art film dichotomy and that between Broadway and the smaller, politically engaged theaters like the Group Theater.[29]
The contradictions of this convergence are evident in the industrial conditions under which these filmmakers were forced to or chose to operate,
and the films they made. Self-consciously borrowing conceits from the foreign art cinema (notably, neorealist themes and style), yet leavening them
with classical Hollywood elements (notably, stars and high melodrama),
the American A art cinema would go through significant permutations.
From studio-based high-art films such as *A Letter to Three Wives* and the
early work of Kazan and others, the "well-made" U.S. art film would undergo
a shift in the mid-1950s to an independently produced variant that was
able to approach, less compromisingly, the foreign art film and which,
together with the increasing legitimation of the B art film, would lay the
groundwork for the Hollywood Renaissance to come.

Joseph Mankiewicz and the Rise of the Studio-Based Auteur

Throughout its history and in its various incarnations, the Hollywood studio system has exhibited considerable pliability in financing and distributing
films that incorporate oppositional content and/or anomalous aesthetics—
provided, of course, that the films in question have commercial potential.
Given the structural and financial turmoil the studios were experiencing
in the post–World War II period, the studios found themselves more
prone than usual to push the thematic and stylistic envelope, even in the
face of heightened political pressures in the early Cold War era to toe the

conventional line.[30] The liberties Fox chief Darryl Zanuck granted Joseph Mankiewicz on *A Letter to Three Wives* to explore issues of class and gender in an unconventional three-part, multiple-flashback narrative form is symptomatic of this more tolerant cinematic climate.[31] As the Zanuck-Mankiewicz exchange also highlights, the climate of tolerance would eventually sour as the studios, Fox in particular, began shifting its emphasis toward the blockbuster at the expense of the A art film. As a result, Mankiewicz, like other independently minded filmmakers such as Kazan, Wilder, and Huston would opt for less security but greater creative freedom by severing ties with the studio.

Because the politically liberal Mankiewicz was a studio insider whose tenure in Hollywood dated from the late 1920s, and because he had avoided membership in radical political organizations in the 1930s and 1940s, his career was not disrupted by HUAC or the blacklist as were those who lacked squeaky-clean credentials.[32] This is not to say that Mankiewicz was unaffected by the reactionary climate that prevailed in postwar Hollywood; rather, like several liberal filmmakers from this decade, he had learned to navigate the New Hollywood shoals by engaging in an oblique critique of the status quo and sophisticated deviation from, but not outright abrogation of, classical aesthetic norms.

Joseph Mankiewicz had followed his older brother Herman Mankiewicz (best known for cowriting *Citizen Kane*) to Hollywood in the 1920s, starting his screenwriting career in 1929 by contributing dialogue to a number of early Paramount anarchistic comedies (*Million Dollar Legs, If I Had a Million* [1932], *Diplomaniacs* [1933]).[33] He became a Paramount-based producer in 1936, moving in the same year to Fox, but it would be ten years before Zanuck gave him a chance to direct *Dragonwyck*, and this only after the film's initial director, Ernst Lubitsch, took ill. After several less than satisfactory assignments directing others' screenplays, Mankiewicz took advantage of the shifting New Hollywood terrain and the rise of the writer-director (Preston Sturges, Wilder, Welles, and Huston had prominently preceded him) and requested, and was granted, writing and directing privileges on his next three films. Mankiewicz didn't disappoint, winning Oscars on two of his first three films: for writing and directing on the first, *A Letter to Three Wives* (1949), and for writing, directing, and best picture (the last award going to producer Zanuck) on the third, *All About Eve* (1950). The spectacular success emboldened Mankiewicz to indulge in a more overtly political, thinly disguised parable about HUAC on his fourth Fox film, *People Will Talk* (1951).

Despite the inevitable studio intervention in the production process (greater than most with the hands-on Zanuck), Mankiewicz was given remarkably free rein. For instance, on both *A Letter to Three Wives* and his second film, *House of Strangers* (also 1949), according to Mankiewicz biographer Kenneth Geist: "Zanuck had permitted Mankiewicz to go to New York to shoot his exterior locations, a rare privilege in an era of movie making when the economic practice was to use either stock footage or a small second unit crew for establishing shots of authentic backgrounds."[34] Whereas the studio producer on the film, Sol Siegel, remained unperturbed by the extravagance, and the film actually came in well within its $1.6-million budget, Zanuck became increasingly frustrated over the amount of creative control he had ceded to Mankiewicz.[35] The studio head voiced his pique in several memos, one of which reminded Mankiewicz that the functions the writer-director had absorbed on *A Letter to Three Wives* and *All About Eve* used to belong to Zanuck as the primary producer, and added that, on principle, he would therefore not take his normal screen credit on the third Mankiewicz film he had produced, *People Will Talk*. (In fact, Zanuck did take credit in the end.)[36]

Mankiewicz's mounting frustration with Zanuck, meanwhile, and with Hollywood studio filmmaking in general, are on ample display in *All About Eve*. Indeed, in a *Life* magazine interview in 1951, Mankiewicz was asked to explain the vast number of insider jokes in *All About Eve* that conveyed an elitist bias for the theater over the film—and television—industries.[37] Mankiewicz tried to defend himself by referring to the scene in the film in which the Broadway director Bill Sampson (Gary Merrill) is about to leave New York to direct a film in Hollywood for Darryl Zanuck (a clear allusion to Elia Kazan, who had left the New York stage to work with Zanuck in 1944).[38] The Broadway star Margo Channing (Bette Davis) asks Sampson disdainfully why he would even consider wasting his talent in this way. Samson's even-handed response is meant to puncture her elitism, Mankiewicz claimed in the interview, but as is clear to any even-handed viewer, this single instance hardly serves to counterbalance the film's overall pro-theater, anti-movie/TV thrust.[39]

As the *Life* magazine interview indicates, Mankiewicz, like other creatively minded filmmakers in the New Hollywood, was struggling to negotiate the motion picture's emerging high-art status vis-à-vis the more established arts and the new low-art foundling, television, while still chomping at the bit of residual studio control and commercial constraints. Mankiewicz's frequent allusions to theater, literature, and classical music via his more snobbish characters thus can be seen as a form of self-criticism, given the unsympathetic treatment of these characters, who are ultimately trapped by their own pretensions. At the same time, like so many of the self-referential filmmakers charted so far, one could argue that Mankiewicz was also employing a strategy of self-referentiality "to undermine the American myths of class consensus and consumer democracy."[40] By revealing the economic engine driving not just the film and television industries, but the institutions of family, marriage, and the romantic couple—all hallmarks of classical Hollywood melodrama—Mankiewicz was foregrounding the popular anti–mass media discourse as a means of exposing a more fundamental critique of postwar capitalist society; or as a *Variety* reviewer succinctly remarks: "He aims barbed darts at the country's favorite institutions."[41]

Crafting an Art Film Out of a Commercial Melodrama: *A Letter to Three Wives*

A Letter to Three Wives was based on a novel by John Klempner that follows three women friends (five in the novel) on a day trip together.[42] Each of the three wives receives a letter from the town flirt, who claims to have run off with one of their husbands. Each wife spends the day recalling the events leading up to this threatening moment and questions any behavior that might have caused her husband to leave her. One of the wives, Rita Phipps (Ann Sothern), is a radio soap-opera writer and the primary breadwinner in her marriage to her classics-teaching husband, George Phipps (Kirk Douglas). Deborah Bishop (Jeanne Crain) the second wife, is a newly married ex-soldier who married her husband while both were in the army and who has trouble adapting to her new suburban, middle-class lifestyle. The third wife, Lora Mae (Linda Darnell), is a poor, working-class secretary determined to marry her rich boss, Porter Hollingsway (Paul Douglas).

George's scathing, antiradio speech to his wife's radio-station bosses, who have been invited to dinner, invokes the typical condescension of the 1950s' mass culture discourse as well as indicating George's resentment toward his wife for her suggestion that he should consider working for the same station:

> The purpose of radio writing, as far as I can see, is to prove to the masses that a deodorant can bring happiness, a mouthwash guarantee success, and a laxative attracts romance. . . . Don't think, says the radio, and we'll pay you for it! Can't spell cat? Too bad—buy a yacht and a million dollars to the gentleman for being in our audience tonight! Worry, says the radio!

Will your friends not tell you? Will you lose your teeth? Will your body function after you're thirty-five? Use our product or you'll lose your husband, your job, and die! Use our product and we'll make you rich, we'll make you famous!

On the one hand, George appears to serve as a mouthpiece for Mankiewicz when he repeats the popular anti–mass culture stance, with its Frankfurt School underpinning given his character's contrasting celebration of classical music, Shakespeare, and the other "high arts." George's biting attack on advertising goes beyond elitist snobbery, however, given its relation to the film's larger critique of gender relations in consumer capitalism through its exposure of the collusion of sexual politics and big business. This critique is translated characterologically in George and Rita's "contractual" relationship: Rita sees her radio job as an opportunity for her husband to take over the role as primary breadwinner for the home; he sees it as a betrayal of his morally and culturally superior job as a school teacher.

George maintains that he has preserved his authenticity and taken the high moral ground by becoming a poorly paid schoolteacher who introduces his teenage students to the merits of great literature. He also perceives his wife as having sold out by becoming a writer for radio soap operas. But the film discloses the hypocrisy of George's high-minded stance by revealing that he is only able to enjoy his love of "the finer things in life" (his tuxedo, for instance) thanks to his wife's bigger paycheck (earned in the broadcasting industry). More crucially, George expects his wife to hide her ambitions, and the moral compromises she has had to make to achieve her economic goals, in order to protect his traditional sense of masculinity as the family's main financial provider. The film's happy ending in which the couple is reunited (with wife Rita seated at George's feet in a position of subservience) is therefore undermined by the degree to which her ambitions have been circumscribed by the social pressure to conform to the homemaker ideal. This ambiguous ending (a rarity by classical Hollywood standards) suggests that his wife can only preserve her marriage (and presumably be allowed to continue working for the ad agency) if she maintains the pretense that her husband is the ultimate authority figure in the household. In other words, the film's reflexive critique of the state of the postwar culture industry is inextricably interwoven with a critique of rigid gender roles that confine women to the home and limit their role to that of primary consumer (rather than wage earner).

Similarly, in a sequence involving Lora Mae and Porter, the film inter-rogates the unspoken class pressures in the early postwar United States to uphold the institution of marriage as a prop for American capitalism. Lora Mae is a secretary without economic means who uses her beauty to trap her boss, a rich and powerful businessman, into marriage. The film spends considerable narrative time portraying her calculating behavior leading to the marriage "deal." Once they marry, both husband and wife must contend with their discomfiture over having committed a social taboo by having brazenly based their marriage on the exchange of sex for money. A crisis in the marriage (the fear of infidelity) prompts each to convey his/her true feelings of love to the other; however, this obligatory if facile resolution does not come until the final moments of the film and fails to erase the memory of the unseemly terms of their marriage contract.

The problematic nature of their romantic relationship is disclosed in the earliest stages of the courtship ritual. After her first quasi-dinner date with Porter (purportedly, they meet to discuss her job), Lora Mae is dis-appointed when he shows no further interest in her as he pulls up to her home. She takes immediate action, using the only weapon at her disposal: her sexual charms. By tearing a hole in her stocking, she seduces Porter (and the audience) by forcing him (and us) to gaze at her suggestively exposed leg, beautifully lit in an artfully framed deep-focus shot as she adjusts her shimmering stocking. Notably, Mankiewicz has revised the convention of the shot-reverse-shot—which, film theorist Laura Mulvey famously argues, tends to empower the male perspective by objectifying the woman—to serve his more subversive political agenda.[43] By substituting a deep-focus shot for the editing convention, the woman's carefully staged sexual trap, and with it her assertion of power over this potent businessman, are liter-ally highlighted.

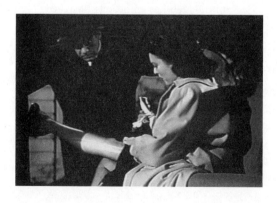

Porter Hollingsway
(Paul Douglas) observes
Lora Mae (Linda Darnell) in
A Letter to Three Wives (1949).

Mankiewicz repeats the sequence a second time to underscore the degree of calculation involved in Lora Mae's seduction of Porter. At the end of their second date, Porter chooses not to get out of the car or even to look at Lora Mae. Concerned that she has lost her sexual hold over him, Lora Mae calls out to Porter so that she can stage yet another seductive "moment of looking." He abruptly stops his car and waits for her to catch up to him. The sound effects of his car screeching to a stop intensify the profound nature of her sexual manipulation of this powerful executive who is now at her beck and call. This time she re-enters the car under the pretense of having left her stockings (the ones he bought her to replace the torn ones) in the back seat. She leans over the front seat, positioning herself so that he can barely (and the audience absolutely cannot) resist ogling her backside. To reinforce her sexual dominance, she follows up with the kiss she has been withholding up till now. By undermining the romantic ideology typically associated with classical Hollywood's conventional representations of men and women, Mankiewicz effectively exposes the class dimensions of the scene and the economic dynamics binding the romantic couple.

Throughout, the film emphasizes Porter as the cold, Machiavellian businessman; however, once again, the film's antibusiness agenda is linked to a critique of postwar gender roles. Unlike most of the other antibusiness films profiled in previous chapters, we never see Porter at work; rather, we see how he has brought his coldly pragmatic, abrasive manner into his home life. When Lora Mae finally extracts a marriage proposal, the scene undermines the conventions associated with marriage in the classical Hollywood text and is therefore disconcerting. Whereas in *The Hucksters*, for example, the social tensions exposed in the film's critique of big business are neatly resolved by shifting focus to the resolution of the couple, in *A Letter to Three Wives*, the marriage proposal marks the beginning of the couple's problems given the blatant economic underpinnings of their relationship. The proposal culminates when they fervently embrace after each has spent New Year's Eve alone and miserable. However, it is a muted victory for Lora Mae, because instead of expressing his love for her, Porter tells her she has "made a good deal" for herself. By using the parlance of the commercial world of business to define the marriage, the film exposes what most Hollywood texts suppress: the oppressive sexual economy of normative romance.

A comparison of *A Letter to Three Wives* to other "gold-digging" films of the period, especially the Fox/Zanuck produced "blockbusters" *How to Marry a Millionaire* (1953) and *Gentlemen Prefer Blondes* (1953), is instructive. While film scholar Maureen Turim argues in "Gentlemen Consume

Blondes" that the characters played by Jane Russell and Marilyn Monroe in these films convey critical self-awareness of their sexual display while on stage, challenging Mulvey's assertion of the objectifying male gaze in classical Hollywood texts, the tone and formal reflexivity inherent in these broad musical comedies tend to evacuate social critique through romantic resolution.[44] For instance, *Gentlemen Prefer Blondes* contrasts Monroe's calculating opportunist methodically pursuing a man for his money with Russell's character who is looking for true love. In *How to Marry a Millionaire*, three women pool their resources to rent a penthouse apartment to trap rich husbands. When they run out of money halfway through the film and must sell the elegant furniture (which belongs to the apartment's owner), in typical Hollywood fashion the real consequences of their poverty are glossed over. In contrast, in *A Letter to Three Wives*, Lora Mae's economic hardship is portrayed graphically. She and her mother live in a ramshackle house so close to the railroad tracks that they must stop whatever they are doing every few minutes while the train passes, shaking the house to its foundation. The film protracts this harsh reality by returning to the scene several times, each time holding on it for an extended period of time, undermining the temporal economy of the conventional Hollywood narrative in which screen time is apportioned according to causality and the imperatives of desire rather than for subtextual resonance. Bill Nichols makes an important distinction in his introduction to Thomas Elsaesser's well-known article on the melodrama genre, "Tales of Sound and Fury: Observations on the Family Melodrama"; whereas the melodramas of Sirk invoke ideological resonance through the constricted focus on the individual and domestic space such that small actions and events accrue meaning, Nichols reminds us that: "This contrasts with metteurs-en-scène, such as Curtiz, Lumet, or Mankiewicz, who aspire to present ideas and value conflicts more directly, as European films do."[45]

Rather than resorting to the commercially "safer" conventions of the musical or anarchistic comedy to explore its core issues of money, marriage, and infidelity, *A Letter to Three Wives* takes them head-on. A variety of postwar themes—the hardworking breadwinner husband, the stay-at-home wife, the benefits and threats posed by new media—are dissected through a mix of social satire and gritty, social realist drama. In addition, the film probes the conventions of romantic melodrama, or "woman's picture," with its suffering female leads, its emphasis on romantic conflict, and its intense emotion, here further complicating these elements by incorporating them into a multiprotagonist, multistrand narrative with extended flashbacks. Despite (or partly because of) its stylistic ingenuity, critics found the film to be "strangely satisfying," and it was "greeted by unusually rapturous reviews."[46] One review acknowledged, and applauded, the film's progressive themes: "Linda Darnell and Paul Douglas . . . fight their way into the golden suburbs—he by building a chain of house ware stores, she by making a marriage license part of her price. Their relationship (pre- and post-marital) is social satire, a form of comment Hollywood seemed to have abandoned entirely."[47]

Not surprisingly, the PCA objected to precisely those aspects most reviewers, the general public, and ultimately the Motion Picture Academy found most welcome: the satirical portrait of the modern American institution of marriage. Memos from the PCA's Stephen S. Jackson to Fox complained about the film's dialogue that overtly exposed the underlying economic basis of the marriage contract:

- The important unacceptable element of this story is the courtship between Porter and Lora Mae. As presently written, the relationship between the two people is completely unacceptable. Porter very bluntly is attempting to seduce Lora Mae; she is toying with him, teasing him, leading him on and dangling her physical attractiveness in front of his eyes, but refusing to submit to him. There are numerous unacceptably blunt references to the fact that Porter desires her sexually, she knows it and she teases him, hoping that he will marry her.

- The motivation and much of the dialogue and accompanying action will have to be carefully rewritten to eliminate the unacceptable flavor if we are to approve the finished picture:

- Please eliminate Lora Mae's line, "Funny you should mention my heart, it's the one part of my body you never showed any interest in."

- Please eliminate Lora Mae's line, "If you'd only made me feel like a woman that a man wanted, instead of a piece of merchandise!" and Porter's reply, "Did you give me a chance to? . . . All you ever showed me was your price tag."[48]

The fact that the film was made with very few concessions to the PCA indicates that the industry's self-censorship bureau was losing its hold on a New Hollywood facing unprecedented financial challenges.[49] Similarly, Fox's willingness to bankroll Mankiewicz's subversive portrait of postwar American life speaks less to the politics or courage of the executives in charge than to the studio's dependence on talented and independent-minded filmmakers for their economic survival at a time of plummeting box-office returns.

Yet even someone like Mankiewicz, by the early 1950s one of Hollywood's most celebrated writer-directors, wasn't immune from the oppressive politics—nationally and in Hollywood—that prevailed during the early postwar period. Shortly after his success with *A Letter to Three Wives* (1949) and an even greater one with *All About Eve* (1950), Mankiewicz became embroiled in the early stages of the Hollywood blacklist when he was elected president of the Screen Directors Guild (SDG) in 1950. While it was mandatory for guild officers to sign a loyalty oath, members were not required to do so. By the late 1940s Cecil B. DeMille, a founding member of SDG, was actively supporting HUAC's anti-Communist vendetta. McCarthy-era scholar Victor Navasky states that Mankiewicz was elected SDG president in part because he was against the mandatory oath.[50] However, DeMille had nominated Mankiewicz precisely because he thought he would be able to influence the younger, newly successful (therefore less secure) director to support the oath. When Mankiewicz refused, DeMille took advantage of Mankiewicz's absence during a critical meeting to force members to publicly vote for the oath. Given the virulent anti-Communist climate in 1950, three years after the first HUAC trial and one year before the second, there was great pressure among SDG members to sign. When Mankiewicz tried to overturn the vote, DeMille initiated a campaign to tarnish Mankiewicz's reputation by hinting to the press that he was a Communist sympathizer. Shortly after the initial vote, Mankiewicz was able to oust DeMille and his supporters from the guild. However, four days later, Mankiewicz capitulated to outside pressure and encouraged members to sign the oath. As the first oath signed by any of the guilds, the SDG action provided significant reinforcement for the blacklist.[51]

Mankiewicz directed one more film under his contract with Fox, *Five Fingers* (1952), an adaptation of a World War II spy melodrama. However, his differences with Zanuck on this and especially on his previous film, the antiracist social-problem film *No Way Out* (1950)—with which Mankiewicz intended to trump Kazan's antibigotry films for Fox, *Gentleman's Agreement* (1947) and *Pinky* (1949)—finally led to their parting of the ways. On his own Mankiewicz made *The Barefoot Contessa* (1954) and *The Quiet American* (1958), distributing through UA; he also took on jobs directing *Julius Caesar* (1953) for Samuel Goldwyn, *Guys and Dolls* (1955) for MGM, and *Suddenly Last Summer* (1959) for Sol Spiegel's Horizon Pictures. Unlike Kazan, however, whose most stylistically and thematically challenging films *(On the Waterfront, Baby Doll, A Face in the Crowd)* were made after he went independent in 1954, Mankiewicz's most creative, and politically provocative work, ironically, was made under the constraints of the studio system. His deterioration during his independent stint, in the ideological realm especially, is nowhere more painfully apparent than in *The Quiet American,* an adaptation of the Graham Greene political thriller set in Saigon, which the allegedly liberal Mankiewicz managed to turn from an anti-American statement into an anti-Communist one. The low point in both Mankiewicz's and Zanuck's careers came, fittingly, when the two rejoined forces on the legendarily ill-fated *Cleopatra* (1963), starring Elizabeth Taylor and Richard Burton, the most disastrous box-office flop in Hollywood history to that time.

Crafting a Blockbuster out of an Art Film: *Woman's World*

Although Mankiewicz was no longer working at Fox at the time, his influence would continue to be felt at the studio. In the making of *Woman's World* (1954), specifically, Zanuck consciously sought to replicate Mankiewicz's critical and financial success on *A Letter to Three Wives* but without having to endure the friction and frustration of working with a gifted but difficult-to-control writer-director. On this project he thus hired five lesser-known writers (Claude Binyon, Mary Loos, Richard Sale, Russel Crouse, and Howard Lindsay) and a director, Jean Negulesco, best known at the time for making, according to Zanuck's specifications, two lavish CinemaScope spectaculars, *How to Marry a Millionaire* (1953) and *Three Coins in the Fountain* (1954).[52] A more devastating change Zanuck made between the two films, at least from an artistic and ideological standpoint, was to alter the original film's gender-role-challenging orientation. Although he initially proposed to retain the focus on the three wives' stories rather than on that of the businessmen, in the end Zanuck reverted to precisely those patriarchal conventions that Mankiewicz's film had sought to undermine. In this and other ways, the Fox chief's efforts epitomize the constantly shifting (if not downright contradictory) response of many studios, indeed the industry as a whole, toward independent-minded talent in the postwar era.

Zanuck had been trumpeted in a 1950 *Time* magazine cover story as "the preeminent Hollywood executive of his generation." Since the war, claimed *Time,* "Zanuck's 20th Century-Fox has consistently led the field in the quality of its films."[53] Much of the praise heaped on Zanuck at this time resulted from the award-winning art films of Mankiewicz and those of Kazan (*A Tree Grows in Brooklyn* [1945], *Gentleman's Agreement,* and *Pinky*). In 1953 Zanuck would once again be celebrated in the press, but this time in the industry trades and not for his creative but rather for his financial achievement. Zanuck, it was now claimed, had helped turn the industry around after making the musical comedy "blockbusters" *Gentlemen Prefer Blondes* and *How to Marry a Millionaire*. The *Hollywood Reporter*'s Wilkerson, wearing his pro-blockbuster hat, applauded Zanuck's return to this type of large-scale, broadly entertaining film as a means of revitalizing a studio system in decline: "Here is a picture *[Gentlemen Prefer Blondes]* that refutes all the arguments that television, and other non-industry factors, are insurmountable obstacles to motion pictures prosperity. . . . The picture makes no effort to deliver a message or oppress the minds and hearts of a trouble-burdened world. It offers just the one basic thing—entertainment."[54] Rather than sticking with the "sheer entertainment" formula, however, Zanuck tried to merge the social-issue characteristics that had earned him his earlier *Time* encomiums with the more blatantly commercial elements that Wilkerson applauded. The result was two big-budget social-problem films, *Woman's World* and *The Man in the Gray Flannel Suit*, which, like the overblown musicals, were lavish, star-studded, CinemaScope releases identified by the trade press as "Zanuck productions." Both films benefited, financially, from the lessons Zanuck had learned on the musicals. As Wilkerson stated about *Gentlemen Prefer Blondes* but which also applies, *mutatis mutandis*, to *Woman's World*: the film's success could be directly attributed to Zanuck's "showmanship," not only in terms of the film's production values and its two big stars, Russell and Monroe, "together in a tuneful carnival of feminine allure that sparkles with fun and bright decoration," but also in terms of the studio's "terrific publicity and advertising aimed at the public, which left no avenue of exploitation unexplored."[55]

As for the artistic side, Zanuck himself admitted that *Woman's World*'s screenplay was poorly conceived and written, certainly no match for *A Letter to Three Wives* on either score. Its indebtedness to the Mankiewicz film lay in its designation for a female audience and it featured three female stars; there the similarities end. *A Letter to Three Wives* features gritty scenes in black and white, contrasts the lives of the working-class poor with those of the professional middle classes, and exposes complex social relationships via suggestively composed deep-focus shots. In contrast, *Woman's World* alternates between close-up glamour shots of its three leading ladies and master shots that emphasize the elegant décor in well-appointed rooms and exotic locales (e.g., a cruise ship, New York landmarks), shopping trips, sightseeing, and many fashion opportunities, all in glorious CinemaScope. Whereas *A Letter to Three Wives* challenges prescribed gender roles, *Woman's World* repeats the type of patronizing list of "do's and don'ts" for married women that prevailed in most women's magazines.[56]

Woman's World's plot centers on three junior executives who are up for a single promotion in a management position at the same firm. Since the employees are all of equal stature in the eyes of their corporate boss, the boss has decided to cast the determining vote after meeting each of the candidates' wives. The wives are forced to compete in scenes that reveal their relative strengths and weaknesses as supportive wives. Katie Baxter (June Allyson) is guilty only of caring too much for her husband, Bill Baxter (Cornel Wilde), so much so that she prefers he take a lesser job so he can spend more time with her and the children. Elizabeth Burns (Lauren Bacall) is determined to temper Sid Burns's (Fred MacMurray) unbridled ambition for the sake of his health. Carol Talbot (Arlene Dahl) portrays the overtly "bad" wife who is so ambitious and money-hungry that she is willing to have sex with the boss in exchange for a promotion for her husband, Jerry Talbot (Van Heflin). A simplistic, morality-tale conclusion resolves the complex social issues by having the boss reward Jerry Talbot with the promotion, contingent upon his divorcing his wife.

In a 1953 memo to Fox executive Ray Klune before the film's release, Zanuck compared *Woman's World* to *A Letter to Three Wives* and *All About Eve* and found the non-Mankiewicz film lacking. As a level-headed studio boss and businessman, Zanuck understandably wanted to repeat the box-office success and critical acclaim of Mankiewicz's two films. He thus forecast that *Woman's World* wouldn't do as well as these films unless it could approach their high level of writing and star power: "Unless this is made with an important box-office cast and unless it is written with the type of writing we had in *A Letter to Three Wives* or *All About Eve*," Zanuck concluded, "it will be absolutely nothing."[57] Zanuck's solution to the writing problem, however, defied his earlier stated conviction that called for an emphasis on the wives' part of the story. His main concern now was that the script placed too much emphasis on the wives. He objected to the story's implication that the women could have a real impact on the men's business lives, specifically that they had too much influence over the boss's decision-making, which he found to be unrealistic.

Zanuck originally had set out to make *Woman's World* because he wanted to avoid yet another story about men seeking success in the corporate world, and presumably also because he wanted to repeat Mankiewicz's success with a film seen from a woman's perspective. And yet, his various memos demonstrate his lack of understanding of what made Mankiewicz's bristling satires on postwar America effective. In one memo dated January 26, 1954, Zanuck tells the executives in the Fox story department to avoid a satire or farce.[58]

With this dictum, he almost guaranteed the resulting comedy would lack the incisive edge of Mankiewicz's films.

Zanuck failed to realize, or chose to dismiss the fact, that much of *A Letter to Three Wives'* success with critics and a segment of the adult audience was a function of its social critique and the film's willingness to subvert classical narrative conventions. Instead of seeking to emulate the earlier film's more incisive look at women's social roles in postwar America, Zanuck resorted to the tired Old Hollywood generic clichés. Zanuck's vacillating between art and commerce tilted squarely, in the end, toward the latter. His choice of writers, director, and cast tipped the studio chief's hand: director Negulesco, at least one of the stars (Lauren Bacall), and four of the six writers had all worked on several of Fox's big-budget, broad-appeal films from 1953 to 1955: *How To Marry a Millionaire* (1953), *Gentlemen Prefer Blondes* (1953), and *Gentlemen Marry Brunettes* (1955).

The creative and political compromises on *Woman's World*'s, as on the subsequent self-referential film *The Man in the Gray Flannel Suit*, were not anomalous; rather, they were symptomatic of the blockbuster strategy that would be pursued with ever-greater diligence at Fox, and other studios, despite recurrent debacles such as *Cleopatra* (a film that brought writer-director Mankiewicz under Zanuck's stewardship one last time), through the mid- to late-1960s.[59] This tilt toward less challenging, more standardized fare was predicated largely, of course, on economics; that is, the search for a cure to Hollywood's stubbornly persistent box-office misery. Significant corollary factors, in the 1950s, included the reactionary political climate, the industry-insider discourse of columnists like Wilkerson, and the pressure applied by high-profile industry leaders like Johnston who questioned whether filmmakers and studio heads had "forgotten that the movie theater is supposed to be a place of entertainment."[60] Despite the forces arrayed against them, however, not all of the artistically minded New Hollywood independents were ready to fold in their tents, as subsequent chapters will reveal.

6.
Elia Kazan:
Caught between HUAC and the "New Hollywood"

Who or what was now safer because this man in his human weakness
had been forced to humiliate himself?

—ARTHUR MILLER, on Elia Kazan's decision to "name names"

Previous chapters described the postwar shift from the Old Hollywood
contract-player system to one in which, because of the lag in production,
the studios were forced to make more single-picture deals with independent producers. Yet the benefits of independence, as we saw with Mankiewicz, were not absolute. Some actually thrived under the greater discipline
still operating within the New Hollywood studio system than under more
full-fledged independence. In addition, although financing was more readily
available to New Hollywood independents than had previously been the
case, given the persistent postwar domestic box-office downturn and the
anti-Hollywood protectionism of many countries abroad, such financing was
never easy to come by and certainly was not a given. Hence, turning a profit
remained a strong motivating factor for the new breed of independent producer, artistic or not. Political deterrents compounded the economic ones,
especially for politically minded independents, who found that the combined impact of HUAC and "falling box-office returns after 1947 discour-
aged innovation."[1] These were the complex and contradictory conditions
under which Elia Kazan found himself working when he came to Hollywood in the mid-1940s from the radical New York–based Group Theater.

Kazan himself is a complex, contradictory, and still controversial figure
in the history of leftist American filmmakers. Although his directing career
began in the late 1930s with the Group Theater and the Communist-
supported Workers Laboratory Theater, his radical credentials, though
significantly not his Hollywood career, were severely tarnished by his cooperative testimony before HUAC in the 1950s and a subsequent open
letter to the *New York Times* defending his actions and urging others to do

the same.[2] Many leftist artists had named names, generally under social or career-threatening pressure, but very few had named names willingly. Several others, including playwright/screenwriters Clifford Odets, Arthur Miller, and John Howard Lawson, directors Nicholas Ray and Martin Ritt, and actor John Garfield, had either refused to testify or suffered pangs of guilt if they did (Garfield actually suffered a heart attack the day before he was to appear before the Committee).[3]

Odets and Miller, in particular, defiantly perpetuated their critique of class relations in capitalist society during their forays in Hollywood. Odets, whose agitprop dramas brought him acclaim as the playwright of the Left in the thirties and forties, allowed several of his plays to be transposed to Hollywood screens, including *Golden Boy* (1939), *Clash by Night* (1952), *Country Girl* (1954), and *The Big Knife* (1955). Although Odets also worked on more mainstream films from 1946 to 1961 *(Deadline at Dawn, Humoresque, Wild in the Country)* and later on mundane television shows like *The Richard Boone Show* (1963–64), he was quite apologetic about having "sold out" to make money.[4] Notably, two of the films Odets wrote are self-referential business films that are also vicious attacks on both the Hollywood film and television industries: *The Big Knife* and *Sweet Smell of Success* (1957). Miller's more circumscribed activities in Hollywood consisted mostly of having his plays adapted to film, including *All My Sons* (1948), *The Crucible* (1956), and *A View from the Bridge* (1962). His only two original screenplays were for *The Misfits* (1961), featuring his then-wife, Marilyn Monroe, and one he had written thirty years before the film was made, *Everybody Wins* (1990). The film version of *The Crucible* was remade in 1996.

In contrast to his Group Theater peers who reluctantly participated in Hollywood filmmaking, when Kazan was first given the opportunity to direct commercial films, he eagerly took whatever assignments he was given by studio heads Jack Warner at Warner Bros. and Darryl Zanuck at Twentieth Century–Fox. He ultimately signed a five-year, five-film contract with Fox in 1944, choosing Fox over Warners because Zanuck, based on Kazan's successful tenure as a theater director, allowed him to start directing prestigious, star-driven, big budget A pictures. At first glance, Zanuck seemed ideally suited to guide Kazan's career, given the studio boss's preference, at the time, for topical stories and films that dealt with socially relevant themes and expressed a "social consciousness"—epitomized by Fox's adaptation of John Steinbeck's progressive-populist Depression-era saga *The Grapes of Wrath* (1940).

Despite Kazan's having been a willing participant of various political and artistic movements or "schools," his theater and film work never remained attached to any one in particular, be it the polemicism of the Group Theater and social realism, the formal excesses of German expressionism, or the "invisibility" of the classical Hollywood style.[5] Kazan's aesthetic fluctuation, as well as his uncertainty about the creative benefits of independent film-making versus the commercial advantages of working within the studio system, epitomizes the quandary faced by many politically liberal, artistically minded filmmakers in the New Hollywood era.

Kazan's early experience at Fox provided him a supportive if still restrictive environment in which he was nonetheless able to adapt his skills as a stage director to filmmaking. He achieved remarkable early success with social-problem films like *A Gentleman's Agreement* (1947), an Oscar winner for Best Picture and the first Hollywood film to openly and extensively confront American anti-Semitism, and *Pinky* (1949), an early and rare examination of southern racism. With Zanuck's help, Kazan managed to turn the social-problem film into a commercially viable mainstream genre film in the postwar era. Starting in 1950, however, Kazan began seeking greater creative autonomy and moved away from the commercially liberal social-problem genre in films like *Panic in the Streets* and *A Streetcar Named Desire*. In this phase, according to Brian Neve, the director began "to combine independent, New York-based filmmaking with the backing of the old Hollywood studio."[6] In this trajectory, Kazan's career ran counter to those of other left-wing filmmakers like Abraham Polonsky and Robert Rossen, whose persistence in making politically charged, socially conscious films, coupled with their decision *not* to "name names" before HUAC, ultimately curtailed their ability to work, much less succeed, in Hollywood. These latter filmmakers, along with many others, were blacklisted for their unwillingness to compromise their political views either in their films or in their dealings with the government investigators or studio heads. A close Kazan collaborator, politically in relation to HUAC and creatively as the screenwriter on both *On the Waterfront* and *A Face in the Crowd*, was Budd Schulberg. As the son of Paramount studio head B. P. Schulberg, Budd Schulberg grew up in and around the stars and glamour of the Old Hollywood, briefly working for the *Hollywood Reporter* and for the Paramount publicity department.[7] In the 1930s he was briefly a member of the Communist Party and, like Kazan, testified as a friendly witness during the second HUAC hearings in 1951.

Much of Kazan's (and Schulberg's) work must be seen in the context of the social-problem film. Most film historians agree that the continuity of the politically progressive filmmaking of the 1930s and early 1940s (in particular Rossen's films made at Warner Bros., and those of Frank Capra and John Ford, among others, at other studios) was broken by the World War II moratorium on filmmaking critical of America.[8] While the early postwar years saw a dramatic increase in social-problem films, the first half of the 1950s saw a steady decline: the number of social-problem films dropped from 21 percent of all Hollywood films in 1947 to 9.5 percent by 1955.[9] The increase in progressive filmmaking immediately after the war can be credited partly to the rise of independent filmmaking in the agency-propelled New Hollywood, and to the need for the studios to rethink their reliance on standard genres in the face of plummeting box-office returns. Other factors include changing postwar attitudes and the influence of Italian Neorealism. In any event, comparatively liberal studio executives like Zanuck and Warner were increasingly receptive during this period to independent and left-wing filmmakers like Kazan, Polonsky, Rossen, Ray, Huston, Wilder, and others who not only explored controversial social themes but also began engaging in stylistic experimentation.[10]

However, the considerable seductions associated with this greater creative freedom were tempered by the mounting threat posed by outside forces like HUAC, which, together with the blacklist, certainly contributed to the drop in social-problem films in the 1950s. Furthermore, in response to studio-union strife and even outbreaks of labor violence in the early postwar period, MPAA head Johnston urged producers to use their media platform to espouse national values in support of American capitalism. Economics, as usual, intersected with politics, as can be seen in Zanuck's concern over the controversial theme of Kazan's *Viva Zapata!* (1952), a pointedly allegorical film about the Mexican Revolution, which stemmed less from aversion to the film's politics than from the studio head's desire to protect Fox's valuable investments—the writers, directors, and stars whose careers were in jeopardy, given the threat of blacklisting.[11]

The Artist as Martyred Rebel

What began as a fruitful association between Zanuck and Kazan on *A Tree Grows in Brooklyn* (1945), at least in terms of commercial and critical success, continued on *Gentleman's Agreement* and *Pinky*. In typical Old Hollywood fashion, the studio head was involved in everything from script to final edit on all three films, and both *Pinky* and *Gentleman's Agreement* were typical of the type of mainstream social-problem film that Zanuck favored (and which may not have thrilled but certainly didn't offend Kazan). As

Neve states, "Zanuck . . . committed his studio to the type of adult pics he felt the war-hardened public wanted."[12] Simultaneously anxious to work in Hollywood but disturbed by his lack of creative autonomy, Kazan thereafter alternated between doing studio-assigned films and returning to Broadway to direct the critically acclaimed and commercially successful plays *A Streetcar Named Desire* (1947) and *Death of a Salesman* (1949). With these two stage successes and the commercial success of his first three films, Kazan received greater creative authority in Hollywood to choose both his projects and the writers with whom he would collaborate.

He first experienced this greater latitude on the film following *Pinky*, *Panic in the Streets* (1950), a controversial and politically ambiguous depiction of postwar life in which a doctor tries to track down a gangster who is the carrier of the bubonic plague. According to Neve, the film, which was shot on location in New Orleans, "combines the studio's [Fox's] semi-documentary tradition with a film noir exploration of the New Orleans underworld."[13] These two styles (social realist and noir) also reappear in *A Face in the Crowd*, but to a different end. In *Panic in the Streets*, noir lighting expresses the mounting pessimism and cynicism of the outside world. The hero is a Public Health Service doctor whose New Deal ethic prompts him to pursue social justice and to serve as an advocate for human rights. In contrast, in *A Face in the Crowd* expressionistic low-key lighting is used to convey the psychological transformation and self-discovery of protagonist Marcia Jeffries, an ambitious, but naïve "armchair liberal" who is caught in the quagmire of conflicting bureaucratic interests in the context of the postwar entertainment industry. In *Panic in the Streets* the stylistic elements are used to emphasize the social world in a state of flux; in *A Face in the Crowd*, perhaps reflecting changes Kazan himself would undergo in the preceding years, they are used to isolate the narrowed world of the heroine's individual psychology.

From the beginning of his Hollywood career, Kazan congratulated himself for resisting the temptation to become a studio contract director. Apparently, for Kazan, the five-year, five-picture contract he had signed with Fox did not constitute "selling out" to the studio.[14] He relished the financial and other perks that came with his association with the studio. For example, the studio system provided him access to financing, to technical resources, and in particular to high-paid talent like playwright Tennessee Williams or novelist John Steinbeck (the latter wrote the screenplay for *Viva Zapata!* [1952]), not to mention stars like Marlon Brando.[15] The lone but significant downside to working for the studios, Kazan felt, was the lack of creative autonomy. Commenting on Zanuck's tendency to interfere in what Kazan considered the director's job, he stated,

> Friends were warning me about Zanuck's tendency to "save" other people's films by taking all kinds of liberties with what was given him. Since film shot on the Fox lot was based on a script Darryl had approved and since he owned more shares of Fox than anyone else, he also owned every foot of stuff shot and could, in the end, do anything he wanted with it.[16]

On the other hand, Kazan's personal respect for Zanuck (the studio executive agreed to make the revolutionary-themed *Viva Zapata!* even after hearing of Kazan's involvement in the Communist Party) is also evident:

> There was no doubt where I stood—with the business boys, with the movie moguls, with the "gonifs" [Yiddish for thieves], with the old, unfeeling, insensitive, crass, vulgar industry barbarians. I trusted them most because I could rely on one thing: If in an open competition I could make an exciting film that people would want to see, they'd go with me. If they thought they could make a bundle, they wouldn't knuckle under to censorship—at least not yet.[17]

Despite his appreciation for Zanuck's support on the political front, after he made *Viva Zapata!* Kazan was determined to free himself from Zanuck's aesthetic micromanagement of his films. Kazan and Steinbeck worked closely on the script and sought "to express [their] feelings of being Left and progressive, but at the same time anti-Stalinist."[18] Despite their fervor and the talents of the entire creative team (the film starred Marlon Brando, Anthony Quinn, and Jean Peters), *Viva Zapata!* was neither a commercial nor a critical success. Some critics argued that Kazan was overly intent on tailoring the film to justify his political shift to HUAC, given his vulnerability as a former member of the Communist Party (a charge that would be leveled at his Oscar-winning *On the Waterfront* [1954] as well).[19] In contrast to Kazan and Steinbeck's precise political goals, Zanuck green-lighted *Viva Zapata!* because he envisioned a big, entertaining epic with clear-cut heroes. Once the film was in production, Zanuck's biggest concern was whether or not the film would be interpreted as pro-Communist, so he requested changes designed to correct such potential "trouble spots." The film's divergent political themes—appearing on the one hand to support the insurgence of its revolutionary hero and on the other to denigrate characters identified as Communist—reflect the complexities and inevitable compromises associated with making a "political" film in the New Hollywood.

The contradictory impulses in Kazan's own career, between artist and producer, between leftist socialist and informer, are epitomized by his decision to testify as a "friendly" witness before HUAC. Kazan had a history of backing left-wing causes throughout the 1930s and 1940s. During his lengthy association with the Group Theater and his brief membership in the Communist Party in 1934, he also helped create a left-wing movement among actors in what was then a very conservative Actor's Equity Association. The association had specific, straightforward goals: to protect the rights of working actors, to secure rehearsal pay for actors, and to limit the time in which the producer could replace an actor without financial obligation.[20] Throughout the early to mid-1940s, primarily through his affiliation with the Group Theater, Kazan became a very public and productive figurehead for the Left.

While never losing sight of his leftist sensibilities, specifically his faith in socialism, Kazan justified his decision to cooperate with HUAC based on his strong rejection of the autocratic direction he believed the Communist Party had taken in the mid-1930s. Perhaps out of stubborn defiance, up to his death Kazan staunchly defended his decision to "name names," including those of his former closest allies with the Group Theater. Zanuck was among the friends and associates with whom Kazan consulted prior to his testimony. As Kazan relates in his autobiography, Zanuck had urged him,

Name the names, for chrissake. Who the hell are you going to jail for? You'll be sitting there and someone else will sure as hell name those people. Who are you saving? He said he could understand it if I was trying to save someone, [like actor John] Garfield for instance, from perjury. (455)

Zanuck went on to explain his own political orientation, or lack thereof, which spoke to his instinct for self-preservation in a competitive business rather than allegiance to a particular political group or ideology. He told Kazan that he had had a good deal of experience in Washington during the war and "the idea there is not to be right but to win" (455). Like many ambitious studio executives, Zanuck understood the value of catering to leftist artists only insofar as they served his commercial agenda of attracting audiences to see his studio's films. Even though Zanuck's loyalty appeared to be self-serving, Kazan appreciated the studio head's forthright agenda:

to preserve the studio's relationship with the talented director. Kazan said about Zanuck:

> I was to find out that there were many conspiracies a filmmaker in our country had to deal with—that of the right, that of the left, that of the self-appointed moralists of the Catholic Church, and that of the men who tend the springs of gold. But for the time being, for that season and that crisis [after telling Zanuck I had been a member of the Communist Party], I preferred to trust Darryl and even Harry Cohn and Jack Warner. (421)

The aftermath of Kazan's very public expulsion from both the artistic Left and the studio establishment following his HUAC testimony (and *New York Times* letter) created an impossible double bind for the troubled director. Furthermore, various leftists, artists, and former associates like Marlon Brando, Arthur Miller, Harold Clurman, Clifford Odets, among others, were also torn between wanting to work with the talented director and remaining true to their leftist sensibilities. These contradictory impulses are nowhere more clearly expressed than in the case of Brando, whose stellar performances in *A Streetcar Named Desire* (Kazan directed him in both the theater and film versions) had elevated the previously unknown actor's stature and fee. Brando revered Kazan, seeing him as a father figure, but when Joseph Mankiewicz told him about Kazan's HUAC testimony, the actor's eyes filled with tears, and he said, "What am I going to do when I see the man next? Punch him in the nose? Because I loved that man." Brando later told Odets (before Odets himself testified): "I'm not going to work with him [Kazan] anymore. But he's good for me. Maybe I'll work with him a couple of times more. At least once" (470–71). In fact, Brando could not resist the opportunity to work with Kazan when offered the lead in *On the Waterfront* two years later. While Brando chose to sacrifice his leftist ideals to make the film with Kazan, he was rewarded with an Academy Award for his performance as the embattled dock worker Terry Malloy. Brando's dilemma speaks to the moral conundrum facing many leftist artists working for Hollywood during this reactionary time: whether to honor the selfless agendas of the Left or indulge the selfish goals of their own careers.

The Faustian bargain was not always so clear-cut, however, as Kazan's case indicates. Kazan's longstanding collaboration with Zanuck and Fox on *A Tree Grows in Brooklyn*, *Pinky*, *Gentleman's Agreement*, and *Viva Zapata!* came to an end after Kazan's HUAC testimony because he was considered damaged goods despite his cooperation. Disingenuously, however, Zanuck cited solely financial rather than political or ethical reasons for not making *On the Waterfront*, claiming that the studio was regrouping from huge financial losses and could no longer afford to risk making anything but obvious crowd-pleasers. Zanuck told Kazan and Schulberg that Fox's new strategy was to make exclusively big-production CinemaScope films that promised broad entertainment (even though earlier Zanuck had told the trades that Kazan's project would be the one exception to that mandate).

At the crucial final meeting to discuss whether Fox would make *On the Waterfront*, Schulberg, Kazan, and Kazan's William Morris agent, Abe Lastfogel, met with Zanuck, who said, "I'm not going to make this picture. I don't like it. In fact, I don't like anything about it." Zanuck went on to describe the various ways in which he had tried to adapt the dark-themed project to what he thought audiences at the time expected: "It's exactly what audiences don't want to see now. . . . Who gives a shit about longshoremen?" Zanuck added that he had tried unsuccessfully to heighten the film's drama, with no success, saying that he had "even tried making Terry [Malloy] a member of the FBI . . . but it didn't work" (508). Zanuck then told the writer and director about the studio's next project: a comic-strip-derived *Prince Valiant*—obviously not the type of socially relevant film Kazan and Schulberg were likely to be interested in.

Not just Fox but all the other studios rejected Kazan's and Schulberg's script for *On the Waterfront*, and for similarly stated reasons: its dark subject matter and social realist themes conflicted with the studios' desperate need to create more broadly appealing entertainment in these financially difficult times.[21] While completely unused to making films outside the studio, Kazan vowed to make the film without the studios and even threatened to shoot the film in 16-millimeter if necessary. Rather than take this principled if commercially challenged route, however, the Kazan-Schulberg team went "independent," turning to a failing producer and German-Jewish émigré, Sam Spiegel (who until 1954 had changed his name to what he felt was the more grandiose—and less Jewish-sounding—S. P. Eagle). Despite the independent producer's often unsavory business tactics, Kazan was impressed with Spiegel's story-editing skills and praised Spiegel for his rigor and intelligence in helping him and Schulberg polish the script. And yet with Spiegel, Kazan also seemed to have simply replaced one form of unscrupulous business manager (the studio mogul) with another (the independent producer). In other words, Kazan apparently had little problem adapting to the new, often more aggressive business practices associated with the New Hollywood as long as they served his artistic and career goals.

In his autobiography, *A Life,* Elia Kazan reflects on his combined contempt and eventual regard for the flashy, manipulative producer who agreed to make *On the Waterfront:*

> [Spiegel] did everything in the world to make directors and writers beholden to him and would in time end up many times richer than any of us. When I was a big success in Hollywood, he placed an upstairs bedroom in his house at my disposal. . . . I appreciated this, and I did feel beholden to him for his favors; in fact, everything was cool between me and S.P. until I began to work with him. Then I got to see his other side, and I alternatively wanted to kill him and embrace him. I have often asked if he was worth the grief and the trouble he was to cause me. In the case of *On the Waterfront,* he certainly was! (514)

Spiegel had a reputation for working with liberal filmmakers like John Huston and Orson Welles; however, at this low ebb in his career, Spiegel agreed to produce Kazan's film because he desperately needed a film, any film, to generate a producer's fee. According to Kazan, everything Spiegel did was tactical, including their first meeting when he invited Kazan to his home while he was preparing to make *The African Queen* (1952) with Huston, in an attempt to woo Huston and Kazan simultaneously. A canny negotiator, Spiegel used Frank Sinatra's interest in playing the lead role in *On the Waterfront* to gain leverage to attach the even bigger star Marlon Brando. Spiegel was confident Brando would say yes to the project because it was good for his career, even though Brando had said publicly that he wouldn't work with Kazan after his HUAC testimony. According to Kazan, Spiegel was not concerned with politics "unless it might stand him in good stead with some lefty writer he was courting to say that he totally disapproved of what I'd done [regarding HUAC]" (515). The producer also played off one studio against another, switching from UA to Columbia, and caused a temporary rift with Abe Lastfogel, Kazan's agent, who also represented the actor Spiegel had used as bait, Frank Sinatra. Despite his disapproval of the producer's unethical tactics, Kazan remained silent because Spiegel was able to secure Brando, the actor Kazan had preferred for the role all along.

Kazan was less impressed with his maverick producer's erratic behavior on the set and ordered him to leave on the first day of shooting. For instance, in an impractical effort to save money, Spiegel secured the rights to shoot on two of the three rooftops needed for the crucial opening scene. (The owners of the middle building were demanding too much money, which Spiegel refused to pay.) This decision caused expensive delays and unnecessary hardship for the crew, who had to carry heavy equipment down five flights and up another five flights rather than proceed directly across the rooftops. On another occasion, Spiegel made a rare appearance on the set, showing up in his limousine with a dinner date, and began lecturing the exhausted crew. This time the crew shouted him off the set (523–24).

While the producer and the director rarely saw eye-to-eye, Kazan was the first to admit to their mutual respect for one another. Kazan and Schulberg had been angry, at the time, when Spiegel requested numerous changes in the script prior to shooting. However, both the writer and director agreed that the producer's persistent efforts to restructure and fine-tune the screenplay, in combination with his casting efforts, contributed substantially to the film's eventual success.[22] *On the Waterfront* helped resuscitate Kazan's sagging reputation after the HUAC controversy and the failure of his two previous films, *Viva Zapata!* and *Man on a Tightrope* (1953). *On the Waterfront* was a phenomenal box-office and critical success and went on to win eight Academy Awards including Best Picture, Best Actor (Brando), Best Director (Kazan), and Best Story and Screenplay (Schulberg).[23]

As much as he had complained about studio interference on all his Zanuck films, and as much as he enjoyed his renewed success with this independently produced, Oscar-winning hit, Kazan eagerly returned to the studios to make his next film, *East of Eden* (1955). Kazan's lingering anger over Zanuck's refusal to make *On the Waterfront* caused him to deliberately snub Zanuck and Fox, however, and to go instead to Warner Bros. This was in spite of the fact that Jack Warner had informed HUAC two years earlier that Kazan and Arthur Miller had been engaged in "subversive" activities with the Group Theater.[24] By this time, Warner's betrayal apparently was of little consequence to Kazan, since his ultimate goal was to return to the comforting, if fading paternalism of the studio system as a paradoxical forum for expressing his artistic rebellion against that system. As Kazan stated at the time:

> [At this] point in my life . . . I was squeezed between conflicting tendencies which tightened around me, pulling and pushing me in opposite directions at the same time. I wanted to be an independent producer and director of films, going my own way without restriction or reservations, but I also wanted the power, equipment, and prestige of a Major Studio behind me. . . . I wanted to write my own story and that of my family, but I also wanted to write about the social history that I'd witnessed in my

time. . . . I wanted to be in with the big shots of the entertainment world, but I also wanted to lead a quiet, reflective life. I wanted money, plenty of it, but I certainly didn't want to pay for that money with onerous services. . . . I wanted to be a lefty, a radical, certainly a socialist—at least that—but I also wanted to be a Democrat, sitting squarely mid-America, loyal and loving to the U.S.A.[25]

The Contradictions of Independence in Postwar Hollywood

Elia Kazan joined John Ford, Alfred Hitchcock, Howard Hawks, Raoul Walsh, William Wellman, John Huston, and Billy Wilder, among others, as one of the former Hollywood contract directors who formed his own production company during the 1950s. However, unlike Hecht-Lancaster, Hal Wallis, Harold Mirisch, Jerry Wald, and other independent producers of the day, Kazan saw his company as serving more of an aesthetic than a financial function. According to Kazan, his primary motivation for forming his own company was less about profits and more about gaining greater artistic freedom, which for him meant the right to find and develop a suitable screenplay and to maintain "final cut" (authority over the final edited version of the film). Determined to assert greater control over the films he directed, starting with *East of Eden*, Kazan formed his own production company, Newtown Productions, in 1956, which he saw as a forum for autonomous filmmaking removed from the capitalist clutches of the studios and through which he produced, as well as directed, all his subsequent films of the 1950s and 1960s. These included *Baby Doll* (1956), *A Face in the Crowd* (1957), *Wild River* (1960), *Splendor in the Grass* (1961), *America, America* (1963), and *The Arrangement* (1969). Despite admitting to being angry with his agent, with Zanuck, and with everyone in Hollywood after allegedly both the studios and his former left-wing allies turned their backs on him following his HUAC testimony, Kazan did not radically change his way of conducting business in Hollywood after forming his own company.[26] He retained the same handlers he had had before (his WMA agent, Abe Lastfogel, his attorney, Bill Fitelson, and others) and simply moved from Fox to Warner Bros. for financing and distribution.

In contrast to the more entrepreneurial attitudes of independent producers like Hecht-Hill-Lancaster, Jerry Wald, or Sam Spiegel, each of whom clearly felt at home with many of the extortionist business practices associated with the New Hollywood, Kazan and Schulberg felt their role was to shape the future of Hollywood as outsiders to the industry. Kazan's 1957 introduction to the published screenplay for *A Face in the Crowd* functions as a political manifesto, celebrating the demise of the Old Hollywood studio system and invoking the consequent liberation of creative people with "something personal and strong to say." Kazan declared that he enjoyed being his own boss and making pictures that were personal rather than homogenized, films that were designed to "disturb, stir up, enlighten and offend":[27]

> Another sign of change is the growing number of small independent units being financed by the big studios and operating with a freedom that was unimaginable ten years ago. The mood is, "Let them try . . ." Kazan said, "I'm one of the ones who's trying. I've formed my own company, Newtown Productions. I like being my own boss. I make my own pictures the way I want to make them. Also, I make my own mistakes. One of the things I've done, against all business advice, is to upset the traditional balance and make the writer more important than the stars. I don't think it's a mistake."[28]

Both Kazan and Schulberg spoke, during this period, with the fervor of artists rather than businessmen. Therefore, when Kazan and Schulberg teamed up again to produce *A Face in the Crowd*, they saw themselves working in a New Hollywood climate of experimentation and unbridled freedom.[29] Unlike Hecht-Lancaster, who balanced economic and creative decision-making in their alternating slate of art films like *Marty* (1955) and star-driven, blockbuster-style, genre films like *Trapeze* (1956), Kazan and Schulberg represented themselves as artists rebelling against the system "all the way." Not completely negating but certainly qualifying this idealistic invocation of artistic rebellion, it is important to remember that a major studio, Warner Bros., financed and distributed *A Face in the Crowd*. By this period, Warners, like most New Hollywood studios, functioned more as a financier and distributor than as a production company, but it still employed the same (if not more aggressive) publicity and marketing techniques to sell its films and the same focus on the bottom line of profits. Furthermore, Kazan and Schulberg's narrow view of themselves as artists does not adequately take into account the creative license Kazan had "earned" by completing a series of commercially viable films during his early days at Fox. On the other hand, going into *A Face in the Crowd*, Kazan could also boast of a string of critically lauded "artistic" films: *On the Waterfront, East of Eden,* and, to a somewhat lesser degree, *Baby Doll.*

In other contexts, Kazan had demonstrated his pragmatic understanding of the value of earning profits for the studios as a means of retaining

his artistic autonomy. Reflecting on his newly won power after the phenomenal success of *On the Waterfront,* Kazan conveyed his impatience with
the naïveté of many leftist artists working in Hollywood. He stated bluntly,

> Don't you get tired of hearing people who live with their mouths pressed
> to the tit of the film and TV industry complaining about their lack of
> artistic freedom? What did they think the rules of the game were? Money
> is magic; very simple. When *On the Waterfront* was filling theatres, my
> "artistic position" as it's called, changed overnight, as if by magic.[30]

After *On the Waterfront,* however, neither of his subsequent Newtown Production films distributed by Warner Bros., *Baby Doll* and *A Face in the Crowd,*
were nearly as successful, especially financially.[31] The critical discourse surrounding the former film emphasized Kazan's battles with the PCA over
its controversial portrait of adultery and its suggestion of deviant sexual
behavior.[32] Reviews of the latter film emphasized the paradox of Kazan
having created a film with leftist themes given his recent cooperation with
HUAC. Thus, while studio marketing departments tried to capitalize on
Kazan's status as a political martyr and a rebel against the system as a tool
to sell his films, these efforts proved largely unsuccessful due to Kazan's
shifting and contradictory political alliances and the films' own mixed artis-
tic/commercial messages.

Kazan's artistic and commercial goals for the films he made under the
Newtown label cannot be considered in isolation, given the complicated
political factors influencing his career choices. Most artists, intellectuals,
and opinion-makers felt intense pressure in the late forties and fifties to
publicly renounce Communism, and not just in Hollywood, when the
McCarthy Senate hearings expanded the anti-Communist probe into the
military, government, unions, universities, and elsewhere.[33] The impulse to
reaffirm the American way of life was particularly strong for Jews and other
immigrants after the war, when ultranationalist sentiment placed these
groups under special duress. As a first-generation Greek immigrant, Kazan
thus might have been moved to "name names" based on a combination of
motives, some self-serving, others more principled, others born of fear.[34]
Kazan himself insists that he testified primarily because of his dislike for
Communism and not to salvage his career; however, the evidence suggests
otherwise.

The link between the pressure to purge himself of subversive suspicions
and remain in good favor in Hollywood was underscored when Kazan took

the unprecedented step of taking out a large ad in the *New York Times*. In the ad he explained in detail (in fact, his wife, Molly, wrote the piece in his name) why he had named seventeen people as Communists, adding a detailed political defense of each of his plays and films. While his cooperation with HUAC did manage to salvage his career, his testimony combined with the letter incurred the wrath of many of his former intellectual and artistic allies from the Left, in particular Arthur Miller, Lillian Hellman, Harold Clurman, and, more ambiguously, Marlon Brando.

The differing responses, and actions, of Kazan and Odets in regard to their HUAC testimony are also telling. Kazan, Odets, and others associated with the Group Theater had begun to lose faith in the political relevance of the theater as a forum for leftist themes as the thirties wore on. Yet, whereas Odets remained apologetic up to his death for capitulating to the temptations of Hollywood, Kazan was adamant to the end in justifying his decision to become a friendly witness. What Kazan did regret was having played a role in convincing Odets, the most staunchly leftist member of the Group Theater, to testify before HUAC. In retrospect, Kazan realized the act of testifying nearly destroyed Odets by undermining the playwright's self-image as a spokesperson for the Left. From that point, Odets punished himself for having sold out to Hollywood, or as Kazan derisively put it, Odets "returned to Hollywood where there was work rewriting the scripts of other men."[35]

Despite his own resolve over his decision to be a friendly witness, Kazan's personal politics—in particular his early years as a member of the Communist Party—continued to haunt him during and after the HUAC trials. Polonsky, for example, observed that all of Kazan's post-HUAC-testimony films were marred by "bad conscience."[36] According to Larry Ceplair, the Kazan films that followed his testimony betray the sensibilities of a cynical former member of the Left. Kazan's heroes are oppressed and misunderstood individuals who must single-handedly rescue a population, which is selfish and easily manipulated.[37] *On the Waterfront*, in particular, was a blatant apologia for Kazan's HUAC testimony, as Brando's dockworker becomes the film's hero when he "courageously" informs on his corrupt union bosses—and is beaten to a pulp for his efforts, though he survives. While *A Face in the Crowd* may be somewhat of an exception to this compromising tendency, Kazan's films from the 1960s and early 1970s tend to leave behind social concerns altogether, instead shifting focus to increasingly personal and autobiographical issues. These films range from *Splendor in the Grass* (1961), about sexual repression in small-town America, to *America, America*

(1963), about Kazan's Greek father's emigration to the United States, to *The Arrangement* (1969), about a hero's search for love and self-fulfillment by rejecting the goals of a materialist society.[38] In his final film, an adaptation of F. Scott Fitzgerald's *The Last Tycoon* (1976), Kazan returned to a critique of Hollywood—albeit, given its 1930s setting, a Hollywood at least two generations removed.

In *Harmless Entertainment: Hollywood and the Ideology of Consensus*, Richard Maltby suggests that Kazan's political ambivalence (he came to define himself in opposition to both the Left and the Right) and his willing complicity with mainstream Hollywood interests complicated his status as a rebel against the factory-like system of production. Odets, in contrast, perceived his own complicity with Hollywood as simply that: selling out for the fame and money. Odets could find no further justification to support his abandonment of his leftist ideals. The hypocrisy Odets felt about expressing his leftist views while still earning a paycheck in Hollywood would manifest itself in his intensely ironic dialogue in *Sweet Smell of Success*. Conversely, Kazan's relative comfort with his complicity with Hollywood resulted in a much less contentious view of the entertainment industry (with the arguable exception of *A Face in the Crowd*). These concessions to the New Hollywood business model may, in fact, be the reason why the professed discontent of Kazan, the artist, was not viewed as antithetical to Zanuck, Warner, and other representatives of mainstream Hollywood's interests. As Maltby states, "Kazan was a valuable financial property who received studio protection against the reactionaries who would bar him from employment. He made himself a martyr at little cost to his career."[39]

"Commercial Liberalism"

Most of Kazan's Hollywood career betrays a consistent effort to capitalize on the studio system while waging war against it on artistic grounds, primarily through films with progressive social themes, a heterogeneous style, and a modernist aesthetic. Kazan's modernist aspirations were analogous to those of other filmmakers working in Hollywood in the 1940s and 1950s—most notably, Orson Welles in *Citizen Kane* (1941), *The Magnificent Ambersons* (1942), *The Lady from Shanghai* (1948), and *Touch of Evil* (1958). James Naremore, in his comprehensive study *More Than Night: Film Noir in Its Contexts*, traces the origins of the modernist aesthetic in Hollywood practices back to a 1920 screening in New York of the German expressionist classic *The Cabinet of Dr. Caligari*. The influence of vanguard European cinema on Americans continued in subsequent decades, with "the most obvious sign of 'artistic-ness' in America during the interwar years ... [being] a slightly UFA-esque or expressionist style . . . [and] the most critically respected film produced in Hollywood . . . after 1941 was Orson Welles's *Citizen Kane.*" American filmmakers incorporated a modernist aesthetic into the classical Hollywood style as a way of revitalizing standardized conventions and genres without alienating the studios, and by extension the public. According to Naremore,

> Each [filmmaker] brought an intense awareness of modernist literature to the making of criminal adventures, and each gained money and fame from the Hollywood studios. Taken together, their work demonstrates how a certain kind of "art thriller" could be critical of the institutions that supported it; but at the same time, their careers reveal that the movie studios needed to lighten or ameliorate the darkness of modernism and mute its intensity.[40]

While for Naremore, "Welles was the most spectacular manifestation of a growing acceptance of modernist values throughout the culture," other postwar filmmakers were taking up the challenge. Kazan, for instance, had been chafing for years under Zanuck's predilection for social-problem films in the "commercial liberal" tradition when he decided to launch his independent company and, at the same time, to begin to indulge in the type of modernist experimentation prevalent on the margins of Hollywood. However, even in his boldest film, *A Face in the Crowd,* TV writer Mel Miller's moralizing dialogue at the end serves the interests of the mainstream. By purporting to resolve the social conflict, Miller's "sermon" falls prey to what Fredric Jameson calls the "profound structural relations" that bind up modernism with the commercialized discourse of mass culture.[41] By making his social critique more accessible to a mass audience, in other words, Kazan was participating in the diminution of its more progressive aspects. Even though Kazan tried to avoid succumbing to "commercial liberalism" in his later, independently made films, his entire Hollywood career and *A Face in the Crowd,* in particular, register a complex dialectic between opposing tendencies: to "be critical of the institutions that supported [his career in Hollywood]," on the one hand; and to respond to a studio system and a mass entertainment which "needed to lighten or ameliorate the darkness of modernism and mute its intensity," on the other.[42]

As for Kazan's extratextual image, a similar "lightening and ameliorating" process was at work: it was far safer and easier to have the press and his mainstream audiences identify with the cause of the martyred artist rebelling against studio executives and the PCA, for instance, than it was for them to identify with a former Communist or political radical in the cautionary 1950s. Kazan's public battles with the PCA over the presence of controversial sexual themes in his Tennessee Williams adaptations, *A Streetcar Named Desire* and *Baby Doll*, for instance, were ultimately good publicity both for the films and the director. As Maltby states,

> The excisions . . . [from *A Streetcar Named Desire*] permitted Kazan to assume a posture that was central not only to the liberal hero, but to the liberal artist compromising himself with an adulterating commercialism. Kazan could become the victimized martyr hero of his own struggles with a philistine establishment; losing ensured that he retained his artistic integrity, since it was he who was compromised in the compromising of the text.[43]

Many film critics and historians have observed, though not fully explained, the fact that the postwar/preblacklist period in Hollywood (1946–50) witnessed a remarkable flourishing of socially critical films before many of the social-problem filmmakers were "silenced, destroyed or driven underground." Naremore adds that it wasn't just the Hollywood Ten or other more radical elements who explored leftist themes. The social-problem film paradoxically reached its apex of respectability during the early postwar period partly through the efforts of studio heads like Darryl Zanuck who were reinforcing the effort "to situate a potentially controversial production within an easily recognizable and mostly liberal genre: the Hollywood social-problem film."[44] The contradiction was not lost on the anti-Communist Right, which derisively termed such fare "commercial liberalism."[45]

Maltby, however, differentiates the social-problem films made by Kazan from those made by unfriendly witnesses. The liberal-leaning Enterprise Studios, as discussed in chapter 1, brought together in the late 1940s a group of soon-to-be blacklisted left-wing actors, writers, directors, and producers including John Garfield, Robert Rossen, Abraham Polonsky, and Robert Aldrich. Although Enterprise disbanded after going bankrupt in 1949, apparently due to what Maltby describes as its "reckless working methods," the company managed to make two of the best-known and most uncompromising social-problem films: *Body and Soul* (1947), directed by Rossen and written by Polonsky, and *Force of Evil* (1948), written and directed by Polonsky.[46] These and other social-problem films made at Enterprise gave forthright expression to leftist politics by exposing and analyzing contemporary social problems, as opposed to Kazan's "artistic rebellion" which resulted in compromised period pieces *(Viva Zapata!)* and out-and-out antiunion diatribes *(On the Waterfront)*. Of the latter, Maltby writes,

> The idea of rebellion was displaced from the specifically political context it had been provided with at Enterprise Studios into a rebellion against the conventional mores of Hollywood and stardom. Brando and Kazan in particular became archetypes of the Rebel as Artist: Brando through his off-screen behavior, Kazan through his insistence on independence from studio control and the "controversial" subject matter of his films. This was an internal rebellion the industry could entirely accommodate within the attitudinal realignment forced on it by its changing economic circumstances.[47]

Whereas the leftist filmmakers associated with Enterprise tended to portray the hero in rebellion against society, Kazan's "social-problem" films glorified method actors for their "rebellion against the conventional mores of Hollywood and stardom."[48] Maltby perhaps overstates his case; however, by turning Actors Studio alumni into the focal point of studio-generated press around his films, Kazan did largely facilitate a transformation in the reception of the post-contract-era stars. As we saw in chapter 1, the rebel image of celebrated actors like Marlon Brando and James Dean derived more from their rebellion against the studio machinery and entertainment press than from their rebellion against society. Kazan helped make the social-problem genre a sanctioned part of mainstream studio production in large part by foregrounding the performance of a new generation of actors whose star quality was paradoxically linked to their rebellion against the studios.

Jameson's comments on the political implications of Method acting are especially relevant when discussing these actors' films as compared with the publicity surrounding the stars. Method acting, Jameson argues, "celebrates the antihero and reduces the politics of marginality to psychologized, personalized alienation. As a result, we do not see class conflict as such but only its individual consequences."[49] Kazan's heroes were largely victimized by their own feelings of alienation rather than by external forces in society. In analogous fashion, in interviews and autobiographical material, Kazan continued to portray himself much like the alienated heroes in his films, as a filmmaker who was victimized by his own feelings of alienation as an artist.

This new perception of the Hollywood actor and director as alienated artists did not take place overnight, nor was it limited to the viewing public. The perceptual shift was symptomatic of changes that were taking place in the critical community as well, particularly among writers for *Cahiers du cinéma*, the French film journal founded in 1951 which first promoted the concept of the director as *auteur* in the early to mid-1950s. While Kazan did not initially fare well with this group of critics, or their American counterpart, Andrew Sarris, the lukewarm response to Kazan's work probably had much to do with his perceived complicity with the studios in the first part of his Hollywood career and with HUAC thereafter.[50] Contemporaneous reviews of *A Face in the Crowd* are symptomatic of this development. Much of the negative reaction toward the film was inextricably linked to journalists' attitudes toward Kazan, the political turncoat/patriot-come-lately. Interestingly, this bad press emanated from both the Right and the Left.

Counterattack (the right-wing watchdog publication formed to identify Communists or Communist sympathizers and to clear the names of those individuals who testified and named names) was of two minds about Kazan: it supported his HUAC testimony but questioned his motives, challenging him to offer more tangible evidence than mere words to prove he was anti-Communist.[51] *A Face in the Crowd* failed to fill the bill. Indeed, *Counterattack* denounced both the film and the filmmakers for making "partisan propaganda," attributing the film's attack on television as a "hang-over from the Communist pasts of Budd Schulberg and Elia Kazan."[52] These "subversive" attitudes, moreover, were seen as symptomatic of a larger social trend among artists and intellectuals bent on producing the previously cited "commercial liberalism." "The commercial liberal has to keep on raving about conformity and thought-control because he doesn't have anything else," *Counterattack* stated, adding that this type of political filmmaker was unified in his irrational fear that

> isolationists, reactionaries and anti-communists are ready to seize power in the United States and throw everybody who voted for Henry Wallace into a concentration camp. It's bunk but it's very profitable bunk and Messrs. Schulberg and Kazan are masters of the art of dispensing it.[53]

While right-wing newspapers attacked both film and filmmakers for being anti-American, the left-wing press attacked Kazan but praised the film. A journalist with the Communist Party's *West Coast People's World* wrote,

When two stool pigeon witnesses before the Un-American Committee conspire to produce one of the finest progressive films we have seen in years, something more than oversimplification of motives is needed to explain it. . . . [A Face in the Crowd] is a hard-hitting exposé of the television industry and the way a hillbilly guitar plucker can be built up to be a national menace. The film will help educate the film audience into an understanding of how public opinion is manipulated in the U.S. and for what purpose.[54]

Kazan found both left-wing and right-wing reviews simplistic in their extremist posturing; however, he regarded the term "commercial liberal" an appropriate term to describe what he called "some of my old friends." Presumably, Kazan was lumping many of his former associates from the Group Theater into this latter category, individuals like Harold Clurman, Clifford Odets, Arthur Miller, and others whom Kazan singled out for their tendency to use narrowly leftist themes to "instruct" audiences. Kazan said about his own work in 1957, "I began to learn not to try to pin a play's meaning down to a didactic theme. We used to do that in the Group; it was the essence of our work as directors. We were 'teaching' the audience with each play."[55] But Kazan refused to admit then what he would confess in later interviews; namely, that many of his own films, even *A Face in the Crowd*, suffered from this same tendency to wrap up complex social problems with a narrow thematic resolution.[56] Kazan and Schulberg's expressed intention in this film was to demonstrate their "anticipation of the power that TV would have in the political life of the nation."[57] They wanted to warn viewers to question what the political candidate says rather than be taken in by his charm or personality. They saw the media's selling of the politician as analogous to its selling of a consumer product. But by giving the liberal writer, Mel Miller (played by Walter Matthau), a closing speech that clarified this liberal message, the film implies that Mel (and by extension the audience) can occupy a position of moral superiority, a "pristine reality" outside the ideologically engridded mass media (notably, a position most antitelevision movies have taken since; e.g., *Network, Wag the Dog, The Truman Show*).[58]

In retrospect, then, Kazan recognized how easily a surface liberalism may have invaded not just the films he had made during Zanuck's stewardship at Fox but which also crept into some of his own later independent work. In both instances he seemed to have replicated Zanuck's tendency to choose topical, liberal themes and make complex social conflict palatable to American audiences by presenting a clearly stated theme and resolution—even in his most daring effort, thematically and stylistically, *A Face in the Crowd*. Yet, despite Kazan's self-criticism about having muted the intensity of this film by using Mel Miller as a spokesman for the didactic political message (and the compromises of Kazan's own career), the film's quite nuanced and ambivalent response to its varied social themes make it stand out as one of the most compelling and complex portraits of the postwar culture industry.

Postwar Independents:
Progressive Texts or "Within the Bounds of Difference"?

David Bordwell, Janet Staiger, and Kristin Thompson's *The Classical Hollywood Cinema: Film Style and Mode of Production to 1960* remains the most comprehensive treatment of Old Hollywood's conventionalized aesthetic style, classical narrative structure, and standardized genres within a specific historical framework.[59] Henry Jenkins's provocative analysis of the anarchistic comedy tradition, *What Made Pistachio Nuts? Early Sound Comedy and the Vaudeville Aesthetic* (1992), deals with the specific historical circumstances impacting a particular genre and decade, the 1930s.[60] Jenkins delineates two opposing theoretical approaches to Hollywood genre study: the post-1968 *Cahiers du cinéma* approach, which tends to treat every aberrant feature of the classical Hollywood narrative as evidence of a radical intent; and Bordwell et al.'s, which explains away all potentially disruptive features as within "the bounds of difference." Within these two extremes, however, lies an approach that "builds upon methodologies and insights drawn from institutional, social, and cultural history . . . [and gives] theoretical rigor and historical specificity to concepts such as formula, convention, formal norms, historical transformation, institutional restraints, intertextuality, and reception."[61]

This "third way," for Jenkins, allows historians to engage in a historical conceptualization of popular genres by means of their formal norms and institutional constraints but also by taking into account the way "generic formulas are . . . also ways of exploiting and resolving ideological tensions." Jenkins also references Stuart Hall's contention, about commercial entertainment in general, that it retains elements of an earlier folk tradition which can be recognized or identified but at the same time, according to Hall, "registers fundamental dissatisfactions within the social formation." According to this view, so-called progressive generic developments do not always signify a radical political intent but rather should be seen as sites of cultural "transformations."[62] For Jenkins, this means "we must also consider the process by which previous social connotations are stripped away, the prevailing ideological order is restored, and cultural respectability is reestablished" when examining films which appear to have strayed from the normal structural and stylistic forms and classical narrative features of any given genre.[63]

My analyses of the more reflexive end of the self-referential business-film cycle undertaken in the remaining chapters—preeminently *A Face in the Crowd* and *Sweet Smell of Success*—are careful to consider the unique production circumstances and historical conditions which informed these films' creation. In so doing, I seek to accommodate both Bordwell et al.'s notion of "bounds of difference" as well as the cultural "transformations" Jenkins and Hall assign to works that stray periodically from the dominant norms of commercial entertainment but eventually are recuperated into the prevailing social order. As the self-referential entertainment-business film evolved to include greater reflexivity toward the end of the 1950s, it increasingly employed aesthetic practices that could be viewed as disruptive to classical narrative conventions. These innovative techniques borrowed elements from a range of existing and emergent forms: the fine arts, theater, vaudeville, nightclubs, radio, television, as well as other national cinemas. Nor was such a cross-cultural approach, by itself, anything new; the ability to absorb a wide range of external, seemingly disparate, and sometimes subversive influences and make them palatable to the masses constitutes a large portion of what Gramsci calls hegemony and Thomas Schatz (following Bazin) calls "the genius of the [Hollywood] system."[64] Classical Hollywood is unthinkable, for instance, without the incorporation of such European modernist innovations as Soviet montage, German Expressionist mise-en-scène, and neorealist style and content. What is different in *A Face in the Crowd* and *Sweet Smell of Success* is that these films' incorporation of outside influences has not been as seamless, not all the subversion has been smoothed over or drained off, some rough edges and residue remain. Coming at the far end of the self-referential business film cycle, *A Face in the Crowd* and *Sweet Smell of Success* (both 1957) are among the most striking examples of all postwar Hollywood films to incorporate a radical modernist (even nascent postmodernist) aesthetic as well as a critique of both of the entertainment industry specifically and the capitalist social order in general.

7

A Face in the Crowd:
Reframing Reflexivity

> As it stands, the picture allows you to take a comfortable position
> and say, "He's obviously a danger." Actually, he's not obviously a
> danger—We're still being caught up in that kind of influence. I'd
> mix things up more, so that the audience is implicated and doesn't
> stand on that safe platform of removal.
>
> —ELIA KAZAN, interview, 1974

The meeting between Kazan and exiled German playwright Bertolt Brecht
in New York and their near collaboration in 1947 are fascinating to consider
in relation to the radical reflexivity of Kazan's *A Face in the Crowd,* made a
decade later.[1] Brecht had invited the Group Theater alumnus and recently
turned Hollywood director to stay in New York to direct one of Brecht's
plays. But Kazan turned down the offer, having already accepted Zanuck's
offer to direct another movie, and he claimed a preference for the unique
challenges associated with working inside the Hollywood system.[2] Nonetheless, the Brechtian influence on Kazan's work is undeniable. By employing Brechtian-type alienation techniques and stylistic excess that subverted
classical Hollywood's genre formulas and "realist" narrative conventions,
Kazan—not alone but perhaps preeminently among artistic-minded New
Hollywood filmmakers—formulated a set of "counter-hegemonic practices
[that], like real political encounters, [can take you] by the shoulders and
shake you out."[3]

Produced in the still-reactionary political climate of the late 1950s and
in a film industry oriented increasingly toward the blockbuster, Kazan's and
Schulberg's reflexive antibusiness film *A Face in the Crowd* was, and remains,
remarkable in its ideological and stylistic boldness. The film fluctuates and
overlaps among at least three distinct aesthetic systems: the "high art" modernism associated with the avant-garde strategies of Brecht and the films
of Orson Welles; the "middle-brow," heavily stylized, though still "realist"
aesthetic of Sirkian commercial melodrama; and the purportedly "low"

popular-culture techniques associated with vaudeville, nightclubs, radio, and television. By juxtaposing these disparate elements, *A Face in the Crowd* looks ahead to postmodernism's pastiche, intertextuality, and the conflation of high and low culture. In its formal experimentation and political forthrightness the film also, together with Odets and Alexander Mackendrick's *Sweet Smell of Success* and to an extent also Wilder *(The Apartment)* and Tashlin *(Will Success Spoil Rock Hunter?)* in their respective self-referential films, limns the outlines of an emerging independent American art cinema movement.

The juxtaposition in *A Face in the Crowd* of an MCA-style talent agent, a corruptible television star, and an independent producer seeking to arbitrate these competing forces, referred self-reflexively back to the complex ideological/industrial crisis facing independent producer-director Kazan and screenwriter Schulberg, who, despite their semi-independence, were still constrained by the corporate environment of the postwar New Hollywood. As demonstrated in previous chapters, the fact that their film targeted television granted Kazan and Schulberg extraordinary leverage to engage in stylistic experimentation and express controversial, anticapitalist themes given the extent to which the "antitelevision" discourse still permeated both the industry trades and popular press in the late 1950s.

The Sheltering Antitelevision Discourse

On its surface, *A Face in the Crowd* is a Frankfurt School–inspired fusillade against the cultural and political depredations of the commercial broadcasting industry. The film's main protagonist, pioneer radio producer Marcia Jeffries (Patricia Neal), "discovers" hobo singer/songwriter Larry Rhodes (Andy Griffith) in an Arkansas jail, renames him "Lonesome" Rhodes to capitalize on his populist appeal, and turns him into a national TV-network superstar. A phalanx of agents, managers, publicists, network executives, and corporate sponsors cultivate Rhodes's Will Rogers–style appeal to sell products and, later, to hawk a right-wing politician with presidential ambitions. Eventually, Marcia brings down the power-mad Rhodes (though not necessarily the corporate boss or politician!) by revealing, live on the air, his previously concealed disdain for his loyal mass audience.

Given the complex set of circumstances governing Kazan's and Schulberg's careers in relation to the social-problem film, the 1950s anti–mass media discourse—which saw television hopelessly mired in false consciousness and the advertising ethos—seems insufficient to explain *A Face in the Crowd*'s iconoclasm. Yet a familiar anti–mass media presupposition informs a 1957 *Hollywood Reporter* review of *A Face in the Crowd*. The review focuses exclusively on the film's critique of the television industry, a target quite congenial to the trade paper's residual anti-television bias:

> [The film] is, in its barest terms, an exposé of one portion of the TV industry, disclosing that medium in its most vulgar reality. But it is also an affirmation of the intrinsic decency and good sense of the people. It is, in Madison Avenue terms, a slaying of the dragon by St. George, and the victory for our side is cheering and satisfying.[4]

The phrase "slaying of the dragon by St. George" suggests that through Marcia Jeffries's courageous act of shutting down the corrupted celebrity Lonesome Rhodes at the end of the film, the will of the people has won out over the television industry's commercial interests.

In fact, the film undercuts this pat resolution in several ways. One of these is the transformation of Joey DePalma's (Anthony Franciosa) character from ambitious errand boy to slick, calculating, cutthroat agent. Moreover, as the screenplay notes explicitly inform us, DePalma was patterned on the MCA "organization man": "Joey is dressed in perfect taste, smoothed out, perhaps with glasses and a waistcoat, like a highly placed, thirty-year-old MCA executive." The critique of the New Hollywood agency is carried further at the end of the film when DePalma tells the network president that he has already found a substitute for Rhodes, who has become damaged goods: "Barry Mills. A young Lonesome Rhodes and a lot easier to handle."[5]

The metaphor of St. George in the *Hollywood Reporter* review is an odd choice to describe *A Face in the Crowd* for another reason, since it presupposes that the ending is definitive and that Marcia's toppling of the false idol of television is unequivocally moral and righteous. In fact, for the bulk of the film Marcia panders to the TV medium to further her own career, doing little to undermine Rhodes even after he has betrayed her romantically and after she recognizes that he poses an obvious danger politically. The review's eagerness to simplify the lines between good guy and bad guy in *A Face in the Crowd* speaks to the 1950s' search for easy targets via the anti-TV discourse. The review's narrow take also invokes the decade's cultural blindness about the downside of American capitalism, and with it, the rise of what Jackson Lears describes as "therapeutic prescriptions offered by advertising and the leisure industries [in general], that have exacerbated the [social] problems, further enmeshing us in a web of consumer interdependence and ego diffusion."[6] *A Face in the Crowd* casts its net far wider than the culture industry; it places commercial television into a broad context that reveals the new medium to be only one aspect, albeit a crucial one, in the development of American corporate capitalism. In the process, far from demonizing TV, the film, as Neve states, "lacks most of the condescension toward mass culture that was characteristic of 1950s educated opinion."[7]

The film contains a strikingly contemporary critique of how politics and entertainment, and the power relations of the media, inform American culture and society. In contrast to the decade's narrow mass-media debate about television, the stylistic reflexivity in *A Face in the Crowd* allows the film to move past the outdated and oversimplified binaries of art versus commerce and high art versus low art by both acknowledging mass culture's strengths and satirizing its excesses. As Kazan, in a 1974 interview on the making of *A Face in the Crowd,* confessed: "There was a great gaiety, making up those ads, the Vitajex sequence. . . . I was both repulsed and attracted by them. TV is always on the verge of being ludicrous; it's always on the precipice—and you say, 'I can't believe they mean that! Are they kidding?'"[8]

The film also mocks its two "intellectuals," Marcia Jeffries and the TV writer Mel Miller, in particular their simplistic left-wing views and naïve celebration of the New Deal populism embodied in Lonesome Rhodes's "country boy" charm. Marcia makes her protégé Rhodes understand that the source of his appeal is his behavioral resemblance to a Will Rogers–style American folk hero who refused to pander to the system. After learning this crucial lesson, Rhodes perpetuates the ruse. Throughout his transition from homespun transient to overbearing and power-hungry celebrity, the film demonstrates how New Deal populism has been undermined in the context of a postwar America devoted to a consensus view of consumer capitalism. Marcia and Mel, however, in their idealistic attempt to reinforce liberal values and the popular over the elitist, fail at first to recognize Rhodes's vulnerability to cooptation by right-wing political forces intent on using his celebrity to further their own reactionary agenda.

Already in its opening moments, the film mocks its college-educated heroine's "armchair intellectual" approach to class relations, when she delivers a lecture to her radio audience (and by extension to the film audience) as an introduction to Lonesome Rhodes's first radio appearance, while still in jail: "[T]he real American music comes from the bottom up. When George Gershwin played it in New York it was black-tie music, but the real beginning of it is from the folks who never owned a tie." Later, she and Mel, her fellow left-wing, college-educated "egghead," compare notes on the return of the Will Rogers–style performer in the figure of Lonesome Rhodes.

> MEL: He's the genuine article, isn't he? Anti-egghead and everything.
>
> MARCIA: Yes, he's it, all right. An old-fashioned mixture of honesty and orneryness and independence and meanness and shirt-off-his-back sentimentality.[9]

This celebration ultimately turns to a warning, of course, when Rhodes's homey populism is adapted to serve a reactionary cause, when the country-bumpkin-turned-national-celebrity instructs his Vitajex sponsor how best to sell their patently phony energy-boosting pills and coaches a charisma-challenged right-wing politician on how to adopt Rhodes's southern "good ol' boy" charm to win votes.

A Face in the Crowd further deconstructs the making of a television star by exploring Rhodes's folksy charm, his charisma, and his ability to act as a spokesman for the common man. These are precisely the personality traits that capture the attention of Marcia, who, thinking she has found the "real thing" in Rhodes, becomes his tireless promoter and "girl Friday." The populist agenda behind Marcia's TV program, *A Face in the Crowd,* is to show "regular people" in everyday settings sans glitzy Hollywood trappings or big production values. Marcia seeks to capitalize on Rhodes's appeal as a vagabond and folk hero who, despite being a drunk whom Marcia finds sobering up in jail, has a natural gift as a storyteller and musician. This weakness on Marcia's part exposes the flaw in the leftist idealization of the proletariat, which in this case is satirically extended to the proletariat's least socially productive component, the lumpen proletariat.[10] Rhodes's trademark song, "Free man in the mornin'," may serve as an anthem for the self-made man, the individual who does not succumb to the trappings of success.[11] But it is sung by a character who, according to screenwriter Schulberg, was conceived "as an amalgam of media-constructed celebrities from the world of entertainment and politics: Will Rogers, Walter Winchell, Arthur Godfrey, Don Carney (radio's 'Uncle Don'), and Huey Long."[12]

In the film's opening scenes, as Marcia takes over managing Rhodes's career and begins the process of turning him into a radio and then a television star, it becomes clear how her nostalgic faith in the populism of a Will Rogers type is out of step in the context of 1950s postwar society. Marcia visits a local jail in a small Arkansas town and arranges with boorish Sheriff Big Jeff Hosmer, who has a crush on her, to let her do her "rovin' reporter" radio show on the prisoners in his custody. Her idealistic goal is to capture the natural intonations of small-town life among society's transients, drunks, and social misfits. She invites the prisoners to "sing a song or tell a funny story," but none of the inmates cooperate until they identify the potential for personal gain. The scene reveals that even society's disenfranchised understand how the system works and are eager to leverage this knowledge to gain not only their freedom but access to a lucrative career in entertainment. In various ways, the prisoners display their jaded understanding of the economics behind the world of show business. When "a scrawny Southern hobo" named Beanie sees the deal Rhodes has struck with the sheriff, he chimes in, saying he is "Rhodes's manager." Trenchantly pointing out a racist clause in the entertainment contract, when the sheriff asks a segregated black prisoner to "do something," he growls, "Just because I got a black skin . . . I'm no minstrel man."[13] Far from narrowly echoing the 1950s anti–mass media debate, then, the film, early on, suggests that while a group of small-town "losers" sees through the "false consciousness" purveyed by the culture industry, it is the educated, liberal Marcia, ironically, who remains in its thrall.

Rhodes, of course, not only sees through the media facade but quickly learns how to manipulate it to his own ends. As he becomes more successful and aware of the function of celebrity within the entertainment business matrix, he begins perpetuating the illusion of his persona's autonomy and individualism by poking fun at the mattress company that sponsors his show. Such a challenge to his corporate handlers, which astonishes Marcia and Mel but endears him to his public, was, of course, also rooted in actuality. Ribbing the sponsor and its slogans was a tried-and-true technique employed by Jack Benny, George Burns, Arthur Godfrey, and other radio and television stars as a means of simultaneously acknowledging and undermining the sponsor's hold over the individual star. At this point in the film, however, Marcia does not yet recognize that the entertainer's ironic distance serves a conservative function, inuring the audience to the economic nature of the implied social contract between the television celebrity and the consumer citizen. This, after all, is to be the central "lesson" of the film for Marcia (and hence the film audience). For while Rhodes's chastising of the sponsor functions initially, on a superficial level, to expose the advertiser-driven economics of the television industry by presenting the celebrity in a posture of rebellion against his corporate "boss," a deeper layer of complexity ultimately is revealed: namely, the ideological infrastructure that supports and propels the construction of the image of the "homey celebrity" in the first place. By unpacking the complex social engridding process that informs television celebrity, the film incrementally shifts the focus away from the celebrity, narrowly conceived, and onto the institutional forces that produce celebrity. And by deconstructing the larger *system* that enables and benefits from the penetration of the advertising message into the home, the film indicts the interrelated political, economic, and institutional components of the culture industry and its ultimate reinforcement of consumer capitalism under the guise of populist entertainment.

The Politics of Brechtian Filmmaking

If the Kazan/Schulberg film succeeds as a critique of mass media that still feels relevant to contemporary audiences, this is not only because of its sophisticated treatment of the subject matter, but perhaps even more because of its stylistic and structural excesses: the complex narrative structure, expressionistic mise-en-scène, and use of ideologically informed reflexivity. As described in the first chapter, reflexivity is not meant here in its more innocuous, purely aesthetic sense, but rather in its progressive political, Brechtian sense. Kazan's early left-wing and New York theater associations had prepared him for a Brechtian-style political approach, even though his new interest in Hollywood filmmaking and his desire to succeed as a movie director diverted this politicized agenda to some extent. Many of Kazan's films, especially the later, more independently conceived ones like *A Face in the Crowd*, represent an uneasy balance between these conflicting agendas.

Kazan's final days' corunning the Actors Studio with Harold Clurman in the mid-1940s were fraught with political and artistic infighting. The collaboration that began during the formation of the creatively vibrant, politically engaged Group Theater was coming to an end. Kazan describes in his autobiography a fateful meeting in which Clurman tried to enlist Kazan's aid in convincing Brecht (still living in exile in the United States) that Clurman should direct Brecht's next play, *Galileo*. Brecht was averse to using Clurman because of his Stanislavskian realist approach: "I don't want mood. . . . Bring me a circus director."[14] Presumably, Brecht preferred Kazan's proven ability to balance the popular and the political. Kazan didn't accept the offer in part because he didn't like the play. But, more significantly, he had just gotten his next offer from Zanuck to direct Fox's "prestige" picture of the year, *Gentleman's Agreement*, which was to be Zanuck's "personal production." In other words, Kazan saw the Fox offer as another building block in his career that would allow him greater power, leverage, and hence, creative autonomy in Hollywood. In contrast, he saw the decision to direct

Brecht's play as a step backward into the world of didactic filmmaking that he had already rejected by going to Hollywood. Kazan not only turned down Brecht's offer, but chose not to speak up on behalf of Clurman as a possible director either, thereby creating the final wedge between the former partners. From his office at Fox, Kazan wrote a letter to Clurman declaring that the partnership was over. Clurman assumed Kazan's decision not to work with Brecht was politically motivated, that Kazan didn't want to be associated with a member of the Communist Party in the reactionary postwar climate. But Kazan states in his autobiography that in 1947 he wasn't yet concerned about HUAC. He implies that at this early phase of his career, before he had so much to lose, that if he had been called to testify he wouldn't have named names. Moreover, he had come, at this point, to see the radical Left as more ineffectual than threatening, epitomized by Kurt Weill's sitting around the Actors Studio talking about the "good old days" in Berlin working alongside Brecht. Kazan was more intrigued with the artistic and political challenges associated with working in the belly of the beast: Hollywood.

The Brecht-Clurman incident and the creative fork in the road it represented for Kazan helps clarify the conflicting political impulses informing Kazan's Hollywood career. For while he may have turned down directing a work by one of modern theater's most influential playwrights, he appears not to have rejected "the master's" aesthetic principles. The mode of political filmmaking that Brecht articulates in his writings on theater, film, and revolutionary art is distinct from the type of liberal filmmaking that Kazan created under Zanuck's stewardship. On the other hand, as Dana Polan explains in "The Politics of a Brechtian Aesthetics," it is a mistake to assume that Brecht's theory allows no place for the type of pleasure and identification present in the classical Hollywood text.[15] Polan argues that, for Brecht, the audience must be able to recognize the conventions of the old traditions in order to recognize the new intervening forces of social critique. Polan goes on to reframe Brechtian theory, which has been misrepresented over the years, into a claim for reflexivity as a set of formal aesthetic practices divorced from the historical specificities associated with the production process. In characterizing Brecht's theories about political art, Polan identifies the two forms of pleasure that are necessary to achieve the preferred third level of "pleasurable instruction":

There is the pleasure of familiarity. This is the pleasure of uncritical, reified realism, the seeing of the world in the ways it has always been seen.

Then there is pleasure that comes from art's dehumanization or from forced self-reflexivity, which I've suggested is little different from the first register of pleasure. This is the pleasure of art as form, as aesthetic emotion in the Kantian sense. This is a pleasure that, as Barthes contends in *Pleasure of the Text*, derives its force from its avoidance of history, by aestheticizing or textualizing it. Then there is the pleasure argued for by Brecht, the pleasure of an art that finally realizes the dream of Horace in his *Ars Poetica* (which Brecht continually refers to): To please and instruct; to please through instruction; to instruct through pleasure. This is an art whose content is a combination of the world and a better version of that world.[16]

According to Brecht's model, the classic Hollywood text's focus on the narrowed world of the individual psychology of the main hero obscures the "social realm" that is invoked in the dialectic between the "realist" and "reflexive" textual systems. In *A Face in the Crowd*, however, Kazan explores the social dimension by foregrounding the institutional forces behind the historically specific changes in the creation of celebrity (including the relationship between the artist and his business representatives) and the power dynamics binding the powerful celebrity to the audience in the television era.

But for Brechtian "instruction" to be effective, it must operate on the level of style as well as content. And indeed, *A Face in the Crowd* is astonishingly inventive and provocative at the level of cinematic technique, exhibiting a consistent self-consciousness about its own methods, often foregrounding a reflexivity that subverts the continuity principles of Hollywood editing and camera. Recapitulating Polan's summary of Brechtian aesthetics, these techniques must incorporate the two types of textual "pleasure"—that associated with the familiar "realist" text, and that associated with formalist aesthetics—to achieve the third, preferred level of "pleasurable instruction" that discloses the social realm. In *A Face in the Crowd*, the film accomplishes the first level in its various, almost documentary-like moments of verisimilitude and in its familiar "rags to riches" story about Rhodes's ascent from a "nobody" to a celebrity. The second level is derived from the aestheticizing of emotion, or art as form, which Kazan accomplishes in most of the sequences depicting Rhodes on the air. For instance, when he first appears in front of a television camera, Rhodes calls attention to the production process by simultaneously engaging his television audience and the floor manager in a conversation. He says to the audience, "Howdy. Y' know I never seen myself on one o' these contraptions before. So if I stop t' admire myself in the whaddicallit—?" Rhodes turns to the floor manager, who answers him, "The monitor."[17] Rhodes tells the floor manager to have the cameraman show the audience what he is talking about by moving to a close-up of his face on the monitor. By exposing the technology responsible for creating the appearance of an unmediated direct address between the celebrity and the audience at home, both the fictional home audience, and by extension the film's audience, can adopt a posture of epistemological superiority.

A Face in the Crowd accomplishes Brecht's third level of "pleasurable instruction" by juxtaposing these two previous approaches (realist rags-to-riches story and formal experimentation) with an additional narrative strand (the romantic storyline involving Marcia and Rhodes), thus creating a dialectical relationship between the realist text and the formal elements. For instance, when performing "live" on the television sound stage, Rhodes appears to be "speaking" directly to his female fans at home in an "impossible" version of the shot-reverse-shot (since Rhodes is not in the same physical space as his mostly female fans watching him on their TV sets at home as they clean stoves, wash dishes, and so on). The scene contextualizes the emotions that bind star and fan by calling attention to the typically "invisible" editorial convention of the shot-reverse-shot. Marcia, however, is always inserted into these exchanges as a third, mediating "voice," articulating the others' relevance.

Producer Marcia Jeffries (Patricia Neal) tells Lonesome Rhodes (Andy Griffith) that he has three minutes left to wrap up his radio show.

Another aspect of the reflexive dialectic in the scenes depicting Rhodes's performances results from Marcia's compositional placement in the middle space of a deep-focus shot between Rhodes in the foreground performing and the other technicians standing far behind. Once the romance between Marcia and Rhodes takes "center stage" in the second half of the film—albeit involving an old-fashioned version of femininity with her support of the male artist/hero—the dialectic between the "realist" drama (involving Marcia and Rhodes as joint owners of "Lonesome Rhodes") and the formalist reflexivity (involving Rhodes's interaction with technicians and audience) is intensified by the literal representation of Marcia's "in-between" status, given her dual role as Rhodes's lover and his "behind-the-scenes" producer.

The Classical Hollywood Romance Revised

In his autobiography, Kazan conveys his nostalgia for an old-fashioned portrait of femininity similar to that which infuses the film's sentimental portrait of Marcia Jeffries and her romance with Lonesome Rhodes:

> Perhaps I was beginning to feel humanly, not think ideologically. The people in my life for whom I'd felt the deepest devotions were three old-fashioned women: my grandmother, my mother, and my schoolteacher. . . . I no longer had a taste for liberal intellectuals. I always knew what they were going to say about any subject. I simply didn't like the reformers I'd been with since 1933, whether they were Communists or progressives or whoever else was out to change the world.[18]

In a 1988 interview, Kazan went further, strongly implying that what he saw as *A Face in the Crowd*'s "secondary story" (the Rhodes-Marcia romance) related, at least partially, to his own relationship to his wife of thirty years, Molly Thatcher.[19]

> The film has an external story, but there is also a secondary story, running concurrently and hiding, as it were, behind the objective one. This "hidden" story has an intimate reference to the emotional life of the author and the director. It is the story of women as conscience. . . . This story, as you can see, has little to do with American politics or even with life behind the scenes of the television industry.

However, while the film certainly indulges in this sentimental portrait of woman as a throwback to the ideal of the "companion wife," it never loses sight of Marcia's more "liberated" proactive role as the "behind-the-scenes" producer orchestrating—literally and figuratively—all the varying story-lines involving Rhodes.[20]

Close analysis of four sequences from the second half of the film clarifies its Brechtian politicized aesthetic and demonstrates how *A Face in the Crowd* ultimately arrives at the "third level of pleasure" Brecht (via Polan) describes. These four sequences correspond to the four phases of Marcia's "education" about the duplicitous nature of the mass media, reflecting her reversion from a dynamic and successful career woman back to a more conservative version of femininity, and her ultimate "rebound" toward a more enlightened progressive position.

In the first half of the film, Marcia's combined professional and romantic interest in Rhodes is carefully orchestrated in deep-focus compositions that foreground (and "rear-ground") that which is typically effaced in the dominant cinema's realist texts: the role of desire in the celebrity/fan relationship. In contrast, in the second half of the film, the scenes dealing with Marcia tend to de-emphasize her role in constructing Rhodes's celebrity and shift to an emphasis on her growing romantic interest in him. By emphasizing the narrowed world of Marcia's individual psychology, the "realist" scenes in the second half of the film tend to put her in the same position as the female fans portrayed in the first half—as victims of the mass media's construction of desire. The distinction is subtle but meaningful. In the first half of the film, Marcia behaves like an on-set producer who critically observes Rhodes "seducing" his female fans on the air from inside the television studio. In these scenes, the film audience can both identify with her character *and* her status as social critic via her growing understanding of the power of celebrity. In contrast, in later scenes, when she watches Rhodes perform on a television set from his penthouse's living room sofa (after, it is implied, having had sex with him the previous evening), she relates to him personally rather than professionally. In the first half of the film, Marcia is portrayed as both an independent woman and a liberal media watchdog, but in the second half her personal motivation for destroying his celebrity—Rhodes's romantic jilting of her—is emphasized. Two of the techniques used to emphasize the romantic love story in the second half of the film are the increased use of close-ups on Marcia and the heightened expressionistic lighting effects, which combine to convey her narrowed psychological world. In the end, however, this seemingly recuperative romantic/psychological strand is torn asunder, revealing both its illusory and socially imbricated nature.

What follows is an analysis of these four sequences that transform Marcia from a idealistic social critic and independent woman (in her role as a producer of a populist television show) to a more conventional portrait of subservient femininity (in her affair with Rhodes) to a chastened but wiser observer of, and hopefully actor in, the social sphere.

Phase I: The Seduction of Marcia

Phase one of Marcia's seduction culminates in the scene, about halfway into the film, when it is implied that Rhodes and Marcia first make love and thus their strictly business relationship becomes a romantic one. The scene takes place in Marcia's hotel, following Rhodes's firing for "crossing the line" in his comments about the mattress company sponsor. In the scenes leading up to the seduction scene, every effort is made to present Marcia as the very model of the "modern" professional woman. She is well educated, sophisticated about a range of topics to do with the origins of culture both popular and high, seems more intelligent than Rhodes, and consistently maintains a position of control over him (e.g., at the jail and in the Arkansas radio-station offices, even in his hotel room early on). She also assiduously, if with some difficulty, avoids his vulgar sexual advances. The script describes Marcia as "a bright, well-groomed local girl in her late twenties whose native Arkansas intelligence has been sharpened by four years of eastern education—Sarah Lawrence, Class of '49. She is tall, brown-haired, handsome."[21]

Rhodes's attempts to undermine Marcia's authority are typically portrayed in deep-focus compositions that explore the power dynamic between the artist and his handler. For instance, while Marcia unpacks Rhodes's suitcase in the foreground of the shot in his small-town hotel room early in the film, Rhodes is initially off-screen, out of view in the bathroom. As she struggles to maintain a businesslike demeanor, Rhodes uses various tactics to try to soften her resistance. From the bathroom, he sings a ribald variation on his theme song, "Free Man in the Mornin'." Then he enters the bedroom, sits on the bed, and pats it suggestively, asking with an impish smile and a reference to his sexually tinged song: "You wanna come over here 'n sorta get acquainted early in the morning?" Marcia, however, does not submit to the obvious come-on.

The next scene depicts Rhodes at the Picket, Arkansas, radio station mocking Marcia on the air for her officious behavior as "management": "The boss-lady of this here program just shoved a piece o' paper under my snoot, says I only got three more minutes. That's what I got against workin'! It's all tangled up with that word hurry." He offers to adapt his populist song to include his oppressed female audience at home: "Shucks, I was just gettin' ready to add on a verse about bein' a free woman in the mornin'. I'll bet a whole lot o' you dream about that sometimes with all them breakfast dishes pilin' up in the sink and those cranky husbands t' get off t' work." This speech is intercut with a shot of a wife listening to Rhodes from her kitchen sink and glaring at her husband in the background of the frame. In a subsequent scene, Marcia reads letters from Rhodes's fans while in the background Rhodes is asleep, snoring. Marcia appears in close-up in the foreground of the shot, her face simultaneously critical of his fans' adulation and proud of her discovery—"her tone scornful, her eyes pleased," as the screenplay describes her expression.

While Marcia has the upper hand in the first half of the film during Rhodes's career ascent, she is eventually overpowered by the sheer force of his personality. By juxtaposing shots of Marcia, the female producer, offstage, with shots of her secretly admiring Rhodes when he is on the air ("putting on airs"), the film initiates the process of undermining Marcia's position of power via Rhodes's imposing celebrity. The film underscores the significance of the transitional moment when she changes from an effective businesswoman to a conventional love interest through an evocative deep-focus long shot of the couple in a hotel hallway. Rhodes, who is intent on leaving town following his firing from his television show, has come to say good-bye to Marcia. She appears at her hotel room door in her nightgown and instructs Rhodes to come to her. Their kiss is just out of view of the camera. She has moved halfway back into the room and their embrace is barely visible in the open doorway. This use of off-screen space heightens the tension in the scene, marking it as a "threshold" event: the end of her dominant professional role and the beginning of her subservient romantic role. His sudden new power over her is punctuated by a close-up of his body filling the frame, with her body all but missing from the shot.

Rhodes's bag remains out in the hallway, marking his sexual conquest graphically and publicly for several different groups of characters in the scenes that follow. A young woman, half of a young military couple who are perhaps on their honeymoon, zeroes in on the suitcase (the overt message: there's a man inside that room who doesn't necessarily belong there, otherwise his suitcase would be inside). When Marcia's unrequited suitor, Mel Miller, spots the suitcase the next morning, he also understands its significance and realizes that he has been one-upped by a more sexually appealing, if also more untrustworthy, male. Finally, when the ambitious young advertising man, Joey DePalma, rushes in, demanding entrance to the taboo setting, he ignores Mel's warning: "Wait a minute, sir, I wouldn't barge in if I were you." DePalma replies, "I'm not you! You're not me!" and pushes his way into the room. Once inside, sensing that Marcia is behind the closed bathroom door, DePalma nonchalantly acknowledges the romantic tryst: "I know. Nice girls do it too but they don't like it to get around. It won't get around." Then he quickly moves on to business with Rhodes: "Honey boy, this is more important! I sold your show."[22] It's clear that Marcia, by having been reduced to a tawdry "love interest," has relinquished her erstwhile power in the eyes of all the males present and has been summarily marginalized from the "man's world" of business.

At this point in the narrative, DePalma, the oily public relations man, is able to step into the power vacuum created by Marcia's sleeping with Rhodes, to "sell" himself to Rhodes as his new business representative. Marcia, meanwhile, has exchanged her potent position as a liberal producer backing a big television star for the impotent position of "companion-wife." DePalma tells Rhodes, "They asked me if you had a New York agent. Would you like to meet your New York agent?" To which Rhodes responds, roaring his trademark "all-knowing, I know you're up to no good" laugh: "Haw! Haw! Haw! A bum outa jail in Pickett, Arkansas, and a Memphis office boy!" DePalma casually hands Rhodes a contract that makes the agent a partner of the TV star and says, "Here, sign this. Just a convenience."[23] While

Joey DePalma (Anthony Franciosa) barges into Marcia Jeffries's hotel room and asserts control over Lonesome Rhodes's TV career as she observes helplessly.

Rhodes signs the contract, still singing a self-mocking ditty about being a rambling gambler, from the rear of the deep-focus composition Marcia looks out of the bathroom as the two men celebrate, sensing DePalma is about to send Rhodes down a blind path to potential disaster.[24] The implication is that by adopting the role of companion-wife, Marcia has literally taken a "back seat" in Rhodes's career, with her subsequent influence reduced to that of providing moral guidance and emotional support. She has taken on the role of the "true woman," much like that seen in countless other postwar Hollywood depictions of the female partner to the ex-soldier-turned-mass media executive (Kay Dorrance, Vic Norman's fiancée, in *The Hucksters*, and Betsy Rath, Tom Rath's wife, in *The Man in the Gray Flannel Suit*).

Phase II: Deconstructing the Institution of Marriage

The second phase of Marcia's edification about the tyrannical power of the romantic ideology (even over an "independent" career woman) takes place in Rhodes's penthouse apartment following the resumption of his success-ful career and directly after his marriage proposal to Marcia the previous night. Marcia finishes her breakfast alone in his apartment, watching an episode of his television show. Whereas normally Marcia would watch his show in her capacity as a producer from within the proximate space of the TV studio, now, with a different kind of vested interest in Rhodes as her prospective husband, she watches the show "one step removed." Coinci-dentally, the subject of that day's show is marriage, and Rhodes sings a song that contains the refrain, "An old-fashioned marriage is my kind of marriage. A marriage that never grows old." Three dancing girls in skimpy attire and wedding veils continue to sing back-up as Rhodes starts talk-ing in his down-home way about the value of old-fashioned marriage. He momentarily turns his attention to the men in the audience, advising them (and presumably also himself) to resist the temptation to "trade in your old cars because a flashy new model catches your eye." Marcia listens intently, clearly musing on the ironic contradictions of the scene in relation to her own situation as both Rhodes's fiancée and lover. She is interrupted by a visit from Rhodes's harsh, vindictive ex-wife (played by Kay Medford), who also saw him on television and has come to extort money by threatening to go to the tabloids.

The scene between the two women is juxtaposed with the scene on tele-vision. On the show, Rhodes reads a letter from a married couple from his home state of Arkansas who are considering divorce. In an exaggeratedly sentimental speech, he tells the audience that he flew the couple out to be

on television with him today. The camera cuts to a bony, plain-looking husband and wife who are now on their second honeymoon as a result of
Rhodes's intervention. The glaring contrast between the television scene,
which sentimentalizes ordinary people, and the decidedly unsentimental
portrait of marriage playing out in his penthouse living room between his
frowsy ex-wife and his unsuspecting fiancée functions on the level of content to expose and debunk the artifice of both the televisual and marital
institutions. On a personal level, the duplicity inherent in Rhodes's television address is underscored, as before, through Marcia's mediating presence,
in a series of close-up shots of her troubled face conveying her growing
realization that the man who is grandstanding in front of the camera is
not the same man she fell in love with in the previous scene. On the "plea-
surably instructive" level of reflexivity, the various framing devices—TV
monitors, cameras, mikes, and other behind-the-scenes apparatuses of the
electronic address in previous scenes, as well as the deep-focus portrait of
the intertwined TV and living-room scenes—by baring the structural basis
of the institutional hypocrisies, expands their critique into the realm of the
social and the ideological.[25] Perhaps most significant from a Brechtian reflexivity standpoint, the savage critique in this scene of the electronic media
and their complicity with the gendered politics of romantic love undermines
the idealized romanticism of the previous night when Rhodes proposed to
Marcia from his penthouse balcony in a more classically organized love
scene. As previously extrapolated from Polan, the audience, according to
Brecht, must be able to recognize the conventions of the old traditions in
order to recognize the new intervening forces of social critique. This is precisely how the two scenes function here. The earlier scene depicted Rhodes's
apparently sincere proposal of marriage using a conventional shot-reverse-
shot exchange between the couple, together with lyrical, nondiegetic music
on the soundtrack: trademark formal devices of the classical narrative text.
In contrast, in the later scene, classical content and style are literally, through
the disjunctive sound editing and multiple points of focus, torn to pieces.
Once the former Mrs. Rhodes enters, she brings with her the objectivity
Marcia has momentarily lost. She sees Rhodes on the television and calls
attention to both the artifice of his stage name and the television portrayal
of the institution of marriage. She turns to Marcia and says, "So you're
Lonesome's new tootsie? 'Lonesome,' that's a hot one. Well, I hope you have
better luck keeping him lonesome than I did."[26] And yet, despite Marcia's
new appreciation of the hidden ideological traps inherent in marriage and
romantic love, she continues to pursue Rhodes romantically in subsequent

scenes, unable, at least immediately, to adapt this scene's epiphany to her own life.

Phase III: The Writers' Room

The third phase of Marcia's consciousness-raising occurs when she enters the television writers' room and the final phase ends with her public "outing" of Rhodes on the air. In the intervening scenes, Rhodes expands both his influence as an entertainer and his betrayal of Marcia, marrying a blonde high-school baton-twirler named Betty Lou (played by a teenaged Lee Remick). Marcia enters the writers' room in a sweeping tracking shot that scans the anonymous writers crowded into the small space, reminding her (and us) of the complex human and technical apparatus that lies behind the construction of Rhodes's celebrity. The scene is chaotic and disorienting, depicting a sea of monitors, typewriters, and alternating between deep-focus compositions and discontinuous editing. For instance, the tracking shot pauses to frame Marcia in close-up, trapped among all the merchandising accessories that her professional creation has spawned. To one side of her face a "Lonesome Rhodes" doll hangs from a noose in the upper foreground of the frame. On the other side is a poster of Rhodes that provides a target for a writer playing darts. Marcia and Mel exchange knowing glances and dialogue in a shot-reverse-shot sequence which indicates their mutual complicity with the commodity-driven television industry. Mel spoofs his anonymity as a television writer for a high-priced celebrity: "Welcome to the Black Hole of Calcutta. . . . Here you see the lepers of the great television industry. Men without faces." He punctuates the uneven power relations between the writer and star by turning the head of another staff writer as if he were a puppet, then continues, "They even slide our paychecks under the door so they can pretend we're not here." As usual, Mel's commentary expresses the savvy, cynical writer's relationship to the media as well as his keen awareness that television writing is considered the lowest form of writing. The writers' room, for example, is noticeably plain (in contrast to Rhodes's elegantly appointed offices). Several self-deprecating signs reveal the workers' lowly occupation as television writers: "Classics Adapted While You Wait—We Also Take in Laundry," "Escape from Freedom," "Please Remove the Straw from Your Hair before Leaving This Room."

Marcia demonstrates her own self-mocking disdain about both the constructedness of the mass media in general and of Rhodes's star persona in particular: "But think of the satisfaction of being even a small cog in the great wheel of humanity we know as Lonesome Rhodes." Mel takes this ironic comment as a sign that she is going to leave the side of management and join up with the faceless writers. However, she reminds Mel that she is involved not just professionally with Rhodes, but romantically as well. Her comment stops their ironic banter, momentarily neutralizing the impact of the film's polemic and its critique of the television industry by shifting focus to the typical Hollywood resolution of social conflict via the melodrama formula's reinforcement of the figure of the couple.

Phase IV: Noir Mise-en-Scène and Its Ideological Effects

In phase four, the film further complicates its attack on the media and corporate capitalism by inserting narrative and aesthetic techniques more closely aligned with film noir—namely, the use of heightened emotionality and expressionistic mise-en-scène—to convey Marcia's inner turmoil over her jilted romance with Rhodes. In contrast to the documentary-style, "social realist" technique used in the opening scenes of Marcia documenting real people for her radio program and through much of the first half of the film, the film's second half adopts increasingly expressionistic lighting effects and visual design.[27] This aesthetic shift serves two main purposes, both relating to Marcia: first, the darker, more stylized lighting reflects the darkness of the story arc concerning Marcia's intellectual awakening about the sinister nature of the mass media; second, it emphasizes her increasingly frayed emotional state as the wronged woman. This altered stylistic representation

Mel Miller (Walter Matthau) and Marcia Jeffries in the writers' room in *A Face in the Crowd.*

of Marcia reappears in several key scenes during the latter part of the film but is crystallized in the scene in which Mel returns from a long absence to tell Marcia about his "tell-all" book about Rhodes and is shocked by her changed appearance. The change in the lighting scheme first occurs, however, after Marcia discovers Rhodes has romantically betrayed her by marrying the baton-twirler. Marcia understands the connection between his personal act of betrayal and the larger betrayal of the mass-media audience when she tells him, "Betty Lou is your public all wrapped up with yellow ribbons into one cute little package. She's the logical culmination of the great twentieth-century love affair between Lonesome Rhodes and his mass audience." The scene seamlessly conflates Marcia's role as the social critic/independent producer (in other words, a stand-in for Kazan and Schulberg) with that of the companion-wife. This conflation of the particular and the general, between the individual psychology associated with the classical Hollywood text and the social domain implied in the modernist aesthetic of reflexivity, is a recurring conceit in the film.

In the scene immediately preceding Marcia's decision to betray Rhodes professionally, her intellectual ally, Mel, shows up at the bar where they used to meet together. This scene marks the beginning of the fourth phase of Marcia's evolution from radical social critic to spurned woman, with the expressionistic lighting invoking her internal state of mind. Mel revels in his newfound freedom as a novelist, able to take revenge, indirectly at least, against the "denim demagogue" Rhodes by writing his exposé. Marcia, in

Mel Miller is alarmed at Marcia Jeffries's altered appearance.

contrast, is still under Rhodes's thumb, working for him and presumably still in love with him. She has been drinking alone, her once cheerful clothing, hair, and mien having been replaced by a severe black dress and skullcap that covers her hair and by the shadowy half-lighting that divides her face in two. Mel, alarmed at her transformation, asks whether she is still working for Rhodes. She turns away from him, her psychological oppression conveyed though her body language and her face hidden in darkness. She justifies her decision to stay, using the parlance of the "true woman" ideology: She is serving as his moral watchdog, moderating his overbearing behavior, toning down his public speeches, protecting those he wants to fire. She momentarily departs from this companion-wife ideal to reveal her professional role, citing all the money she is making as one further justification for staying with him. Stylistically, structurally, and now thematically the film interweaves these disparate strands—the modernist and classical Hollywood "realist" texts, the social and individual psychological realms, the independent career-woman and companion-wife images.

Expressionistic mise-en-scène persists as one of the stylistic tools used to reinforce this collapsing of meanings around the figure of Marcia in future scenes as well. In the final, climactic sequence, when Marcia is in the control booth and decides to expose Rhodes to his unwitting public, the half-lighting first splits her face in two, then replaces it with a keylight from above, giving her face an angelic glow. In this way, the aesthetics of the film idealize her role as simultaneous social critic and wronged woman, giving her act of stopping Rhodes an aura of manifest destiny. Her benevolence is sharply contrasted to the shots of Rhodes on the television screen. His duplicity is conveyed by foregrounding television's technology as his representation alternates between his cohesive televised image and his split, duplicitous image filmed against a myriad of cameras, frames, and other distancing devices—combining reflexivity with an expressionistic "doubling motif." Not only is Rhodes's beaming face framed by the television set, another frame is created within that frame as he slides his face in front of and behind a pole on the set. Adding another dimension to the doubling and splitting, the image and sound are also split, alternating between Rhodes's incongruously saccharine facial expression and poisonous words. The multiple framing and doubling devices foreground the layers of artifice behind the constructed television address, which is replicated in the character's psychological "doubling" (as loyal, populist hero and monstrous, untrustworthy lover), thereby reinforcing and foregrounding the highly constructed nature of the film address as well.

Several film noir directors—both politically liberal ones like Huston and Welles, and later-blacklisted ones like Polonsky, Rossen, and Dassin—used expressionist mise-en-scène, among other stylistic and structural elements, to portray the criminal underside of society and to counter the popular press's optimistic portrait of the American way of life. In *A Face in the Crowd,* the expressionistic effects seem traceable more to Kazan's penchant for melodrama (arguably, an element present in much of noir as well),[28] which, through its very familiarity provides, at least theoretically, the necessary grounding for reflexive subversion. Expressionism, by definition, is concerned with the externalization of internal states, and by extension can serve to reveal characterological as well societal flaws, flaws that are typically suppressed in the classical Hollywood text. In *A Face in the Crowd,* expressionistic strategies focus attention both on the fractured moral universe represented by the mass-media celebrity Lonesome Rhodes and on the psychological ambivalence of Marcia Jeffries in her romantic and business relationship with Rhodes. The effect of this stylistic bifurcation is to collapse these two sets of meanings: private and public; personal and professional; cohesive classical narrative world and disruptive, multiple, constructed reality.

The final result of this complex combination of classic and modernist elements is to expose the mediating voices inherent in television's production of meaning as well as the ideological effects of the classical Hollywood text. In this way, the film realizes the oppositional potential of the Brechtian reflexive aesthetic by foregrounding and subsequently subverting classical style and content, most resoundingly in the "secondary story"—Marcia's status as a jilted lover—thereby reinforcing and enriching the larger critique of postwar consumer capitalism.

In the final scene, Mel tells Marcia, "You were taken in. The way we were all taken in. But we get wise to 'em. That's our strength. We get wise to 'em." By having Mel deliver a "feel good" message about the people getting wise to the media, the film's third-level reflexive potential "to please through instruction, to instruct through pleasure," is momentarily derailed. As we saw, Kazan himself later regretted his decision to give the "intellectual" Mel the last word.[29] However, in fact, the film's last words belong to Rhodes, who pathetically rants, unseen, from his penthouse apartment, calling down to the woman who served, simultaneously and schizophrenically, as both his loyal "companion-wife" and his professional "handler." The dramatic effect of the extreme-low-angle shot (from Marcia and Mel's street-level POV) of the imposing steel-and-glass skyscraper and Rhodes's disembodied voice howling into the night is quite chilling. The ideological effect is punctuated by the final image of a large, blinking-neon Coca Cola sign—in all, a fitting conclusion to a film that both reverses the classical Hollywood movie romance and disassembles corporate capitalism's consumerist underpinnings. How much of this challenge to the status quo can be attributed to the aesthetic aspirations and conflicted politics of Elia Kazan (and Budd Schulberg) is difficult to assess. What can be asserted is that in *A Face in the Crowd* a mainstream Hollywood film was made that managed to assault, if not to explode, some of the industry's and the country's most sacred cows.

Whereas Wilder's and to an even greater extent Tashlin's early postmodernist films fail to radically deconstruct the narrative (à la *both* Brecht and Godard), and instead introduce an ironic, so detached, identification with the heroes of their films, in *A Face in the Crowd,* Kazan and Schulberg are pursuing an effective balance of avant-garde and pulp, by simultaneously allowing the audience to adopt a comfortable position of identification with Marcia's romantic angst (as both a populist hero and as a jilted woman) *and* to accept their implication in (and hence the need to critique) the ideological forces at work in postwar capitalism. While Kazan's instincts of commercial self-preservation may have prevented him from replicating the type of countercultural aesthetic adopted by Brecht and Godard, whose films, as indicated at the beginning of this chapter, "like real political encounters, can take you 'by the shoulders and shake you out,'" he aspired to achieve something approximating those filmmakers' level of political engagement and radical opposition to the dominant ideology of Hollywood; however, at this stage of his career, when he had so much to lose and when he had already sacrificed everything to maintain his ties to the Hollywood power elite, Kazan was unwilling to jettison this last vestige of commerciality—the mollifying presence of the melodrama genre, or to forfeit the film's nostalgic portrait of an old-fashioned femininity.

8.

When Talent Becomes Management:
The Making of *Sweet Smell of Success*

If the new modus operandi of the independents was . . .
"packaging"—star-driven alliances between actors, directors,
producers, and writers—HHL, constantly guided by Wasserman,
was showing the industry how. . . . [T]he fact that Lancaster and
Hecht articulated a particular vision of what the movies needed
in this transitional time reinforced their image—and bankability—
as seeming prophets of a new celluloid age.

—KATE BUFORD, *Burt Lancaster: An American Life*

As with *A Face in the Crowd*, the analysis of *Sweet Smell of Success* is divided
into two parts. This chapter examines the careers of Burt Lancaster, Harold
Hecht, James Hill, Clifford Odets, Alexander Mackendrick, and Ernest
Lehman: the primary above-the-line players involved in the making of the
film. The purpose is to clarify the film's methodological underpinnings and
ideological parameters as they relate to an emerging American independent art cinema. Chapter 9 is devoted to a close reading of the film text as
another key exemplar of the ideologically reflexive entertainment-business
film. Made by another prominent talent–turned–independent producer
working with other politically liberal and artistically ambitious filmmakers
in a genre combining the social problem film with the romantic melodrama,
Sweet Smell of Success, like *A Face in the Crowd*, registers the filmmakers'
seemingly incompatible goals: to make a commercially viable film that
simultaneously confronts and challenges the status quo. Ultimately, as with
the Kazan-Schulberg effort, *Sweet Smell of Success* succeeds as an uncommonly bold reflexive entertainment-business film largely due to the uncommon conditions of its production.

Hecht-Hill-Lancaster Productions—The New Hollywood Moguls

Formed in 1948 at the cusp of the New Hollywood, Hecht-Norma Productions (named after Burt Lancaster's former agent, Howard Hecht, and

Lancaster's wife Norma) was among the first and most successful of the independent agent-actor combinations (shortly changing its name to Hecht-Lancaster).[1] Lancaster biographer Kate Buford details the specifics of "the Lancaster deal":

> [UA] gave Lancaster special domestic distribution terms (the cut taken by the distributor, usually off the top, for the middleman costs of brokering the movie from the producer to the exhibitors) of 23 percent rather than the industry standard of 30 or even the 27.5 percent of the Warner contract; foreign distribution remained at 40 percent. Eight months later, on February 7, 1954, UA . . . signed an even bigger deal with what was now renamed Hecht-Lancaster (HL), giving the independent $12 million to produce seven pictures, five of which would star Lancaster).[2]

The tremendous box-office (and later Academy Award–winning) success of *From Here to Eternity* (1953) and the potential for even greater profits on the soon-to-released *Apache* (1954)—both Lancaster-starring films, the latter also an H-L production—gave Lancaster-agent Wasserman considerable leverage to force UA to provide a lucrative "gross percentage" deal on behalf of his rising-star client. In fact, *Apache*, Lancaster's first film made under the terms of a new deal between H-L and UA, already conveys the indie company's conflicting aims: "to make a broader statement on the injustice of racism" rather than simply another profitable star vehicle.[3] After an initial period of freewheeling spending on the part of the H-L team, a disheartened UA demanded greater fiscal responsibility, which it generated through "cross-collateralization" terms added to the initial agreement.[4] Such an arrangement assured UA that losses on one H-L film would impact the production company's share of gross profits on another. The need for such contingency protection proved largely unnecessary, at least during the early years of the UA/H-L partnership, and the studio reaped substantial profits—in large part because of Lancaster's commercially potent star power.

Hecht-Lancaster changed its name to Hecht-Hill-Lancaster Productions (H-H-L) in 1957, the Hill referring to producer James Hill, who became the third partner that year, just prior to the making of *Sweet Smell of Success*.[5] The establishment of talent-controlled production companies (especially when the talent was politically liberal, like Lancaster) gave liberal directors and writers who worked for them hope that they would be given a greater opportunity to express themselves freely than if they were working for the studios.[6] However, screenwriters Clifford Odets and Ernest Lehman, who both worked for H-H-L on *Sweet Smell of Success*, felt in this case that they had merely traded in the old moguls for an even more competitive, arrogant, and pernicious breed of taskmaster. Such disappointments notwithstanding, *Sweet Smell of Success* emerged as one of the 1950s', if not American cinema history's, most vitriolic portraits of the entertainment industry.

Sweet Smell of Success was directed by Briton Alexander Mackendrick, known for several intelligent and distinctive Ealing Studio comedies including *The Man in the White Suit* (1951) and *The Ladykillers* (1955). The final screenplay was written by Odets, based on a short story and first screenplay-draft by Lehman. The film tells the story of sleazy press agent Sidney Falco (Tony Curtis), who does the bidding of the ruthless, powerful gossip columnist J. J. Hunsecker (played by Lancaster, modeled on Walter Winchell). Falco's moral weakness and opportunism extend to his planting drugs and inflammatory Communist literature in the pockets of Steve Dallas, a young, idealistic jazz musician (Martin Milner) and beau to Hunsecker's oppressed sister, Susie Hunsecker (Susan Harrison). Hunsecker, the archvillain of the piece, holds a powerful sway not only over Falco, Susie, and Steve, but over everyone in the New York–based segment of the entertainment industry: actors, singers, dancers, comedians, and musicians, as well as over their various representatives—agents, managers, and press agents (and even a U.S. senator who is having an affair with an attractive would-be-starlet). Falco bows to Hunsecker's pressure and agrees to break up Steve and Susie's relationship in order to satisfy the columnist's borderline incestuous obsession with his sister. Ultimately, the ineffectual press agent is done in by Susie, who finally acts out her rage against her manipulative brother and his "errand boy" by staging a rape scene that implicates Falco. The film ends by intercutting scenes of Falco being hauled away to jail by the corrupt police (also under Hunsecker's control) and Susie walking away from her megalomaniacal brother's control.

H-H-L first hired Lehman to write and direct *Sweet Smell of Success*, though eventually Odets and Mackendrick replaced Lehman as writer and director, respectively. Conflict among the creative team did not cease with the change in personnel. The West Coast "new moguls" Hecht, Hill, and Lancaster, liberal sympathies notwithstanding, were products of the New Hollywood's entrepreneurial business practices; East Coast playwright Odets, like Kazan, was a product of the radical populism of the New York Group Theatre (Lehman, while also a New York liberal, had not been associated with the Group Theater). Mackendrick, meanwhile, was a European-style art director used to having artistic control. This clash of cultures created tensions that can be traced both in the filmmakers' working relationship and in the film itself, which, like *A Face in the Crowd*, juxtaposes classic Hollywood conventions with satirical subject matter and reflexive technique. Also like the Kazan/Schulberg film, the Lehman/Odets/Mackendrick/Lancaster collaboration evinces a prime paradox of postwar Hollywood: namely, that an attempt by liberal filmmakers to salvage their political and artistic integrity through thematic and stylistic experimentation, while somewhat diluted by the commercial and ideological imperatives of the Hollywood system, was also enabled by the uncommon pliancy of that system in a period of tumultuous social and institutional change. What compounds the contradictions for *Sweet Smell of Success* is that whereas the positions of writer, director, and producer were combined in *A Face in the Crowd* among two people (Schulberg and Kazan) sharing the same political and aesthetic persuasions, these positions in *Sweet Smell of Success* were split among four people, or groups of people (Lehman, Odets, Mackendrick, and H-H-L) operating from not diametrically opposed but still conflicting perspectives.

Internal conflicts experienced by individual members of the creative team further complicated the situation. Lancaster, by the mid-1950s a major movie star and one of the most successful of the talent-turned-producers, exemplified the ideological fissures of the postwar Hollywood independent. On the one hand, he personified the "rags-to-riches" American success story. Raised by working-class parents in a tough East Harlem section of Manhattan, he left behind a college sports scholarship to perform as an acrobat in circuses, vaudeville, and nightclubs. When he was "discovered" and cast in a Broadway play and later in a Hollywood film, Kubrick's *The Killers* (1946), he was immediately dubbed a rising star; however, rather than sign a studio contract, in 1948 he became one of the first postwar film actors to become an independent producer. Once he had established a power base via his production company, Lancaster frequently used his fledgling clout to fight against his mainstream star persona, gravitating to unconventional roles (such as that of Alvro Mangiacavallo in *The Rose Tattoo* [1955]). Therefore, one could assume, Lancaster had aligned himself with the liberal creative community against the reactionary postwar forces. Yet, as a big-time star, Lancaster not only retained some of the "class stratification" inherent in the star system, but his position atop the pyramid of power had actually been enhanced through his promotion to management as an independent producer. These conflicting working-class and capitalist sensibilities expressed themselves in Lancaster's work to a striking degree: in his fluctuation between serious and more mainstream fare in general, and in the backstage and on-screen dramas of *Sweet Smell of Success* in particular.

The disparity between 1930s radicalism and 1950s liberal pragmatism was the dilemma Odets confronted when he was brought on to rewrite Lehman's screenplay adaptation of Lehman's novella, *Sweet Smell of Success*. Coming from the Group Theatre, whose uncompromising political and artistic sensibilities placed it in passionate opposition to Hollywood, Odets, like Kazan, John Garfield, and others who made the leap to Tinseltown, bore a sense of treachery for their "defection." Thus Odets was horrified to discover that *Sweet Smell of Success* would be shot in New York where he might run into Harold Clurman, Stella Adler, and other Group Theater loyalists. Clurman had been trying to get Odets to return to the New York theater for years, but Odets argued that the days when liberal theater was a real force in shaping the American social agenda were gone. On the other hand, he remained apologetic to the end for "going Hollywood," decrying a feeling of "weightlessness" that accompanied his material success; he was especially ashamed of having "lowered himself" further by working for network television.[7]

In his 1940 play *The Silent Partner*, Odets dramatized what he saw as the ideological fault lines within the Group Theater by fictionalizing four of the Group's one-time principals: Clurman, Kazan, Lee Strasberg, and himself. Since, by 1940, only Clurman remained of the original core group, Odets saw the source of this disintegration in the abandonment of the Group's principles. In particular, Odets feared that the Group was selling out to Hollywood's merchandising of art. In a 1939 letter to Clurman, Odets challenged Clurman's decision to join forces with Hollywood: "Summer is for plays like *The Silent Partner*, not for movies. Pictures equal fame and money. Yes, but leading to what?" Quoting a character from his play, Odets stated, "If this theatre leads to a people's theatre, to repertory, to a radical critical attitude to the society around it, it's for something. Otherwise it's nothing!"[8] And yet, the fame and fortune of Hollywood had already wooed Odets as well (and would continue to until his death in 1963). His Hollywood work began with the screenplay for *The General Died at Dawn* (1936) and the play on which the film *Golden Boy* (1939) was based. He later wrote and directed *None but the Lonely Heart* (1944), wrote *Deadline at Dawn* (1946, directed by Clurman) and *Humoresque* (1947, starring Garfield), and wrote the plays that were adapted for *Clash by Night* (1952), *The Country*

Girl (1954), and *The Big Knife* (1955). After *Sweet Smell of Success,* he would go on to write and direct *The Story on Page One* (1959) and *Wild in the Country* (1961).

The high art/low art argument made by Odets, somewhat hypocritically, in his letter to Clurman in 1940 was echoed, more narrowly, within Hollywood itself at the time of Hecht-Norma's formation in 1948. The issue in the industry was not whether art was possible in mainstream movies but rather whether long-term studio contracts compromised artistic integrity by providing the security of a steady paycheck. Samuel Goldwyn, who was among the more artistically ambitious of the independent producers, argued, perhaps self-servingly, that this indeed was the case. Using the lure of entrepreneurial independence and profit participation, he tried to convince screenwriters and other "talent-for-hire" that they could reclaim creative autonomy and earn more money by writing screenplays on a speculative basis rather than receiving a guaranteed salary for work completed.[9] (This then-novel distinction between "work-for-hire" and "spec"—the latter being original works written without upfront guarantee of payment—remains very much in place in the new New Hollywood of today.) Goldwyn challenged the screenwriter to take the same risk as the independent producer (and as other writers such as playwrights and novelists), who only makes substantial money if the picture gets made and is a success at the box-office. Goldwyn urged screenwriters to create for themselves "an atmosphere of artistic freedom and an opportunity for even greater financial rewards for the future" by being willing to take the same chance.[10]

Goldwyn's manifesto for artistic freedom found a receptive audience. In *Class Struggle in Hollywood, 1930–1950,* Gerald Horne describes the late 1930s and early 1940s in Hollywood as a period when writers were beginning to object to a system in which "studios own everything a writer creates—plays, novels, radio scripts, poems—if written while he is under contract, and [a] contract for one year calls for three months without pay." Furthermore, Horne notes, writers during this period were becoming more "union-conscious and world-conscious."[11] These "liberated" attitudes among writers and other creative personnel, especially as they began to be realized in the late forties and fifties due to the changing power dynamics of the New Hollywood, led to a backlash among the studio bosses.[12] As we saw in the Zanuck-Mankiewicz relationship, Zanuck balked at the relinquishment of creative control to the newly powerful writer-director. The studio financing and distributing the project should still be able to maintain control over the creative process, he argued, adding that even Kazan, an internationally recognized and award-winning stage director, had been *assigned* his first two scripts, *Pinky* and *Gentleman's Agreement*.[13]

Creative conflicts between studio and talent, as Horne indicates, had long been intertwined with politics. British émigré journalist Cedric Belfrage, when he first arrived in Hollywood in the 1920s, noted that "class stratification was a signal aspect of the film colony, and the ostentatious luxury in which so many lived helped to engender a rampant fear that the great unwashed might seize it all; this fear in turn sparked a desperate desire for an ever-growing apparatus of repression."[14] The leftist movements of the 1930s, although sparked mainly by the Depression, were additionally fueled in Hollywood by the mainly right-wing-headed studio regimes (Warners was an exception), whose antiunion crackdowns, led by MGM's Louis B. Mayer, were notorious.[15] Labor struggle in the entertainment media and the arts, in turn, was not confined to Hollywood. Odets and other leftist artists working in New York in the 1930s published a pamphlet that decried "police terrorism: nightsticks, tear-gas, riot calls and jails," and other indications of authorities reacting to fears that Depression-influenced art was too oriented toward working-class radicalism.[16]

The Hollywood studios adopted various strategies to contain labor radicalism, culminating in exploitative labor contracts that capitalized on the glamour associated with the movies. According to one guild official, "It's nice to be able to call the stars by their first names, but when the reward for 15 years' service is a salary of $40, the privilege was hardly worth it." As World War II approached, and the United States aligned itself with the Soviet Union, a broad array of leftist elements joined forces to fight the fascists. In this environment, the Writer's Guild (WGA) and the less vocal Screen Actors Guild (SAG) formed a unified front in support of the progressivism of Roosevelt.[17]

Throughout the 1930s, the WGA had been among the most politically active of the guilds, engaging in constant battles with producers to preserve their autonomy. Leftist screenwriter John Howard Lawson, the WGA's first elected president in 1932, fellow future–Hollywood Ten member Ring Lardner Jr., and then twenty-one-year-old Budd Schulberg were among progressive writers who joined the Communist Party in 1934, declaring that "the best hope for mankind lay with the Soviets." While certain WGA members objected to the guild's radical contingents dabbling in international politics rather than focusing their efforts on their local union, most writers in the 1930s and 1940s, and the occasional studio mogul such as Jack Warner, agreed that "[t]he country is in chaos. There is revolution in

the air. We need a change." As anti-Communist sentiment grew in the early
1940s, despite the wartime U.S.-Soviet alliance, Warner changed his tune.
Taking his cue from the chair of the California State Senate's Un-American
Activities Committee, Jack Tenney (himself a former leftist), who declared
that the Writer's Guild was being "promoted and controlled by the Communists," Warner now also denounced the WGA's leaders as "communists,
radical bastards and soap-box sons of bitches."[18] Despite the more conservative national climate, the social activist mood persisted, culminating in the
movie industry strikes of 1945. The FBI and a variety of government agencies monitored the leftist trends and, along with conservative studio heads
and right-wing ad hoc organizations such as the Motion Picture Alliance,
initiated an aggressive campaign to extirpate leftist elements via the 1947
and 1951 (through 1954) HUAC hearings, and, of course, the blacklist.[19]

As for the effect of the reactionary postwar climate on Odets, we have
already seen how his cooperative HUAC testimony in 1952, albeit more
apologetic than Kazan's, had a far more detrimental psychological impact.
As Kazan stated,

[Odets] gave away his identity when he did that; he was no longer the
hero-rebel, the fearless prophet of a new world. It choked off the voice
he'd had. The ringing tone, the burst of passion, were no longer there. . . .
I believe he should have remained defiant, maintained his treasured identity, and survived as his best self. He was to die before he died.[20]

Arthur Miller, who had defied HUAC and written the anti-McCarthy
allegory *The Crucible,* and who met with Odets in Hollywood in 1958,
believed that *Sweet Smell of Success* served his fellow playwright as a means
of assuaging the guilt associated with his perceived craven capitulation
to HUAC. As Kazan observed in recounting the Miller-Odets meeting:
"For Odets, *Sweet Smell of Success* was a way of striking back at this public
humiliation."[21]

Another player in the *Sweet Smell of Success* backstage drama, for whom
the film represented a chance to vindicate his HUAC role, was agent-turned-
producer Harold Hecht. Hecht had been a Communist and head of the
Federal Theater Project from 1937 to 1939. Later, after becoming a Hollywood agent and a partner in Hecht-Norma and Hecht-Lancaster, he
earned the nickname "the Mole" for naming names before HUAC.[22] Hecht's
testimony also resulted in the sacrifice of the company's primary development executive, Roland Kibbee, who was supposedly next in line for a

partnership with Hecht-Lancaster until named by Hecht.[23] Deeply cynical about his fall from grace in those politically troubled times, Hecht frequently answered the phone: "Mole speaking."[24] James Hill, who became Kibbee's replacement (and would later marry Rita Hayworth), had almost no experience in Hollywood when he met Lancaster. He was dubbed "Burt Lancaster's boy" and was regarded as under the thumb of the powerful star.[25] In many respects Hill's relationship to Lancaster replicated the relationship between Falco and Hunsecker in *Sweet Smell of Success*. Hill's primary function was to keep peace between Lancaster and Hecht, who rarely got along. Rumors circulated that the burly Lancaster not only verbally abused his former agent but once threatened to hurl the much smaller man out the window. Like Falco, Lancaster's younger, untried protégé, Hill, loved engaging in Hollywood-style power mongering, such as when he pretended to be drunk to extract information from reporter Ezra Goodman and photographer Sam Shaw. According to Goodman, "We [Goodman and Shaw] came to the conclusion that he [Hill] was not drunk at all and that, under the pretense of being high, had been trying to provoke from us any lowdown, classified information we had about Hollywood and H-H-L that might prove tactically helpful to him in his business operations."[26]

Ernest Lehman and the Literary Origins of *Sweet Smell of Success*

Before writing the novella *Sweet Smell of Success*, Lehman had spent four years in Manhattan as a Broadway press agent, both dependent on and fearful of New York's powerful gossip columnists (including Walter Winchell). After writing and publishing the novella in *Cosmopolitan* in 1952 (under the name *Tell Me about It Tomorrow*, since editor Herbert R. Mayes would not use a title with the word "smell" in it), Lehman feared retaliation that never came. Nonetheless, Lehman was convinced that no Hollywood studio would dare approach the material, even though he had carefully masked references to the real people in what were ultimately thinly veiled fictional characters. But the studios were interested, specifically Paramount, as was the independent company Hecht-Lancaster. When they first approached Lehman in 1952, H-L had little clout, but by 1956, after having won multiple Oscars for *Marty*, Lehman decided to sign with the up-and-comers.[27]

The culture clash between the New York artistic community and the Hollywood movie crowd, alluded to in regard to Odets, was experienced in spades by Lehman. At his first meeting with Lancaster, for example, the actor-producer allegedly entered the room zipping his fly and grinning triumphantly because the latest woman he had sexually assaulted had decided to settle out of court. Later meetings were devoted to procuring women for the three producers. The happily married Lehman was ashamed to be associated with the raunchiness: "There we were, scratching around for women. They were the most corrupt group. I really sank into the depths when I decided to work with them."[28] Lehman, who initially wrote *Sweet Smell of Success* to expiate his guilt over having worked in the seamy world of PR and gossip, ironically felt that he had recapitulated to a similarly distasteful milieu by joining forces with H-H-L.

Lancaster and his partners, like many of the nouveau riche of the New Hollywood, were big spenders, filling their offices and apartments with expensive antiques and art work, and they were notorious womanizers. Upon acquiring the former William Morris offices in Beverly Hills for $750,000, they turned the space into a showplace. "It was paved with acres of white broadloom and furnished in the quasi-oriental style known as L. B. Ming and Metro-Goldwyn-Medici," according to *Life* magazine journalist Shana Alexander.[29] Lancaster, in particular, didn't limit his opulent displays of power, wealth, and fame to conducting business. He also used these assets, along with his movie star looks, to attract and frequently inflict violence on women. In 1955 the fan magazine *Confidential* published an article on Lancaster's propensity for sexually tinged violence, recounting one incident in which he had ripped the sleeve off an expensive dress worn by actress Francesca de Scaffa (former mistress to the Shah of Iran) when she met him about a role in a movie. As *Confidential* writer Charles Wright put it, "Burt's tendency toward clobbering cuties is rapidly becoming no secret at all among dames in the know in Hollywood."[30] Wright had earlier maintained that "international playgirl" Zina Rachevsky had joined Lancaster in his bungalow at the Palm Springs Racquet Club in 1951, and when he got physically abusive, she "bit the actor in an undisclosed body part, resulting in his hospitalization."[31] There appears to be a thin line between the physical hostility Lancaster unleashed against women in real life and the verbal and emotional hostility toward them his character J. J. Hunsecker displays in *Sweet Smell of Success*.

According to various accounts, violence was always just below the surface on the *Sweet Smell of Success* set. The eighteen-year-old actress Susan Harrison, who played Susie Hunsecker, was apparently already emotionally unstable when hired for the film and became overwhelmed by the oppressive mood created by the various warring factions. Many suggested that the fragility she exhibited on film was close to her real state of mind on the volatile set. Harrison once admitted to director Alexander Mackendrick "a fascination with high buildings—she had an impulse to throw herself off."[32] Mackendrick is reputed to have capitalized on her moodiness and suicidal tendencies in directing her on the final scene when she threatens to hurl herself out of the top floor of her brother's penthouse apartment.

The male violence and competitiveness, the womanizing, and the casting of a fragile, unstable actress to play Susie Hunsecker were symptomatic of the contradictory constructions of gender and sexuality in general in the fifties. On the one hand, women were frequently represented in the popular media as docile and demure in the Victorian tradition of "true womanhood." Yet the lighthearted tone of the fan magazines toward the hostility male stars exhibited toward women reveals both the hypocrisy and darker truths about the ramifications of gender stereotypes. Thus, the representations of women as alternately victimized and victimizers in *Sweet Smell of Success* speaks to a situation in which 1950s women were revered and resented in equal measure.[33]

The parallels between the on-screen and off-screen worlds of *Sweet Smell of Success* are not limited to violence against women. More than mere grist for the gossip mill, the film's backstage dynamics reflect the actual climate of angst and paranoia that prevailed both on and off screen. *Vanity Fair*'s 1999 interviews with several of the major players, including Lehman, Hill, and Curtis, reiterate these themes, even with forty-two years' distance. Despite his reservations about his bosses' base morals, Lehman realized that these men were nonetheless receptive to his social critique of the media's abuse of power. Furthermore, Lehman was impressed that they were willing to take on this Winchell-bashing exposé in an era when many in Hollywood were fearful of crossing the powerful columnist. Therefore, Lehman resigned himself to colluding with the enemy, convinced that H-H-L were probably the best—perhaps the only—Hollywood producers willing and able to bring his vision to the screen. After all, they were living the corrupt world he was depicting in the actions of the morally bankrupt Sidney Falco and J. J. Hunsecker.[34]

As for Lehman's suitability for H-H-L, Lehman's former boss, *Hollywood Reporter* columnist Irving Hoffman, allowed Lehman to write his own plug as the ideal screenwriter for the project in Hoffman's column:

> The world I want to see on film is the world of Toots Shor's at lunch-hour, Sardi's at 11 of an opening night, Lindy's at 2 o'clock of any morning . . . the world of Winchell and Wilson, Sullivan and Sobol . . . of columnists on the prowl for items, press agents on the prowl for columnists. . . .

Now I may be wrong (and I don't think I am), but just off his past performances I would say that Ernest Lehman is the guy who can write this kind
of picture.[35]

Self-promotion notwithstanding, shortly after he was hired as writer-
director of *Sweet Smell of Success*, Lehman was fired as director. The official
story was that UA fired him because they had just been burned by Lancaster's previous failed venture as a first-time director on *The Kentuckian*.
More likely, however, H-H-L simply blamed the studio rather than admit,
as Hill did years later, that the powerful producers never intended to let
Lehman direct. They had offered him the world to assure they got the rights
to his original story. In fact, once Lancaster agreed to play Hunsecker, the
project became increasingly important to the company. Lehman, still under
contract to do rewrites, buckled under the mounting pressure from the creative team at H-H-L and began developing a severe ulcer. Mackendrick
was hired as the director and, while Lehman was recuperating from his
stomach ailment, Mackendrick proposed that Odets come on board to do
additional rewrites. When Lehman finally returned to Los Angeles, he
found out that he had been replaced as both director and writer on the project and had been "demoted" to one of the producers. When he told the
aggravating news to his agent, Lew Wasserman, the super-agent informed
Lehman that he already knew. Indeed, Wasserman, as it turns out, had
played a key role in determining the creative team behind *Sweet Smell of
Success*, including the decision to fire Lehman, one of Wasserman's less valuable clients (this in spite of the fact that Lehman had already written such
acclaimed screenplays as *Executive Suite* [1954], *Sabrina* [1954], *Somebody
Up There Likes Me*, and *The King and I* [both 1956]). "That was the trouble with MCA in those days," Lehman later observed, "because Wasserman was also their [H-H-L's] agent! So they made me a producer instead
of a director."[36]

Hollywood, then as now, is accused of developing material to death, of
depleting it of originality by hiring multiple writers and subjecting them
to a multitude of executives' story notes. However, studio interference was
not an issue with *Sweet Smell of Success*, distributed by the hands-off, artist-
friendly United Artists.[37] Instead, most of the fighting for control took place
among the creative team of writer, producer, star, and director, who all
worked closely to shape the project into a finely tuned and structurally taut
film. According to accounts, there was no end of heated arguments. Elmer
Bernstein, composer on the project, creates a vivid portrait of the set:

I wasn't privy to everything, but the combination of people on that movie—Harold Hecht, Burt Lancaster, Cliff Odets who was crazy—good crazy, but crazy—it was a snake pit. There was a cultural distance between Burt and Sandy [Mackendrick]. It was like Sandy's heart beat at a different rate. Burt was really scary. He was a dangerous guy. He had a short fuse. He was very physical. You thought you might get punched out. I mean, I was in the projection room once and I saw Burt chasing someone around. Sandy was a lovely man. It was a miracle that he finished that film. In fact, I think that film is what finished Sandy—as a film-maker.[38]

The production company was forced to begin shooting without a finished screenplay because of the demands of stardom (Curtis and Lancaster had other film commitments after they completed *Sweet Smell of Success*), and the expense and complications attending location shooting in New York. An unfinished script exacerbated the frenzied pace and heightened tensions on the set. Originally hired only to polish the dialogue, Odets did a substantial rewrite of Lehman's original adaptation of his own novella. According to Mackendrick, "What Clifford did, in effect, was dismantle the structure of every single sequence in order to rebuild situations and relationships that were much more complex, had much greater tension and more dramatic energy."[39] Despite his ambitious goals, Odets's expansive vision of the characters was compromised by the financial constraints facing the company. Furthermore, Odets's negative experience of working for Lancaster was heightened by the star-producer's unpredictable and, according to Odets, "downright schizophrenic" nature. Odets provided *Life* writer Alexander a sardonic and detailed list of Lancaster's autocratic personality traits, which included "Enigmatic Burt," "Cocksure Burt," and "Wild Man Burt," just to name a few.[40]

The Changing Role of the Hollywood Press Corps

To better understand the social context from which Lehman's novella's and the film's critique of the entertainment industry publicity machine emerged, it is useful to compare reports of industry insiders from the period in which *Sweet Smell of Success* was made with the film itself. In his 1961 book *The Fifty-Year Decline and Fall of Hollywood*, former journalist Ezra Goodman chronicles the relationship between talent and press agent, which, while never much to write home about, had deteriorated further in the New Hollywood:

Today [in 1961] one is allowed to express oneself with relative impunity even about Ike [Eisenhower] and Nikita [Khrushchev] and to intimate that they might have just a few human failings and foibles. But if one so much as presumes to utter a single word against Jayne Mansfield and Tuesday Weld—or George Stevens and William Wyler—one is given the bum's rush from all corners of the ball park. Perhaps the motion picture, as the last, desperately held myth of our times, with its mythological gods and goddesses, the movie stars, is considered, in this sense, to be above criticism, somewhat like Mother Love (although that has come in for plenty of harsh words in recent years, and the word "mother" has taken on overtones that are not indicated in the unabridged dictionary).[41]

Such friction between talent and their "handlers"—the press agents, gossip columnists, agents, and managers who act as gatekeepers of the talents' success—is a major subtext in *Sweet Smell of Success* as well. Indeed, discontent on the part of talent with industry middlemen, and vice versa, permeates the film, as each side trades insults and jockeys for position.[42] For instance, when Steve, the jazz musician, conveys his personal distaste for press agent Falco's occupation and manner, Falco reminds him that they are bound together in a business relationship as client and publicist: "Let me apologize for getting you that press spread. It's been an honor to serve you gratis."[43] Another client reminds Falco of the press agent's subservient role as the talent's employee, working for a fee: "Take your hand out of my pocket, thief!"—followed by: "It's a dirty job, but I pay clean money for it, don't I?"[44]

Exacerbating the already rocky relations between talent and press agent in postwar Hollywood was the fact that despite the dramatic changes in entertainment journalism that had occurred—notably the separation of the press agents, gossip columnists, and fan magazines from the old studio publicity departments that used to control them—the fascination with movie stars' on- and off-screen exploits persisted. Yet paradoxically, as I have argued, the stars' iconic status derived largely from Old Hollywood publicity techniques that were often compromised once the stars "moved up" by joining forces with management and becoming heads of their own companies, or "moved down" by appearing on television. These contradictory pressures—to preserve the movie stars' iconic status while also capitalizing on their fame in competing industries like television—added to the burdens on the press agent.

Further pressure resulted from press agents' dual responsibilities: to their star clients and to the gossip columnists. Celebrities hired press agents to keep their names in front of the public and the industry. But press agents also performed an invaluable role for the columnists by providing juicy news items, acquired by frequenting the same nightclubs and restaurants as the celebrities. As Goodman wryly notes: "[It] is not surprising that most of the journalists do not write their copy alone. . . . One long-time syndicated columnist, who almost never writes his own copy, was heard upbraiding a press agent about a story that the publicist had submitted to him: 'This is not up to my usual standard.'"[45]

A similar complaint is uttered in *Sweet Smell of Success* by Falco, when he insinuates that he essentially does columnist Hunsecker's job for him by feeding him material.[46] Making matters worse for the press agent, his dual role entailed a double bind, for the agents' two tasks were frequently diametrically opposed: keeping their star clients' noses clean and showing them in the best possible light, on the one hand; digging up dirt on the other. Confronted by these internal and external pressures, press agents, as a group, according to Goodman, became "cynical, tired, and corrupt so that even the most elementary facts about the movies rarely get into print. Hollywood press coverage is compounded almost entirely of apathy, ignorance, imagination, wishful thinking, press agentry and soft soaping.[47]

Goodman recognized that the plight of the press agent was endemic to the Hollywood system, but some significant changes had occurred in the postwar publicity regime. The demise of the studio-run fan magazines went hand in hand with the decline of the studio system that had controlled all releases about their stars. Thus, while stars remained off-limits to negative reporting as late as 1960, as Goodman noted above, once the fan magazines became independent, they were no longer beholden to the studios and hence no longer expected to protect the stars with fanciful cover-up stories (although they were still part of an industry that fed off success; and they were still dependent on stars). Ultimately, as gossip columnists and their fan magazine counterparts became less accountable to studios and more accountable to their own bottom line, media "reporting" became the province of independent scandal-sheet journalism, which eventually evolved into today's *Star* and *National Enquirer*.

The upshot of all these developments, paradoxically, was the demise of the all-powerful, much-feared gossip columnist, such as the legendary Louella Parsons, Sheila Graham, Hedda Hopper, and Walter Winchell (the latter providing the model for the scurrilous J. J. Hunsecker). Goodman relates how Parson's power, for example, had weakened, though not dissipated completely, by 1960:

Since the death of her boss, William Randolph Hearst, and the advent of powerful television publicity outlets, Parson's stranglehold on Hollywood has loosened somewhat. But she still has her lifelong contacts with the movie tycoons. . . . Testifying to her power over "old Hollywood," Walter Winchell once suggested it ought to be retagged "Lollywood."[48]

Stars attended testimonial dinners to Parsons in 1960 for fear of reprisal in her column. Eddie Cantor said: "I am here for the same reason everyone else is: they were afraid not to come."[49] Of course this "lighthearted" blackmail had taken a more sinister turn in the late 1940s and 1950s, when Winchell was using his column, and his radio and television shows, to smear suspected leftists.

Television proved the death knell of the once-dreaded gossip columnist, as the new medium by the late 1950s came to dominate the star-building activities once controlled by the old-style journalists.[50] For instance, in 1959 Ed Sullivan, then both a syndicated columnist and popular television variety-show host, fought with competitor Hedda Hopper over the issue of paying television guest stars from the film industry. Sullivan charged that Hopper was "using plugs" in her column "to get performers free" on her short-lived television show. He challenged what he called "her reign of terror out there in Hollywood," adding, "Parsons and Hopper [and presumably Winchell] are through and they don't know it. They think they are still important, but they are nowhere what they once were. It's just the ridiculous press agents who cater to them and keep the myth alive."[51]

It is this turbulent transitional moment in the culture industry that is being explored in *Sweet Smell of Success*—a moment when the media publicity machine was being overhauled and the power of gossip-mongers like Parsons, Hopper, and Winchell to make or break a career through a single publicity item was waning. But as we have seen with other self-referential entertainment-business films, *Sweet Smell of Success*'s aim went beyond a narrow antimedia diatribe. Through the character of Steve, the high-minded artist and jazz musician, for example, the film provided a liberal mouthpiece to articulate a critique not only of the corrupt publicity machine but of the reactionary forces in the industry, and American society, it represented.

The Hecht-Lancaster Style: Getting It Both Ways

Hecht-Lancaster's success in 1956 can be measured by its new, lucrative arrangement with United Artists. On April 13, 1956, UA guaranteed the production company $40 million for eighteen pictures over a four-year period, making their deal, according to *Variety,* "the biggest indie production-distribution deal in film history." In the mid-1950s, the company was profusely praised in the *Hollywood Reporter* for imitating (and often outdoing) studio publicity techniques in support of UA's releases, culminating in the *Trapeze* campaign in 1956.[52] For *Trapeze,* UA committed to a $2 million ad campaign when the typical advertising and promotion for major films was between $300,000 and $400,000. *Trapeze* earned $4.1 million in its first week, making it the largest seven-day gross in the history of the film industry to that time. It eventually earned between $10 and $11 million in its initial release and was the company's most profitable film. The premiere in Los Angeles for *Trapeze* included a two-ring circus on the sidewalk and a midnight party at the former Warners studio lot with the stars and director in attendance. When the following week, Lancaster and Curtis appeared on the *Ed Sullivan Show,* one reviewer effused, "Lancaster and Curtis, gag after gag, line after line, built up that tremendous TV audience's desire to see *Trapeze.*"[53]

The producers had proved equally adept at nurturing the quite different *Marty* (1955), a small-scale film based on a highly touted TV drama written by Paddy Chayefsky, which UA initially treated like a limited "art film" release in selected theaters rather than providing a broad release. Encouraged by *Marty's* strong reviews, the producers pushed for an aggressive marketing campaign for the modest-scale film. Despite its low budget of $350,000, the film grossed $6 million, its success attributable in large part to Hecht-Lancaster's encouraging UA to spend $400,000 on promotion and advertising (with $75,000 going to the Oscar campaign alone).[54] The pre-Oscar hype and the fact that the film won the Best Picture, Best Director (Delbert Mann), Best Actor (Ernest Borgnine), and Best Screenplay (Chayefsky) awards for 1955 didn't hurt.

Hecht-Lancaster's ecumenical brand of success—mixing the commercial with the arty and scoring on both fronts—played particularly well in the conservative 1950s. Just how well can be seen by the contrasting trade press responses to star-producer Lancaster and the new breed of more overtly rebellious stars like Marlon Brando, James Dean, and Marilyn Monroe. While celebrating Lancaster and company's showmanship and marketing strategies, the *Hollywood Reporter's* Wilkerson chastised (by implication, rather than actually naming them) the latter group of actors who were raking in big salaries and participating in profits but who refused to cooperate in the marketing of their pictures. Brando and Dean, for instance, were notorious for either not showing up to scheduled press interviews or purposely sabotaging the interviews by refusing to answer questions. Wilkerson blamed such behavior for contributing to the downward spiral of the motion-picture industry in the late fifties. "The men and women doing this type of thinking should extend their brainwork a bit and delve into the plight of the movie business, which means their own projected drop in high salaries and the possibility of less work at ANY salary, in the not too distant future."[55] Monroe, especially, was seen as exploiting the studios for her own short-term benefit rather than the long-term health of the industry. While one can easily counter Wilkerson's complaints by pointing to the demonstrable success of many of these "ungrateful" stars' films which, if anything, helped the struggling film industry survive, more important for our purposes is how the stars' "acting out" their ambivalence with the New Hollywood revealed the ideological fissures inherent in the new system.

In thrall to the lucrative benefits of his independent star-producer status and not inclined to jeopardize them, Lancaster recognized the value in being a "team player" with the studios—and the feeling was mutual.[56] Independent production companies like Hecht-Lancaster were increasingly important to the survival of the studios in the postwar era, given the prolonged slump in audience demand for movies yet the continued need to fill distribution pipelines.[57] Thus, as with MCA, Hecht-Lancaster was praised for its "gray-flannel" business approach which prioritized the bottom line, whereas independent talent that received high salaries and a share of studio profits but did not experience the risks taken by producers were criticized for their selfish indifference to the survival of the industry.

In his own acting career, Lancaster literally played it both ways, working on his own company's films but also signing on with independent producer Hal Wallis at Paramount in order to gain added security and guaranteed income.[58] In fact, in the early days of his production company, Lancaster was obliged to alternate between projects for his own company and ones for Wallis. In experiencing the actor-producer relationship from both sides, Lancaster came to appreciate the benefits of the Hecht-Lancaster approach, given that his work for Wallis ended up costing him $50,000 of his $100,000-per-picture salary by 1954.[59] However, this insight into the inequities of the New Hollywood system didn't prevent Lancaster from replicating them in his own company's talent arrangements, wherein he eagerly followed Wallis's lead by signing actors under contract to create additional revenue streams. Lancaster and company's decision to cast Ernest Borgnine, a relative unknown at the time, in *Marty*, instead of Rod Steiger, the Emmy-winning star of the television version, was also driven more by marketplace than artistic considerations. By putting the not-yet-a-star Borgnine under contract with their production company, Hecht-Lancaster could start loaning the actor out to other studios for a fee. Martin Milner, who played the jazz musician in *Sweet Smell of Success,* and Susan Harrison, who played Hunsecker's sister, were also under contract with Lancaster's company.[60]

Lancaster's brand of "independence," therefore, was that of an "organization man" whose profit-maximizing mentality was supremely compatible with the interests of the New Hollywood. The rise of independent producers in the context of the postwar era thus must be expanded beyond the Wilder, Mankiewicz, and Kazan/Schulberg variety to include the Hecht-Lancaster type of team player whose interests were largely identical to that of the (old and new) studio executives. This latter type was less concerned with granting writer-directors unprecedented freedom to express their personal vision—a trend that would take place on the margins of the dominant cinema with filmmakers like John Cassavetes and Shirley Clarke in the late 1950s and 1960s. Instead, Lancaster's company, Hal Wallis, and other successful independent producers who prospered in the 1950s learned to balance their liberal views and desire for artistic freedom with the cutthroat commercial instincts of the studios upon which they relied (as independent producers still do today) for the financing, marketing, and distribution of their films.

Independent producers who came to power in the 1950s were therefore not necessarily more benevolent than their studio counterparts. The "indies" may have offered a degree of artistic freedom unavailable under the Old Hollywood regime, but this was rarely a wholly altruistic gesture on behalf of artists who had been oppressed by the studios, but rather, part of an overall business strategy. Borgnine, for example, sued Hecht-Lancaster in 1956, claiming that he had indeed signed a "loan-out" clause, "but nothing is said [in the contract] about them keeping the salary I earn, and they have." He sued the company again a few months later, claiming that he was entitled to 2.5 percent of the profits for *Marty,* which in their accounting reports was understated by $250,000.[61] Perhaps harboring residual anger over this perceived mistreatment, Borgnine later claimed that Lancaster and company had only made *Marty* for tax purposes (rather than for its artistic merit) and planned to shelve it halfway through production until their accountant insisted it must have a theatrical release before they could earn tax credits.[62] Borgnine's actions convey the contradictory attitudes many members of the above-the-line talent held toward the "new moguls."

By 1957 Hecht-Hill-Lancaster had grown into one of Hollywood's biggest independents, with expensive offices in Beverly Hills and New York. The company "hired stringers abroad, financed Broadway plays, founded a music publishing company, put actors and directors under contract, and even created television pilots for *The Bachelor Party* and *Vera Cruz*."[63] All this activity required a large staff and huge overhead. Ultimately, the company overreached, purchasing more properties than it could manage to produce (by the end, H-H-L had an inventory of $2.5 million worth of unproduced scripts). This was a far cry from the company's original modus operandi in 1948, when Hecht and Lancaster personally nurtured each project and survived in offices provided by whatever studio they were affiliated with on a particular project. Several box-office failures, most notably that of *Sweet Smell of Success*, led to a severe cash crunch at the company. Despite having seriously overextended themselves, many argue that the principles failed to capitalize on their potential when, in 1958, a floundering MGM offered to buy up the company.[64] Instead, the producers opted to stay independent and continued their pattern of overspending by developing high-profile properties. UA began questioning whether to continue subsidizing the company's future projects after adding up the company's combined loss of $2.6 million on *Sweet Smell of Success*, *Bachelor Party* (also 1957), and *Run Silent, Run Deep* (1958). While denying rumors that they were in trouble, the principles began scaling back their operations and dismantled their overseas offices. In 1959, the *New York World-Telegram* delivered a flattering "obituary" for the faltering company, calling it: "the biggest of the independents . . . [that] triggered the new era of film making, with stars heading companies that rivaled the major studios."[65]

Following the company's collapse in 1959, some industry commentators began questioning H-H-L's previously lauded strategy of balancing seemingly surefire box-office hits with "art-house" films—a strategy apparently prompted by the singular success of *Marty*, which deviated from the company's earlier efforts to capitalize on Lancaster's physical prowess and movie-star persona. After *Marty*, according to Vincent Canby of the *New York Times*, "For each mass-market entertainment film he [Lancaster] made, there was always one comparatively risky 'artistic venture.'" Indeed, such a ping-pong approach did characterize the company's post-*Marty* output: along with every *Trapeze*, *Vera Cruz*, and the submarine movie *Run Silent, Run Deep* came a black-and-white film with a darker theme and starring roles for character actors with average looks like Ernest Borgnine, or roles that undermined Lancaster's movie-star looks like those in *The Rose Tattoo*, *Come Back, Little Sheba*, and, most prominently, *Sweet Smell of Success*.[66]

In his history of United Artists, Tino Balio echoes Canby's caveat, describing H-H-L's efforts to replicate the success of *Marty* with *The Rabbit Trap* (1959), *Take a Giant Step* (1959), and *Cry Tough* (1959) as ill-founded, given that all three went over budget and lost money. Balio concludes that there was no market for these types of films and calls *Marty* a "fluke."[67] While Balio's conclusion may be accurate if relying exclusively on a simple business formula of profits and losses, it fails to account for another less manifest dynamic at stake in this period. Another reason for an independent like H-H-L to pursue more difficult projects was to differentiate its product from mainstream studio fare, which meant occasionally venturing into untried waters and flexing its creative muscles, and also meant currying the favor of talented (and successful) filmmakers. Just as longtime studio chief Zanuck was forced to adjust his management style to accommodate, however grudgingly, Mankiewicz's and Kazan's desire for creative autonomy, the new breed of independent producer also had to cater to talented writer-directors' ambitions for more challenging cinematic fare. Talent, after all, had become the primary leverage for deal-making in the New Hollywood's shift from "producer-unit" to "package-unit" production.

A Matter of Style? The Added "Cost" of Achieving an Ideologically Reflexive Aesthetic

Besides H-H-L's purchase of controversial source material in Lehman's anti-entertainment-business novella, and in enlisting the services of tarnished radical screenwriter Odets and foreign director Mackendrick, the company took some risk and spared no expense in hiring acclaimed, but "arty," cinematographer James Wong Howe to shoot *Sweet Smell of Success*. Howe ended up using striking chiaroscuro black-and-white images of New York, actually shot at night rather than the more typical and cost-efficient day-for-night, to evoke the seedy underside of Broadway's nightlife.[68] To emphasize the connection between characters and the environment, and with one another, he also employed extensive and highly evocative deep-focus cinematography.

Critics generally credit cinematographer Gregg Toland with pioneering the innovative use of deep-focus on Welles's *Citizen Kane* (1941). However, in "Technological and Aesthetic Influences on the Development of Deep-Focus Cinematography in the United States," Patrick Ogle notes that Howe had used deep-focus technique ten years earlier in William K. Howard's *Transatlantic*. Howe claims that his use of deep-focus was influenced by the realistic work of photojournalists in popular magazines such as *Life* and

Look.[69] Ogle also cites the influence of the various technological and aesthetic developments of the German expressionist filmmakers who immigrated en masse to Hollywood in the 1920s and 1930s. Strikingly absent from Ogle's account, however, is any analysis of the broader industrial context in which these aesthetic strategies emerged.

For instance, Toland was granted far greater time and expense to experiment on *Citizen Kane* in large part because Welles's reputation for experimentation in theater and radio made him eager to explore innovative filmmaking techniques on this, his first feature film.[70] Similarly, Howe's hiring on *Sweet Smell of Success* enhanced H-H-L's reputation as "creative producers" by seeming to promote artistic experimentation. By the time he joined the creative team on *Sweet Smell of Success,* Howe's artistic gifts were not only recognized among his peers, but he was also one of the few cinematographers whose name was recognized by the public. Nicknamed "Low Key Howe" partly for his Asian ethnicity but mostly for his low-key cinematography strongly associated with his 1940s Warner Bros. films (e.g., *Kings Row, Yankee Doodle Dandy*),[71] Howe had shot two previous Lancaster company films, *The Rose Tattoo,* for which he won an Academy Award, and *Come Back, Little Sheba.* While known for his stylistic experimentation, Howe's two decades of work perfecting his techniques had helped make many of them accepted conventions in the classical American cinema. Therefore, by hiring the bold but time-tested Howe, the producers were once again hedging their bets: promoting artistic integrity, within the bounds of commercial viability.

While Howe by himself may have posed no serious threat to the art/commerce balance, the "creative package" in its entirety may have given H-H-L more than they bargained for. The jaundiced view of the entertainment business that Lehman and Odets brought to the mix has already been touched upon. What Mackendrick seems to have contributed is an extreme stylistic self-consciousness, reinforced through Howe's modernist mise-en-scène, that expands the film's formal reflexivity—much as Kazan did in *A Face in the Crowd*—to *mise-en-abyme* proportions.[72] The climactic TV-studio scene described in the chapter on *A Face in the Crowd* is emblematic of this heightened self-consciousness. The use of deep-focus long take and subverted point-of-view editing in two other scenes from both films are further examples.

At key points in both films, as the film's protagonists, Falco and Marcia, stand on a precipice between selfish and selfless behavior, their moral ambivalence is reflected in the deep-focus compositions that complicate the static, clearly delineated power relations evoked by the classic shot-reverse-shot format, thereby "democratizing" meaning. The deep-focus compositions "collectivize" the situations by implicating the viewer in these moments of deliberation: Will Falco plant the Communist literature in Steve's coat per Hunsecker's request or will he have a change of heart? A more conventional shot-reverse-shot configuration would have conveyed the character's narrowed options conforming to the preexisting logic of the narrative. Instead, the intercutting of complex deep-focus compositions reinforces the impression that the viewer is morally complicit in the larger social themes on display, such as in the case of the greedy Falco, the ruthlessly competitive capitalist system in which he and his ilk operate.

Mackendrick's (and Howe's) intricately choreographed deep-focus shooting was facilitated, from a practical standpoint, by having movable parts on the interior sets to allow for more fluid camera movement. Lancaster occasionally objected to the large costs incurred by such experimentation, such as when "a scene that would run only six minutes on the screen" took "thirty-five camera moves on a dolly." Lancaster further complained, "The whole floor was taped. We had to hit marks like crazy." While budget was a factor, Lancaster "put up with it because you put up with Babe Ruth even if he's drunk. We respected Sandy [Mackendrick]; he was a little kooky, but he was good."[73]

In retrospect, Mackendrick himself felt he may have gone overboard on some of the shots. This comment is useful in determining how the film failed in one half of its mission: to reach a large mainstream audience. Mackendrick's interest in deep-focus over more conventional "coverage" of a scene (master shot, medium, close-up) had a direct relation to the industrial context in which the film was made. On the one hand, Mackendrick was taking advantage of Howe's expertise with this kind of shooting, the culmination of the cinematographer's years of technical and aesthetic experimentation. On the other hand, the British director's ulterior motive for orchestrating the placement of characters in deep-focus compositions was in effect to edit the film "inside the camera." Working for Lancaster, Mackendrick and Howe assumed that they would have greater creative freedom given that their star-producer also prided himself as a filmmaker, but this freedom ended up being compromised by the fact that Lancaster the filmmaker was also part of management. Given that H-H-L had contractual right to "final cut," and the film's editor, Alan Crosland, had informed Mackendrick of the producers' intention to take full advantage of this right, Mackendrick minimized the chance for any tampering with his vision by shooting in intricately composed shots with little additional "coverage," thus providing scant alternative editing options.[74]

Such an approach was actually an old Hollywood trick that can be traced back to directors like John Ford, notably one of the few filmmakers who was granted "final cut" in the classical period. However, in this transitional moment from the "producer-unit" to the "package-unit" system with its "emerging auteurist tendency to attribute particular stylistic innovations to a single worker (producer, director, writer)," one can see how a lesser-known (in America) director like Mackendrick, who was hoping to make his mark here, would have been drawn to a technique which both set his work apart and granted him a measure of creative control.[75]

Given the precedents for modernist aesthetic practices such as expressionist mise-en-scène and deep-focus composition, these discrete stylistic and structural devices cannot, by themselves, have produced a progressive text. What additionally seems to have occurred, as with *A Face in the Crowd,* is that the mainstream social problem genre, briefly popular in the late 1940s before the McCarthy era and the blacklist nipped it in the bud, has been reflexively recontextualized and reconfigured. A filmmaker like Kazan, for example, who had made his name on "commercially liberal" social problem films like *Gentleman's Agreement* and *Pinky* in the late 1940s, responded to the changed industrial conditions of the 1950s (some freeing, some constraining) by turning his critique "inward," both exploiting and challenging the very conditions that fomented his critique but that also made it possible in the first place. A similar dynamic, and problematic, appears to have informed the complex and contradictory contributions of Lehman, Odets, Mackendrick, and Lancaster to *Sweet Smell of Success*—the cinematic results of which will be explored in the next chapter.

Conclusion: A Battle of Wills

The various factors contributing to the emergence of an independent American art cinema in the context of the New Hollywood—the enhanced clout and creative freedom of the talent-turned-independent producer; the "gray flannel" corporate culture of the mega-talent agency (preeminently MCA); the antitelevision critique of the ideologically reflexive entertainment-business film; and the reactionary climate generated by the HUAC hearings and the blacklist—converge in the 1957 Hecht-Hill-Lancaster production *Sweet Smell of Success.* The creative clashes between the entrepreneurial producers, especially Burt Lancaster, and the more politically radical members of the creative team during the development, production, and marketing phases of *Sweet Smell of Success,* underscore the complications attending industrial relations in the postwar film industry. Yet, as with *A Face in the Crowd,* what emerged from these tensions was one of the most scathing attacks on the mass media and the corporate capitalist system ever produced in Hollywood. The added irony with *Sweet Smell of Success* is that the film's textual critique of the culture industry was mirrored by an extratextual struggle of similarly epic proportions. The familiar "battle of wills" between filmmaker and studio, such as Kazan and Schulberg had experienced, was now reconceptualized as a battle *among filmmakers,* one of whom, producer-star Burt Lancaster, was also a part of management.

The textual analysis of *Sweet Smell of Success* that follows in the next chapter foregrounds, per Gramsci, the ways in which society's major institutions (prominently but not exclusively the mass media) are able simultaneously to reinforce and subvert the dominant values of a particular era. More specifically, the film, as a discursive project, demonstrates, per Foucault, how the disciplinary impulses inherent in mass media have infiltrated our everyday lives via the institutions of family, marriage, the workplace, and other social institutions, producing an "engridding" process that operates through spoken language as well as through the various, increasingly complex communicative practices that constitute our social relations in the world.

9.

Sweet Smell of Success: Punishing Privileges
of the Professional–Managerial Class

In an industry in which practices are frequently not on the highest
plane, this type of tactic is considered good business by many of
MCA's competitors and even by some of the victims thereof. "This
is a tough, dog-eat-dog field," said one victim, "and if they're smart
enough to clip me, it's my own fault and my hat's off to them.
I wish I had some of their executive talent working for me."

—BILL DAVIDSON, "MCA: The Octopus Devours the World"

Presentation and Representation in *Sweet Smell of Success*

As with *A Face in the Crowd*, classical Hollywood conventions vie with ideologically reflexive technique in *Sweet Smell of Success* to produce complex,
contradictory, and ultimately progressive meanings. By imposing a Brechtian aesthetic on the classical, character-driven narrative relating to the rise
and fall of press agent Sidney Falco, *Sweet Smell of Success* conflates the individual psychological facet with its broader social dimension: the power
dynamics of the artist/business relationship. For example, in the scene where
Falco attempts to win an account with the aging vaudevillian Herbie Temple (Joe Frisco), who wants to break into television, complex visual cues
seemingly irrelevant to causality and logical narrative flow serve instead to
foreground the film's critique of the culture industry. Temple is talking backstage to his future press agent, Falco, and his current manager Al Evans
(Lewis Charles), as the comedian waits for a movie playing onstage to end
so he can go out and perform. The reflexive allusion to behind-the-scenes
Hollywood deal making, created by the spatial demarcation and the juxtaposition of presentational and representational forms, is heightened by
the odd angle from which the onstage movie screen is shot, which distorts
the flickering black-and-white images. Whereas the classical Hollywood
"film within a film" scenario generally privileges either the representational
or presentational aspect of the production/reception conjunction by focusing

219

on the audience facing the movie screen or onstage performer, here the presentational/representational and onstage/backstage binaries are simultaneously displayed and deconstructed, as are these binaries' connections to the New Hollywood and to American consumerist capitalism.

Another aspect of the presentational/representation dialectic is disassembled in the subsequent scene where Falco "stages" a phone call to Hunsecker (actually Falco's secretary on the other line) while Temple and his manager, unaware of the hoax, look on. Here the classical text's clear, "common sense" separation of communicative space is once again shattered, this time underscoring how mediated communication has replaced interpersonal, face-to-face contact and revealing the complex power relations underlying the exchange. The purpose of Falco's "performance" is to create the impression that he has the power to get Hunsecker to feature Falco's clients in Hunsecker's column. This despite the fact that previous scenes have betrayed the opposite message: that Falco has virtually no influence over Hunsecker; indeed, quite the opposite. The phone scene further fractures the classical text in its subversion of the "invisible" editing convention of the shot-reverse-shot combination, which in its classical context is intended to bind character and viewer together in a seamless, identificational nexus. Here, however, the falsity of the situation reveals the fallacy of the formal device. Discontinuity rather than continuity is the upshot of Falco's "phony" call, a discontinuity which is extended spatially when Falco's secretary, at first confused by the call, soon realizes that Falco is not speaking to her and sets the phone on the desk while going about her job. Temple, on the other hand, falls for the ruse and insists that his more skeptical manager hire Falco on the spot to be his press agent. The multiple associational levels—formal and thematic, self-referential and reflexive—on which the mendacity and manipulation of media and interpersonal relations are conveyed in this scene are ideologically reflexive to the extreme.

In *Sweet Smell of Success*, Sidney Falco (Tony Curtis) stages a phone call to win over the aging vaudevillian Herbie Temple (Joe Frisco) as his skeptical manager Al Evans (Lewis Charles) observes.

The Disciplinary Power of the Gaze

The film further unpacks power relations in its exposure of the marginalization and subjugation of "lesser lights": women, artists, the below-the-line craftsmen in the film and television industries, and a highly impressionable radio and television home audience. These hierarchical relations are critiqued, on the level of content, through the demonization of the despotic and despicable Hunsecker, not merely as an individual but as chief representative of the professional-managerial class. On the level of form, the uneven power dynamic is foregrounded through an undermining of classical Hollywood stylistic conventions that typically serve to naturalize the status quo. The "disciplinary gaze," for instance, is associated with Hunsecker from the very opening of the film: a dazzling montage depicting the hustle and bustle of downtown New York as the early edition of the *Globe* newspaper carrying Hunsecker's column is readied for delivery.

Nearly every shot incorporates Hunsecker's representational image, or his name, in some way, thereby conveying both his centrality to the narrative and connoting his godlike "all-seeing-ness" (and omnipresence) as Lord of the Media.[1] As workers load bales of newspapers from the *Globe* building onto delivery trucks, we see painted on one truck's side a pair of spectacles with heavy rims and disembodied eyes—the logo for Hunsecker's column, as well as for his radio and television broadcast shows—peering out at us and the city as the truck rumbles off. Next Hunsecker's face appears, on the banner atop his column that Falco is reading. As for Hunsecker's aural dominance, as we follow Falco through his city beat, we hear Hunsecker's name invoked repeatedly by various people, typically with fear or reverence. Images of Hunsecker's bespectacled eyes and face on trucks, newspapers, and posters, and the overawed invocation of this name, are recurrent motifs throughout the film. This textual redundancy serves to reflexively highlight what is normally obscured in the classical Hollywood text: the ideological implications of the gaze.[2]

Falco's comparative lack of power in relation to Hunsecker's persona is conveyed early on when one of the newspaper bundles hits the street and Falco impatiently instructs the almost blind (thus marginalized) newsstand owner, Iggy, to hurry up. Iggy makes a bad joke with sexual connotations— about "two rolls [getting] fresh with a baker! Hey, hot, hot, hot"—which he suggests Falco should pass on to Hunsecker for his column. Both the vulgar play on words and the flippant suggestion trivialize Falco's role as a professional, suggesting that anybody can do his job. Iggy's even greater insignificance, of course, is conveyed by his poor vision and his inability to use language effectively. This is just the beginning of a series of insults and put-downs Falco will suffer in the opening ten minutes of the film from various people, including current and past clients, as Falco carries out myriad tasks on behalf of the representationally ubiquitous but physically still absent Hunsecker.

As Falco circulates through the city in a frustrating attempt to locate Hunsecker, the power of the columnist's "internalized" gaze expands its domain to include the audience as well. For just as Falco is compelled by career concerns to seek out Hunsecker, the viewer is impelled by a cinematic desire to meet "in the flesh" the man about whom so much is being made. When Falco finally "locates" the columnist at the Twenty-One club, Hunsecker's physical introduction is further postponed and the viewer's visual gratification further deferred. Falco must call Hunsecker from a phone at the club: another ignominious act which the phone operator points out to the press agent. Our first contact with Hunsecker's actual person is thus aural rather than visual, as we hear his voice on the phone ominously attacking Falco: "You're dead, son, get yourself buried!" When we are finally granted the satisfaction of seeing the "great man" himself, it is in a deep-focus composition that foregrounds Hunsecker's imposing figure to the point of almost filling the screen—and literally overshadowing (and upstaging) Falco standing behind him. As the film progresses and Falco goes from a "dead man," torn from Hunsecker's good graces, to fawning sycophant to power broker trading on information he has on Hunsecker's sister Susie, the same basic organizational principles prevail, constructed around and dependent on the omnipresent and omnipotent gaze.

A later scene extends the range of Hunsecker's tyrannical power to include the broadcast media and the other main characters—Steve, his manager Frank D'Angelo, and Susie—and serves to draw attention to the changed power dynamics in the postwar culture industry. In what I call the "threshold scene," Steve and D'Angelo leave the "democratic" streets of New York to enter Hunsecker's sphere of influence: the television studio building where the columnist broadcasts his show. As the artist and his manager enter the lobby of the steel-and-glass building, they pass multiple copies of the same poster for Hunsecker's show, *It's a Wonderful World*. The posters depict Hunsecker, his bespectacled gaze directed at the viewer, standing next to a globe, conveying both the international reach and authoritative nature of television celebrity. Not only are the posters behind reflective steel-and-glass cases, but Steve and D'Angelo must pass through the glass doors of the modern high-rise building. The overall effect of this icono-graphic redundancy (multiple images of "Big Brother" Hunsecker in com-bination with layers of literally reflexive and metaphorically imprisoning framing devices) is a sense that the two men have entered the transparent yet tightly controlled "engridding" system that Hunsecker oversees in his "panopticon" capacity as media guru.[3] An additional "carceral" dimension is embedded in the title of Hunsecker's show, *It's a Wonderful World*, which, in its analogy to Capra's *It's a Wonderful Life*, demonstrates how easily Capra's New Deal populism could be co-opted by the media into an emblem for postwar corporate capitalism.[4] This latter reactionary political aspect, of course, is a pointed jab at notorious McCarthyist stooge Walter Winchell, on whom Hunsecker's character was based.

Steve and D'Angelo's entrance into the studio building thus embodies a passage across two thresholds: a physical passage from the hectic, teem-ing streets of New York to the controlled (and controlling) environment of the television studio; and a spiritual passage from the exploratory world of the independent, idealistic artist to the confining world of the manipula-tive, commercially driven, and conservative mass media. In the lobby, Steve and D'Angelo meet up with Susie, who had been waiting there for them; while Falco, Hunsecker's emissary, arrives from the studio to play the role he will play into the next scene and beyond: that of mediator between (the subjects) Steve, Susie, and D'Angelo, and (the subjugator) Hunsecker.

The longer "wedding scene," following directly upon the "threshold

Steve Dallas (Martin Milner) and his manager Frank D'Angelo (Sam Levene) join Susie Hunsecker (Susan Harrison) to meet J. J. Hunsecker at his television studio in the "threshold scene."

scene," is a particularly complex elaboration of the institutionalized and internalized system of discipline and punishment embodied in Hunsecker but applying to the culture industry and U.S. society at large. Taken together, the "threshold" and "wedding" scenes reflexively articulate the ways the mass media in the television age have collapsed the personal and the public by imbricating Hunsecker's control of public opinion as a television opinion-maker (in the "threshold scene") with his control of Susie's private life as it relates to her romance with Steve (in the "wedding scene"). The imbrication is reinforced stylistically by means of reflexive modernist technique that configures the main characters, in their various "private" relationships with Hunsecker, against the physical backdrop of the television studio.

In the "wedding scene," Steve, D'Angelo, Susie, and Falco meet with Hunsecker in the TV studio. The motivation behind the meeting, on Steve's part, is to gain Hunsecker's approval to marry Susie; Hunsecker's aim, to the contrary, is to push Steve to the breaking point so that he can justify a vendetta against him that will force Susie to break off their relationship in order to spare Steve's career. Various formal devices (dialogue, point-of-view editing, deep-focus composition, and other aspects of mise-en-scène) expose, through excess and contradiction, the insidious methods by which Hunsecker, stand-in for the culture industry, operates.

The Disciplinary Function of Language

In analyzing the dialogue—that is, the function of language—in the "wedding scene," extratextual factors again come into play. Despite having been the one to propose Odets as "script doctor" on the film, even director Mackendrick had trouble balancing the playwright's theatrical, archly stylized dialogue with the "seamlessly realistic" conventions of the classical Hollywood film.[5] As it turned out, the "stagey" language is one of the most effective reflexive components in the film, in that it emphasizes the meaning rather than the mimesis of speech, challenges the delimited individual psychology typically foregrounded in the classical text, and highlights the corrupt social forces impeding the characters' exercise of free will.

Language, inarguably, is one of the prime mechanisms of social control. One of the prime ways this control is exercised is through an internalized "engridding" process—per Foucault, an institutionalized system of internal discipline of monitoring and maintenance based on discursive rather than purely material systems.[6] In the "wedding scene," language functions precisely in this manner, both as a reflector and reproducer of the scene's power dynamics. Hunsecker, whose business—as columnist and TV-radio show host—*is* language, uses it masterfully here to manipulate and control, discipline and punish, all the other characters. Hunsecker's first words to Steve appear to flatter his "rival" by emphasizing Steve's separation from the dark side of popular culture, while they actually serve to discipline not only Steve's dissenting voice but any other potential dissenters among the other characters:

> Serious as a deacon. . . . I like it. I like your style, son! In a world of old rags and bones, I like it! For instance, take Sidney. . . . If Sidney got anywhere near Susie I'd break a bat over Sidney's head! Sidney lives so much in a moral twilight that, when I said you were coming here, he predicted disaster. You wouldn't take my favor—you'd chew up the job, he said, and spit it right back in my face![7]

The "bat breaking" gibe at Falco (and, by association, at Steve) aims to bring back into line an underling who is threatening to stray from the "docile body"—Foucault's term for those who have submitted to the oppressive institutional forces of society like faceless soldiers marching mindlessly in formation.[8] A prime means of reining in the rebellious lackey through language is to threaten violence, as Hunsecker does here. Another means is to prey on the lackey's moral weakness and confusion. Hunsecker uses this tactic on Falco in a later scene when he blurts, "Sure you're in jail, Sidney. You're a prisoner of your own fears, of your own greed and ambition; you're in jail."[9] Here, with Steve, he uses a variation on the technique by implying that the purportedly morally upstanding musician has the potential for violence as well: "Sidney told me you'd chew it up, spit it back in my face." Who would be favored to come out on top in a battle between spit and a baseball bat is also clear, but the overarching point, from a psychological (and ideological) standpoint, is that whoever controls the discourse wins the war.

Susie is a more complex case, given her complete subjugation to her brother's will. She epitomizes the "docile body" whose domination is accomplished by "individualizing discipline" to "eliminate individual difference."[10] While every stylistic, structural, and thematic tool is used to convey Susie's (and thus women's) oppressed state, language, more vividly than any other formal device, expresses Susie's psychological imprisonment. Whenever she does battle with her sadistic and manipulative brother, she is reduced to whimpering silence. In this scene again, Susie looks on helplessly "from the sidelines" while the men verbally duke it out, literally taking her own

victimization "sitting down." Steve at least puts up a fight. His initial strategy is to try to extricate himself from Hunsecker's tight web of influence
over him and the larger artistic community by emphasizing the personal
over the professional: "I'm not here as an artist. I'm here as an average Joe,
who happens to love your sister." Hunsecker deftly counterpunches: "Well,
just be careful you don't knock her off her feet." Hunsecker's comeback is
really a one-two punch: first, it insinuates that being an average Joe carries
with it connotations of male brutishness; second, the phrase "knock her off
her feet" is scandalously close to "knock her up"—a reversal of "knock her
down" (the original language in the screenplay and changed during filming)—which even more disturbingly conjoins sexuality and violence. The
multiple shades of meaning here are historically instructive, combining nostalgia for "old-fashioned" femininity with men's fear, as commonly expressed
in the postwar popular media, of being trapped into shotgun marriages
through women's false claims of pregnancy.[11] When Steve responds to Hunsecker's malicious insinuations with his usual honesty and directness, Hunsecker again counters with pugilistic metaphors: "Frankly, son, you lost me
on that last hill. Just give us the punch line."[12]

The scene highlights how Hunsecker, the master manipulator, maintains
his position of power by keeping the world of logic and morality shifting
under Steve's feet. Although he indulges in sinister metaphor and double-
entendres, Hunsecker acts as if language is simply a form of storytelling,
hence innocuous; Steve, in reaction, struggles to uphold "pristine reality" by
speaking simply and straightforwardly. However, as the scene pointedly illus-
trates, there is no such a thing as harmless speech or pristine reality, since
all language derives from and redounds to social "griddings" that both reflect and reproduce systems of power and knowledge.[13] Eventually, Steve
takes off the gloves himself, recognizing that if he is going to resist Hunsecker's efforts to manipulate him, he needs to engage the columnist on his
own terms. Resorting to innuendo, he asks Hunsecker about Falco: "Do you
think, sir, when he dies he'll go to the dog and cat heaven?" Steve's demeaning turn-of-phrase flatters Hunsecker by affirming that Sidney is Hunsecker's
lapdog and therefore beneath him in power and stature. Continuing on the
offensive, Steve shows an awareness of the columnist's "rules of engagement" by using metaphor on Hunsecker himself: "Wait a minute. I haven't
handed over punishing privileges to you yet. Just lay the whip down and
maybe I'll respect what you're saying." But in playing by Hunsecker's rules,
Steve undermines his greatest asset: his moral integrity. By identifying language as the foundation of power relations, he may have temporarily gained

the upper hand in his struggle with Hunsecker, but in lowering himself to the columnist's level, he also has left himself open to further degradation.

Once Steve has crossed this line, tempers flare and the mudslinging begins; now Hunsecker is really in his element. Falco plays into the columnist's hand by relating how, just moments earlier, Steve had tried to strike Falco over the press agent's alleged role in the smear campaign against Steve. Hunsecker challenges Steve to justify this violent outburst. As Hunsecker had intended, Steve finally explodes and hurls insults at the columnist, although some of the verbal barbs (directed, by the filmmakers, as much at Walter Winchell as at Hunsecker) cut close to the bone: "You think of yourself, you and your column . . . as a national glory . . . but to me, and thousands of others like me, you and your slimy scandal, your phony patriotics—to me, Mr. Hunsecker, you are a *national disgrace!*"[14]

Genuinely stung by Steve's criticism but also seeing his big opening, Hunsecker goes for the jugular, threatening to publicly destroy the young musician's career and his reputation in the community in his gossip column and on his broadcast shows. Susie, realizing that this is no idle threat, throws in the towel for her true love's sake. In an aside with Hunsecker, she agrees to break things off with Steve (a pact she makes good on in a subsequent scene). Steve thus emerges from the verbal fracas with his integrity intact, but Hunsecker, who didn't have any to begin with, emerges triumphant.

The "wedding scene" is a pivotal moment in the film, in that it demonstrates Hunsecker's, and thus the media's, ability to control discourse through the manipulation of language on both the verbal and "virtual" levels—that is, institutional power is shown to derive not merely from the force of that which is actually expressed but, perhaps even more so, from the *threat* of that which might be expressed in the future. As with the gaze, the effectiveness of disciplinary language is shown to come from an internalized *mechanism* of control.

Deep-Focus Composition in the "Wedding Scene"

The manipulation of character relations through a complex interplay of deep-focus cinematography and disorienting editing is an additional reflexive device used in the "wedding scene" to unpack the power dynamics at work in the scene. As Nick Browne has argued, the sequence of shots in the classical text, and specifically the pacing and direction of gazes within the sequence, can produce ideological effects that are not always commensurate with Mulvey's "determining male gaze."[15] Browne focuses on a scene from John Ford's *Stagecoach* (1939) in which deep-focus sequence shots,

alternating with the shot-reverse-shot figure, induce a realignment of identification from the conventionally heroic pair (the cavalry officer's wife and
her chivalrous escort) to the outcast couple (the prostitute and the fugitive
gunslinger). This realignment, by shifting audience sympathy characterologically from "center" to "periphery," also shifts the center of gravity ideologically from the psychological to the social.

In applying Browne's approach to the "wedding scene," a similar rhetorical shift can be seen occurring and through much the same technical means.
In this scene also, viewers are encouraged to realign their identification from
the dominant and powerful Hunsecker to the marginalized, less powerful
Steve and Susie. As we transition from the "threshold" to the "wedding
scene," Hunsecker stands high on the stage in the foreground, his back to
the camera, while Steve and Susie walk toward him along the theater aisle.
Hunsecker's position of dominance in the frame serves to further mock and
undermine Steve's mission, as does Hunsecker's line, "Looks like a wedding!"—shouted before Steve has a chance to pose the question. Indeed, the
shot of the couple, with Sidney and the manager close behind, looks like a
wedding procession. As the verbal set-to ensues, Falco, the film's antiheroic
protagonist, is present in nearly every shot, although, tellingly, he rarely
speaks. His positioning in the scene, like his narrative role, is highly ambiguous. In the "A" series of shots, featuring Hunsecker as the source of the
controlling gaze and originator of the shot-reverse-shot figure, both the
connection between him and Falco and their hierarchical relationship is

As Steve Dallas and Susie Hunsecker approach, J. J. Hunsecker (Burt Lancaster) remarks,
"Looks like a wedding."

indicated by having Hunsecker sit in the front row of theater seats and Falco sit behind him in the second row. Also, when Hunsecker speaks to the off-screen couple about Falco without directing his gaze at him, Falco's presence is simultaneously affirmed and negated. Hunsecker's superior power position is underscored through his verbal salvo directed at Falco (his threat to break a bat over Falco's head), and through his belittling demand to be serviced: "Match me, son." The master-servant scenario culminates with Falco solicitously reaching up to light Hunsecker's cigarette. (This servile gesture is rhymed in a later scene in which Falco tries to assert his independence from Hunsecker by *refusing* to light his cigarette.)

In the "B" series of shots, the camera circles in a series of deep-focus sweeps around Hunsecker in the foreground squaring off with Steve, while Falco alternately stands or sits on the stage in the background wedged between the players, his arms crossing and uncrossing, his expression sometimes surly, sometimes amused. He cuts a decidedly (unsym)pathetic figure, a third wheel in the two-way conversation between Hunsecker and Steve, while also tacitly supporting Hunsecker's threatening words with their undercurrent of physical violence. Notably, Odets's advice to actor Tony Curtis was to portray Falco's amoral ambition and frustrated desire for power through constant movement, whereas power itself, Odets argued, was stationary.[16] In the deep-focus counterpoints to the shot-reverse-shots, and as visual corollary to Hunsecker's verbal dominance, Mackendrick choreographed the scene so that the other characters constantly shift position within the frame, while Hunsecker remains comparatively static, reinforcing the impression that Hunsecker's power serves as the pivot point to which everyone else gravitates and around which they revolve.

Falco's role as "middle-man" in the scene is conveyed through shifting camera angles. In the "A" series of shots, Falco's temporarily enhanced social standing through his connection to Hunsecker is achieved by coupling the two men in two-shots. However, in the "B" series of shots (those portraying Steve, Susie, and D'Angelo), Falco is frequently portrayed behind and between these three characters as a reminder of Falco's role as mediator, but also to implicate him in Hunsecker's agenda of "dividing" the romantic couple. In addition, Falco's presence in the background of these shots can be read as an indication of his fleeting alignment with the socially disempowered; in other words, he too, is controlled by Hunsecker's gaze.

The shifting viewer alliances produced by the complex interplay between shot-reverse-shot and deep-focus compositions complicate viewer understanding of Falco. Moreover, given his dual role as insider and outsider,

Sidney Falco aligns himself with J. J. Hunsecker in the "A" series.

antagonist and protagonist, Falco's fluctuating status and moral ambiguity defy the norms of the classical text—but in a manner quite different from *Stagecoach*. Unlike in the Ford film, which, in keeping with the New Deal populist spirit of the time, encouraged viewer empathy with marginalized members of society, *Sweet Smell of Success*, in the context of the ideologically fraught 1950s, sanctions viewer identification neither with the outsiders (Steve and Susie), the insider (Hunsecker), nor with the outsider/insider (Falco). The interplay of deep focus and shot-reverse-shot makes personal identification fleeting and unfocused, undermining full affiliation with any particular character. Identification is further complicated by the silent presence throughout the scene of a group of studio grips, visible in the background or on the margins of most shots, busily rearranging cameras, lights, and other equipment. Just as the vacillating figure of Falco splits the difference between center and periphery among the main characters, adding a dialectical "third term" to the binary, the workmen/audience, like a mute Greek chorus, contribute another unsettling ideological component to the scene.

While the marginalized workers can be taken as a nod to Marx and the exploited proletariat, clear-cut leftist values on the whole have been replaced by a complex and conflicted identification with an amoral businessman who, on the one hand, descends from the hoary "Horatio Alger type" yet, on the other, reflects the 1950s "organization man's" partial complicity with and opposition to the corrupt business world of postwar America. The film, if perhaps to a lesser extent than Falco, refuses to a take a firm stand either.

Instead, its ideologically reflexive technique "democratizes" viewers' choices between siding with power and with powerlessness, and allows Falco to emerge as the apotheosis not only of his own but of America's ambivalence.

In earlier scenes which featured deep-focus/shot-reverse-shot combinations, such as when Falco planted Communist literature in Steve's pocket, the viewer was implicated in Falco's moral confusion. In the "wedding scene," by contrast, the constantly moving characters within the deep-focus/shot-reverse-shot dialectic are anchored in the tyrannical figure of Hunsecker. Whereas the earlier examples left room for moral choices, the later, more complex "wedding scene" reveals how easily Falco (and by extension the viewer) can get swept up in the power dynamics of the corporate capitalist system. Hunsecker's implacable ability to "infect" the group with his maliciously self-serving personal agenda is reinforced in the "wedding scene." As Hunsecker shifts between the symbolic roles of audience member (seated in the theater) and powerful celebrity orchestrating the group dynamic, viewers themselves become implicated in this re-enactment of the mass media institution's imposition of discipline and punishment under the guise of news and entertainment. As in *A Face in the Crowd*, however, the mass-media critique is a red herring. The culture industry is not the only oppressive system being indicted; the conventions of the classic Hollywood text are exposed as yet another institutionalized means of controlling dissident voices. Here, as in *A Face in the Crowd*, visual and aural devices associated with reflexivity offer the possibility of disclosing the apparatus and pointing

Falco demonstrates his fluctuating status and shifting alliances by joining the "B" series with Steve Dallas, Susie Hunsecker, and Frank D'Angelo.

to a progressive alternative; or as Brecht explains it, popular media imbued with reflexivity can present the world *and* a better version of the world.[17]

Portrait of a New Hollywood: Insider Responses to *Sweet Smell of Success*

Increasingly aware that American film in the mid-1950s was starting to take up issues of scandal-mongering and sensationalism in the entertainment press, the *Hollywood Reporter*'s Wilkerson engaged in a concerted effort to shore up the fading studio system in his regular column. Two weeks after the release of *Sweet Smell of Success*, he complained that industry insiders were to blame for perpetuating their own negative press (presumably by making films like this): "Have you ever stopped to consider that . . . the downbeat propaganda about the motion picture business, started by men in the business and infiltrating into the press . . . [has become] something of a topic in the public's conversations?"[18] Wilkerson was not alone in contrasting the current state of affairs with an alleged golden age when robust studios and glamorous stars made "feel good" films that won the hearts and minds of the mass audience; however, as we have seen, he was inconsistent in his views on how best to return to the "good-old days" in the face of continuing box-office gloom.

A similar uncertainty pervaded overall reception to *Sweet Smell of Success* in the trade and popular press at the time of the film's release. The *Hollywood Reporter* itself had placed ad copy hailing the film as "The Story of a Vicious Gossip Columnist who Trafficked in Sensation and Scandal."[19] As for reviews, several, such as one from Richard Gertner in *Motion Picture Daily*, saw the film as part of a trend in dark tales about the entertainment industry:

Telling their "Inside Story" about the private lives of prominent personalities in show business is popular subject matter for films this year. First there were "The Great Man" and "A Face in the Crowd," which purported to expose the venal nature of radio and television stars. . . . Now the Hecht-Hill-Lancaster organization is providing a look underneath the surface of another aspect of the Broadway scene.[20]

Variety noted the same trend, but looked unfavorably on H-H-L's particular rendition of it:

In a market apparently bullish on pictures devoted to violence and the seamier side of life, Ernest Lehman's novelette about an arrogant, dictatorial columnist and a boot-licking press agent must have seemed a likely prospect for filming. Unfortunately, as produced by James Hill for Hecht-Hill-Lancaster, the characters and situation are so overdrawn as to fail to engender any audience identification or sympathy.[21]

Other industry trades were more upbeat about the film and its prospects, recommending that the distributors capitalize on the box-office strength of the two stars along with "the gimmick that the picture offers a 'behind-the-scenes' view." In general, reviews were mostly positive, but one notice in the *Hollywood Reporter* reflected Wilkerson's concern, from an industry vantage point, in releasing films with a pessimistic message. One solution, this notice proposed, was a happier ending: "This mood of unrelieved ugliness could have been lightened by a final scene between Miss Harrison and Milner. It would not have harmed the honesty of the picture and would have heightened the happy note that is already implicit." Once again, however, ambivalence shone through in the review's conclusion that, downbeat ending notwithstanding, the film "should be a gratifying box office success—if you will pardon the word success."[22] This recognition of the fraught attitudes toward success in the New Hollywood and 1950s America, underscores the aesthetic/commercial paradox underlying ideologically reflexive films like *Sweet Smell of Success* and the new generation of manager-artists engaged in making them.

The overall "insider" press's strategy toward a harsh entertainment-industry satire like *Sweet Smell of Success*, as with *A Face in the Crowd*, was to emphasize both the commercial upside and the ideological rectitude of the film—thereby not only boosting the financial bottom line in the short run but also sheltering the creative capital of artistic filmmakers like Lancaster and Kazan in the longer run. One way trade reviewers managed to achieve this analytical duplicity was by emphasizing the films' melodramatic over their modernist aspects. For example, trade reviews tended to isolate the actions of the two films' two main women characters, Susie Hunsecker and Marcia Jeffries, even though both are secondary characters in dramatic terms (Susie more than Marcia) to their imperious leading-male counterparts, J. J. Hunsecker and Lonesome Rhodes. By privileging the female characters' narrative functions and casting them as upholders of the films' moral universe, reviewers recuperated traditional gender roles enshrined in the melodramatic formula and downplayed the film's anti-American critique.[23]

The ability of the ideologically reflexive films to skirt by relatively unscathed in the critical discourse brings to mind Naremore's claim, following Jameson, that many postwar American "art" films reinforced

the "profound structural relations" between modernism and the new economy . . . [by combining] a type of modernism and type of commercial
melodrama. . . . Especially in Hollywood, melodrama is a conservative or
sentimental form associated with stalwart heroes, unscrupulous villains,
vivid action, and last-minute rescues. Certain attributes of modernism (its
links to high culture, its formal and moral complexity, its disdain for classical narrative, its frankness about sex, and its increasingly critical stance
toward America) threatened this type of film and were never totally absorbed
into the mainstream. High modernism and Hollywood "blood melodrama"
nevertheless formed a symbiotic relationship that generated an intriguing
artistic tension.[24]

While the specific reference here was to film noir, such an analysis applies
equally to *Sweet Smell of Success* and *A Face in the Crowd*. Maintaining the
ideological tension between art and pulp, "high modernism and blood melodrama," as I have argued, was not only crucial to the artistic and commercial
success of these independently produced, studio-distributed, proto-auteurist
works, but would have substantial impact on future generations of Hollywood filmmakers engaged in shaping the outlines of a more truly independent American cinema.[25]

Postwar Precedents for the Hollywood Renaissance:
Marketing Marginal Texts

Industry trade reviewers' discomfort with *Sweet Smell of Success*'s negative
portrait of the entertainment industry was partially mollified by their appreciation for H-H-L's attention to the "big picture": the bottom line and the
financial interests of the studio, UA, which had financed and was distributing the film. In other words, the "businessmen-filmmakers" were excused
their momentary lapse into cynicism because of the soundness of their overall, long-term commercial strategy. Despite its scabrous themes, *Sweet Smell
of Success* was at least intended to turn a profit, which, alas, it failed to do.
According to Lancaster biographer Kate Buford, "*Sweet Smell of Success*, despite being named one of the best movies of 1957 by *Time*, was a box-office
failure. To the *Marty*-obsessed industry the movie represented a lot of things,
principally what happens when a $600,000 labor of love balloons into a
$2.6 (maybe $3.4) million disaster."[26]

In the 1960s and 1970s, studio production heads and their development
and marketing teams would become increasingly adept at managing these
"monstrous" mixtures of art, exploitation, and star-studded genre films,

as director-auteurs like Arthur Penn, John Frankenheimer, and Stanley Kubrick in the 1960s, and Robert Altman, Francis Ford Coppola, and Martin Scorsese in the 1970s played even greater havoc with classical Hollywood conventions. As these postmodern juxtapositions of art-house, exploitation, and classical Hollywood film types became the norm in this period, the studios learned to manage these excessively subversive combinations of art and pulp by targeting the now, mostly young, increasingly rebellious audience that preferred films that gave cultural expression to the social turmoil associated with the era.

In 1957, a prescient *Variety* reviewer simply listed in the byline as "Gene," provided a clue as to how best to access the narrow, but highly committed urban audience for *Sweet Smell of Success*. Gene understood the film's potential appeal for the emerging art cinema crowd and the antiestablishment sensibilities of the so-called beat generation, whose vanguard was starting to make itself known in the bars, coffeehouses, and nightclubs of New York, San Francisco, and other urban centers.

> Hecht-Hill-Lancaster is at hand with a savage indictment of a powerful and unscrupulous syndicated columnist and an unconscionable, slippery press agent. This is strong material. "Success" is by nature a "big city" story, not alone in the Gotham locale, but also in the popular bistros visited, the showbusiness and nightlife characters encountered and the events that come to pass. It all may be pretty remote to rural area citizenry. But the dramatic wallop it packs assures good boxoffice, particularly in key burgs.[27]

In "instructing" his industry cohorts on how best to manage this "niche" product, Gene was essentially describing the "platform" distribution strategy and "word-of-mouth" marketing techniques that would eventually become associated with the "specialized" independent film business in ensuing decades. Once distributors caught on, and the beat generation morphed into the counterculture, the platform was in place for the studios (and the public) to embrace the anomalous, innovative, and oppositional aesthetic of the Hollywood Renaissance.

Blockbusters and Backlash (against the "Indigestible" Art Film)

At the same time that *Variety*'s Gene was envisioning a type of specialized studio release for films like *Sweet Smell of Success*, the *Hollywood Reporter*'s ever-fluctuating owner-columnist Wilkerson was arguing the opposite case, advising studios to cease making such challenging, difficult-to-market fare.

On June 19, 1957 (the same day that *Sweet Smell of Success* was released and reviewed by the *Hollywood Reporter*), Wilkerson revised his erstwhile tack in support of an American art cinema. No longer aligning himself with the bold independent producer who often served as a magnet for talented filmmakers, he objected instead to those who "seem to have forgotten that the movie theatre is supposed to be a place of entertainment."[28] Two days earlier, his column had decried the declining state of the industry due to the current focus on difficult, "indigestible pictures" over broadly entertaining ones. He described watching Old Hollywood movies on television and marveled at the broad appeal of these formula pictures:

> [O]ne thing you can't escape is that the stories generally are 1000 percent better than the ones now being used to attract people into theaters and you may wonder how we steered so far away from the plots that brought us in so much money in the early days, replacing them with so many disagreeable subjects that not only do NOT entertain or attract but send the few customers that do go to our theaters home unhappy with what they saw and a determination to skip movies until something comes along they really want to see. . . . Why not a switch to formulas that DID bring in the masses and brought the industry a lot of money.[29]

While it is facile to presume that the release of *Sweet Smell of Success* could single-handedly prompt a backlash among studio heads, thereby re-energizing their commitment to broadly entertaining films with mass appeal (i.e., the blockbuster), Wilkerson's comments nonetheless remind us that "alternative and Hollywood cinemas are always somehow interconnected and interdependent."[30] His nostalgic re-assertion of Old Hollywood moral values in the face of New Hollywood films that portray the industry as corrupt, indicates the threat posed by the alternative film practices such as those of *Sweet Smell of Success* and *A Face in the Crowd*.

As the 1950s progressed, and the Hollywood studios continued to struggle, industry insiders like Wilkerson become increasingly critical of the commercial consequences for the studios of their support for the emerging alternative cinema. This conservative backlash had some very immediate reinforcements. Wilkerson's latest series of anti-Hollywood jeremiads occurred only days after a crucial and highly symbolic luncheon of film companies and sales executives at Hollywood's Roosevelt Hotel, where MPAA head Johnston delivered an address titled "America's Traveling Salesman." In the speech, Johnston described the American motion picture as "the great stimulator of mass production" at home and abroad and cited the screen as "the pioneering and still tireless agent for American democracy and the fruits of democracy throughout the world." Offering a historical gloss, Johnston added, "Although the movies set out with only one purpose, to entertain, their unique power of suggestion soon made them the greatest selling force in the world." Their "suggestion of new styles, new devices, new methods" that appeared in the very first pictures, Johnston concluded, created demands of the most powerful sort, stimulating manufacturers of everything from clothing to luxurious homes; what's more, he insisted, this force was still at work today more than ever: "Those who come out for the show will stay out to shop. What's more, they'll be in a mood for shopping."[31] Johnston's brazen articulation of the consumerist project underlying the postwar entertainment industry is symptomatic of the quantum leap Hollywood was undergoing at this historical juncture—away from simply producing mass entertainment to reproducing mass consumption in the U.S. and abroad. Independent art films that questioned unbridled consumerism or in other ways cast aspersions on the American way of life were bad business all the way around.

As Hollywood's box-office woes persisted into the next decade, and with the dramatic arrival of the French New Wave and other national "new cinemas," renewed concern was expressed in the early 1960s about Hollywood's ability to compete with foreign films that seemed to strike a chord with younger audiences due to their innovative technique, sexual content, and dark themes. That these films were having a significant impact on American films is evident from a 1961 *Variety* article decrying the new negativity in the "sicko" movies coming out of the New Hollywood whose box-office success came at the expense of its "happier" fare.[32] A corollary concern was that the new-wave trend was going to have a devastating impact on "family entertainment," which had been the primary source of Hollywood's mass appeal for decades. According to Monaco: "By the end of the . . . [1960s], industry pundits claimed that features aimed at the 'family' market could no longer attract the adolescents and young adults who had become the mainstay of the movie theater box office. . . . Films that appealed to one niche were not just ignored by other portions of the potential audience, but were frequently condemned by them."[33]

As the 1960s wore on, the detrimental commercial impact of European art films on the American film industry in one direction was compounded by another damaging effect in the other direction: runaway production. For the year 1960, Monaco notes, "forty percent of all movies financed by the

Hollywood majors were shot overseas . . . [and] the following year, Hollywood companies produced 164 features in the United States and ninety abroad."[34] While American producers were enjoying all the tax-savings, favorable foreign exchange rates, and other incentives created by foreign governments to encourage American filmmakers to shoot in their countries, American union employees were losing out. The search for alternative sources of production financing and savings abroad, coupled with the emergence by the 1960s of a coherent art-house distribution and exhibition system in the United States, prompted many in the industry to question whether such "Europeanization" was ultimately in Hollywood's best interests.

A 1960 *Variety* article summarized Wilder's uniquely cynical take on the European cinema, which he claimed was having its biggest impact on certain sexploitation films, not on the art or commercial cinema. Recapping Wilder's comments during a press conference publicizing *The Apartment,* the headline read: ". . . France Has New Wave, U.S. Has Zugsmith."[35] Albert Zugsmith epitomized the shameless exploitation producer. Although he had begun his film-producing career with such impressive outings as Welles's *Touch of Evil* (1958) and Douglas Sirk's *Tarnished Angels* (1958), Zugsmith had quickly switched to the more lucrative field of cheap sensationalistic films with sleazy sexual overtones such as *Female Animal* and *High School Confidential* (also both 1958). Wilder was equally disparaging of the so-called modernist aesthetic practices associated with the European new waves. As *Variety* recounted: "He thought that much of what is taken as the new wave type of filming is simply 'the second time around,' meaning a return to a self-conscious type of film direction which was popular in Europe in the late 20s and 30s. 'You know what I mean,' he said, 'photographing a scene through the flames in the fireplace (the Santa Claus [point of view]) or a hospital room through a syringe.'"[36]

Wilder's provocative critique of the modernism derived from the European art cinema (and a major influence, as we've seen, in *Sweet Smell of Success* and *A Face in the Crowd*), while partly attributable to the filmmaker's notorious pessimism and misanthropy, is also representative of a more widespread controversy surrounding U.S. filmmakers' absorption of European aesthetics. Wilder's comments also point to the increasingly thin line dividing art and exploitation films as filmmakers on both sides of the generic divide began exploring more controversial sexual themes and experimental techniques to reach an increasingly overlapping audience demographic. Near-complete convergence would be realized during the Hollywood

Renaissance of the mid-1960s through mid-1970s, with a cinema that openly played with and around the margins of art and exploitation.[37]

But the studios would not go quietly into the good night. The backlash against an American independent art cinema articulated by *Variety*, Wilkerson, Johnston, and studio heads such as Zanuck would find increasing cinematic expression in the 1960s-style blockbuster, whose upsurge would overlap with, occasionally overwhelm, but ultimately—if only temporarily—feed into the art cinema trend. Some blockbusters such as *The Guns of Navarone* (1961), *The Longest Day* (1962), and especially *The Sound of Music* (1965) lived up to their name and proved box-office (and, for the latter, also Oscar) gold; others, like *Cleopatra* (1963) were abject critical and financial failures. Most all of the big-budget spectaculars aimed to attract a mass audience, both here and abroad, through old-fashioned Hollywood production and moral values. When disastrous misfires began to overtake successes in the late 1960s with several heavily capitalized *Sound of Music* wannabes (*Doctor Doolittle* [1967], *Star!* [1968], and *Hello, Dolly!* [1969]), the bifurcated strategy gave way, out of desperation, to a single-minded one favoring low-budget, youth-oriented, often quite experimental art movies, thereby ushering in the Hollywood Renaissance.[38]

Conclusion

Nowhere was the clash between leftist ideology and conformist pressure more evident than in the production circumstances attending the making of *Sweet Smell of Success*, a highly polemical attack on the self-made man and the politically suspect, commercially-driven postwar entertainment industry. The workplace tensions and ultimate supremacy of the newly empowered professional-managerial classes, embodied in the film on-screen in the omnipotent character of J. J. Hunsecker and off-screen in the equally unassailable figure of Burt Lancaster, expose the mounting 1950s' "class struggle" between managers and media artists. Frequently, producers and/ or studio heads pressured filmmakers to forego forthright critiques of the American way of life in favor of procapitalist reinforcement of Hollywood's commercial enterprise. Yet in this ideologically reflexive film, the repressive tactics of the reactionary old guard, here represented by the powerful columnist Hunsecker, to control jazz musician Steve Dallas by using anti-Communist politics as its club—echoing the behind-the-scenes battles among Lehman, Odets, and Mackendrick on the one side and the purportedly liberal Lancaster on the other—are severely critiqued.

Sweet Smell of Success, in its textual/extratextual conjunction, serves as a prototype for John Caldwell's notion of the "industrial intertext," which posits the necessity, for any thoughtful textual analysis, to engage the cultural artifact's production circumstances. In this instance, the circumstances included the commercially oriented/politically liberal/artistically inclined H-H-L, which "packaged" a group of cultural workers, many of whom had strong affiliations with the political Left and/or Hollywood's more innovative technical operations. The goal of this merging of art and commerce was to create a media product that merged the mainstream and the alternative, the dominant and the marginal, in a way that, for the producers, maximized profits and, for the artists, cast their message wide. The film's production history also highlights one of the chief paradoxes of New Hollywood independence: that corporate-minded honchos like Wasserman, in facilitating the ascendance of talent-run independent production companies like H-H-L, thereby helped create a cinema of political engagement intrinsically opposed to the corporate capitalist ethos.

As for the fates of the main creative collaborators on *Sweet Smell of Success*, the slighted Lehman went on to a major career in Hollywood as screenwriter and occasional producer on some of the most high-profile, and generally successful, films of the next few years (e.g., *North by Northwest* [1959], *West Side Story* [1961], *The Sound of Music, Who's Afraid of Virginia Woolf?* [1966], and *Hello, Dolly!*). Mackendrick, on the other hand, seemed exhausted by the New Hollywood ordeal and made very few films, of any sort, thereafter, eventually becoming dean of the California Institute of the Arts. As for Odets, the one-time radical political firebrand wrote several more screenplays in Hollywood and, far from proudly, several teleplays for *The Richard Boone Show* (1963–64); he died six years after the release of *Sweet Smell of Success* at the age of 57.

There is a certain poignancy associated with the inexorable process whereby Hollywood manages to absorb and make commercially palatable the aesthetic innovations and progressive worldviews of politically radical film artists. In analyzing this phenomenon, however, the tendency has been to extol the "genius of the system" or to critique the depredations of hegemony. Left out of the equation is the human fate of the compromised cultural practitioners themselves. Arthur Miller's observations about Odets in 1957 serve to reinscribe the personal into the political: "There was something so utterly American in what had betrayed him—he had wanted everything." Miller went on to compare Odets to Miller's wife, Marilyn Monroe: "Like her, he was a self-destroying babe in the woods absentmindedly combing back his hair with a loaded pistol." As Odets himself said to Lancaster,

"Hell, you can get killed just yearning for Hollywood."[39] These sentiments bare witness to the painful dilemma facing many Hollywood filmmakers and other members of the artistic Left in the post–World War II era, as they struggled to survive McCarthyism and, through their cultural work, to reconcile the self-serving seductions of success with the altruistic desire to do right by their fellow human beings.

Conclusion

Stimulated by the national cinemas, the various New Waves of the 1950s, and the growing popularity of the art film circuits . . . [the Hollywood Renaissance's responsiveness to social change and to formal] innovations such as overt reflexivity that fractured invisible narration passed into the commercial vocabularies of both film and television. . . . The desire and the ability of the art or the political cinemas to maintain autonomy from the industry was, with few exceptions, entirely eroded by the late 1970s.

—DAVID JAMES, "Alternative Cinemas"

This book's central project has been to analyze the ascension of a new generation of professional-managerial cultural workers, the New Hollywood independents, during a period of industrial crisis and transformation in the post–World War II American film industry. This transitional period saw the evolution of film production from the classical, studio-governed, factory-like "production unit" system to an entrepreneurial, one-shot-deal "package" system in which an independent producer assembled a "creative team"(often including himself as star, director, and/or writer) to use as leverage in obtaining financing and distribution from a studio or independent production company. Out of this new arrangement, which encouraged greater creative freedom, emerged a nascent form of independent art cinema. Besides the achievement of this cinema in its own right, one also can discern in it the seeds of the more truly groundbreaking work of the Hollywood Renaissance of the 1960s and 1970s.[1] Alongside the New Hollywood's art cinema strand, however, other alternatives to the classical system emerged, most significantly, in terms of the state of the industry today, a blockbuster strand that would fade briefly during the Hollywood Renaissance period but would return, in retooled form, to become the dominant form from the mid-1970s on.

Postwar Precedents for a Cinema of Political Engagement

As I have shown, several of the prime thematic and stylistic markers of Hollywood Renaissance–style cinema were clearly presaged by the ideologically reflexive entertainment-business film of the late 1950s.[2] The challenging of traditional gender roles is one of the most prominent of these markers. As our analysis of both the self-referential and reflexive films has shown, faith in traditional female tropes such as the stay-at-home wife and moral arbiter were in deep trouble well before the unofficial launch of the women's movement with the 1963 publication of Betty Friedan's *The Feminine Mystique*. In the reflexive films especially, the subversion of these tropes, and their linkage to a corporatized culture industry and U.S. society, are only minimally contained by residual narrative traces of the melodrama formula.

Marcia Jeffries in *A Face in the Crowd* is symptomatic of this crossroads in the portrait of male-female (and class) relations. Marcia is simultaneously Lonesome Rhodes's business and sexual partner, his biggest advocate, and the jilted woman who ultimately punishes him for his betrayal—both romantically and professionally—by removing him from his position as a (male) TV star with the power to influence (primarily women) consumers. When Rhodes leaves her for a young baton twirler, Marcia is unwilling to forfeit her investment in the business and, to Rhodes's shock, demands 50 percent of the proceeds in Lonesome Rhodes, Inc., which she helped create, indicating an unseemly complicity with the television industry but also a commencement of women's rights. Rhodes's ambivalent response aptly describes the strain Marcia's "liberated" actions pose for traditional gender roles: "All these new-look women a-tellin' off their men folks, a grabbin' a hold of men's jobs and even takin' to wearin' pants. . . . But there's no use getting yaself all het up about somethin' ya can't change."[3]

A similar reversal of classical gender and class relations is at the core of *Sweet Smell of Success*. The film's later scenes juxtapose the ambitious "self-made man" (Falco) and the "true woman" (Susie Hunsecker) in ways that show how each has become a perversion of the traditional ideal. What is left of the "true woman" in these scenes is the pathetic Susie, a woman stripped of her power, her voice, her pride, and thus forced to stoop to the same level of corruption as her male counterparts when she stages a rape scene to destroy her nemesis Falco. However, in the process of exposing Falco as her brother's henchman, Susie acquires the moral strength not only to rid herself of the accoutrements of her brother's wealth and power (which is signified in the film by the act of removing the fur coat he gave her as a gift) but to walk out on her once-invincible brother and begin her life anew. The final images of the film alternate among Hunsecker, alone in his penthouse apartment and stripped of his power, Falco cornered like a rat in the middle of Times Square—the dirty heart of a city overrun by bums, cheats, and liars—and Susie, who escapes the city in the first ray of sunlight in an otherwise oppressively dark urban landscape.

The marginalized, put-upon types juxtaposed at the end of *Sweet Smell of Success*—the victimized, stay-at-home woman and the maligned middle-class working man—both seek to escape the oppressive control of the new class of salaried manager, personified by Hunsecker, who uses his TV celebrity to inflict politically reactionary views on a passive and unsuspecting public. Such ideological exploitation on the part of the entertainment industry is similar to that which Jackson Lears ascribes to the advertising industry at the time: "[D]eliberately or unconsciously, dominant social groups could use gender, race, ethnicity, [class,] and other barriers to screen out entire subcultures by dismissing or ignoring them."[4] The entire process of sociocultural elision is strikingly resonant with Gramsci's notion of hegemony, as Lears explains in a way that bears directly on the social formation of the New Hollywood:

> The essence of hegemony is not manipulation but legitimation. It does not require a vision of a scheming elite and a passive populace. Rather, cultural hegemony is exercised by what Gramsci called a "historical block"— a loose coalition of groups cemented by cultural as well as economic bonds. It is possible to argue that in postwar America a hegemonic historical bloc was formed by the groups often characterized as a "new class" of salaried managers, administrators, academics, technicians, and journalists—people who manipulated symbols rather than made things, whose stock in trade consisted of their organizational, technical, conceptual, or verbal skills. . . . By 1950, Lionel Trilling was able to observe that "intellect has associated itself with power, perhaps as never before in history, and is now conceded to be itself a kind of power."[5]

From this perspective, the self-referential and reflexive films' dark portrayals of powerful managers and middlemen invading the entertainment industry can be seen as an indictment of a hegemonic system in which the filmmakers themselves were participating. It was a system that relegated *non-* or *semi-*managers—women like Susie Hunsecker, Tom Rath's wife Betty in *The Man in the Gray Flannel Suit*, and elevator girl Fran Kubelik in *The Apartment;* men like Tom Rath, Sidney Falco, and Kubelik's co-worker Bud Baxter—to the margins of society. In *Sweet Smell of Success,* the predicament foregrounded in the text—that of one social group's dominance by another—mirrored the filmmakers' extratextual attempts to defy or circumvent the producers' authority on the set—for example, using stylized dialogue and deep-focus sequence shots to circumvent Lancaster's right to final cut.

The major back-screen bogeyman, but also a significant enabler, for the New Hollywood independents was the mega-talent agency epitomized by MCA. As Wilkerson put it in 1957, "Making pictures to entertain the people of the world is a big job, and requires top management and control, much of which the studios have passed to the big agents."[6] Film texts such as *Sweet Smell of Success* and *A Face in the Crowd* indicate, by association, artistically inclined filmmakers' growing awareness of the Faustian conditions inherent in their qualified independence as mediated by mega-agencies like MCA. These creative and moral conflicts are referenced in the films through the clash of artistic aspiration, personal ambition, economic interest, and political persuasion. In *A Face in the Crowd,* the populist singer-humorist Lonesome Rhodes is portrayed as a "regular Joe" corrupted by his own weakness of character but also by an entertainment system that exploits celebrity for commercial gain. In *Sweet Smell of Success,* Hunsecker's (and his sidekick Falco's) embodiment of the culture industry's corrupt publicity machine brings low the artist Steve Dallas, also a "regular Joe" but an "authentic artist."

In both films, industrial forces are not represented as wholly evil; the middleman type is split between a good and a bad representative; however, both films also suggest that the "good" talent representative is a nostalgic holdover from the idealistic populism of the 1930s that must be replaced by a more hard-headed pragmatism to survive, much less to succeed. In *A Face in the Crowd,* the wide-eyed Marcia Jeffries recognizes from the start the ruthlessness of self-serving middleman Joey DePalma, but only in the end does she see through the more invidious façade of the seemingly altruistic Rhodes. In *Sweet Smell of Success,* the aggressive New Hollywood–style agent Sidney Falco is set against the fatherly Old Hollywood–style manager Frank D'Angelo. Similarly, Falco's cold, calculating attitude toward the comedian Herbie Temple, like DePalma's toward Rhodes, is symptomatic of the increasingly mercenary relationship between talent and their representatives in 1950s Hollywood. Just as MCA brought certain comedians like George Gobel to fame not because of his inherent talent as a performer but as a means to build yet another production company and hence another potential revenue stream, so do DePalma's promise of overnight show-business success to Rhodes or a similar promise by Falco to Temple reflect the no-holds-barred venality of the New Hollywood.

In addition to similar self-referential thematic elements, both *A Face in the Crowd* and *Sweet Smell of Success* incorporate a variety of ideologically reflexive devices that invoke a social space outside the narrative, offering perspectives on the relationship between the artists and their business representatives that have implications beyond the diegesis. These reflexive techniques function in a Brechtian sense as aesthetic levers to pry open the classical Hollywood text and release some of its progressive potential. The elements in the classical style most antagonistic to such a release are delineated by Bordwell, Thompson, and Staiger: "causality, consequence, psychological motivations, the drive toward overcoming obstacles and achieving goals. Character-centered—i.e., personal or psychological—causality is the armature of the classical story."[7] Polan, however, has shown that a social dimension can be elicited in the classical Hollywood text, despite its emphasis on the narrative trajectory of the individual hero, through the incorporation of ideologically reflexive technique.[8] While *A Face in the Crowd* and *Sweet Smell of Success* are hardly standard-issue classical texts, even in these highly experimental films, the ambitious and ambivalent hero(ine) and business representatives—Marcia and Falco—are "punished" for their transgressions in the end, and the social order appears to be restored. But the "restoration" is fraught with residual tension and unanswered questions regarding gender roles and the business/artist relationship. By not offering a neat resolution but rather by creating a dialectic between oppositional systems—classical Hollywood's melodrama formulas and ideologically reflexive aesthetics—*A Face in the Crowd* and *Sweet Smell of Success* shift the focus of their critique away from the narrow world of individual psychology and onto the larger social domain.

The End of the Entertainment-Business Film Cycle?

According to Naremore, the evolution of the film noir cycle from the mid-1940s through the early sixties can be characterized as a movement from the idealization of the criminal in a corrupt society in the early neorealist-style films of Huston, Polonsky, and Rossen to a more contradictory societal critique rendered in a radical modernist aesthetic as in Welles's *Touch of Evil* (1958). The cycle culminates in films like John Frankenheimer's *Manchurian Candidate* (1962) in a final "piling on of self-referentiality," or what Jonathan Rosenbaum describes as "allusion profusion": the effect of which is to undermine any simple thematic resolution and instead to provoke a range of possible interpretations given the proliferation of social tensions exposed.[9]

A similar evolutionary arc can be discerned in the self-referential and reflexive entertainment-business films surveyed here. This cycle, which began with the redemption of the adman hero in *The Hucksters*, developed through various permutations into the tainted, entrepreneurial anti-heroes in *A Face in the Crowd* and *Sweet Smell of Success*. These last two films, which correspond thematically and stylistically to the hyper-self-referentiality in Welles's film, thus can be seen as representing the last phase of the postwar self-referential entertainment-business cycle. Both *A Face in the Crowd* and *Sweet Smell of Success* struggle to balance a modernist aesthetic—incorporating elements of stylistic and structural excess—with a concern for individual psychology derived from the classical Hollywood "realist" text.[10] Unlike the "commercially liberal" self-referential films favored by the studios in the late 1940s and early 1950s (e.g., *The Hucksters, It Should Happen to You, Executive Suite*), or the later, more "commercially conservative," blockbuster films favored by Darryl Zanuck (e.g., *Woman's World, The Man in the Gray Flannel Suit*), *A Face in the Crowd* and *Sweet Smell of Success* do not provide easy resolution to the complex social issues they explore. Rather, the ironic "piling on of self-referentiality" in these two films is, as was said of *The Manchurian Candidate*, "in fact so numerous that one cannot be sure whether . . . [the director] and his collaborators were purveying old myths or making fun of them."[11]

The foregrounding of the gaze, stylized language, and complex camera movement in *A Face in the Crowd* and *Sweet Smell of Success* were by no means unique to these two American films during this time period. Similar techniques were prevalent in, if not pioneered by, the hyper-reflexive melodramas of Douglas Sirk (e.g., *Magnificent Obsession* [1954], *All That Heaven Allows* [1955], *Written on the Wind* [1956], *Imitation of Life* [1959]). Also to be reprised are Frank Tashlin's self-referential anarchistic comedies such as *Artists and Models, Hollywood or Bust*, and *Will Success Spoil Rock Hunter?*, and Billy Wilder's acerbically self-referential *Sunset Boulevard, Ace in the Hole*, and *The Apartment*. Given the commercial success of many of the Sirk, Tashlin, and Wilder films, however, one could argue that their aesthetic "excesses" lay more safely within Bordwell, et al.'s acceptable "bounds of difference" in classical Hollywood genres. *Sweet Smell of*

Success, on the other hand, despite subsequent critical acclaim, performed poorly at the box office, suggesting that despite the popularity of certain liminal texts in the 1950s, the troubled H-H-L production was too much of an anomaly with its heavy quotient of "art" juxtaposed to prominent B-film/noir elements and its brutal laying bare of the workings of show business. Complicating matters, the presence of two major movie stars, a spiraling budget, and the high-priced cinematographer "Low-Key Howe," created an awkward hybrid that did not qualify as either an art film, exploitation film, or commercial, mainstream A film. This confluence of competing agendas caused the film to miss its mark both with the mainstream and the art-film audience. *A Face in the Crowd*, meanwhile, which did manage to turn a profit, succeeded financially by taking the *Marty* route (ironic, given that Hecht-Lancaster had pioneered the technique)—that is, the Kazan-Schulberg film balanced its difficult subject matter and challenging technique with a reasonable budget and targeted art-film promotion. The emphatically anti-heroic performances of stars Lancaster and Curtis in *Sweet Smell of Success*, however, coupled with the film's strange brew of blood melodrama and high modernism, art and pulp, movie star vehicle and postmodernist "allusion profusion," was more than the movie marketers at UA could mediate and virtually guaranteed—at least in 1950s' America—commercial disappointment. Yet, as I have attempted to show, not only was the investors' loss posterity's gain, but the massive affront to the classical Hollywood text, the culture industry, and corporate capitalism as a whole in *Sweet Smell of Success*, as in *A Face in the Crowd*, succeeded in the long run by providing, if not exactly a model, at least the inspiration for even more rigorous assaults to come.

What Price New Hollywood: Art Film or Blockbuster?

In 2000, more than three decades after helping usher in the Hollywood Renaissance with the ground-breaking *Bonnie and Clyde* (1967), the talent-turned-independent-producer (and later director) Warren Beatty commented, "You could make a case that the Hollywood artistic community was more liberal in the 1950s and 1960s than it is now. Since the demise of the contract system, the creative community, to a greater extent, has become management."[12] As this study has shown, Beatty's historical gloss is anachronistic: the complicity between the artistic community and management that began with the talent-MCA affiliations in the mid-1940s was already firmly entrenched by 1960. Moreover, the culture clash and moral ambivalence this unholy alliance generated was amply registered in the self-referential and reflexive business films we have surveyed.

The films of the New Hollywood—art film, blockbuster, and variations in between—emerged in a climate of vast industrial and societal change. As we have seen, the industry trades alternated between lauding and lamenting this transformation and, by association, the new breed of talent-turned-independent-producers who had drastically altered the power dynamics of the Old Hollywood studio system and opened the door for more challenging cinematic fare. Further complicating matters was the rise of the corporate middle-managers: talent agents, attorneys, accountants, et al. The increased ability of filmmakers to critique the status quo was thus problematized by their increased enmeshment in "the system." One short-lived solution was to direct one's critique not at the film business or the society at large but at a scapegoat—television—which became both an easy target and an effective metaphor for addressing the unsettling industrial and societal conditions and one's own conflicted attitudes about them.

By the end of the 1950s, the "insider" discourse about the transition from Old Hollywood's mogul-based paternalism to New Hollywood's increasingly brand-oriented, corporate-style of doing business was no longer controversial; it permeated not only the self-referential and reflexive films but routinely appeared in comic monologues and skits on early television shows (formats which themselves were replacing the celebrity-gossip shows hosted by Winchell, Hopper, Parsons, and other Old Hollywood dirt-dusters). And yet, while the ruthless, take-no-prisoners ethos of the New Hollywood power elite may have become "second nature" inside and outside the entertainment industry, a resistant cultural strain in the form of an emergent American art cinema production and audience base also evolved. This new cultural formation would not only withstand intense political repression and commercial pressure to produce compelling work of its own; it would pass the torch to "the dark, disturbing, intelligent, provocative, and quirky" films of the decades to come.[13]

The "alternative cinemas must be contextualized," David James cautions, "by a summary of the history of the [Hollywood] film industry, for when it was not their ambition, it was their antagonist." James is speaking of the avant-garde, but a similar caveat can be applied to the American art cinema, whose aversion/attraction to the two poles, alternative and mainstream, has never been clear-cut. Rather, Hollywood filmmakers find themselves "constantly negotiating and renegotiating various degrees of autonomy and

control, each continuously fracturing and reforming under the stress of internal contradictions and external pressures."[14] In the transitional era, these
stresses, while easing on one hand, proliferated on the other, as politically
liberal, artistically-oriented filmmakers, in particular, found their internal
conflicts compounded by battles with the studios, the agencies, the MPAA,
the PCA, the Catholic Legion of Decency, and HUAC.

By the time of the Hollywood Renaissance, indeed a prerequisite for
it, many of the external stresses—PCA, Legion of Decency, HUAC—had
been relieved. Internal conflict remained, however, as did the need for compromise. Industry figures such as Beatty and even certain historians have
highly selective, often nostalgic memories of the late 1960s, and therefore
prefer to see a monocausal relation between the radical social movements
of the 1960s and the cultural radicalism of the American New Wave. In
fact, the films of the Hollywood Renaissance were much more balanced
affairs, responding both to marketplace conditions and the prevailing zeit-
geist. It made good business sense for an industry in financial disarray and
at the cusp of the counterculture to give the green light to creatively risky,
but lower-budget efforts rather than to continue throwing good money after
bad on exorbitant would-be blockbusters that were routinely failing at the
box-office. For their part, however, Hollywood Renaissance filmmakers, like
their 1950s art-cinema counterparts, were not necessarily interested in emulating, to the letter, European or other foreign auteurist models. Ultimately,
what distinguishes the American art cinema most from those of other
nations is rooted in Hollywood filmmakers' acute, perhaps ingrained awareness of the commercial realities driving the U.S. film industry. Hollywood
Renaissance and New Hollywood independents alike, if each in their own
way, sought to balance two traditions, art and mainstream, either by alternating between one or the other type of film ("one for the Pope, one for
me") or through attempting fusions of both tendencies in the same work.
It was the best of the latter attempts, as I have argued in regard to the self-
referential and ideologically reflexive entertainment-business films, which
emerged as the most aesthetically original and ideologically progressive cinematic achievements of the early New Hollywood era.

The New Hollywood independents, some recent transplants from the
New York–based political theater, others veterans of the contract era, were
all eager to carry on the 1930s populist tradition and, to varying degrees,
to infuse their work with elements of the European art cinemas, classical
B-genre and social problem films, and early television. Eventually, in the

mid-to-late 1960s, these trends coalesced in the more consistently innovative and commercially viable Hollywood Renaissance, propelled by a new generation of filmmakers who emerged from and spoke to the counterculture and who, at their best, sought "to remake Hollywood into a democratically responsive, forward thinking, and even potentially subversive set of cultural institutions."[15]

Notes

1. Charting a Path of Independence in a Corporate Wilderness

1. David O. Selznick said to Ben Hecht in 1951: "Hollywood's like Egypt, full of crumbled pyramids. It'll never come back. It'll just keep on crumbling until finally the wind blows the last studio props across the sand." Cited in J. A. Aberdeen, *Hollywood Renegades: The Society of Independent Motion Picture Producers* (Van Nuys, Calif.: Cobblestone Entertainment Press, 2000), 239.

2. Universal adapted its factory-like production techniques to create standardized, inexpensive programming for television starting in the midfifties. See Christopher Anderson, *Hollywood TV: The Studio System in the Fifties* (Austin: University of Texas Press, 1994), 60–62.

3. For the range of meanings associated with the phrase "New Hollywood" see Gerald Mast and Bruce F. Kawin, *A Short History of the Movies,* 8th ed. (New York: Longman, 2002); Thomas Schatz, *Old Hollywood/New Hollywood: Ritual, Art, and Industry* (Ann Arbor, Mich.: UMI Research Press, 1983); Schatz, "The New Hollywood," in *Film Theory Goes to the Movies,* ed. Jim Collins, Hilary Radner, and Ava Preacher (New York: Routledge, 1993); Steve Neale and Murray Smith, eds., *Contemporary Hollywood Cinema* (London: Routledge, 1998); Jon Lewis, ed., *The New American Cinema* (Durham, N.C.: Duke University Press, 1998); Geoff King, *New Hollywood Cinema: An Introduction* (New York: Columbia University Press, 2003). King uses the designation "New Hollywood, Version I and II" to refer to the films of the Hollywood Renaissance and blockbuster eras, respectively.

4. Schatz writes: "In terms of budgets, production values, and market strategy, Hollywood has been increasingly hit-driven since the early 1950s. This marks a significant departure from the classical era, when the studios turned out a few 'prestige' pictures each year and relished the occasional runaway box-office hit, but relied primarily on routine A-class features to generate revenues. The exceptional became the rule in postwar Hollywood, as the occasional hit gave way to the calculated blockbuster." Schatz, "The New Hollywood," 8–9. Definitions of an American "art cinema" (what it is and when it began) vary among historians. Most, like Merritt, trace it back to experiments made in the teens or even earlier, emphasizing

nonstudio releases; others focus on the films of the Hollywood Renaissance (also known as the American New Wave). Greg Merritt, *Celluloid Mavericks: A History of American Independent Film* (New York: Thunder's Mouth Press, 2000). Still others, like Naremore, use the phrase "art movie" to describe artistically ambitious film noir made in the 1940s and 1950s. James Naremore, *More Than Night: Film Noir in Its Contexts* (Berkeley: University of California Press, 1998), 139.

5. See Justin Wyatt, "From Roadshowing to Saturation Release: Majors, Independents, and Marketing/Distribution Innovations," in *The New American Cinema*, ed. Lewis, 64–86; and Lisa Kernan, *Coming Attractions: Reading American Movie Trailers* (Austin: University of Texas Press, 2004), 30. Both distinguish between the two types of late 1960s films (and trailers)—the large, roadshow productions and smaller independent cinema—and trace these developments back to the 1950s.

6. Two major exceptions are: Schatz, *Old Hollywood/New Hollywood*, 187; and Tino Balio, *United Artists: The Company That Changed the Film Industry* (Madison: University of Wisconsin Press, 1987), 150–53.

7. David E. James is cited in Chris Holmlund, "Introduction to 'Critical Formations,'" in *Contemporary American Independent Film: From the Margins to the Mainstream*, ed. Chris Holmlund and Justin Wyatt (London: Routledge, 2005), 26.

8. Lea Jacobs explains the inconsistencies in the A and B system based on production values, box office performance, and so on. Cited in Naremore, *More Than Night*, 141.

9. See Richard Maltby, *Hollywood Cinema*, 2nd ed. (Malden, Mass.: Blackwell, 2003), 132.

10. Freeman Lincoln, "The Comeback of the Movies," quoted in *The American Film Industry*, ed. Tino Balio (Madison: University of Wisconsin Press, 1976), 371; Balio, *United Artists*, 150.

11. For instance, Merritt calls Kazan, John Huston, Robert Aldrich, and others "semi-independent" given their dependence on the studios for financing, distribution, and even exhibition. Merritt, *Celluloid Mavericks*, 94–97.

12. Ibid.

13. Paul Monaco, *The Sixties: 1960–1969* (Berkeley: University of California Press, 2003), 24.

14. "UA Releasing 65 Features in 18 Months: Krim Announces Record Schedule: 34 Completed; 32 in Color, Some in 3-D," *Hollywood Reporter*, April 10, 1953.

15. See Wyatt, "From Roadshowing to Saturation Release," 67.

16. A typical strategy employed by exploitation companies was to make inexpensive versions of successful titles. For instance, *Hot Rod Rumble* was a knock-off of *The Wild One* with a lead actor who adopted Marlon Brando's mannerisms from that film. Roger Corman directed and produced forty-five low-budget exploitation films between 1953 and 1970, and produced or executive produced another thirty films.

17. Holmlund, "Introduction," in *Contemporary American Independent Film*, ed. Wyatt and Holmlund, 5.

18. Merritt, *Celluloid Mavericks*, 155–56. Merritt writes: "In the late sixties, 'Cinema 5' became synonymous with 'art films.'"

19. Wyatt, "From Roadshowing to Saturation Release," 68.

20. See, for instance, Peter Biskind, *Easy Riders, Raging Bulls: How the Sex-Drugs-and-Rock 'n' Roll Generation Saved Hollywood* (New York: Simon and Schuster, 1998).

21. Wilder is quoted in Aberdeen, *Hollywood Renegades*, 249.

22. *Hollywood Reporter* columnist W. R. Wilkerson states, "To give you some idea of the influence and the power of the big agency operation currently, take the case of the forthcoming 20th-Fox production of *The Young Lions*, which will star Marlon Brando and Montgomery Clift, both clients of MCA." He continues: "Instead of using one of its promising contract players in a part that would start his stride to stardom, 20th had to give in to MCA's demand and that's what we meant yesterday in our yarn on the power of the big agencies and how the major studios have given in to that power." Wilkerson, "Trade Views" (daily column), *Hollywood Reporter*, June 14, 1957, 1.

23. Edward T. Thompson, "There's No Show Business Like MCA Business," *Fortune*, February 1960, 52.

24. Robert Phillip Kolker, *A Cinema of Loneliness* (New York: Oxford University Press, 1980), 5; quoted in Schatz, *Old Hollywood/New Hollywood*, 200.

25. "Indie Packaging Gets Tougher," *Hollywood Reporter*, June 25, 1954, 1.

26. Richard Dyer MacCann, *Hollywood in Transition* (Boston: Houghton Mifflin, 1962), 53.

27. Balio is quoted in Kate Buford, *Burt Lancaster: An American Life* (New York: De Capo Press, 2000), 136.

28. Lancaster appeared in nonstar turns in two films made by independent producer Hal B. Wallis: *Come Back, Little Sheba* (1952) and *The Rose Tattoo* (1955). After Wallis left Warner Bros. in 1943, he formed Hal B. Wallis Productions, releasing his films through Paramount. In order to supplement his income, Lancaster signed a contract with Hal Wallis Productions and initially alternated between making films for Wallis and for his own company, imitating Wallis's strategy by alternating between star roles and nonstar turns at H-L.

29. James Hill was named a partner in 1956 (and the company became Hecht-Hill-Lancaster). Hill is also credited with producing three of the company's more mainstream films during 1954–56.

30. In today's consolidated entertainment industry, most specialty divisions (e.g., Fox Searchlight, Warner Bros. Independent, Focus Features) are owned by media giants. The distinctions between mainstream and specialty films continue to narrow as bankable stars like Bruce Willis and Bill Murray dramatically reduce their salaries to appear in smaller films like *Pulp Fiction* (1994) and *Lost in Translation* (2004).

31. Gary Fishgall, *Against Type: The Biography of Burt Lancaster* (New York: Scribner's, 1995), 174.

32. Lea Jacobs explains the inconsistencies in the A and B system that allowed certain B films with better-than-average production values and/or box-office performance to be given an "A" release. She also describes a category called "intermediates," which cost between $250,000 and $500,000. For a more complete discussion, see Lea Jacobs, "The B Film and the Problem of Cultural Distinction," *Screen* 33,

no. 1 (Spring 1992): 1–13; cited in Naremore, *More Than Night*, 141. In the 1950s, certain independent production/distribution companies like Allied Artists were making "intermediates" to become more competitive with the studios.

33. These statistics are compiled from the following sources: Schatz, "The New Hollywood," 13; Balio, *United Artists*, 126; and Corbbett Steinberg, *Reel Facts: The Movie Book of Records* (New York: Vintage Books, 1978), 345–48. Steinberg's domestic film rentals were gathered from *Variety*, *Motion Picture Herald*, *Motion Picture Daily*, and *Film Daily*.

34. Schatz, "The New Hollywood," 12.

35. Peter Lev, *Transforming the Screen: 1950–1959*, History of American Cinema 7 (New York: Scribner's, 2003), 62. Lev describes the way certain 1950s films (e.g., *Singing in the Rain* and *Gentlemen Prefer Blondes*) "fled social controversy by situating stories in a nostalgically remembered past." Balio lists several big-budget A films, including "[United Artists'] *The African Queen*, MGM's *Quo Vadis?*, and Paramount's *The Greatest Show on Earth*, which smashed box-office records. Cinerama and 3-D boosted business in 1953 and, following the introduction of CinemaScope, a turnaround was in the making . . . [with the release of *The Robe* in CinemaScope in 1953]." Balio, *United Artists*, 124–25.

36. Schatz, "The New Hollywood," 11.

37. Critic/historian James Harvey is quoted in Lev, *Transforming the Screen*, 217.

38. Ibid., 241. Lev identifies a group of fiction films (e.g., *On the Waterfront*, *Marty*, *Blackboard Jungle*), which used black-and-white and emphasized "realism" as a reaction to the mid-1950s' trend toward color and widespread spectacle. The budgets for these films tended to be under $1 million; for example, *Marty*'s budget was $360,000; *On the Waterfront*'s budget was $900,000. Some studios made slightly bigger-budgeted art films (in the more typical A-film price range of $2–4 million) if the package contained one or more marketable elements (e.g., a major director, star, or pre-sold literature) to help offset the risks.

39. The budgets for film adaptations of significant plays by established playwrights, such as Tennessee Williams and William Inge, were often directed by artistically ambitious directors and ranged from $1.8 for the WB release of the Elia Kazan–directed *Streetcar Named Desire* (1951) to $3 million for the Columbia release of the Joseph Mankiewicz–directed *Suddenly, Last Summer* (1959).

40. Welles's "value" was volatile, prompting the budget for *Lady for Shanghai* to go up to $2 million whereas *Mr. Arkadin* had to be made for very little money outside the studio system; *Touch of Evil* was capped at $830,000 (much higher than Welles's "rate" given the presence of Charlton Heston, who impelled the studio to accept Welles as director).

41. Not just *Cahier du cinéma* and *Positif*, but other, less-prominent publications were also targeting Wilder, Huston, Preminger, Kazan, Mankiewicz, and others. See, for instance, Lino Lionello Ghirardini, "Post-War American Cinema Studies," in *Il Cinema del Dopoguerra Americano: The Big Carnival* e Billy Wilder, in *Storia Generale del Cinema, 1895–1959* (Milan: Dott. Carlo Marzorati, 1959), 2:943–48; cited in Steve Seidman, *The Film Career of Billy Wilder* (Boston: G. K. Hall, 1977), 121.

42. Monaco, *The Sixties*, 25.

43. Murray Smith, "Theses on the Philosophy of Hollywood History," in *Contemporary Hollywood Cinema*, ed. Neale and Smith, 5.

44. Ibid., 3. Also see Henry Jenkins, *What Makes Pistachio Nuts? Early Sound Comedy and the Vaudeville Aesthetic* (New York: Columbia University Press, 1992), 18–19.

45. Smith, "Theses on the Philosophy of Hollywood History," 3.

46. After returning from the war in 1945, Zanuck was convinced that the postwar moratorium on social problem films would end and hired Elia Kazan to direct several commercially liberal social problem films: *Gentleman's Agreement* (1947) on anti-Semitism and *Pinky* (1949) on race relations.

47. Wilkerson, "Trade Views," August 12, 1953. Wilkerson states: "Audiences, since the advent of TV, insist that the pictures they pay for in theatres have to be better than those they can get on TV for free. Result: the elimination of the small pictures with their low budgets UNLESS a little picture has what it takes to attract the customers. The big studios found out long ago that the in-between picture means nothing. Not only did they lose money, but they dragged the important profits away from the hit films."

48. The details of this unique campaign are described in Buford, *Burt Lancaster*, 47–50. Also see Balio, *United Artists*, 82.

49. Buford, *Burt Lancaster*, 148.

50. Ibid., 150.

51. In Lev, *Transforming the Screen*, 216, 197–216, the author states: "By 1958 and 1959, at least four important strategies for attracting and sustaining audiences had been developed: the road show, the traditional first-run, the art movies, and the drive-in movie." The "road show" refers to the special handling given to the certain high-profile films (e.g., the prestige/blockbuster-style epics) at a prestigious A theater, usually on a reserved-seat basis and at a higher-than-normal admission price. The "first-run" refers to the first screening of all other A films at select A-film theaters, often at a higher price, before they were exhibited at neighborhood theaters. The "art house" refers to the small, urban theaters that screened either classic revivals, or new, mostly European, films of limited box-office appeal.

52. Corrigan is describing post–Vietnam era Hollywood, whereas I am tracing the evolution of this business model back to the post–World War II era. Timothy Corrigan, *A Cinema without Walls: Movies and Culture after Vietnam* (New Brunswick, N.J.: Rutgers University Press, 1991), 80–98, 103.

53. Wilkerson, "Trade Views," November 16, 1954, 1. Wilkerson attempts to mediate the star's costs/benefits on behalf of media practitioners: "[Marlon Brando is] probably a screwball to a lot of producers whose efforts to get him on a set in a picture meet with little success. His personal life might differ from the general conception of a young fellow at his age. BUT he's an actor and might well add up to one of the big ticket-sellers of all times because he has the knack of picking GOOD PICTURES for his participation and this plus his ability is a cinch to make him the big draw."

54. Cited in Aberdeen, *Hollywood Renegades*, 239.

55. After making independent, socially critical films that were box-office disappointments (e.g., *Monsieur Verdoux* in 1947 and *Limelight* in 1952) and given his

unpopular support of Russia as part of the Allies in World War II, Chaplin, like Welles, was accused of being a Communist supporter. While abroad in 1952 supporting the release of *Limelight*, Chaplin was barred from returning to the States by the U.S. Immigration and Naturalization Service. Aberdeen, *Hollywood Renegades*, 232–33.

56. Gerald Horne, *Class Struggle in Hollywood, 1930–1950: Moguls, Mobsters, Stars, Reds and Trade Unions* (Austin: University of Texas Press, 2001), 218. The CSU had to battle not only the studios but the established union, the International Association of Theater and Stage Employees (IATSE), headed by the rabidly anti-Communist Roy Brewer.

57. Thom Anderson, "Red Hollywood," in *Literature and the Visual Arts in Contemporary Society*, ed. Suzanne Ferguson and Barbara Groseclose (Columbus: Ohio State University Press, 1985), 187; quoted in Naremore, *More Than Night*, 130.

58. According to Hamilton, "After the original 'Hollywood Ten' went to jail in 1947, the hearings resumed in 1951. Then the avalanche of reluctant witnesses naming names began in earnest." Among them were Budd Schulberg, Clifford Odets, Elia Kazan, Robert Rosen, Larry Parks, Lee J. Cobb, Edward G. Robinson, and Sterling Hayden. Hayden said, "I was a real daddy longlegs of a worm when it came to crawling." Ian Hamilton, *Writers in Hollywood* (London: Heinemann, 1990), 298.

59. Nancy Lynn Schwartz, *The Hollywood Writer's Wars* (New York: Knopf, 1982). Schwartz is quoted in Naremore, *More Than Night*, 106.

60. Brian Neve, *Film and Politics in America: A Social Tradition* (London: Routledge, 1992/2000), 174.

61. Bertolt Brecht, the only one among the initial eleven of the Hollywood Ten to testify who hadn't been a member of the Communist Party, afterwards was in tears. "[H]e wanted to take the same position as the rest of [the Hollywood Ten] had and refuse to answer the Committee's questions. . . . [A]fterwards [he] took a flight to Paris and never returned to the U.S." Hamilton, *Writers in Hollywood*, 291.

62. According to Crowdus, "the threat of being cut off from his supply of celluloid shaped many of the important aesthetic choices [Wilder] made in his career." Crowdus continues, "He was haunted by the fate of Von Stroheim, haunted by the fear that one day the corporate money men would take his camera away." Gary Crowdus, in *The Political Companion to American Film*, ed. Crowdus (Chicago: Lakeview Press, 1994), 480. Sikov points out that Wilder knew to avoid Robert Rossen as a potential writing partner when his then-agent made the suggestion; Wilder had thus far escaped the HUAC. Ed Sikov, *On Sunset Boulevard: The Life and Times of Billy Wilder* (New York: Hyperion, 1998), 332.

63. Buford cites several attempts by right-wing organizations to target Lancaster for his tendency to hire leftist filmmakers—writers, directors, and executives—and the company's track record of making films with controversial themes. A 1951 *American Legion Magazine* article, "Did the Movies Really Clean House?," singled out Lancaster, along with John Garfield, Judy Holliday, Jose Ferrer, Shelley Winters, Arthur Miller, and Clifford Odets as "unexposed big-name sympathizers" overlooked by HUAC. Lancaster paid a large sum to his attorney Martin Gang of

the Los Angeles firm of Gang, Kopp, and Tyre to draft a letter avowing his patriotism. In January 1952, *Counterattack* also challenged Lancaster. Buford states, "Via Norma Productions, he was accused of hiring Norman Corwin, a top writer/producer at CBS who had 'over 50 instances . . . [of] support of CP fronts and causes.'" Finally, according to Buford, an informant wrote a letter to the FBI, stating "The Reds are just as active as ever," citing Norma Productions as an example of "the way the Reds help each other." Buford, *Burt Lancaster*, 120–21.

64. Early in his career, Joseph Mankiewicz learned to balance his personal politics with the studio's focus on profits when he served as the in-house producer of F. Scott Fitzgerald's first and highly polemic Hollywood screenplay, *Three Comrades* (1938). To Fitzgerald's utter dismay, the Breen office had asked the writer to turn the film's rampaging street gangs (identified as Communists) into the "heavies." At first, Mankiewicz protected Fitzgerald's political vision, but later made major cuts in the unwieldy screenplay. Hamilton, *Writers in Hollywood*, 146.

65. See Lary May, *The Big Tomorrow: Hollywood and the Politics of the American Way* (Chicago: University of Chicago Press, 2000), 211–12; May, "Movie Star Politics: The Screen Actors' Guild, Cultural Conversion, and the Hollywood Red Scare," in *Recasting America: Culture and Politics in the Age of Cold War*, ed. Lary May (Chicago: University of Chicago Press, 1989), 146–49; and Ezra Goodman, *The Fifty-Year Decline and Fall of Hollywood* (New York: Simon and Schuster, 1961), 251–53.

66. According to May, "Hope spoke of the country as an 'Uncle Sugar'" and justified the Marshall Plan as a way of reinforcing the "wonderful Shangri La we are living in here." Hope also justified the Cold War belief that "we should share our resources with the Europeans before others [i.e., communists] move in and make them our enemies." Bob Hope's quote originally appeared in "Tomorrow Is a New Day," in *The American Magazine*, March 4, 1949, 21, 134–36; cited in May, *The Big Tomorrow*, 178–79.

67. A number of postwar histories emphasize the social-problem film and film-noir genres. In addition to Neve, *Film and Politics in America*, see Peter Roffman and Jim Purdy, *The Hollywood Social Problem Film: Madness, Despair, and Politics from the Depression to the Fifties* (Bloomington: Indiana University Press, 1981). Naremore points out that "the blacklist helped to create some of the finest and most socially outraged examples of film noir, as if the material that government officials and Hollywood censors were trying to repress had managed, in Metz's language, to get through, one way or another" (*More Than Night*, 130).

68. Neve explains how "the *Screen Writer* magazine and the scholarly *Hollywood Quarterly* gave considerable space to liberal and radical aspirations for better, more creative and more socially responsible post-war filmmaking." Neve notes that in the face of HUAC, Eric Johnston, head of MPAA since 1945 and a former businessman, delivered a speech in March 1947 arguing that "We'll have no more *Grapes of Wrath*, we'll have no more *Tobacco Roads*. We'll have no more films that show the seamy side of American life" (*Film and Politics in America*, 89–90).

69. May, *The Big Tomorrow*, 2. Steve Ross, *Working Class Hollywood* (Princeton, N.J.: Princeton University Press, 1998).

70. The concept of "ideologically reflexive" (discussed at length in chapter 7) is derived from Polan's reading of Brechtian reflexivity and is based on a tri-part relation to textual pleasure in Dana B. Polan, *The Political Language of Film and the Avant-Garde* (Ann Arbor: UMI Research Press, 1985), 98. According to this schema, audiences potentially experience pleasure on three levels. The first two levels, those resulting from mimetic recognition and formal appreciation, are a part of the pleasure produced by all classical texts. The third level, "pleasurable instruction," inserts a didactically entertaining (or entertainingly didactic) dimension into the text, through which it performs its ideological "work"—or as Polan puts it, "This is an art whose content is a combination of the world and a better version of that world."

71. By way of contrast, certain social realist films like *Marty* and *On the Waterfront* (both 1954) were being singled out both by the Academy and by various international film festivals.

72. Naremore, *More Than Night*, 139.

73. A variation on this theme is the appearance in certain 1950s films of "oppositional figures—the beatnik, the artist, the juvenile delinquent . . . all [of which] express sympathy for the new rebels [a] broad but unfocused rebelliousness [that] would become a crucial part of 1960s popular culture." Lev, *Transforming the Screen*, 255.

74. The two leading postwar distributors of independent productions were UA and Warner Bros. "[Surpassing UA, . . . Warner Brothers] investments in independent productions for distribution climbed from less than two million dollars in 1946 to roughly twenty-five million dollars ten years later." Schatz, *Old Hollywood/New Hollywood*, 174.

75. Zanuck served as head of Twentieth Century–Fox from 1934 to 1956 when he was replaced by production head Buddy Adler. From 1956 to 1962 Zanuck ran his independent production company: Darryl F. Zanuck Productions. In 1962 Fox's board asked Zanuck to resume control of the studio to help guide it out of its post-*Cleopatra* economic downturn. However, explaining the change that prompted Zanuck to quit in 1957, a Fox executive stated: "It is no longer possible to filter the total production of one company through the mind of one man"; Eric Hodgins, "Amid Ruins of an Empire a New Hollywood Arises," *Life*, June 10, 1957, 147.

76. Corrigan, *A Cinema without Walls*, 81.

77. Many 1950s films mock classical Hollywood film traditions from which they derived. See, for instance, the films of producer-director John Huston: *The African Queen* (Horizon [Huston-Spiegel]/UA, 1952), featuring Humphrey Bogart and Katharine Hepburn, both of whom undermine their star personas by playing a drunk and a spinster, respectively; also see, for example, Huston's English-Italian-American coproduction, *Beat the Devil* (Horizon/Santana/Romulus Ltd./Rizzoli-Haggaig/UA, 1954), a farcical take on *Maltese Falcon*–type movies, written by Truman Capote, and featuring Bogart, Gina Lollabrigida, and Peter Lorre (also mocking earlier noir performances).

78. Michael Ovitz, the head of CAA in the 1980s and 1990s, cites Lew Wasserman as one of his primary role models. Much like MCA in the 1950s, Ovitz and CAA dominated the entertainment industry in the 1980s and 1990s, acting as the

behind-the-scenes negotiator in two significant transactions: Sony's purchase of Columbia and Matsushita's purchase of Universal.

79. The narrowed gap between independent and dominant cinema practices is particularly striking in the modern era. Most industry analysts agree that mini-majors Miramax and New Line have forgotten their "art-house" roots and are using stars, budgets, and marketing campaigns that are comparable to those of the majors since they were bought by Disney and Warner Bros., respectively, in the mid-1990s; Jeffrey R. Sipe, "Year End Wrap 2001: The Indies," *Hollywood Reporter*, January 4–6, 2002.

80. John T. Caldwell, "Critical Industrial Practices: Branding, Repurposing, and the Migratory Patterns of Industrial Texts," *Television and New Media* 7, no. 2 (May 2006): 99.

81. For instance, Wilkerson praises Disney's business practices, writing, "One of the chief factors enabling Walt Disney to maintain his consistently high average in the mass-appeal quality of his product is a realistic system conducted right on his own lot among all employees. This calls for 'testing' and 'previewing' all picture ideas from their origination through their development and completion" (Wilkerson, "Trade Views," April 30, 1953, 1).

82. Caldwell, "Critical Industrial Practices," 24. Caldwell is referring to the vast array of interstitial information generated by contemporary television networks about their activities, including the publicity materials between programs, on network Web sites, during "up-fronts," and so on).

83. Denise Mann, "Spectacularization of Everyday Life: Recycling Hollywood Stars and Fans in Early Television Variety Shows," in *Private Screenings: Television and the Female Consumer*, eds. Lynn Spigel and Denise Mann (Minneapolis: University of Minnesota Press, 1992), 44.

84. An ad for *Saturday Evening Post*, "Pete's done it again!," *Hollywood Reporter*, May 22, 1956, 24, compared readership among *Saturday Evening Post, Life*, and *Look*, the three major popular magazines covering the entertainment industry during the fifties. *Saturday Evening Post (SEP)* exceeded 1,500,000 newsstand sales compared to *Look* and *Life* at 800,000 and 900,000, respectively. The ad features a series of quotes from major industry journalists celebrating *SEP*'s sales, including *Hollywood Reporter*'s Mike Connolly, who states: "*Time* had 33 men on its Monroe story. In spite of which *SEP*'s Pete Martin was not outnumbered." Goodman, *The Fifty-Year Decline and Fall of Hollywood*, 224, cites the article Goodman wrote in *Time* (1956) about Monroe called "Marilyn." Jack Hamilton, "Rita Hayworth: Out of 'Bondage,'" *Look*, January 21, 1959, 50–54.

85. Mann, "Spectacularization of Everyday Life," 53–55.

86. For a more in-depth discussion, see Lynn Spigel, *Make Room for TV: Television and the Family Ideal in Postwar America* (Chicago: University of Chicago Press, 1992).

87. Ibid.

88. *Variety*, September 19, 21, and 25, 1950. Notably, several years later, Tashlin has Martin and Lewis enact a "tribute" to motion picture fans across the globe in the preamble to their last film made together, *Hollywood or Bust* (1956). Fashioned

like a comedy-variety monologue, Martin stands on stage next to a spinning globe and introduces Lewis, who portrays viewers of different nationalities (e.g., Chinese, Russian, American) in a series of highly stereotypical comedy bits.

89. Naremore traces the lines of continuity between 1940s and 1950s "film noir" and their contemporary counterparts. For instance, he shows how Neil Jordan's *The Crying Game* (1992) shows traces of Welles's *Mr. Arkadin* (1955), and Quentin Tarantino's *Reservoir Dogs* has allusions to Godard and Kubrick, among others. Naremore continues, "Like *T-Men* in the late 1940s, they mixed generic conventions with artistic effects, blurring the line between exploitation and sophistication" (*More Than Night,* 165–66).

90. Schatz provides this type of sweeping analysis of a vast array of films (1940s–1970s) that experiment with genre. Schatz, *Old Hollywood/New Hollywood,* 67–187.

2. Backstage Dramas

1. For detailed histories of MCA, see Dennis McDougal, *The Last Mogul: Lew Wasserman, MCA, and the Hidden History of Hollywood* (New York: Crown, 1998), and Connie Bruck, *When Hollywood Had a King: The Reign of Lew Wasserman, Who Leveraged Talent into Power and Influence* (New York: Random House, 2003). For a detailed history of the William Morris Agency, see Frank Rose, *The Agency: William Morris and the Hidden History of Show Business* (New York: Harper-Collins, 1995); and for an overview of talent agencies in general, see Whitney Stine, *Stars and Star Handlers: The Business of Show* (Santa Monica, Calif.: Roundtable Publishing, 1985).

2. In 1948 *Variety* described the studios' more dependent relationship to stars at the end of the contract-era as "a last ditch effort to win back the lost audience by emphasizing the stars." "Studios Star-Stud Pix to Bolster Limp Box-Office," *Variety,* April 27, 1948.

3. Douglas Gomery, "Hollywood Corporate Business Practice and Contemporary Film History," in *Contemporary Hollywood Cinema,* ed. Neale and Smith, 47–57.

4. According to one trade account, the current circumstances reveal "the extraordinary leverage that movie stars held over the studios"; *Variety,* April 27, 1948. Other relevant articles include "Stars Hitting the Skids," *Daily News,* 1954, and "End of Era for Stars," *Variety,* January 3, 1951.

5. *Hollywood Reporter,* January 20, 1953, 1.

6. In 1945, when a federal district court judge in Los Angeles filed the first antitrust suit against MCA, calling it the "octopus" to characterize the extent of its monopoly over talent, MCA was forced to pay damages to Larry Finley, an operator of a ballroom in Mission Beach, California, who claimed he couldn't book talent since MCA had an exclusive contract with a rival owner. David Gelman and Alfred G. Aronowitz, "MCA: Show Business Empire," *New York Post,* June 4, 1962, 27. Also see McDougal, *The Last Mogul,* 108–9.

7. *Hollywood Reporter,* May 24, 1957, 1.

8. Michele Hilmes, *Hollywood and Broadcasting: From Radio to Cable* (Champaign: University of Illinois Press, 1990), 118–20.

9. Thompson states: "In February 1958, MCA bought the Paramount backlog of pre-1948 features and a year later it bought the Universal lot. MCA paid $10 million cash for the Paramount backlog and gave a note for $25 million more to be paid in annual installments of about $2 million over 12 years." He continues: "MCA had already sold some or all of the films in at least eighty of the hundred major U.S. TV markets for a total of about $60 million. By the time the company gets to the remaining domestic markets and the untapped foreign markets, its contracts seem sure to top $100 million." Thompson, "There's No Show Business like MCA Business," 165.

10. Gelman and Aronowitz, "MCA: Show Business Empire," *New York Post*, June 8, 1962, 45.

11. McDougal, *The Last Mogul*, 212.

12. Ibid., 115.

13. Florence Jacobowitz, "Joan Bennett: Images of Femininity in Conflict," *CineAction!* (December 1986): 23–34.

14. According to Neve, both the Mark Hellinger unit (a former studio producer at Warners) and Diana Productions had their production company deals at Universal International. "[Eager] to exploit its wartime prosperity to achieve 'big five status,' Universal-International was to make A pictures exclusively with budgets rising toward $1m—and to become a home for independent producers. . . . With the beginning of the market downturn, supervision of productions was tightened in 1947, and Universal returned to a low cost 'assembly line strategy' in 1949" (Neve, *Film and Politics*, 119).

15. MacCann, *Hollywood in Transition*, 53.

16. Gillette writes: "The glamour is being taken out of the movies in more ways than one." Don Carle Gillette (who replaced W. R. Wilkerson), "Trade Views," *Hollywood Reporter*, March 12, 1960, 1.

17. Goodman, *The Fifty-Year Decline and Fall of Hollywood*, 251.

18. See May, *The Big Tomorrow*, 183–89.

19. Several directors boycotted the Academy Award ceremonies of 1936 due to the studios' refusal to recognize the talent agency guilds. The studios didn't officially grant the unions recognition until required to under the provisions of the Wagner Labor Relations Act. Mason Wiley and Damien Bona, *Inside Oscar: The Unofficial History of the Academy Awards* (New York: Ballantine, 1986).

20. May, "Movie Star Politics," in *Recasting America*, ed. May, 125–53, 128–29.

21. Goodman, *The Fifty-Year Decline and Fall of Hollywood*, 252.

22. Ibid., 252–53.

23. McDougal, *The Last Mogul*, 275.

24. Bruck, *When Hollywood Had a King*, 84–85.

25. Bruck quotes long-time agent Marty Baum (currently at CAA), who says about the era: "MCA was saying, 'Take this money, come with us, you'll be part of the biggest agency—and if you don't we'll take away your clients.'" Bruck, *When Hollywood Had a King*, 73–74.

26. Alva Johnston, "Hollywood's Ten Per Centers," *Saturday Evening Post*, August 8, 1942, 37.

27. McDougal writes: "In an ambitious three-part series titled 'Hollywood's Ten Per Centers,' . . . journalist Alva Johnston devoted over 12,000 words to Hollywood's 'flesh peddlers,' naming every major player in town . . . except MCA" (*The Last Mogul*, 86).

28. Johnston, "Hollywood's Ten Per Centers," *Saturday Evening Post*, August 15, 1942, 38, and August 22, 1942, 23.

29. Jacobowitz, "Joan Bennett," 23–34.

30. Gaines writes, "One of the predominant versions of star-making was the myth that Hollywood promotion made 'something out of nothing.'" For instance, "there was the discovery which featured a Svengali who trained and outfitted the star mentioned. The success of Jane Russell, Lana Turner, and Rita Hayworth all include a tribute to the exquisite taste and sense of timing of agent, manager, producer, or husband"; Jane Gaines, "The Popular Icon as Commodity and Sign: The Circulation of Betty Grable, 1941–55," Ph.D. diss., Northwestern University, 1982, 131.

31. Gaines describes studio publicity efforts to "bring the stars down to earth" so as to avoid envy. For instance, "the way to bring down Lana Turner was to report that she returned her rented sable to the furrier after every party" (ibid., 471). In other cases, publicity that depicted stars aligned with noncelebrities reinforced their "everyday" qualities over their "aristocratic" standing, such as when *Look* magazine reports that Clark Gable, "unlike other stars . . . likes to hang around and talk with 'lower echelons'"; Joe McCarthy, "Clark Gable: How He Became King of Hollywood," *Look* 19, November 1, 1955, 104.

32. Goodman writes: "Studio press agents have a punitive weapon in the official 'accreditation' they hand out through their committee on the AMPP. . . . If a journalist steps out of bounds, he may be barred by the AMPP publicity boys from studios and press showings." Invoking the unspoken requirement that journalists preserve the stars' "auratic" qualities, he writes: "[I]f one so much as presumes to utter a single word against Jayne Mansfield and Tuesday Weld—or George Stevens and William Wyler—one is given the bum's rush from all corners of the ball park." Goodman, *The Fifty-Year Decline and Fall of Hollywood*, 42, 44.

33. See, for instance, Maria LaPlace, "Bette Davis and the Ideal of Consumption," *Wide Angle* 6, no. 4 (1985): 34–43; and Jane Gaines, *Fabrications: Costume and the Female Body* (New York: Routledge, 1990).

34. Johnston, "Hollywood's Ten Per Centers," August 8, 1942, 9.

35. According to Johnston's account, "the modern Hollywood agent, who differs widely from the earlier theatrical and picture agents, came into being in 1927." Ibid., 10.

36. Ibid., 9, 38. Notably, much of the anti-agent language used in the *Post* article and elsewhere is strikingly similar to the period's anti-Semitic descriptions of Jewish businessmen in general—a bitter irony in an industry noted for the disproportionate number of Jews in its ranks, from the moguls on down.

37. Johnston, "Hollywood's Ten Per Centers," August 22, 1942, 24.

38. Johnston, "Hollywood's Ten Per Centers," August 8, 1942, 38.

39. Stine, *Stars and Star Handlers*, 123–28. While the 1942 *Saturday Evening*

Post article, "The Star-Spangled Octopus," emphasized only the negative attributes of agents, most publications emphasized Hayward's uniquely aristocratic bearing. The tall, worldly, debonair agent Hayward had previously courted other female clients, including Katharine Hepburn, a romance that started after he had negotiated her salary at RKO for *Bill of Divorcement* (1932).

40. Bruck, *When Hollywood Had a King*, 74–75.

41. The documentary, *It's All True*, remained unfinished (until it was released in 1993). Johnston, "Hollywood's Ten Per Centers," August 22, 1942, 23.

42. McDougal, *The Last Mogul*, 138.

43. Ibid., 139.

44. David G. Wittels, "The Star-Spangled Octopus," *Saturday Evening Post*, 4 parts, August 10, 17, 24, and 31, 1946.

45. According to McDougal, "If Wittels had any hard evidence of Stein's long-rumored ties to the Capone mob, his global monopolistic aspirations, or MCA's extortionate business practices, it didn't show up in the *Saturday Evening Post*" (*The Last Mogul*, 124).

46. Ibid., 126.

47. Richard Dreyer, *Heavenly Bodies: Film Stars and Society* (New York: St. Martin's Press, 1986), 1–18. See further evidence of the contradictory impulses inherent in the manufacture of star images in Christine Gledhill, ed. *Stardom: Industry of Desire* (New York: Routledge, 1991); and Gaines, "The Popular Icon."

48. Bruck, *When Hollywood Had a King*, 80.

49. McDougal, *The Last Mogul*, 386.

50. Ibid., 137. For a lengthier discussion of Lazar's flamboyant tenure as an agent, see Irving Lazar, *Swifty: My Life and Good Times* (New York: Simon and Schuster, 1995).

51. McDougal, *The Last Mogul*, 284.

52. Ibid., 86.

53. Johnston, "Hollywood's Ten Per Centers," August 8, 1942, 10.

54. Thompson, "There's No Show Business Like MCA Business," *Fortune*, July 1960, 112.

55. Stine, *Stars and Star Handlers*, 297–98.

56. McDougal, *The Last Mogul*, 246.

57. Ibid.

58. For a more detailed account of studio accounting practices in contemporary Hollywood, see Pierce O'Donnell and Dennis McDougal, *Fatal Subtraction: The Inside Story of Buchwald v. Paramount* (New York: Doubleday, 1992).

59. Stewart won the New York Film Critics' Best Actor award for *You Can't Take It with You* (1938), *It's a Wonderful Life* (1939), and *Mr. Smith Goes to Washington* (1939). In 1940 he won an Academy Award for *The Philadelphia Story*.

60. McDougal, *The Last Mogul*, 155.

61. Ibid.

62. *Hollywood Reporter*, January 20, 1953, 1.

63. Stine, *Stars and Star Handlers*, 299.

64. Ibid., 242–44.

65. Today, "re-born" stars like former Sweathog John Travolta ask and get "not just a minimum salary of [then] $17 million plus, but demands what has become the new standard in star contracts—an array of perks so outlandish that executives could only roll their eyes. And agree"; *Variety*, June 27, 1997, 1. The top salaries for the top box-office drawing stars like Tom Cruise, Jim Carrey, and others have risen to $30 million plus at the time of this writing.

66. Bruck, *When Hollywood Had a King*, 120.

67. Bruck points out that SAG's existing regulations "did contain a mechanism by which an agent could apply for a waiver to produce a movie on a case-by-case basis, and that, presumably, could be applied to television as well; but it would be far too restrictive for [Wasserman]. What Wasserman wanted was untrammeled freedom: a blanket waiver that would allow his talent agency to engage in television production for many years to come." Ibid., 119.

68. According to McDougal, "The unfair advantage MCA had in its cozy waiver with Screen Actors and Writers Guilds was a sour note that rang through several weeks of similar testimony from representatives of William Morris, rival producers from MCA competitors like Four Star and Danny Thomas Productions, and several other television executives" (*The Last Mogul*, 292).

69. Gelman and Aronowitz, "MCA: Show Business Empire," *New York Post*, June 19, 1962, 4.

70. During the 1958–59 television seasons, Desilu surpassed Revue Productions in terms of the number of shows on the network schedule with Screen Gems coming in third. The three television production giants were frequently neck-and-neck throughout the fifties. Coyne Steven Sanders and Tom Gilbert, *Desilu: The Story of Lucille Ball and Desi Arnaz* (New York: Quill, 1993), 155.

71. McDougal, *The Last Mogul*, 291.

72. Albert R. Kroeger, "The Winning Ways of Sonny Werblin," *Television Magazine*, September 1961, 58–59.

73. Ibid.

74. Since 2000 the Association of Talent Agencies (ATA) has been in still-unresolved negotiations with SAG to allow them to become deregulated and "to sell themselves to—or invest in—motion picture producers, distributors and networks. . . . Agents also can own indirect stakes in production companies." Echoing 1950s' attitudes toward the SAG waiver, one insider describes the new, pending waiver as "seeing the wild wild West again," and warns, "Agencies will push the envelope on the new rules as hard as they can until some regulatory agency or SAG tells them they've gone too far." *Variety*, February 21, 2000.

75. Kroeger, "The Winning Ways of Sonny Werblin," *Television Magazine*, September 1961, 66.

76. Ibid., 67.

77. Thompson writes: "No MCA 'fiduciary relationship' is better hidden than the economics of its TV activities. MCA frequently sets up its own clients—mostly actors—in the TV film business, sometimes as fifty-fifty partners." Thompson, "There's No Show Business Like MCA Business," *Fortune*, July 1960, 115.

78. McDougal, *The Last Mogul*, 203–5.

79. Ibid., 282.

80. Ibid.

81. Gelman and Aronowitz, "MCA: Show Business Empire," *New York Post,* June 5, 1962, 27.

82. Ibid.

83. Gelman and Aronowitz, "MCA: Show Business Empire," *New York Post,* June 8, 1962, 45.

84. Gelman and Aronowitz, "MCA: Show Business Empire," *New York Post,* June 7, 1962, 29.

85. Emphasizing his self-deprecating stance toward his role as advertising spokesman, Jack Benny routinely opened his Jell-O-sponsored radio show from 1934 to 1942 by saying, "Jell-O again."

86. Bill Davidson, "MCA: The Octopus Devours the World," *Show Magazine,* February 1962, 52.

87. Ibid.

88. Congratulatory articles on Wasserman's contributions to the entertainment industry appear as early as 1957 in Hodgins, "Amid Ruins of an Empire a New Hollywood Arises." Positive accounts are even more frequent after Wasserman leaves the talent agency and becomes head of Universal Studios: e.g., D. Zeitlin, "Meanwhile Back in Hollywood, Efficiency Takes Over," *Life,* December 20, 1963; John McPhee, "New Kind of King," *Time,* January 1, 1965.

89. McDougal, *The Last Mogul,* 310–11.

90. According to Gelman and Aronowitz, "To obtain the indictment, the Justice Department had to send a steady stream of FBI agents to question everybody who had conducted business with MCA—which was everybody in Hollywood. The witnesses included a number of MCA's estimated 800 clients and a number of MCA's estimated 300 ex-clients." Gelman and Aronowitz, "MCA: Show Business Empire," *New York Post,* June 8, 1962, 45.

91. McDougal, *The Last Mogul,* 288.

92. Ibid., 157.

93. "Screen Gems and William Morris Might Get Together in TV," *Hollywood Reporter,* June 5, 1957, sec. 1.

94. May, *The Big Tomorrow,* 269; McDougal, *The Last Mogul,* 432–33; Stephen Prince, *Visions of Empire: Political Imagery in Contemporary American Film* (New York: Praeger, 1992).

95. McDougal, *The Last Mogul,* 293.

96. Ibid., 319. (Dan Glickman, former congressman and Agriculture secretary in the Clinton administration, succeeded Valenti as MPAA chief in July 2004.)

97. "What we've done," says MCA president, Lew Wasserman, "is what every other agency has tried to do, but we like to think we've done it better." In a business deal, the winner is always the villain." "When Ford sells cars," says Schreiber, "they allocate. You have to sell so many trucks with your cars or you don't become a dealer. There has always been in business a method of increasing your sales by the most prudent, intelligent marketing methods." He continues: "You talk about Jack Benny selling other shows from his company? J. Walter Thompson had just the

year before, when it acquired Perry Como's show for Kraft, bought summer shows through Como's company, bought some pilots and made as broad a deal as they could make." He boasts, "Look at Warner Brothers and ABC. Never before has one company sold eight programs to one network." Gelman and Aronowitz, "MCA: Show Business Empire," *New York Post*, June 8, 1962, 45.

3. The Gray Flannel Independent

1. MacCann, *Hollywood in Transition;* Hodgins, "Amid Ruins of an Empire a New Hollywood Arises," 146–66. Hodgins states: "A glamorous era ended in disaster, but men of Talent, aided by agents and tax experts, inherited the movies and are making them pay."

2. Janet Staiger, "Individualism Versus Collectivism," *Screen 24*, vol. 4–5 (July–October 1983), 76.

3. According to Rosten, the typical producer-unit during the studio contract era consisted of an executive in charge of production or executive producer (e.g., Darryl F. Zanuck at Twentieth Century–Fox), who oversaw a staff of contract producers, also known as "A producers" (e.g., Hal B. Wallis at Warner Bros., Buddy de Sylva at Paramount), and "B producers" (e.g., Bryan Foy at Warner Brothers; and Sol Wurtzel at Twentieth Century–Fox). Zanuck was atypical because he served as both an executive in charge of production and an "A producer," micro-managing everything from story decisions to budget to postproduction. Leo Rosten, *Hollywood: The Movie Colony, The Movie Makers* (New York: Harcourt, Brace, 1941), 262.

4. Aberdeen describes how Hollywood talent became available on a freelance basis when producers first began setting up movies as "collapsible corporations," a practice that was popularized by Samuel Goldwyn. Aberdeen, *Hollywood Renegades*, 248.

5. Anderson, *Hollywood TV*, 158; also see, "WB in Record Indie Financing: 21 Independent Films Now on Slate: Open for More, Says Jack Warner," *Hollywood Reporter*, November 17, 1954, 1. Aberdeen, *Hollywood Renegades*, 241.

6. David Bordwell, Janet Staiger, and Kristin Thompson, *The Classical Hollywood Cinema: Film Style and Mode of Production to 1960* (New York: Columbia University Press, 1985), 330.

7. Rosten, *Hollywood*, 262.

8. Ibid.

9. See Christopher Anderson, "Disneyland," and "David O. Selznick and the Making of Light's Diamond Jubilee," in *Hollywood TV*, 133–55, 101–32; Janet Wasko, *Understanding Disney: The Manufacture of Fantasy* (Malden, Mass.: Blackwell, 2001); and Eric Smoodin, ed., *Disney Discourse: Producing the Magic Kingdom* (New York: Routledge, 1994).

10. Anderson, *Hollywood TV*, 5.

11. Sam Spiegel started producing in the forties and hit his stride in the fifties with *On the Waterfront, The Bridge on the River Kwai,* and *Lawrence of Arabia* (all Academy Award–winning films). Starting in 1951 Walter Mirisch produced low-budget features for Monogram. In 1957 he and his two brothers, Harold and Marvin, formed the Mirisch Company, Inc., a financing entity known for granting creative autonomy to independent producer-directors.

12. Leonard J. Leff, *Hitchcock and Selznick: The Rich and Strange Collaboration of Alfred Hitchcock and David O. Selznick in Hollywood* (New York: Weidenfeld and Nicolson, 1987), 144. Selznick remarked as early as 1937, "What makes Hitchcock so important is that he is a producer as well as a director actually." Also see W. R. Wilkerson, "Trade Views," June 27, 1954, 1. Wilkerson describes Hitchcock's understanding of budget and cost saving using the example of *Rear Window* (1954), which Hitchcock was able to shoot on a set for a mere $89,999 (vs. a studio production, which might have cost $200,000+).

13. There are several well researched accounts of producer-talent partnerships, including Matthew Bernstein, *Walter Wanger, Hollywood Independent* (Minneapolis: University of Minnesota Press, 2000); Leff, *Hitchcock and Selznick;* Natasha Fraser-Cavassoni, *Sam Spiegel: The Incredible Life and Times of Hollywood's Most Iconoclastic Producer* (New York: Simon and Schuster, 2003). Also see *The Velvet Light Trap* 22 (1986), a special issue on Hollywood independents, and Staiger, "Individualism Versus Collectivism," 68–79.

14. After instigating the anti-trust decrees, the SIMPP organization lost focus and was disbanded by the early sixties. Aberdeen, *Hollywood Renegades,* 20.

15. Jacobowitz, "Joan Bennett," 23–34.

16. Aberdeen, *Hollywood Renegades,* 230–31.

17. When Selznick refused to be involved with Ford's next film, *Stagecoach* (1939), Ford turned to producer Walter Wanger, who granted the director 20 percent of the profits in what turned out to be one of Ford's most critically and commercially successful films. Ibid., 146.

18. Spiegel was the first to raise money independently by selling foreign rights (from the British distributor Romulus Films, Ltd.), a technique that remains in place today. Ibid., 151.

19. Ibid., 152.

20. Rosten, *Hollywood,* 262.

21. Neve, *Film and Politics,* 126.

22. Aberdeen, *Hollywood Renegades,* 148.

23. Leff, *Hitchcock and Selznick,* 90.

24. William H. Whyte Jr., *The Organization Man* (New York: Simon and Schuster, 1956), 404.

25. Jackson Lears, "A Matter of Taste: Corporate Cultural Hegemony in a Mass-Consumption Society," in *Recasting America,* ed. May, 45.

26. Richard Wightman Fox and T. J. Jackson Lears, eds., *Power of Culture: Critical Essays in American History, 1880–1980* (Chicago: University of Chicago Press, 1993), xii.

27. Whyte cites several pre-1956 (when his book was published) novels and films, such as *Patterns* and *The Man in the Gray Flannel Suit.*

28. Whyte, *The Organization Man,* 12.

29. For a more detailed discussion of the intimate relationship between suburban middle-class family sitcoms and a postwar consumer economy, see Mary Beth Haralovich, "Sit-coms and Suburbs: Positioning the 1950s Homemaker," in *Private Screenings,* ed. Spigel and Mann, 111–42.

30. Joseph Satin, ed., *The 1950s: America's "Placid" Decade* (Boston: Houghton Mifflin, 1960). The phrase, "The Morale of the Cheerful Robots," is taken from C. Write Mills, *White Collar* (Oxford: Oxford University Press, 1951); "Arise, Ye Silent Class of '57" appears in an editorial from *Life*, June 17, 1957; and "The Leisured Masses" is reprinted from *Business Week*, September 12, 1953.

31. John G. Cawelti, "Dream or Rate Race?," in Cawelti, *Apostles of the Self-Made Man* (Chicago: University of Chicago Press, 1965), 201–36.

32. Ibid., 270–71.

33. Cawelti surveys an extensive list of titles written by 1950s' intelligentsia such as Wright Mills, David Reisman, and Vance Packard, all devoted to critiquing postwar American capitalism. They include Howard R. Bowen, *Social Responsibilities of the Businessman* (New York: Harper and Brothers, 1953); Marquis W. Childs and Douglas Cater, *Ethics in a Business Society* (New York: Harper and Brothers, 1954); Thurman Arnold et al., *The Future of Democratic Capitalism* (Philadelphia: University of Pennsylvania Press, 1950); Frederick L. Allen, *The Big Change* (New York: Harper and Brothers, 1952); Mills, *White Collar;* David Riesman, *Individualism Reconsidered* (Garden City, N.Y.: Doubleday, 1955), and *The Lonely Crowd* (Garden City, N.Y.: Doubleday, 1955); Wright Mills, *The Power Elite* (New York: Oxford University Press, 1956); Michael Harrington, *The Other America: Poverty in the United States* (New York: Macmillan, 1962); Elijah Jordan, *Business Be Damned* (New York: Henry Schuman, 1952); William H. Whyte Jr., *Is Anybody Listening* (New York: Simon and Schuster, 1952) and *The Organization Man;* David E. Lilienthal, *Big Business: A New Era* (New York: Harper and Brothers, 1953); Peter Viereck, *The Unadjusted Man: A New Hero for Americans* (Boston: Beacon Press, 1956); Vance Packard, *The Status Seekers* (New York: D. McKay Co., 1959); and Mark Hanan, *The Pacifiers* (Boston: Little, Brown, 1960).

34. Cawelti, *Apostles of the Self-Made Man*, 271.

35. Ibid., 205–6.

36. Ibid.

37. "New Industries: They Are a Miracle of Design," *Life*, November 25, 1946, 32–33.

38. These postwar economic trends are discussed in detail by Marty Jezer in *Life in the United States, 1945–1960* (Boston: South End Press, 1982), 117–27.

39. For an analysis of credit-card spending and its representation on television, see George Lipsitz, "The Meaning of Memory: Family, Class, and Ethnicity in Early Network Television Programs," in *Private Screenings*, eds. Spigel and Mann, 71–110.

40. William H. Whyte Jr., "Bugetism: Opiates of the Middle Class," *Fortune*, May 1956, 134. For an analysis of Ernest Dichter's social construction of the homemaker ideal by fusing expert opinions from consumer science and psychology to consumer product designs targeting women, see Haralovich, "Sit-coms and Suburbs," 126–27.

41. Thomas J. McCormick is cited in Steven Cohan, *Masked Men: Masculinity and the Movies in the Fifties* (Bloomington: Indiana University Press, 1997), ix.

42. May, *The Big Tomorrow*, 230. May uses the term "cultural radicalism" to

describe a group of postwar films that revive populist New Deal themes and presage the social movements of the late sixties. Ibid., 215–56.

43. Ibid., 224.

44. Lynn Spigel and Michael Curtin, eds., *The Revolution Wasn't Televised: Sixties Television and Social Conflict* (New York: Routledge, 1997), 9.

45. Staiger adapts Foucault's historical methodology (in, e.g., *Discipline and Punish* and *The Birth of the Clinic*) to media studies, demonstrating how discursive sites (i.e., language, mass cultural products) act as encoding systems that reinforce the dominant ideology associated with monolithic institutions (e.g., the prison system, medicine, psychoanalysis) and can indicate transformative moments of resistance to the dominant ideology. Janet Staiger, *Bad Women: Regulating Sexuality in Early American Cinema* (Minneapolis: University of Minnesota Press, 1995), xvii.

46. Crowdus, *Political Companion to American Film*, 34–40.

47. Ibid. Notably, both Ford and Wood were Republicans. Wood ended up cofounding the right-wing, anti-Communist Motion Picture Alliance for the Preservation of American Values.

48. Honey examines various cooperative ventures among the Bureau of Campaigns, OWI, and various government war agencies. Maureen Honey, *Creating Rosie the Riveter: Class, Gender, and Propaganda during World War II* (Amherst: University of Massachusetts Press, 1984), 34–35.

49. May, *The Big Tomorrow*, 142–44. According to May, examples of cooperation between OWI and wartime production include films like the Warner Bros. *Confessions of a Nazi Spy* (1939) and the participation in "Victory Parades" by countless movie stars.

50. Cawelti and Whyte openly critiqued the postwar "organization man"; however, even the more temperate Whyte writes: "the success cult's glorification of hired managers . . . [which he traces back to the 1920s is] at the very least a retreat from the traditional ideal of independence [associated with the Carnegie model]." Whyte, *The Organization Man*, 169.

51. Warren Susman, "Did Success Spoil the United States? Dual Representations in Postwar America," in *Recasting America*, ed. May, 19–37.

52. Roland Marchand, "Visions of Classlessness, Quests for Dominion: American Popular Culture, 1945–1960," in *Reshaping America: Society and Institutions: 1945–1960*, ed. Robert H. Bremner and Gary W. Reichard (Columbus: Ohio State University Press, 1982), 163–90.

53. Serafina Kent Bathrick, "The True Woman and the Family Film: The Industrial Production of Memory," Ph.D. diss., University of Wisconsin, Madison, 1981; Spigel, *Make Room for TV*, 34–35.

54. May comments on the difficulty that June Allyson had living up to her popular screen image as "America's Sweetheart," and "the girl the soldiers most want to marry." Her screen roles replayed this persona over and over again, as did the popular press when describing her marriage to screen idol Dick Powell. However, after her husband's death, Allyson entered a psychiatric clinic and confessed to having had multiple affairs and to having engaged in heavy drinking to escape a husband who "wanted to control all things." May, *The Big Tomorrow*, 172–73.

55. Rod Serling, *Patterns: Four Television Plays with the Author's Personal Commentaries* (New York: Simon and Schuster, 1957), 34.

56. Ibid. In a later (1959) television interview with Mike Wallace just before the *Twilight Zone* series went on the air, Serling is visibly defensive about his decision to leave the world of "quality" live television in New York and move to Hollywood to create what would become an extremely successful telefilm series. This taped interview is available on the *Twilight Zone* (boxed set) featuring "The Howling Man" and "Eye of the Beholder" episodes.

4. Self-Referentiality

1. The box-office results of the three releases reveal a number of postwar trends. *The Hucksters* was number twelve in the box office for 1947, earning only $4.7 million compared to *The Best Years of Our Lives*, which was number one in the box office and earned $11.5 million; Clark Gable's "un-heroic" adman as postwar returning hero may have contributed to the smaller returns. Three lavish "blockbusters": *Guys and Dolls* ($9 million), *The King and I* ($8.5 million), and the H-H-L production, *Trapeze* ($7.5 million) topped the charts in 1956. Surprisingly, the more modestly budgeted, black-and-white, independent production, *The Man with the Golden Arm* (Otto Preminger) tied with Twentieth Century–Fox's lavish, Cinema-Scope, "blockbuster" production, *The Man in the Gray Flannel Suit* at number thirteen, with each earning $4.6 million. In 1960, *The Apartment* was number seven, earning an impressive $5.1 million, despite its dark themes and difficult subject matter. The source of the statistics is Steinberg, *Reel Facts*, 344–48.

2. Lev sees the "new American realist" cycle of films (e.g., *On the Waterfront, Marty, Blackboard Jungle, The Bachelor Party, Trial, Night and the City, Twelve Angry Men,* and *Shadows*) as a reaction to the mid-1950s color, widescreen movie spectacles. Peter Lev, *Transforming the Screen: 1950–1959*, History of American Cinema 7 (New York: Scribner's, 1990/2003), 241. Walter Mirisch's early attempt in 1951 to sign name directors while at the "B+" movie company Allied Artists failed. In contrast, after he formed Mirisch Company, Inc., in 1957, he was able to sign lucrative, multiple-picture contracts with Billy Wilder, John Sturges, Robert Wise, and George Roy Hill. Balio, *United Artists*, 162–65, 169–70.

3. Late in life, Wilder disputed Izzy Diamond's claim that the Jennings Lang/Joan Bennett affair was the primary inspiration for *The Apartment*. Cameron Crowe, *Conversations with Wilder* (New York: Knopf, 1999), 136.

4. May, *The Big Tomorrow*, 241.

5. MGM was no doubt eager to replicate that film's critical and box office success by adapting another novel dealing with a returning veteran.

6. Frederic Wakeman, *The Hucksters* (New York: Rinehart and Company, 1946), 111. (This joke appeared in the novel but not in the film.)

7. McDougal, *The Last Mogul*, 127–28. Notably, MCA client and *Huckster* producer Arthur Hornblow Jr.'s son was a playmate of Wasserman's daughter.

8. Don Carle Gillette (who had taken over for Wilkerson), "Trade Views" *Hollywood Reporter,* May 12, 1960, 1.

9. Spigel, *Make Room for TV,* 7.

10. Christopher Anderson, "Hollywood in the Home: TV and the End of the Studio System," in *Modernity and Mass Culture,* ed. James Naremore and Patrick Brantlinger (Bloomington: Indiana University Press, 1991), 89, 80–102.

11. Ibid., 87.

12. Neve, *Film and Politics in America,* 197. Neve makes this claim about *A Face in the Crowd.* I argue that something similar can be said of most of the self-referential films about television cited in this study.

13. Wilkerson, "Trade Views," December 5, 1952, 1. In 1952 Wilkerson offered several reasons why Hollywood stars shouldn't cross over to TV: 1. "Why should people pay to see a star that they can get once a week for nothing? 2. No matter how good the star is, the public can get too much of him or her. 3. Appearing on TV in complete programs running a half hour or so cannot be considered good promotion in the same sense as appearing in a film trailer because the trailer gives the viewers just enough to arouse curiosity and anticipation. 4. The more shows a star has to put on, the greater percentage of below-part entertainment he or she is bound to deliver."

14. Anderson, *Hollywood TV,* 2.

15. Wilkerson, "Trade Views," March 12 and 13, 1953, 1.

16. Dan Jenkins, "On the Air" (column), *Hollywood Reporter,* June 12, 1953.

17. Anderson, *Hollywood TV,* 46–47.

18. Schatz, "The New Hollywood," 9–10; Eileen Meehan, "'Holy Commodity Fetish, Batman!': The Political Economy of a Commercial Intertext," in *The Many Lives of the Batman: Critical Approaches to a Superhero and His Media,* ed. Roberta E. Pearson and William Uricchio (New York: Routledge, 1991), 47–65.

19. Wilkerson, "Trade Views," April 30, 1953, 1. Disney did not pioneer early film testing. Rather, Gallup was being used to quantify audiences as early as the 1930s. See Susan Ohmer, "The Science of Pleasure: George Gallup and Audience Research in Hollywood," in *Identifying Hollywood's Audiences: Cultural Identity and the Movies,* ed. Melvyn Stokes and Richard Maltby (London: BFI, 2000).

20. Other studios were also advertising their movie trailers on television by 1953. "Pix in All-Out TV Advertising," *Hollywood Reporter,* July 3, 1953, 1.

21. See, for instance, "H'wood Sells Democracy Abroad Without Subsidy, House Hears," *Hollywood Reporter,* April 14, 1953, 1. Not only MPAA head Eric Johnston, but Representative John J. Dempsey (D.-N.M.) repeated the conservative, patriotic message that "Hollywood films do a tremendous job abroad for America and export of our films should be encouraged."

22. For a more detailed account, see Mann, "Spectacularization of Everyday Life," 41–70.

23. Anderson, "Hollywood in the Home," 57; "Holden Entering Music Publishing, TV Production," *Hollywood Reporter,* April 3, 1956, 1.

24. Wilkerson, "Trade Views" April 23, 1956, 1. Wilkerson praises independent producer Stanley Kramer for the expert "showmanship" in the selling of his films (and chides the majors for their lack of ingenuity). In another column, Wilkerson writes: "If a producer is able to sell a big network sponsor an idea to build a show around his picture, to get that picture before the eyes of probably 85% of the

nation, in the hope that those viewers will want to see the picture, he has done a good job for his picture and the industry that needs this type of exploitation." Wilkerson, "Trade Views," May 29, 1956, 1.

25. "*Trapeze* Set in 375 Dates: $2 Million Ad Campaign Sets Up Expected Greatest First Week of Any Pictures: New York," *Hollywood Reporter,* May 25, 1956, 1. The article continues: "Four hundred prints have been ordered to meet the dates. . . . The vigorous and highly successful publicity campaign by the Hecht and Lancaster forces, achieving results mindful of *Gone with the Wind* days, carry *Trapeze* into its early openings."

26. "Tonight's World Premiere *The Wonder Show of the World* Hecht and Lancaster present *Trapeze* Fox-Wilshire 8:30 PM Benefit Variety Boys Club of Los Angeles," *Hollywood Reporter,* May 29, 1956, 5–6. A two-page ad for the film included reference to this cross-promotional TV event.

27. Mann, "Spectacularization of Everyday Life," 44.

28. Charles Sinclair, "Should Hollywood Get It for Free?" *Sponsor* 9, no. 2 (August 8, 1955): 102.

29. "Johnston Calls for Meeting of Studio Heads, Ad Directors to Implement Film Jubilee," *Hollywood Reporter,* June 25, 1957, 1. *Hollywood Reporter* features a number of positive accounts of the increasing integration of the two industries. See, for instance, "65 Million TV Spot Biz Here: Major Facilities, Talent Bringing 90% of Commercials to Hollywood," *Hollywood Reporter,* July 5, 1957, 1.

30. Jenkins celebrates synergistic possibilities such as "the current influence of the all-pervading TV screen on motion picture thinking" given "the use of TV personalities as box office bait for motion pictures (e.g., Lucy and Desi's *The Long Long Trailer,* and *Forever Darling,* and TV star Bob Cummings and Marie Wilson, star of "My Friend Irma" in *Marry Me Again*)." Dan Jenkins, "On the Air," June 10, 1953, 8.

31. Sloan Wilson, *The Man in the Gray Flannel Suit* (New York: Simon and Schuster, 1956), 300.

32. George B. Leonard Jr., "The American Male: Why Is He Afraid to Be Different?" *Look,* February 18, 1958, 95, 97.

33. Frank Tashlin's *Will Success Spoil Rock Hunter?* contains a similar scene of a businessman-hero receiving the ultimate 1950s emblem of success: the key to the executive bathroom. In Tashlin's film, the passage is treated in an over-the-top satiric manner as Tony Randall's organization man sheds tears of happiness while an angelic light shines over the scene and a choir sings on the soundtrack.

34. Zanuck to Nunnally Johnson, conference note, November 25, 1956, *The Man in the Gray Flannel Suit* file, Twentieth Century–Fox Scripts file, Arts Special Collection, UCLA.

35. John McCarten, "Abe Lincoln on Madison Avenue," *New Yorker* 32 (April 21, 1956): 75–76. In his sardonic *New Yorker* review of *The Man in the Gray Flannel Suit,* McCarten epitomizes this view. He writes: "As played by Jennifer Jones, the lady is so persistently surly that it's hard to imagine why the fellow doesn't clear out, particularly in view of the fact that some years before we encounter him he has enjoyed the favors of a beautiful and sweet-tempered girl in Rome (Marisa Pavan)."

36. Roland Marchand, *Advertising the American Dream: Making Way for Modernity, 1920–1940* (Berkeley: University of California Press, 1985), 96, 248–54; Spigel, *Make Room for Television*, 36–72. In the late 1920s "Lucky Strike extracted endorsements from an amazing assortment of public figures, from business tycoons and society women to athletes and movie stars."

37. In contrast, by 1960, the *Hollywood Reporter* unapologetically underscores this collapse of meanings in a two-page ad for CBS. "We have an eye for the ladies and they have an eye for us," The ad continues: "It is always pleasant to learn that you are more appealing to women than the next man—and if you are a broadcaster or an advertiser it has its practical advantages." CBS ad, *Hollywood Reporter,* May 1, 1960, 6–7.

38. Wakeman, *The Hucksters,* 43. Norman says this in the novel but not the film. Tom Rath says something equally cynical about the advertising profession in the 1955 novel *The Man in the Gray Flannel Suit;* however, unlike Norman, Rath is resigned to the requisite insincerity of his job: "It's absurd to think of these things," he thought. "I could get a job in an advertising agency. I'll write copy telling people to eat more corn flakes and smoke more and more cigarettes and buy more refrigerators and automobiles, until they explode with happiness." Wilson, *The Man in the Gray Flannel Suit,* 180.

39. *The Hucksters* file, Photographs, Special Collections, Margaret Merrick Library, Los Angeles.

40. Dana Polan, *Power and Paranoia: History, Narrative and American Cinema, 1940–1950* (New York: Columbia University Press, 1986), 18. Polan shows how in most postwar Hollywood films, women who are overly "carnal preempt themselves from the world of classic narrativity"—they can never be a member of the classical couple. In fact, Kerr's character in the novel version of *The Hucksters* was an adulterous wife. In the Hollywood adaptation, however, Production Code officials demanded that she be turned into a war widow to reconcile the film's portrait of femininity with the standards of the day. See McDougal, *The Last Mogul,* 127–28.

41. In addition to producing *The Hucksters,* Arthur Hornblow Jr., a Paramount-based producer, and later a MGM-based producer, became an independent producer in the midfifties and was responsible for Cukor's *Gaslight* (1944), Huston's *The Asphalt Jungle* (1950), and Wilder's *Witness for the Prosecution* (1957), among other films that challenged accepted norms.

42. Lev, *Transforming the Screen,* 235. Lev explains that in the late 1950s, "male anxieties, mental illness, homosexuality, and racism were [among the new themes] added to the melodrama's traditional concerns." "Male anxiety" is already a major theme of several "returning vet" films in the late forties.

43. For analyses of women's traditional roles and domestic ideology, see Barbara Welter, "The Cult of True Womanhood: 1820–1860," *American Quarterly* 18, no. 2, pt. 1 (Summer 1966): 151–74; and Bathrick, "The True Woman and the Family Film."

44. MGM studio publicists struggled to reconcile the divergent goals associated with the workplace and home using a publicity still for *Executive Suite* that literally collapses public and private spaces. It depicts Holden and Allyson in a romantic clinch behind the transparent door to Holden's corporate office. The copy reads:

"after-office hours are brilliantly spotlighted in the exciting new film, in which William Holden and June Allyson reveal that 'big business' has a heart." *Executive Suite* file (photographs), MGM Collection, Margaret Merrick Library, Los Angeles; courtesy of Academy of Motion Picture Arts and Sciences.

45. "Top Performances, Great Screenplay Mark 'Flannel,'" *Hollywood Reporter*, March 30, 1956.

46. Wilkerson "Trade Views," April 2, 1956. "In all the thirty years that Darryl Zanuck has been in pictures, he has never been associated with the production of a picture of such excellence. . . . It's a big picture, reported to have cost around $4,000,000 and it looks every penny of it and more."

47. For a detailed discussion of this phenomenon, see Jenkins, *What Makes Pistachio Nuts?*

48. As discussed in chapter 1, two major changes in studio publicity department operations took place in the postwar era: the studios relinquished control over the New York–based fan magazine publications and the waning popularity of the powerful newspaper entertainment columnists (e.g., Hedda Hopper, Louella Parsons, and Walter Winchell), who had dominated the Hollywood and New York–based gossip circuit throughout the 1930s and 1940s.

49. As discussed in chapter 2, media practitioners in the fifties and sixties expressed great concern over the fact that MCA appeared to treat its clients as interchangeable objects.

50. Charles Eckert, "The Carole Lombard in Macy's Window," in *Stardom: Industry of Desire*, ed. Christine Gledhill (London: Routledge, 1991), 39.

51. McDougal states: "Most Americans would never know that the monolithic agency called Talent Ltd. in the movie was patterned after MCA, or that its founder, the fictional Dave Lash, was a smooth autocrat who looked far too much like Dr. Jules Stein to be a coincidence" (*The Last Mogul*, 126).

52. McDougal tracks several insider jokes about Wasserman and MCA in popular media of the day. For instance, he cites a popular joke about Wasserman as Ali Baba, and his agents as the Forty Thieves. Another describes an actor running from the police. "Where can I hide?" he breathlessly asks another actor. The latter responds, "Join MCA. Nobody'll hear from you or see you again." With unintended irony, singer and MCA client Mel Torme once told an interviewer, "It's such a gigantic organization [that] personal attention is difficult to get, unless you're a Danny Kaye." McDougal, *The Last Mogul*, 247–48.

53. Ibid., 172, 249.

54. Edward T. Thompson, "There's No Show Business like MCA Business," *Fortune*, June 1960, 152.

55. McDougal, *The Last Mogul*, 127, 156.

56. Wakeman, *The Hucksters*, 189.

57. McDougal, *The Last Mogul*, 166.

58. Ibid., 247–49.

59. "In the Picture: Bergman and Wilder," *Sight and Sound* 28, no. 3 (Summer/Autumn 1959): 134; "The Wilder Shores of Hollywood," *Variety*, June 8, 1960, 1. For a useful bibliography, see Seidman, *The Film Career of Billy Wilder*. For biographies,

see Sikov, *On Sunset Boulevard;* Maurice Zolotow, *Billy Wilder in Hollywood* (New York: G. P. Putnam's Sons, 1977); Crowe, *Conversations with Wilder.*

60. Frank Tashlin's agents at MCA negotiated a contract with Fox for his services in 1955, the same day that shooting began on the Hal B. Wallis production *Artists and Models* at Paramount. He was in such high demand that he had to complete his obligations to Wallis, including *Hollywood or Bust* (1956) before returning to Fox to make *Will Success Spoil Rock Hunter?* (1957). It is during this same period that Frank Tashlin becomes the topic of a special issue of *Positif,* signaling the European scholarly community's recognition of the radical aesthetic implicit in films that the Americans trade magazines see as simply crowd-pleasing comedies. Roger Garcia and Bernard Eisenschitz, "Chronology," in *Frank Tashlin,* ed. Garcia and Eisenschitz (Locarno: Editions du Festival international du film de Locarno and BFI, 1994), 192–93.

61. John T. Caldwell, *Televisuality: Style, Crisis, and Authority in American Television* (New Brunswick, N.J.: Rutgers University Press, 1994), 39.

62. Ad for Tashlin *Will Success Spoil Rock Hunter?, Hollywood Reporter,* August 7, 1957. A full-page ad honors the director: "20th Century–Fox Congratulates Frank Tashlin on His Third Consecutive Box Office Boffo for the Studio!" The ad depicts three buxom blondes in each of the three movie ads depicted for *The Lieutenant Wore Skirts, The Girl Can't Help It,* and *Will Success Spoil Rock Hunter?* For a more complete discussion of Godard's appreciation of Tashlin, see Roger Garcia, "Introduction: Hollywood or . . .," in *Frank Tashlin,* ed. Garcia and Eisenschitz, 15–19.

63. Kodak ad, *Hollywood Reporter,* July 7, 1960, 8–9. The copy on the Kodak ad exclaims: "Everywhere in the world . . . because it's on film! Remember . . . people are people—Guatemala, Salzburg, Rio—everywhere! They all 'go to the movies!' And the things they like, they tell their friends about." As evidence of the careful line Tashlin was forced to walk between satirizing and celebrating the film industry, the previous year, *Hollywood or Bust* (1956) featured Lewis and Martin on stage delivering a "tribute" in direct address to movie fans around the world during the opening moments of the film.

64. "Tashlin Production Packed with Laughs," *Hollywood Reporter,* July 29, 1957, 3.

65. After the negative press that followed the release of *Ace in the Hole,* Wilder was determined not to make films that compromised his position as a commercial director. When *The Apartment* first opened, he once again faced mixed reviews; however, once that film began winning awards, followed by good word of mouth, UA responded by increasing the publicity and number of theaters across the country.

66. Garcia and Eisenschitz, eds., *Frank Tashlin,* 16. The authors describe Godard's various homage to Tashlin; for example, Godard's *Vento dell'Este* (1969) depicts a man inviting us into the picture, repeating a similar conceit in the opening credit sequences of Tashlin's *The Girl Can't Help It* and *Will Success Spoil Rock Hunter?* Godard would later invoke Tashlin's *Who's Minding the Store?* as part of his analysis of France and capitalism in *Tout va bien* (1972).

67. Jonathan Rosenbaum, "Tashlinesque," in *Frank Tashlin,* ed. Garcia and Eisenschitz, 26–27.

68. Other early Tashlin social-realist comedies include *Son of Paleface* (a 1952 Bob Hope vehicle), *Marry Me Again* (1953), and *Susan Slept Here* (1954). Garcia and Eisenschitz, eds., *Frank Tashlin*, 157. Tashlin has said: "One of the reasons he wanted to go work at Disney [1938–1941] was to help the cause of the union. Ted [Pierce] was the first president of the Screen Cartoonists Guild, as it was called then, and I was vice-president, and we used to meet in cellars—it was like Communist cell meetings." Bill Krohn, "The First Films," in *Frank Tashlin*, ed. Garcia and Eisenschitz, 34.

69. Garcia and Eisenschitz, eds., *Frank Tashlin*, 213.

70. Mann, "Spectacularization of Everyday Life," 59–60.

71. Douglas Kellner, "The Frankfurt School and British Cultural Studies: The Missed Articulation," *Illuminations*, http://www.uta.edu/huma/illuminations/kell16 .htm, 2.

72. Ibid. Caldwell, "Critical Industrial Practices," 24.

73. Kellner, "The Frankfurt School and British Cultural Studies," 2.

74. Naremore, *More Than Night*, 166.

75. See, for instance, Colin Young, "The Old Dependables," *Film Quarterly* 13, no. 1 (Fall 1959). Young interviews Wilder, Ford, Zinnemann, and Milestone. John Gillett, "Wilder in Paris," *Sight and Sound* 26, no. 3 (Winter 1956): 142. Fernaldo DiGiammatteo, "L'Audacia de Billy Wilder," *Bianco E Nero*, no. 12 (November 1951): 5–17. According to Seidman, this is "the most comprehensive exploration of the influence of German Expressionism on Wilder's American films," 118.

76. Naremore, *More Than Night*, 88.

77. Wilder biographer Sikov states: "It was an idea close to Billy's heart: a fiercely ambitious newspaper reporter stuck in the middle of nowhere pulls a scam and ends up stewing, then dying, in his own self-contempt. *Ace in the Hole* would not be relieved by light comedy. It would, instead, reveal American culture as the shithole Wilder saw it to be. And thanks to his own authority as the nation's most successful writer-director, Billy would finally be able to shove American's faces right into it." Sikov, *On Sunset Boulevard*, 311, 319.

78. Charles Brackett, "A Matter of Humor," *The Quarterly of Film, Radio and Television* 7, no. 1 (Fall 1952): 52 (cited in Seidman, *The Film Career of Billy Wilder*, 119); Sikov, *On Sunset Boulevard*, 326; Young, "The Old Dependables"; Seidman, *The Film Career of Billy Wilder*, 121, 123. On Wilder's balancing art and industry see, for instance, "Wilder Hits at Stars, Exhibs, Sees Pay-TV as 'Great Day,'" *Daily Variety*, December 13, 1961, 3.

79. Jenkins's *What Makes Pistachio Nuts?* demonstrates how the anarchistic comedy genre tradition emerged in the late 1920s and 1930s as a reaction to the crisis and transition associated with the shift from silent to sound films. Studios adopted certain stars, performance techniques, and narrative strategies from vaudeville. Analogously, I argue that media practitioners sought out certain of television's stars, style, and narrative techniques to broaden the appeal of their films during a comparable period of crisis and transition from classical to post-classical films. For instance, long-time studio producer-turned-independent-producer Hal B. Wallis was initially stumped when faced with the challenge of adapting Martin and Lewis's

nightclub performance (their "rowdy, unrestrained antics on stage") to the screen. Screenwriter Cy Howard suggested adapting the well-known radio show, *My Friend Irma,* to the screen in 1949. The radio-show format lent itself more easily to the alternation of narrative and long sequences of pure comedy spectacle that became a trademark of all anarchistic comedies involving Martin and Lewis. James L. Neibaur and Ted Okuda, *The Jerry Lewis Films: An Analytical Filmography of the Innovative Comic* (Jefferson, N.C.: McFarland, 1995), 22–23.

80. Seidman, *The Film Career of Billy Wilder,* 37–38. Notably, when asked to describe his film role models, Wilder compared himself to both von Stroheim and Ernst Lubitsch; however, Seidman and other critics have noted Wilder's stronger kinship with Lubitsch, given both directors' preference for techniques which emphasize classical Hollywood's heightened artifice over its "social realist" mode of filmmaking.

81. "*Apartment* Provocative Pic with Strong B.O. Pull: Wilder Production Blistering Comedy—The Apartment (Mirisch-UA)," *Hollywood Reporter,* May 18, 1960, 3.

5. Two Emergent Cinemas

1. While the terms "art film" and "blockbuster" were not yet being widely used in the late forties and early fifties to characterize these two distinctive types of studio release, the terminology is being used here as a descriptive means of identifying cultural trends in their earliest formulations.

2. As Monaco explains, the Hollywood majors were allowed to own movie theaters in other countries and had well-established distribution and marketing branches around the world. In the face of competition with television, Hollywood cultivated its business opportunities abroad so that by 1960 "over half of their total revenues came from abroad." Paul Monaco, *The Sixties,* 10.

3. Zanuck, a pro-Eisenhower Republican, who is nonetheless known for his politically liberal social-problem films ranging from *Grapes of Wrath* (1940) to *Gentleman's Agreement* (1947), had to learn how to balance the often-radical politics of certain of their films (e.g., Kazan's *Viva Zapata!* [1952], about a working-class peasant's rise to power during the Mexican revolution, and Mankiewicz's *People Will Talk* [1951]), with the studio's more commercial agenda by insisting on famous stars (e.g., Marlon Brando and Cary Grant, respectively) and by foregrounding familiar genre elements (an action-filled war epic and melodrama, respectively).

4. Elia Kazan, *A Life* (New York: Knopf, 1988), 508.

5. "'On the Waterfront' Packs Terrific Wallop for B.O.: Spiegel-Kazan Film Ace Gangster Drama," *Hollywood Reporter,* July 14, 1954, 3. Eager to label this unique production with a familiar genre, the trade reviewer aligns this independently produced film with the popular 1930s Warner Bros. gangster film tradition. The review states: "This brutal, violently realistic drama, set against the sordid background of the New York waterfront, packs a terrific wallop that results in topflight entertainment. After so many costume dramas, it may be just what the box-office needs, for 'On the Waterfront' is so stark and gripping that it can only be compared with 'Little Caesar' and 'The Public Enemy.' It seems sure to create a new vogue

for gangster pictures, since it offers the exhibitor a rare chance to cash in on something different." The film earned $4.2 million in domestic theatrical revenues, making it one of the top-earning films of 1954. Steinberg, *Reel Facts*, 346.

6. Granted, the tide would switch back in favor of the low-budget personal films by auteurs in the late sixties; however, the schism that formed in the fifties is symptomatic of future developments when the blockbuster would once again prevail in Hollywood and art-house films were marginalized.

7. See "Mankiewicz Bows as Indie with 2 UA-Backed Pictures," *Hollywood Reporter*, May 12, 1953, 1. UA agreed to finance Mankiewicz's first writer-director-producer credit, *The Barefoot Contessa* (1954), under the new arrangement for $1 million. *The Barefoot Contessa*, like *Letter to Three Wives*, was self-referential and a highly cynical portrait of the entertainment industry. Explaining Mankiewicz's goals as an independent producer, *Hollywood Reporter* writes: "he'd use the corporate setup and UA tie-up to interest other directors and writers in independent production . . . [and was discussing] such joint ventures through Figaro with Elia Kazan . . . among others."

8. Richard Dyer MacCann is quoted in Monaco, *The Sixties*, 15.

9. Monaco, *The Sixties*, 3.

10. Each of these titles is a top-earning film for its year. Steinberg, *Reel Facts*, 344–47.

11. As previous chapters have revealed, several postwar filmmakers, such as Welles, Kubrick, and Aldrich, were committed to an "engaged cinema" but were marginalized by the studios if their films failed to exhibit commercial promise. Similarly, Enterprise Studios represented a failed experiment in political filmmaking for studio release when too many of the independent production company's films failed to deliver at the box office.

12. Buford, *Burt Lancaster*, 172.

13. Merritt, *Celluloid Mavericks*, 144.

14. See, for instance, Naremore, *More Than Night*, 140–55. Naremore provides a detailed discussion of the relationship between "B-film" production and noir as well as the distinctions between budgets assigned to different films/filmmakers in the "B" category. For instance Fritz Lang's *Secret Beyond the Door* (1948) was budgeted by Republic Pictures at $615,064 and is described by Naremore as "bargain-basement noir." In contrast, most of the westerns, Charlie Chan series, and so on, made at Republic, Monogram, PRC, and other Poverty Row companies were held to budgets of less than $200,000.

15. Naremore, *More Than Night*, 157. While Naremore attributes the "avant-garde" features of Kubrick's films to cost-cutting measures, an avant-garde film tradition was emerging at around the same time, as Merrick observes, started in part by filmmaker Maya Deren in New York around this time. She also helped found a number of film societies and prompted a number of scholarly publications, such as *Film Culture*, to form around these works. Merritt, *Celluloid Mavericks*, 104–6.

16. Naremore, *More Than Night*, 158. Film theorist and critic André Bazin started the highly influential *Les Cahiers de cinéma* in 1951, launching *la politique des auteurs* (the auteur theory), which was a major influence for the filmmakers associated

with the French New Wave, including, in particular, the films of Jean-Luc Godard, Francois Truffaut, Claude Chabrol, and Eric Rohmer. Sarris was an American theorist and critic for the New York newspaper *Village Voice* (1960–89). He introduced American readers to the auteur theory in his columns and in Andrew Sarris, *The American Cinema: Directors and Directions, 1929–1968* (New York: E. P. Dutton, 1968).

17. These films did, however, become identified as significant noir art-house masterpieces by the French intellectual filmmaking community.

18. Naremore, *More Than Night*, 137.

19. Review of *A Letter to Three Wives*, *Theatre Arts* 33, nos. 6– (April 1949). The review begins, "For a happy change, the most satisfying film to appear recently is an American product. Called 'A Letter to Three Wives,' it has been greeted by unusually rapturous reviews. . . ."

20. A quick survey of the budgets assigned to Mankiewicz's film and Bogart's film reveals that the studios did not conceive Bogart's film as an exploitation film. Instead, *Letter to Three Wives*, a somewhat daring take on the "women's film" formula of the 1940s, budgeted $1.6 million, was slightly lower than the typical A film and was cast with several relatively new contract players (such as Kirk Douglas and Linda Darnell) and a theater actor (Paul Douglas). In contrast, Bogart was considered a major star by the late forties, having routinely appeared in a number of commercial, studio A-genre films at the higher $2–4 million budget range; these include: *Treasure of Sierra Madre* (1948), an action-drama starring Bogart and directed by director-auteur John Huston, made for $3.8 million, and released by Warner Bros.; *Sabrina* (1954), a romantic comedy starring Bogart, William Holden, and newcomer Audrey Hepburn, directed by director-auteur Billy Wilder for $2.2 million at Paramount; and *Desperate Hours* (1955), a crime drama starring Bogart and directed by studio director William Wyler, made for $2.3 million at Paramount.

21. Schatz, *Old Hollywood/New Hollywood*, 186. After working together on *Knock on Any Door*, Bogart was eager to work with Nicholas Ray again on another Santana-produced, Columbia-distributed film, *In a Lonely Place* (1950). Notably, *Knock on Any Door* (Nicholas Ray, 1949) was the first movie Bogart made following *Key Largo* (1948), a similar noir thriller directed by John Huston and released by Warner Bros. (Bogart went on to make another Huston film: *Treasure of Sierra Madre* [1948].)

22. Review of *A Letter to Three Wives*.

23. Ibid.

24. Ibid.

25. Ibid.

26. See Kenneth L. Geist, *Pictures Will Talk: The Life and Films of Joseph L. Mankiewicz* (New York: Scribner's, 1978), 145. Mankiewicz admitted that the ending was a mistake. When Deborah (Jeanne Crain) is given a message that her husband won't be home that night, Porter (Paul Douglas) confesses to the group that he was planning to leave with the flirtatious Addie but decided to stay with Lora May (Linda Darnell) after all. Most audience members assume that Porter is telling a lie to protect Deborah's feelings.

27. Wilkerson, "Trade Views," September 9, 1954, 1.

28. Wilkerson "Trade Views" September 24, 1954, 1. Otto Preminger produced and directed *The Moon Is Blue*, a controversial film that defied the Production Code ban for using the then-taboo words "virgin" and "pregnant."

29. The discussions among Kazan, Odets, Arthur Miller, and other Group Theater members about the differences between the New York–based theater and Hollywood are a recurring theme in Kazan's autobiography, starting in the mid-1940s when Odets encouraged Kazan to join him in Hollywood. Kazan, *A Life*, 160. Mankiewicz, in contrast, was headquartered in Hollywood, but admired and emulated Kazan's involvement in theater. See Robert Coughlan, "15 Authors in Search of a Character Named Joseph L. Mankiewicz," *Life*, March 12, 1951. Also see Geist, *Pictures Will Talk*, 163.

30. As Neve points out, studio heads in the postwar era were probably less concerned with being "politically correct" than with being first in line to reap box office revenues on a topical subject. Zanuck, the liberal studio head and producer who first tackled the issue of anti-Semitism in *Gentleman's Agreement*, was just as eager to make the first anti-Communist film, *The Iron Curtain* (1948). Neve, *Film and Politics*, 187.

31. Mankiewicz made very little effort to veil his criticism of HUAC in his social comedy *People Will Talk* (1951). According to Neve, the film was "a comment on America at the time, including references both to McCarthy and to the dispute in the Screen Directors Guild—of which he was chairman—over loyalty oaths." Neve, *Film and Politics*, 182.

32. Herman Mankiewicz's skepticism toward idealistic causes and Joseph's self-proclaimed "political illiteracy" prompted both brothers to steer clear of "the political or charitable causes that regularly besieged affluent figures in the film community." Geist, *Pictures Will Talk*, 174.

33. Notably, Mankiewicz began his career as a staff writer, creating dialogue and jokes for *Diplomaniacs*, one of the anarchistic comedies that Jenkins cites as evidence that Hollywood incorporated performance-centered vaudevillian comedy in response to the crisis and change prompted by the introduction of sound. Jenkins, *What Makes Pistachio Nuts?*, 185.

34. Geist, *Pictures Will Talk*, 153.

35. Ibid. Sol Siegel brought the underlying story material for both *A Letter to Three Wives* and *House of Strangers* to Mankiewicz and Zanuck at Twentieth Century–Fox. Siegel left Paramount to become a studio-based producer at Fox starting in 1947. He didn't become an independent producer until the 1960s.

36. Geist, *Pictures Will Talk*, 211.

37. Coughlan is quoted in Geist, *Pictures Will Talk*, 159.

38. Ibid., 152–53. Mankiewicz admired and envied Kazan's theater credits and later tried to outdo him by directing a antiracist social-problem film, *No Way Out* (1950), which he considered far more hard-hitting and graphic than the more tepid social-problem films about prejudice that Kazan directed for Zanuck in the late forties (e.g., *Gentleman's Agreement* [1947] and *Pinky* [1949]).

39. Ibid., 163–64. Mankiewicz saw Broadway theater as a more sophisticated medium in part because there were fewer strictures on language and sexual reference.

Film tended to fare better than television among fifties' intellectuals debating the degrees of artistic integrity associated with the popular arts, but nonetheless, theater was viewed as a more serious, artistic endeavor. In *All About Eve*, Eve voices her utter contempt for television; when asked, "Do they have auditions for television?" she replies, "That's all television is, my dear. Nothing but auditions."

40. May, *The Big Tomorrow*, 241. While May refers here to Wilder and Huston, similar claims could be made about Mankiewicz's self-referential films.

41. Cited in Leslie Halliwell, *Halliwell's Film Guide* (London: HarperPerennial, 1991), 651.

42. John Klempner, *A Letter to Five Wives* (New York: Scribner's, 1946).

43. Laura Mulvey, "Visual Pleasure and Narrative Cinema," *Screen* 16, no. 3 (Autumn 1975): 6–18.

44. Maureen Turim, "Gentlemen Consume Blondes," *Movies and Methods*, vol. 2, ed. Bill Nichols (Berkeley: University of California Press, 1985), 369–78.

45. Bill Nichols, introduction to Thomas Elsaesser, "Tales of Sound and Fury: Observations on the Family Melodrama," in *Movies and Methods*, ed. Nichols, 165.

46. Ibid.

47. Review of *A Letter to Three Wives*, *New Republic* 120, no. 31 (February 7, 1949).

48. *A Letter to Three Wives* clipping file, May 7, 1948, Margaret Merrick Library, Academy of Motion Picture Arts and Sciences, Los Angeles.

49. In a series of exchanges between Stephen S. Jackson at the Production Code Administration and Col. Jason S. Joy at Twentieth Century–Fox on May 7, 13, and 25, 1948, Jackson emphasizes two major objections: references to Deborah's (Jeanne Crain's) excessive drinking and references to Lora Mae's (Linda Darnell's) overtly sexual behavior designed to trap department-store tycoon Porter (Paul Douglas) into marriage. According to Stephen S. Jackson, Colonel Joy and producer Sol Siegel (and Mankiewicz himself in one case) made several visits to the Production Code Administration offices, with Spiegel in particular winning Jackson over and causing him to marvel over "the friendly spirit of cooperation exhibited" in these meetings. While the filmmakers ultimately "forfeited" several references to Deborah's drinking, the objectionable lines involving the Lora Mae–Porter relationship remained intact in the final version of the film. *A Letter to Three Wives* file, May 7, 13, and 25, 1948. Academy Library Core Collection.

50. Navasky, *Naming Names*, 179–81.

51. In fact, Elia Kazan, then a prominent feature and theater director and former member of the Communist party, warned Mankiewicz to stay clear of him to protect his friend's career. Kazan, *A Life*, 323. When DeMille demanded that SDG members swear a loyalty oath and asked for a show of hands of directors who supported the resolution, only Wilder and Huston refused to raise their hands. Huston said the "meeting changed his life," and he never returned. May, *The Big Tomorrow*, 235–36.

52. The five writers hired register Zanuck's schizophrenic goals for this film. Claude Binyon's most recent credit prior to this film was an episode of the *United States Steel Hour*, a prestigious live TV drama series known for grappling with social issues. In contrast, Russel Crouse and Howard Lindsay were best known as playwrights

of widely popular musicals and plays. Finally, Mary Loos and Richard Sale were both hired to write *Gentlemen Marry Brunettes* (1955), the less-successful follow-up to *Gentlemen Prefer Blondes* after working on *Woman's World*. *Woman's World* director Jean Negulesco directed *How to Marry a Millionaire* the previous year.

53. Lev, *Transforming the Screen*, 1.

54. Wilkerson, "Trade Views," August 11, 1953, 1. The column begins: "Those professional mourners who have been looking forward to Hollywood's early demise should take a look at the grosses 'Gentlemen Prefer Blondes' is piling up all around the country and toss away their pallbearers' gloves."

55. Wilkerson, "Trade Views" August 11, 1953, 1.

56. See, for instance, Evelyn Mills Duvall, Ph.D., and Reuben Hill, Ph.D. , "If You Are Getting Married . . .," *Look*, June 16, 1953, 93.

57. Zanuck, memo to Ray Klune, January 29, 1953. *Woman's World*, Twentieth Century–Fox Scripts file, Art Special Collection, UCLA. Despite the problems with the script, Zanuck spared no expense when attaching many of the leading stars: Clifton Webb, June Allyson, Van Heflin, Arlene Dahl, Lauren Bacall, and Fred MacMurray.

58. Zanuck, memo to Charles Brackett, David Brown, and Jean Negulesco, January 26, 1954. *Woman's World*, Twentieth Century–Fox Story file. Special Collection, UCLA.

59. Reviewers in *Motion Picture Daily, Daily Variety, Hollywood Reporter*, and *Weekly Variety* (each published on September 29, 1954) project big box-office results for *Woman's World*, given the film's big name cast and "travelogue" tour of New York, comparing it favorably to another recent CinemaScope release, *Three Coins in the Fountain*. *Woman's World* file. Academy Library Core Collection.

60. Wilkerson, "Trade Views," June 19, 1957, 1.

6. Elia Kazan

1. Neve, *Film and Politics*, 84–85.

2. At the end of his days with the Group, Kazan said he no longer believed the play could be directed by a collective, that it needs the singular voice of the artist in charge. Kazan, *A Life*, 322. Formed in the 1930s by Harold Clurman, Cheryl Crawford, and Lee Strasberg, the Group championed the socially conscious plays of John Howard Lawson, Clifford Odets, and others. Neve, *Film and Politics*, 6.

3. For useful book-length studies of the Hollywood blacklist, see Larry Ceplair and Steven Englund, *The Inquisition in Hollywood: Politics in the Film Community, 1930–1960* (Berkeley: University of California Press, 1983); Navasky, *Naming Names;* Hamilton, *Writers in Hollywood;* Schwartz, *The Hollywood Writer's Wars*.

4. *Deadline at Dawn* (1946), a murder mystery starring Susan Hayward, represents Group Theater's Harold Clurman's only effort as a director in Hollywood. *Humoresque* (1946) features John Garfield playing an ambitious violinist and Joan Crawford as his unstable patroness. *Humoresque*, like *Sweet Smell of Success* and *The Big Knife*, contains a thinly disguised attack on the concessions an artist must make to earn a living in modern capitalism. Odets's last screenplay, *Wild in the Country* (1961), features Elvis as a rebellious country-boy with literary aspirations!

5. Naremore and Brantlinger characterize the contradictory status of modernist art as "sharply critical, even deconstructive, of certain high-culture values . . . [prompting the artist to cultivate] what Adorno (a modernist himself) described as an 'autonomous' social role." Naremore and Brantlinger continue: "Artistically, the early modernists were proponents of a media-specific formalism; politically, they were opposed to any social organization—whether industrial capitalism or state socialism—that would prevent artists from functioning as unacknowledged legislators." Naremore and Brantlinger, *Modernity and Mass Culture*, 9. Kazan describes his often-contradictory artistic/political goals in the preface to *A Face in the Crowd*, i–xv, and in a passage in his autobiography (which is quoted at length later in this chapter): Kazan, *A Life*, 533.

6. Neve, *Film and Politics*, 189.

7. Schulberg (the son of a studio-head father and talent-agent mother) had numerous run-ins with Billy Wilkerson in the 1930s. Budd Schulberg, *Moving Pictures: Memories of a Hollywood Prince* (New York: Stein and Day, 1981). His scathing, anti-Hollywood novel was modeled in part on producer Jerry Wald. Schulberg, *What Makes Sammy Run?* (New York: Random House, 1941).

8. For more on Rossen and Capra, see Neve, *Film and Politics*, 14–27, 28–55.

9. Ibid., 85.

10. Despite his early preference for social-problem films, Zanuck, along with Sam Goldwyn, Jack Warner, and Lew Wasserman, was a supporter of the Eisenhower ticket. McDougal, *The Last Mogul*, 182.

11. After Kazan was called before HUAC, Zanuck's advice was to save his career by testifying—an attitude, Zanuck explained, which he'd learned while working closely with the government as part of the war effort. Kazan, *A Life*, 455.

12. Neve, *Film and Politics*, 85.

13. Ibid., 189.

14. Indicating his ambivalence about aligning with the studio, Kazan writes, "What a narrow escape! I might have ended up a Fox staff director. My first film had been a great success, and Zanuck was hot after me. My long-term contract would have been eagerly 'adjusted,' that is, enriched. I could have had a lovely, spacious home in Bel Air in any one of a number of styles. I could have had a numbered bank account in Switzerland and a press agent to see to it that I was showered with praise. . . . I could have had my name in the *Hollywood Reporter* once a week like so many others." Kazan, *A Life*, 272.

15. Kazan frequently portrays himself as an "enlightened" artist having to do battle with Zanuck, the "unenlightened" studio executive. Kazan writes, "John [Steinbeck] and I had been brought to the Springs to confer with Darryl [Zanuck] on the script for *Viva Zapata!* If this was an incongruous setting for a conference on the story of a Mexican revolutionist, it hadn't occurred to Darryl. 'It's just a big western,' he was to say to me later." Ibid., 395.

16. Ibid., 259.

17. Ibid., 421.

18. Neve, *Film and Politics*, 222.

19. Vanderwood writes: "No documents better reveal the problems of political

focus which beset the intellectual left in postwar America than the succession of Steinbeck/Kazan screenplays which preceded the filming of *Viva Zapata!* What began as an endorsement of revolution with determined leadership as the means to social change ended up as a rejection of power, strong leadership and rebellion in favor of grass-roots democracy which promises little, if any, change at all." Paul J. Vanderwood, "An American Cold Warrior: *Viva Zapata!*" in *American History/ American Film: Interpreting the Hollywood Image*, eds., John E. O'Connor and Martin A. Jackson (New York: Ungar, 1979), 183–201.

20. Kazan, *A Life*, 473. Page numbers for subsequent quotations from this source appear in the text.

21. Prior to the HUAC trials, Kazan and Arthur Miller had been set to collaborate on *Hook*, a script written by Arthur Miller about longshoremen, but Miller retreated, given his anxiety over the mounting anti-Communist fervor in Hollywood. Ibid., 410–12.

22. Spiegel demonstrated his ability to collaborate effectively with strong writers and directors on three key films from the period, *On the Waterfront* (1954), *The Bridge on the River Kwai* (1957), and *Lawrence of Arabia* (1962).

23. Kazan notes, with pride, that as a testament to the intense audience interest in the film, three hundred people stood in line beginning at 9 A.M. for the film's opening several hours later at the Astor Theater in New York. Kazan, *A Life*, 528. Also see Schulberg's foreword to *On the Waterfront*, ed. Joanna E. Rapf (New York: Cambridge University Press, 2003), xv–xxii.

24. Kazan wrote, "I'd find out only much later that two years before, Jack Warner had confidentially offered this astonishing statement to the House Committee: 'Arthur Miller and Elia Kazan worked on Broadway where they practiced some sort of subversion.'" Ibid., 421.

25. Ibid., 533.

26. Michel Ciment, "Working with Schulberg: *On the Waterfront* (1954), *A Face in the Crowd* (1957)," in *Elia Kazan Interviews*, ed. William Baer (Jackson: University Press of Mississippi, 2000), 180.

27. Kazan, "Introduction," in Budd Schulberg, *A Face in the Crowd* (New York: Random House, 1957), xv.

28. Ibid.

29. Kazan and Schulberg epitomize the paradox of postwar independence in that the benefits of greater creative autonomy were enjoyed primarily by above-the-line personnel while below-the-line craftsmen saw some pay increases, but also lost the job security associated with regular studio employment.

30. Kazan, *A Life*, 533–34.

31. Lloyd Michaels, ed., *Elia Kazan: A Guide to References and Resources* (Boston: G. K. Hall, 1985), 13.

32. For an insightful, in-depth examination of these issues, see Vincent Brook, "Courting Controversy: The Making and Selling of 'Baby Doll' and the Demise of the Production Code," *Quarterly Review of Film and Video* 18, no. 4 (2007): 347–61.

33. Neve, *Film and Politics*, 173.

34. Larry Ceplair, "Elia Kazan," in *The Political Companion to American Film*, ed. Crowdus, 234.

35. Kazan, *A Life*, 463.

36. Neve, *Film and Politics*, 89.

37. Ceplair, "Elia Kazan," 232–35.

38. *The Arrangement*, an homage to Kazan's wife Molly who died the previous year, documents the midlife crisis of advertising executive (played by Kirk Douglas), who chooses a path to personal self-fulfillment over the pursuit of materialism.

39. Richard Maltby, *Harmless Entertainment: Hollywood and the Ideology of Consensus* (Metuchen, N.J.: Scarecrow Press, 1983), 275–86.

40. Naremore, *More Than Night*, 47–48.

41. Ibid., 48. For a more comprehensive discussion of the relationship between modernism and mass culture, see Naremore, "Modernism and Blood Melodrama," in ibid., 40–95.

42. Naremore uses case studies from noir narratives to explore the links between modernism and mass culture. I use this theoretical premise to make an analogous case for the evolution of Kazan's "social-problem" films.

43. Maltby, *Harmless Entertainment*, 276. The exchanges between PCA executive Geoffrey M. Shurlock and Kazan during the making of *A Face in the Crowd* reveal Shurlock's admiration for the critically acclaimed director and Kazan's eagerness to cooperate (through polite written exchanges, if not by making substantive changes to his film). The first letter from Shurlock (dated July 10, 1956) states PCA's objections to the sexually suggestive references to Marcia and Lonesome's relationship. Shurlock writes Kazan nine months later (on April 1957, presumably while the director was already in production) to say that he spoke with Schulberg and all his objections have been met. The lines cited are present in the final film. They include several references to intimacies between Marcia and Lonesome; Kiely's (Joey DePalma's) line, "Don't mind me, I know—Nice girls do it too . . ."; a modified version of the ex–Mrs. Rhodes's comment that Larry feels he has to sleep with every woman he meets; and the scene depicting Lonesome undressing in front of Marcia with the intention of sleeping with her. The following month (May 22, 1957), Kazan writes Shurlock, explaining he plans to remove other, potentially controversial material during editing. In a follow-up letter to Kazan, Shurlock thanks the director for writing him personally (noting it wasn't necessary since the PCA already gave him certification). Shurlock exchanges niceties about the film and says he hopes the critical response will be good. *A Face in the Crowd* file. Academy Library Special Collections—Manuscripts.

44. Naremore, *More Than Night*, 106, 120.

45. While Kazan applies the term "commercial liberal" to some of his old friends (presumably he means Clifford Odets, Arthur Miller, and so on), Kazan nonetheless criticizes himself for his tendency to resolve conflict in many of his films through easy narrative resolution. Kazan, *A Life*, 567.

46. Maltby, *Harmless Entertainment*, 278.

47. Ibid.

48. Ibid.

49. Cited in Bill Nichols's introduction to Fredric Jameson, "Dog Day Afternoon as a Political Film," in *Movies and Methods*, ed. Nichols (Berkeley: University of California Press, 1946–85), 2:716.

50. Sarris, in *The American Cinema*, places Mankiewicz, Kazan, Wilder, David Lean, William Wyler, and Fred Zinnemann in a category called "Less Than Meets the Eye." For additional discussion, see Michel Delahaye, "Interview with Elia Kazan, 1966" (from *Cahiers du cinéma in English*, March 1967), reprinted in *Elia Kazan: Interviews*, ed. Baer, 72–103. This 1966 interview, published by *Cahiers du cinéma*, is an attempt "to set the record straight" on Kazan.

51. Kazan, *A Life*, 475. While never wavering from his position that he testified to register his contempt for Communism, Kazan admitted that he experienced shame when right-wing organizations and publications such as *The World-Telegram* ran an editorial commending his testimony. Ibid., 470.

52. Ibid., 567.

53. Ibid.

54. Ibid., 566–67.

55. Ibid., 505. Kazan's quote about Odets continues: "Clifford Odets felt it necessary in his third acts to grab the audience by their shoulders, shake them, and say, 'Don't you see what all this means?' 'No? Well, I'll tell you.'"

56. Stuart Byron and Martin L. Rubin, "Elia Kazan Interview/1971," in *Elia Kazan: Interviews*, ed. Baer, 145.

57. Kazan, *A Life*, 568.

58. Dana Polan provides useful insights into how best to apply Foucault's theories of discourse to film studies. He writes: "For Foucault, we are never in contact with a pristine reality that would exist outside our griddings" (*Power and Paranoia*, 7).

59. Bordwell, Staiger, and Thompson, *Classical Hollywood Cinema*.

60. Jenkins, *What Made Pistachio Nuts?* Coining the phrase "anarchistic comedy," Jenkins analyzes the continuity between vaudeville and a subgenre of comedy films from the thirties during this period of institutional transition and crisis in Hollywood. Other notable, historically informed, industry-informed, single-genre studies that Jenkins cites are Lea Jacobs, *Reforming Women: Censorship and the Female Ideal in Hollywood, 1928–1942* (Madison: University of Wisconsin Press, 1991), Donald Crafton, *Before Mickey: The Animated Film, 1898–1928* (Cambridge: MIT Press, 1982); Paul Kerr, "Out of What Past? Notes on the B Film Noir," in *The Hollywood Film Industry*, ed. Kerr (London: Routledge and Kegan Paul, 1986), 20–44; and Thomas Doherty, *Teenagers and Teenpics* (Boston: Unwin and Hyman, 1988), 13.

61. Ibid., 12–19.

62. Hall is cited in Jenkins, *What Makes Pistachio Nuts?* 20.

63. Ibid., 20–21.

64. Antonio Gramsci, *Lettered al cacere*, ed. Sergio Caprioglio. Elsa Fubini. Torino: Einaudi, 1965. Schatz cites Bazin: "The American cinema is a classical art, but why not then admire in it what is most admirable, i.e., not only the talent of this or that filmmaker, but the genius of the system," in Thomas Schatz, *The Genius of the System: Hollywood Filmmaking in the Studio Era* (New York: Pantheon Books, 1988).

7. A Face in the Crowd

1. In the 1974 interview quoted in the epigraph, Kazan gives pragmatic expression to Brechtian theories of art. He writes: "I think I let the audience off too easily, in a position where they could patronize him, where they could look down on him, and say: 'Oh, those jackasses! How could they be taken in by that man!' . . . I think that's the single failure of the film." Ciment, "Working with Schulberg" 184.

2. Kazan, *A Life*, 322–23.

3. C. Kraus, *I Love Dick* (New York: Semiotext(e), 1997), 156. Kraus is quoted in Joan Hawkins, "Dark, Disturbing, Intelligent, Provocative, and Quirky: Avant-garde Cinema of the 1980s and 1990s," in *Contemporary American Independent Film*, ed. Holmlund and Wyatt, 93. Hawkins argues that the avant-garde cinema of the 1980s and 1990s is the cultural descendant of the late 1950s and 1960s counter-cultural movement and underground cinema movement, but that unlike that group, the current generation (e.g., Todd Haynes, David Lynch) "rarely try to disrupt the narrative or block traditional processes of spectator identification."

4. Review of *A Face in the Crowd, Hollywood Reporter,* May 28, 1957.

5. Ibid.

6. T. J. Jackson Lears, "From Salvation to Self-Realization: Advertising and the Therapeutic Roots of Consumer Culture, 1880–1930," in *The Culture of Consumption: Critical Essays in American History, 1880–1980,* eds. Richard Wightman Fox and T. J. Jackson Lears (New York: Pantheon Books, 1983), 4; cited in Lynne Joyrich, "All That Television Allows: TV Melodrama, Postmodernism, and Consumer Culture" in *Private Screenings,* ed. Spigel and Mann, 237.

7. Neve, *Film and Politics,* 197.

8. Ciment, "Working with Schulberg," 187.

9. Schulberg, *A Face in the Crowd,* 43.

10. In some respects, the film can be seen as an allegory about the Left and Kazan's own evolution away from Communism.

11. Schulberg, *A Face in the Crowd,* 12.

12. Ibid. Schulberg and Kazan frequently expressed greater concern for television's capacity to sell right-wing political ideology than its capacity to sell a consumer lifestyle. Nora Sayre, "A 1957 Film Speaks of Watergate," *New York Times,* September 8, 1975, 1, 13; cited in *Elia Kazan,* ed., Michaels, 117.

13. Schulberg, *A Face in the Crowd,* 6.

14. Kazan, *A Life,* 323.

15. Polan provides a useful and articulate discussion of Brecht's various works: *Brecht on Theater, About Realism, About the Cinema,* and *The Arts and the Revolution* in "The Politics of a Brechtian Aesthetics" in *The Political Language of Film and the Avant-Garde,* 79–100.

16. Ibid., 98.

17. Schulberg, *A Face in the Crowd,* 44.

18. Kazan, *A Life,* 597.

19. Kazan, "Private Notes, January 4, 1958," in *Elia Kazan: An American Odyssey,* ed. Michel Ciment (London: Bloomsbury, 1988), 112.

20. Both *A Face in the Crowd* and *On the Waterfront* resort to didactic speeches

by principal characters (Mel Miller and Father Barry [Karl Malden], respectively) and to romantic subplots (Marcia Jeffries in *A Face in the Crowd*, Edie Doyle [Eva Marie Saint] in *On the Waterfront*) to resolve complex social conflict.

21. Schulberg, *A Face in the Crowd*, 4.

22. Ibid.

23. Ibid., 66.

24. Ibid. While cut from the final film, Schulberg wrote a sequence in which Marcia reminds DePalma to put in the contract that "Larry [Lonesome Rhodes] can say anything he wants. Remember he's his own man." In the meantime, Rhodes continues his self-referential ditty: "Ramble. Ramble. Brother, I'll scramble their commercials and I'll ramble their vice presidents . . . we'll start a Brother's Keeper Department, honey." The "mindless" refrain reveals Rhodes's implicit understanding of the divergent responsibilities of his two "representatives." Whereas DePalma is responsible for leveraging the power Rhodes has amassed, Marcia is to help him preserve (superficially, at least) the impression of a populist agenda, protecting the common man against corporate advertisers.

25. The irony inherent in this scene is intensified in a later scene when Rhodes restages his marriage to Betty Lou on his television show, complete with dancing girls, sexy costumes, and young boys in cowboy suits holding up the bride's wedding veil.

26. Schulberg, *A Face in the Crowd*, 88–89.

27. Kazan started as a director of left-wing documentaries and later expressed a desire to return to this more personal form of filmmaking. Rex Reed, "For Elia Kazan, Life Begins at 62," *New York Sunday News*, February 6, 1971, S9, cited in *Elia Kazan*, ed. Michaels, 115.

28. Kazan's popular melodramas include *A Streetcar Named Desire*, *East of Eden*, and *Splendor in the Grass*.

29. Byron and Rubin, "Elia Kazan Interview," 145. Kazan stated in the 1971 interview, "I feel the picture is at several points over-explicit. I'm not sure I like all of Matthau's speech at the end, when he says to Griffith, 'I know what will happen to you. Someone else will take your place,' and all that. I think telling the audience, 'This is what the picture means,' instead of letting them find out what it means, is of that time, not of our time."

8. When Talent Becomes Management

1. See chapters 4 through 7 in Buford's well-researched biography on Lancaster's production company in its various permutations. Buford, *Burt Lancaster*, 83–195.

2. Ibid., 136–37.

3. Ibid. H-L hired Robert Aldrich, an alumnus of Enterprise Studios, to direct *Apache*. Among the leftists writers H-L hired were Roland Kibbee, a long-time head writer for Norma Productions who was later called before HUAC, Paddy Chayefsky, J. P. Miller, Ernest Lehman, John Gay, Phil Leacock, Julius Epstein, Roger MacDougal, and Ray Bradbury. Ibid., 110, 172.

4. Buford quotes portions of Krim's memo to Benjamin (voicing his concerns about the H-L contract): "I have the completely helpless feeling of not knowing

enough about the internal operations of Hecht-Lancaster [including the] purchase and development of other properties . . . personal withdrawals for themselves . . . money [spent] unnecessarily on overhead or in any other direction." Ibid., 139–40.

5. The final credits reveal the complex, multiple "talent" deals (each with its own company, capital gains tax structure, and profit participation) associated with most 1950s independent productions. For instance, *Sweet Smell of Success* is an H-H-L production, a Norma-Curtleigh Production (Curtis and wife Janet Leigh's production company), and a United Artists release, and was produced by James Hill.

6. In 1957 Joseph Vogel, the new president of Loew's, Inc., wanted to hire Hecht, Hill, and Lancaster as "special consultants" to MGM; however, his conservative board of directors "bridled at the autonomy on which Lancaster, Hecht, and Hill insisted and at the partners' rather avant-garde program." Fishgall, *Against Type*, 166.

7. Odets wrote some episodes of *The Richard Boone Show*. Sam Kasner, "A Movie Marked Danger," *Vanity Fair*, April 2000, 431.

8. Margaret Brenman-Gibson, *Clifford Odets, American Playwright: The Years from 1906–1940* (New York: Athenaeum, 1981), 552–54.

9. "Goldwyn Offers Scribes Cut of Pix Profits, No Salaries," *Variety*, April 22, 1948, 3. Goldwyn contrasts playwrights and novelists to Hollywood writers who "turn on their talents like faucets only when payment is guarantee."

10. Ibid. *Variety* goes on to state that Goldwyn excludes "writers of westerns and whodunits"—that is, the factory-produced B genre fare that prevailed in the "old Hollywood" era—from his remarks. In this context, playwrights and novelists were portrayed as more "authentic" than writers who received weekly paychecks for writing films and television shows.

11. Horne, *Class Struggle in Hollywood*, 17.

12. Characterizing Columbia studio head Harry Cohn's begrudging acceptance of the greater leverage talent holds in postwar deal making, Hodgins writes: "It is hard on the Harry Cohns, not just because their power is waning but because they are losing it to the men who were once their hired hands: the stars, the directors, the producers and even—this last being the most galling of all—the writers." Hodgins, "Amid Ruins of an Empire," 147.

13. By 1954 Kazan would form his own production company, Newtown Productions.

14. Horne, *Class Struggle in Hollywood*, 40–41.

15. This anti-union animus receives fictionalized treatment in Schulberg's *What Makes Sammy Run?* A recent column in the *Los Angeles Times* discusses the analogies between the 1941 novel and present-day Hollywood. Patrick Goldstein, "How Sammy Still Runs," *Los Angeles Times*, June 5, 2005, 1.

16. Horne, *Class Struggle in Hollywood*, 41.

17. Ibid., 45, 56–57.

18. Hamilton, *Writers in Hollywood*, 106, 113.

19. This confluence of events leading up to the HUAC hearings and the leftist backlash expressed by filmmakers is discussed in greater detail in chapters 5, 6, and the epilogue of May's book. May, *The Big Tomorrow*, 175–269.

20. Kazan, *A Life,* 463.

21. Kasner, "A Movie Marked Danger," 428.

22. Eric F. Goldman, *The Crucial Decade and After: America, 1945–1960* (New York: Vintage Books, 1956), 192.

23. Buford relates "a story that circulated around Hollywood for years [claiming] that when Kibbee turned to Hecht for advice on how to handle his HUAC summons, Hecht graciously obliged, and then turned around and named him." Hecht also named John Howard Lawson, Albert Maltz, Budd Schulberg, and Frank Tuttle. Buford, *Burt Lancaster,* 131.

24. Ibid., 173.

25. Kasner, "A Movie Marked Danger," 423. A *Look* magazine article on Hayworth collapses the categories of business and romance, industry analysis and gossip, comparing her unhappy fourth marriage to Dick Haynes to her professional "break" from Harry Cohn, president of Columbia Pictures. Hamilton, "Rita Hayworth," 50.

26. Goodman, *The Fifty-Year Decline and Fall of Hollywood,* 192, 194.

27. Lehman would have understood the significance of the combined artistic and financial success of the low-budget *Marty,* whose respective earnings exceeded the more mainstream (and much more expensive) *Vera Cruz.* Fishgall, *Against Type,* 142.

28. Kasner, "A Movie Marked Danger," 425.

29. Cited in Fishgall, *Against Type,* 143. Hecht's office featured works by Corot, Utrillo, and other modern French masters. According to Shana Alexander (cited in ibid.), "Lancaster's office was more modest, though it did contain a half dozen Rouault paintings of circus acrobats, a barbecue, and a real waterfall." The men's room had marble walls, onyx fixtures, and towels with H-L embroidered in gold.

30. Cited in Kasner, "A Movie Marked Danger," 425.

31. Fishgall, *Against Type,* 136.

32. Kasner, "A Movie Marked Danger," 426.

33. For detailed analyses of the ambivalence expressed toward women in 1950s popular culture, see Elaine Tyler May, "Explosive Issues: Sex, Women and the Bomb," in *Recasting America,* ed. May, 154–69; Leila J. Rupp, "The Survival of American Feminism: The Women's Movement in the Postwar Period," in *Reshaping America,* ed. Bremner and Reichard, 33–65; Wini Breines, *Young, White and Miserable: Growing Up Female in the Fifties* (Boston: Beacon Press, 1992).

34. Paddy Chayefsky, who had just finished making *Marty* with H-H-L, commiserated with Lehman during the making of *Sweet Smell of Success.* "He and Lehman would go on long walks together and trade horror stories." Kasner, "A Movie Marked Danger," 426.

35. Ibid., 423.

36. Ibid., 426. One version of the events is that UA fired Lehman because they'd just been hurt by another first time director (i.e., Burt Lancaster, who directed *The Kentuckian*). Lehman claims he dropped out due to severe stomach problems, which he implies were caused by H-H-L. Odets and Lehman, *Sweet Smell of Success* (London: Faber and Faber, 1998), viii.

37. Hodgins writes, "United Artists will finance any type of producer, once it is

satisfied with the 'commercial appraisal' of his property and his ability to cast. It will work with him in juggling scripts, directors and stars until these essentials are brought into some sort of balance." Hodgins, "Amid Ruins of an Empire," 164–65.

38. Cited in James Mangold, "Afterword" to Odets and Lehman, *Sweet Smell of Success*, 176. Contemporary director James Mangold *(Heavy, Copland, Girl, Interrupted)* was Mackendrick's student at the California Institute of the Arts.

39. Fishgall, *Against Type*, 161.

40. Cited in ibid., 162. Odets gave a laundry list of personality types Lancaster displayed, "No. 1 is Enigmatic Burt, the Inscrutable One . . . No. 2 is Cocksure Burt . . . No. 3 is Wild Man Burt . . ., No. 4 is Old Father Burt . . . No. 5 might be labeled, 'Mr. Hyde,' cutting, searing Burt, who is remarkable not so much for his vulgarity—which can be spectacular, but for the destructive quality of his cruelty. No. 6 is the Marquis de Lancaster . . . No. 7 is Snake Oil Burt, con man, mischief-maker, and light-hearted rogue."

41. Goodman, *The Fifty-Year Decline and Fall of Hollywood*, 44.

42. The uneven power dynamics are frequently expressed in the film as that of man to dog. For instance, Hunsecker's secretary says to Sidney, "The next time you want information, Falco, don't scratch for it like a dog—ask for it like a man." Susie Hunsecker says to Sidney, "Who could love a man who keeps you jumping through burning hoops, like a trained poodle?"

43. Odets and Lehman, *Sweet Smell of Success*, 23.

44. Ibid., 36.

45. Goodman, *The Fifty-Year Decline and Fall of Hollywood*, 39.

46. For example, Sidney explains his job to a senator and his "date," "Sure, columnists can't get along without us. Only our good and great friend, J.J., forgets to mention that. We furnish him with items." Odets and Lehman, *Sweet Smell of Success*, 48.

47. Goodman, *The Fifty-Year Decline and Fall of Hollywood*, 46.

48. Ibid., 22.

49. Ibid., 27.

50. Many of these developments originated on radio, where 1930s' shows like *Hollywood Hotel*, hosted by gossip columnist Hedda Hopper, and *Forty-Five Minutes* made by Paramount and RKO, respectively, promoted Hollywood stars and movies.

51. Goodman, *The Fifty-Year Decline and Fall of Hollywood*, 26.

52. "*Trapeze* Set in 375 Dates," 1.

53. Fishgall, *Against Type*, 150.

54. Ibid., 136.

55. Wilkerson, "Trade Views," May 29, 1956, 1. Wilkerson continues: "Everyone in the business knows they are in a declining industry. . . . But, these important people whose names mean a lot in attracting ticket sales, simply refuse to lend a hand in getting people to see the pictures they have worked on."

56. Monroe also formed a production company but was far less active in maintaining it.

57. Kirk Douglas's Bryna Productions was almost on a par with H-H-L in its aggressive efforts to emulate the studio-level product, budgets, and talent deals.

H-H-L and Bryna Productions were jointly involved in producing *The Devil's Disciple*. Kirk Douglas's value was higher than Lancaster's at the time. UA gave Douglas the starring role. Buford, *Burt Lancaster*, 190–91.

58. Wallis stepped down as head of production at Warner Bros. in 1942 to form Hal Wallis Productions at Paramount. He had "profit participation, a producer's fee, and complete autonomy in making [his] films," making his the first truly independent company in the business and a model for future independent film production companies (like H-H-L). Fishgall, *Against Type*, 46.

59. Ibid., 133.

60. The young actor, Milner, later became famous in the popular television show *Route 66* and then *Adam-12*. Ibid., 162.

61. Ibid., 179–80.

62. In spite of Borgnine's claims about H-H-L's profit motives for making *Marty*, studio head Bob Blumofe and director Delbert Mann insist it was a "labor of love" for Harold Hecht, in particular. Ibid., 130–31.

63. Ibid., 194.

64. "Loew Studio Board Meet Details are Disclosed," *Hollywood Reporter*, July 12, 1959, describes the film grosses of all H-H-L productions and the new terms H-H-L forged with MGM in 1959. "The four pictures to be made by H-H-L would be cross-collateralized and participation between MGM and H-H-L in profits would be 50–50. This deal was submitted by Lew Wasserman of MCA."

65. Buford, *Burt Lancaster*, 195.

66. To "de-glamorize" the movie star, Howe cast shadows from the glasses onto Lancaster's face, giving his face a gaunt, skull-like frame.

67. Balio, *United Artists*, 153.

68. Howe had already used many of the camera techniques "pioneered" in *Citizen Kane*, including shooting the actors from extreme low angles so they seemed to be "knifing up through the air, poised for the kill." Kasner, "A Movie Marked Danger," 424.

69. Patrick Ogle, "Technological and Aesthetic Influences on the Development of Deep-Focus Cinematography in the United States," *Movies and Methods*, ed. Nichols, 2: 61, 70. Toland himself had used deep focus in an earlier John Ford film, *The Long Voyage Home* (1940).

70. Ogle, "Technological and Aesthetic Influences," 70.

71. Ephraim Katz, *The Film Encyclopedia* (New York: HarperCollins, 1994), 651.

72. This French variation on *mise-en-scène* literally means "placing of the mirror" and refers to an "endless mirroring" effect such as occurs when two mirrors are placed across from one another. The effect is literalized in *Citizen Kane* in the scene where Kane walks down a dark corridor past two adjacent mirrors and his image—the last time we will see it—is replicated into infinity.

73. Fishgall, *Against Type*, 162–63.

74. Ibid.

75. The tradition of granting the studio production executive "final cut" can be traced back to the origins of "the producer-unit system" in Old Hollywood in 1931. Bordwell, Thompson, and Staiger, *The Classical Hollywood Cinema*, 326. The

battle between the studio (or producer representing the interests of the studio) and directors over who has "final cut" began in the 1930s and has persisted in today's Hollywood, as satirically depicted in *An Alan Smithee Film: Burn, Hollywood, Burn* (Alan Smithee, 1998). Leonard Maltin, *Movie and Video Guide* (New York: Signet, 2003), 19.

9. Sweet Smell of Success

1. See Mangold's analysis of the opening sequence in "Afterword" by James Mangold, cited in Odets and Lehman, *Sweet Smell of Success*, 163.

2. For a fuller discussion of the significance of the gaze, and in particular, Vivian Sobchack's conceit of the "giant, disembodied eyeball," see Linda Williams, *Viewing Positions: Ways of Seeing Film* (New Brunswick, N.J.: Rutgers University Press, 1995), 1–2.

3. My use of "the disciplinary gaze" is derived from the theories of Michel Foucault, specifically those formulated in his genealogy of the prison system, *Discipline and Punish* (1979), which offers an especially apt conceptual frame for analyzing the New Hollywood power dynamics on display in *Sweet Smell of Success*. See, in particular, Foucault, *Discipline and Punish* (New York: Pantheon Books, 1999), 174, 195–228.

4. See May's account of Capra's complex political conversion. While fighting accusations of being a radical, Capra made conservative films like *State of the Union* (1948) to "celebrate corporate liberals as the engines of postwar reform." May, *The Big Tomorrow*, 171–72. A similar compression takes place in Hunsecker's on-air denunciation of smear campaigns. Hunsecker says, "The man has a right to face his accusers . . . that's the American way. From Washington through Jefferson, from Lincoln and FDR, right up to today. The Democratic way of life, that's what the man said, nowadays, it doesn't export too well, but you know and I know that our best secret weapon is D-E-M-O-C-R-A-C-Y." Odets and Lehman, *Sweet Smell of Success*, 113.

5. Kasner, "A Movie Marked Danger," 429.

6. See for instance, Foucault's description of discipline as the "power of mind over mind." He quotes Bentham: "[I]ts great excellence consists in the great strength it is capable of giving to any institution it may be thought proper to apply it to" (*Discipline and Punish*, 206). Also, see Polan's discussion of Foucault in *Power and Paranoia*, 7–10.

7. Odets and Lehman, *Sweet Smell of Success*, 118–19.

8. The references to "docile body," and to specific social formations that enforce this state of being in society, such as the soldier walking in formation, originate in Foucault's *Discipline and Punish*, 169.

9. Odets and Lehman, *Sweet Smell of Success*, 136.

10. Foucault, *Discipline and Punish*, 199.

11. *A Place in the Sun* (1951) gives vivid expression to this fear when George Eastman (Montgomery Clift) feels trapped by plain, needy, factory-worker Alice Tripp (Shelley Winters) after he discovers she's pregnant with his child. A cartoon in *Look* magazine depicts two businessmen surrounded by female employees. They

discuss the family portrait on one of the two men's desk. He explains: "I don't know whose family it is. I just put it there to protect myself." *Look,* May 10, 1960, 76.

12. Odets and Lehman, *Sweet Smell of Success,* 120–21.

13. As Dana Polan explains, "For Foucault, we are never in contact with pristine reality that would exist outside our griddings. The stabilities of our social languages work to cut up space in precise ways to govern our behavior, to calculate which things (practices, ideas, speech-acts, etc.) we can produce and which ones we can't. Our perception is an effect of our social place and everything we do is readable in relation to a system of inclusions and exclusions that work to make up our social reality" (*Power and Paranoia,* 7).

14. Odets and Lehman, *Sweet Smell of Success,* 127.

15. Nick Browne, "The Spectator-in-the-Text: The Rhetoric of Stagecoach," *Movies and Methods,* ed. Nichols, 2: 458–75.

16. Kasner, "A Movie Marked Danger," 428.

17. Polan, *The Political Language of Film and the Avant-Garde,* 98.

18. Wilkerson, "Trade Views," July 2, 1957, 1.

19. *Hollywood Reporter,* June 17, 1957, 5.

20. Richard Gertner, review of *Sweet Smell of Success, Motion Picture Daily,* July 19, 1957. *The Great Man* (1956), based on a novel of the same name, was directed by and starred Jose Ferrer (and featured Ed and Keenan Wynn). Ferrer's character prepares a memorial show for a much-loved TV star only to find out the star was a despicable phony.

21. Review of *Sweet Smell of Success, Variety,* June 19, 1957.

22. Review of *Sweet Smell of Success, Hollywood Reporter,* June 19, 1957, 3.

23. As Elsaesser explains, both impulses are often present in 1950s' melodramas (e.g., Sirk), which function "not only as critical social documents but genuine tragedies, despite, or rather because of, the 'happy ending': they record some of the agonies that have accompanied the demise of the 'affirmative culture.'" Elsaesser, "Tales of Sound and Fury," 188.

24. Naremore, *More Than Night,* 47, 48.

25. For instance, Naremore examines contemporary filmmaker Quentin Tarantino, who "makes densely hypertextual movies that reproduce the 'underground' quality of 1960s criticism. His *politique* consists of tributes to European auteurs such as Godard, Fassbinder, and Jean-Pierre Melville: Americans such as Scorsese, Schrader, and Sam Peckinpah; old fashioned tough guys such as Hawks and Samuel Fuller; and contemporary specialists in blood melodrama such as John Woo and Abel Ferrara." Naremore, *More Than Night,* 216, 167–219.

26. Buford, *Burt Lancaster,* 183. After the success of *Marty,* Hecht stated in an interview for *Hollywood Reporter* that the ideal price tag for studio-distributed art films was $300,000. However, once two movie stars (Lancaster and Curtis) were attached, and the egos of all the players clashed, the budget soared and suddenly a subversive art film was being made at blockbuster prices.

27. Gene's (only the last name of the journalist is listed) take identifies the film's "art film" qualities. Gene, review of *Sweet Smell of Success, Variety,* June 19, 1957.

28. Ibid.

29. Wilkerson, "Trade Views," June 17, 1957, 1.

30. Holmlund, "Introduction to 'Critical Formations,'" 26.

31. "Film Company Toppers Join Johnston and Sales Execs in Industry Campaign Kickoff," *Hollywood Reporter,* May 29, 1957, 1, describes MPAA head Eric Johnston's address, "America's Traveling Salesman."

32. Cited in Monaco, *The Sixties,* 44.

33. Monaco quotes Jerry Lewis, who continued making movies for families, asserting testily "that there were 'only twenty sophisticates in the world' and that he wasn't interested in making movies for them." Monaco also notes that Katharine Hepburn rejected the pretensions of "arty features made by European directors." As my previous chapter suggests, so did Billy Wilder during this same period in the early 1960s. Monaco, *The Sixties,* 44.

34. Ibid., 14.

35. "The Wilder Shores of Hollywood," 1; Monaco, *The Sixties,* 59. Monaco notes that *Irma La Douce* was saddled with a "B" rating (meaning "morally unacceptable, in part, for all") by the Catholic Legion of Decency (as was the blockbuster *Cleopatra*). Wilder's sudden cynicism toward European cinema's provocative sexual themes may be explained in part by his own concerns, expressed in the *Variety* article, about the racy content of his next film, *Irma La Douce,* based on a Broadway musical, with the film re-teaming Jack Lemmon, playing a French gendarme, and Shirley MacLaine, playing a prostitute.

36. *Variety,* June 8, 1960, 1.

37. King, *New Hollywood Cinema,* 40. The formal techniques that Wilder mocks became a signature element of the films of the Hollywood Renaissance in the late 1960s; however, as Geoff King and other critics have noted, the use of New Wave techniques by American filmmakers does not always maintain the same radical, counterhegemonic intent.

38. By the mid-1970s, the blockbuster trend would re-emerge with the successful release of *Jaws* (1975), *Star Wars* (1977), and others.

39. Kasner, "A Movie Marked Danger," 428, 431.

Conclusion

1. See, for instance, Andrew Schroeder, "Strategies of Cinema: Cultural Politics in the New Hollywood, 1967–1981," Ph.D. diss., New York University, 2002.

2. Holmlund, "Introduction to 'Critical Formations,'" 23–26.

3. Schulberg, *A Face in the Crowd,* 147.

4. Lears, "A Matter of Taste," 49–50.

5. Ibid., 50.

6. *Hollywood Reporter,* June 13, 1957, 1.

7. Bordwell, Thompson, and Staiger, *The Classical Hollywood Cinema,* 13.

8. Polan, *Power and Paranoia,* 7.

9. Jonathan Rosenbaum, "Allusion Profusion," *Chicago Reader,* October 21, 1994, 12, 25–26; cited in Naremore, *More Than Night,* 34–35.

10. In *Sweet Smell of Success,* the filmmakers appear to indirectly satirize their own aesthetic ambitions when Steve tries to escape an "Intellectual Young Woman

in spectacles, a much-too-earnest devotee of progressive jazz," who tells him: "I'm terribly interested in jazz—serious jazz. . . . This is such an interesting fusion of the traditional, classical form with the new progressive style." Odets and Lehman, *Sweet Smell of Success*, 17.

11. Naremore, *More Than Night*, 134.

12. "When Politics Met Glamour," *Los Angeles Times*, August 13, 2000, 78.

13. These terms are frequently used by specialty division marketing teams to describe the films of David Lynch, Todd Solondz, and other filmmakers who are carrying on the cultural-intellectual legacy of the late 1960s avant-garde. Hawkins, "Dark, Disturbing, Intelligent, Provocative, and Quirky Avant-garde Cinema of the 1980s and 1990s," 89–105.

14. Ibid., 62.

15. Schroeder, "Strategies of Cinema," vi.

Index

Denise Mann is head of the Producers Program and associate professor in the Department of Film, Television, and Digital Media at UCLA.